FATHERS AND SONS IN SHAKESPEARE:
THE DEBT NEVER PROMISED

Frontispiece Sir Walter Ralegh. Unknown artist, 1602. National Portrait Gallery, London.

FRED B. TROMLY

Fathers and Sons in Shakespeare

The Debt Never Promised

UNIVERSITY OF TORONTO PRESS
Toronto Buffalo London

© University of Toronto Press Incorporated 2010
Toronto Buffalo London
www.utppublishing.com
Printed in Canada

ISBN 978-0-8020-9961-7

Printed on acid-free, 100% post-consumer recycled paper with vegetable-based inks.

Library and Archives Canada Cataloguing in Publication

Tromly, Frederic B., 1943–
    Fathers and sons in Shakespeare : the debt never promised / Fred B. Tromly.

    Includes bibliographical references and index.
    ISBN 978-0-8020-9961-7

    1. Shakespeare, William, 1564–1616 – Criticism and interpretation.
    2. Shakespeare, William, 1564–1616 – Characters – Fathers and sons.
    3. Fathers and sons in literature. I. Title.

    PR2992.F3T76 2010   822.3'3   C2009-907520-2

This book has been published with the help of a grant from the Humanities and Social Sciences Federation of Canada, through the Aid to Scholarly Publications Program, using funds provided by the Social Sciences and Humanities Research Council of Canada.

University of Toronto Press acknowledges the financial assistance to its publishing program of the Canada Council for the Arts and the Ontario Arts Council.

University of Toronto Press acknowledges the financial support for its publishing activities of the Government of Canada through the Book Publishing Industry Development Program (BPIDP).

For Luke and Ben

With a Father's Tongue-Tied Love

And now, beholding the good deeds of his sons, he confesses that
they are greater than his own, and rejoices to be surpassed by them.
Ovid, Metamorphoses, *XV, trans. Miller (with an added son)*

Contents

Preface

The double portrait of Sir Walter Ralegh and his son Walter (frontis-piece) depicts a relationship that is immediately familiar but also deceptively foreign.[1] Both qualities manifest themselves in a single motif: the son's studious imitation of his father. With fresh-faced solemnity, the eight-year-old Walter ('Wat' to his family) emulates his father's casually aristocratic, hand-on-hip pose. Clearly the boy is proud of the sword and hanger he wears, a scaled-down version of his father's and a symbol of the manhood to which he prematurely aspires. Only a year earlier, he was probably still in the unisex clothing that Elizabethan boys wore until they were 'breeched' at seven. Though Sir Walter's expression is difficult to read, we may suspect him to be both pleased with and a little amused by the studied seri-ousness of his son. Perhaps in the boy's set countenance, the warrior and explorer – now past his prime – catches a glimpse of himself in *his* youth.

But we should resist the impulse to turn the Elizabethan portrait into a Norman Rockwell painting of an adoring boy and his proud dad. These figures are not our contemporaries. We notice Wat's sur-prisingly modern-looking brush cut only because his hat is in his hand – an act of deference demanded of Elizabethan sons in the presence of their fathers. Close as they are, father and son do not touch. That the relationship is more hierarchical than intimate is suggested by the positioning of the two figures, as young Walter is literally under the arm of his imposing, splendidly dressed father. Indeed, Sir Walter is so dominant that the painting may have been intended less as a double portrait than a portrait of the lord with his son present mainly as a sig-nifier of paternal authority. This interpretation is supported by the legend in the upper left-hand corner, which identifies the elder Walter and lists his titles without any reference to Master Walter; the only comment on Wat is an abbreviation (under his sword hilt) that indicates his age without mentioning his name.[2] At the time of the painting (1602), he was Ralegh's only living son, and the fact that he bears his father's first name suggests that in good part his identity derives from his status as successor. The paternity of Sir Walter is confirmed by the fact that his son bears his image as well as his name.

When we consider that it may not be of his own choosing, young Wat's solemn paternal imitation loses some of its charm. In early modern England the mutually reinforcing voices of religious, political, and pedagogical authority insisted that it was the duty of sons to emulate and indeed replicate their fathers. Nor, as we will see in chapter 1, were Elizabethan patriarchs reluctant to exhort their male progeny to use them as models of virtue, thus ensuring that their noble lives would be reproduced. While one commentator may exaggerate when he says that the Ralegh portrait 'proclaims that children are the images of their parents,' it certainly reflects an ethos that defines filial virtue in terms of how truly sons imitate their fathers.[3] Of course, as sons grow older and develop a need for autonomy, the duty of paternal imitation becomes more burdensome than a child like Wat could imagine. A good deal of colourful evidence indicates that in fact the relationship of the two Walter Raleghs did become much less harmonious as the fractious son approached the manhood that the portrait depicts him as imagining.[4]

A defining (if possibly apocryphal) moment in the Raleghs' relationship was recorded in one of John Aubrey's anecdotes. Before dinner at a great lord's table, Aubrey's story goes, Sir Walter chastised his son for being such a 'quarrelsome, affronting creature' and declared that he was ashamed to be seen in public with 'such a bear.' Young Walter was suitably contrite, humbling himself before his father and promising to 'behave himself mightily mannerly.' For the first half of the dinner, Wat was a model of filial decorum, but then he suddenly announced that he had made a visit to a prostitute that very morning: 'I was very eager of her, kissed and embraced her, and went to enjoy her, but she thrust me from her, and vowed I should not, "For your father lay with me but an hour ago." Sir Walter, being so strangely surprised and put out of his countenance at so great a table, gives his son a damned blow over the face; his son, as rude as he was, would not strike his father, but strikes the face of the gentleman that sat on the other side of him, and said "Box about, 'twill come to my father anon."'[5] With breathtaking effrontery young Ralegh skewers paternal hypocrisy, and by endorsing his father's choice of courtesans he mocks the idea that a boy becomes a man by following in his father's footsteps. But wicked as Wat's tongue is, there are limits to his rebelliousness, and so he chooses to retaliate in an indirect fashion. While ostensibly deferring to his father's authority, he delivers a blow that will make its roundabout way to his father.

In Shakespeare's plays, the depiction of fathers and sons encompasses both the celebration of paternal authority in the painting and the savouring of filial rebellion in the anecdote. In Shakespeare's most interesting depictions of sons, both the patriarchal ideal and the impulse to subvert it are, in varying degrees, present. These sons are marked by their ambivalence toward their fathers, being more defiant than the young Wat of the painting but also more deferential than the rebellious Wat of the anecdote. Typically, they are outwardly obedient but inwardly restive, chafing against the strictures of paternal authority but not willing (or able) to reject them outright. The dilemma of these sons is that they have internalized the very values they find oppressive; the enemy they would resist is already within the gates. They are, as Elizabethans said and as we say, their fathers' sons. The complex nature of the paternal burden they bear is suggested by the fact that most of the sons in Shakespeare are eldest or only sons who, like young Walter Ralegh, carry their father's Christian name. To the extent that these sons are capable of rebelling against the fathers and the culture that shaped them, they do so in ways far more circumspect than Wat's rousing call to 'Box about.'

The current study attempts, for the first time, to focus attention on Shakespeare's depictions of divided sons and their fathers as a group. Following the two opening chapters on interpretive strategies and on Elizabethan-Jacobean contexts, the book traces the arc of Shakespeare's examination of these relationships, a single play at a time. Arranged in the order. that the plays were composed, the analytic chapters begin with young John Talbot and his father Lord John Talbot in *1 Henry VI* (chapter 2) and move to Henry Bullingbrook and his father John of Gaunt in *Richard II* (chapter 3), Prince Hal and King Henry IV in *1 Henry IV* and *2 Henry IV* (chapters 4 and 5), Prince Hamlet and King Hamlet's Ghost in *Hamlet* (chapter 6), and Edgar and the Earl of Gloucester in *King Lear* (chapter 7). As the analyses stress, these central relationships are counterpointed by other literal or figurative father-son connections in each play, which are of crucial importance.[6] In their cumulative insight, these depictions amount to one of the great accomplishments in Shakespeare's canon and constitute the most sustained exploration of the father-son relationship in any literature.

After *King Lear*, these complex sons rapidly disappear from Shakespeare's plays, being replaced by a series of simpler, more conventional depictions, many of which are discussed in the penultimate chapter. The final chapter shifts the focus from the plays to their author, since it is natural to wonder (impossible *not* to wonder) whether the recurrent representations of troubled fathers and sons reflect Shakespeare's experience with his own father, John. Finally, appendix 1 examines the close connections between the relationships studied in the body of the book and that of a father (Edward III) and son (Edward the Black Prince) in *Edward III*, a play that in recent years has been frequently ascribed to Shakespeare, while appendix 2 considers the veracity of an important seventeenth-century anecdote characterizing the relationship of Shakespeare and his father.

The recurrent, core features of these relationships will be laid out in the introduction. For now, suffice it to say that none of these characters is entirely new. They all have sources in and are namesakes of forebears appearing in sixteenth-century chronicles and plays. But in every instance Shakespeare has created them anew by complicating the depiction he inherited. In these plays, he represents the father-son relationship as being less harmonious than do his sources, where an orthodox, unproblematic bond of natural affection holds sway. Ironically, critical commentary has often undone what Shakespeare did, reducing his fathers and especially his sons to the conventional figures that he found in his sources – and transformed.

Acknowledgments

First come my students at Trent University, who have buoyed me up through the years with their energy, goodwill, and fresh perceptions. In the text and notes I have quoted from a number of (unpublished) essays written by students in my Shakespeare courses, and I appreciate their permission to cite this material. But I want to stress that this group represents only a small cohort of the many memorable students who helped me think about Shakespeare and much else.

Even in an uncommonly collegial English department, Zailig Pollock has been remarkable for his sustained generosity. A number of observations in this book had their origin in the give-and-take of Shakespeare courses that we team-taught over the years; my references to him in the notes do not begin to do justice to the breadth of his contribution. Though he unwisely compounded his complicity by commenting on early versions of most of the chapters, he should not be held responsible for the book's shortcomings.

Special thanks go to Trevor Silverstone, MD, who read the entire manuscript with an eagle eye and pounced on an embarrassing number of professional deformations in word and thought. Without a doubt, this book would have been stronger if Sheldon Zitner, my friend and best teacher of Shakespeare, had lived longer and seen more of the manuscript.

For timely help with various aspects of the manuscript, I am indebted to Elisabeth Young-Brühl and Christine Dunbar, Murray Schwartz, Scott Tyrer, Orm and Barbara Mitchell, Florence Treadwell, James Neufeld, Margaret Owens, and Danièle Cybulskie. With a forbearance bordering on the saintly, Didi Pollock solved my recurrent desktop problems and expertly formatted several stages of the text.

My mother, Ruth Pierce Tromly, has championed my educational goals from the beginning and remains an inspiration; my lamented father, Fred Tromly, is always with me. Also, I value the steady and steadying support of my extended family and friends, especially those tactful ones who resisted asking me too often how it was going.

This book benefited greatly from the detailed reports of the anonymous readers for the University of Toronto Press. For the second time, I am grateful to Suzanne Rancourt of the Press for her commitment to my work and for her deft overseeing of the entire process. Barb Porter saw to it that the various stages of editing were relatively painless (to me). I also appreciate the assistance of Dr Kel Morin-Parsons, the program manager of the Aid to Scholarly Publications Program of the Canadian Federation for the Humanities and Social Sciences. Two grants from Trent University's Social Sciences and Humanities Research Committee helped to set this project in motion.

I could not have written this book without access to the excellent collections of the Robarts Research Library of the University of Toronto and the Centre for Reformation and Renaissance Studies at Victoria University in the University of Toronto. At a number of key moments, the staff of the Interlibrary Loans Office of Bata Library (Trent University) tracked down elusive materials for me. Also, my thanks go to the staff of the Folger Shakespeare Library for help during a fruitful visit and to Erica Wylie, the Librarian of the Thomas Plume Library (Maldon, Essex) for reproductions of manuscript material.

At various stages of this lengthy project, lectures gave me the opportunity to test ideas, beginning with an exploratory talk at the Royal Military College (Kingston, Ontario) in 1998. Further opportunities at Trent University came in the form of presentations for the Department of English Literature's Colloquium Series and in 2004 for the annual Humanities Research Day. In the summer of 2006, I was invited to speak on fathers and sons in 1 Henry IV at the Stratford (Ontario) Shakespearean Seminars organized by McMaster University. That such knowledgeable playgoers as the seminarians found my ideas plausible was extremely encouraging.

Finally, and foremost, there is always Annette, who is not only my most practised critic but also the co-author of the book's dedicatees and the source of much else that gives life meaning.

A Note on Texts

Unless otherwise noted, all quotations of Shakespeare are from the second edition of *The Riverside Shakespeare*, ed. G. Blakemore Evans et al. (Boston: Houghton Mifflin, 1997). It should be noted that the *Riverside* prints a single, conflated text for plays that appeared in both Folio and Quarto versions – a practice frowned on by some editors. For the purposes of the present study, the differences between Folio and Quarto texts are significant with regard only to *Hamlet*, and the issue is addressed in my discussion of the play. In all instances I have removed the distracting square brackets that the *Riverside* editors inserted to distinguish between different textual strata.

To prevent the language of Shakespeare's contemporaries from appearing more ancient and quaint than the modernized *Riverside* text, I have reluctantly modernized the spelling and punctuation in all Elizabethan quotations, including those taken from edited old-spelling editions. The original spelling is retained only in the titles of books.

With the exception of *The Famous Victories of Henry the Fifth*, I have quoted Shakespeare's sources from Geoffrey Bullough's *Narrative and Dramatic Sources of Shakespeare*, which is cited parenthetically in the text. For the *Famous Victories* I have used the text with corrected lineation in *The Oldcastle Controversy*, edited by Peter Corbin and Douglas Sedge.

FATHERS AND SONS IN SHAKESPEARE

Introduction:
Interpreting Shakespeare's Sons –
Ambivalence, Rescue, and Revenge

Any book purporting to say something new about the meaning of major Shakespearean plays merits immediate suspicion, especially if its subject is as apparently accessible as the relations of fathers and sons. Although there has never been a comprehensive study of the topic (unlike fathers and daughters in Shakespeare), a good deal of ink has been spilled on it, and one may wonder why additional commentary is called for. The simple answer is that there is more to Shakespeare's central depictions of fathers and sons than meets the eye, even the critical eye. The principal interpretive difficulty is posed by the sons, who are often more complex and more elusive than their fathers; unlike paternal pronouncements in the plays, which are usually unambiguous, filial responses tend to be guarded, devious, and hard to parse. Concealment and indirection are at the heart of these young men. Indeed, their avoidance of undisguised expression is so thoroughgoing that an interpretation based on taking word or even deed at face value is likely to be mistaken. And mistaken in a particular way. What is hidden or repressed in these sons is invariably more complex (and more critical of paternal authority) than the sentiments that find direct expression.

With some notable exceptions, criticism has failed to pay adequate attention to the complexity of Shakespeare's sons, or – especially in the case of Hamlet – has misconstrued the nature of that complexity. This oversight has led to many exaggerated accounts of inter-generational harmony and reconciliation in the plays. Thus, in a 1932 British Academy lecture entitled 'Paternity in Shakespeare' that could have been written fifty years earlier, Sir Arthur Quiller-Couch praised the 'magnificent *simplicity*' of *Hamlet* and divined 'a higher strain of paternal feeling and of correspondent filial affection growing through the Plays.'[1] An avoidance of psychological complexity attends many historically oriented studies that examine the father-son relationships not only in the light of, but also as manifestations of, official Elizabethan views on family hierarchy, including the naturalness of the bond linking the male generations.[2] Similar simplifications appear in comparative studies that examine Shakespeare's fathers and sons in the heroic, larger-than-life context of myth and classical epic; a study entitled *Shakespeare's Epic of Fathers and Sons* stresses the centrality of 'the son who toils for his father's sake, who strives for his father's ideal.'[3] In another register, psychoanalytic criticism is also capable of eliding differences between father and son, as in an eminent practitioner's rather alarming discovery of a Shakespearean pattern in which 'the son becomes almost literally the father's genital.'[4] Also, less strikingly, there is a characteristic exaggeration of achieved harmony between father and son in critical studies that stress the importance of identification with the father in male ego development.[5] It is probably not a concidence that, beginning with Coppélia Kahn's ground-breaking study of masculine identity in Shakespeare, *Man's Estate*, a disproportionate amount of the most clear-sighted commentary on fathers and sons in the plays has been written by women.[6]

Because his approach is predicated on an intense analytic engagement with Shakespeare's language, the critic who has cast the most light on individual pairs of fathers and sons in the plays is Harry Berger Jr. In rebutting the argument that close attention to language is misguided because it is impossible to maintain during theatrical performance, Berger distinguishes between what he calls the plays' 'theatrical' and 'textual' meanings, arguing convincingly that Shakespeare has given us 'a text which is overwritten from the standpoint of performance and the playgoer's limited perceptual capacities.'[7] Several of his essays carry the subtitle of 'Text Against Performance,' and his work demonstrates the value of concentrating carefully on language, especially when it may differ from, or even undercut, the ideology conveyed by the play performed in the theatre. Despite its many trenchant local observations, some of which are cited in the chapters to follow, Berger's valuable treatment of fathers and sons has a limitation: the relationship emerges more as a prime site for exploring the richness of the 'overwritten' text than as a subject for sustained thematic study.[8]

The present study attempts to do something obvious but apparently unprecedented: to identify and study as a group the most complex and divided sons in the plays. Though there has been surprisingly little critical recognition of this grouping, their commonality is not hard to find.[9] Incipiently in young John Talbot and Henry Bullingbrook, and then much more fully in Prince Hal, Hamlet, and Edgar, we see differing versions of a recurrent figure: an intelligent, recently come-of-age young man who is an eldest or an only son and often a prince, and thus the designated inheritor of the paternal fortune and reputation. The fact that usually this son is named after his father highlights both the similarity (often of temperament) and the difference (often of values) between the two, and often there are hints of a prolonged separation between them. To compound the challenge faced by the son, the father – who has always been a commanding figure – is threatened by advanced age and deadly enemies, thus becoming beleaguered as well as authoritarian. The son feels the need to save his vulnerable father but also to assert his own fragile autonomy.

The mixture of deference and defiance in these sons stands in sharp contrast to the relatively unalloyed attitudes of Shakespearean daughters toward their fathers. Notwithstanding the Elizabethan stereotype of daughters as obedient and silent, the plays often depict them as quite capable of unqualified, outspoken defiance, as Joan of Arc's father discovers to his dismay (1H6:5.4.1–33). The most comprehensive monograph on Shakespeare's fathers and daughters observes that the latter must choose between 'domination by father figures or defiance,' and accordingly it devotes separate chapters to 'Dominated Daughters' and to 'Defiant Daughters.'[10] While in some instances the assignment of daughters to either the Dominated or the Defiant category can be challenged, the distinction remains useful. But binary pairings will not do justice to Shakespearean sons. In the responses of the two unjustly banished children in King Lear, we can see in microcosm the differences between the paternal attitudes of Shakespeare's daughters and sons: while Edgar's anger toward Gloucester is deeply disguised (perhaps even from Edgar himself), at the beginning of the play Cordelia confronts Lear with passionate indignation. Late in the play both Cordelia and Edgar attempt to rescue their fathers from despair, her intervention proving to be less hedged and much more intimate than his. The openness of Cordelia's early anger conduces to the fullness of her eventual reconciliation with Lear.

Perhaps because their minds and loyalties are divided, Shakespeare's sons excel at the very activity that Cordelia refuses to engage in: they disguise their feelings by adopting roles. It is no coincidence that Hamlet, Prince Hal, and Edgar are some of the most accomplished actors in Shakespeare's plays and that each is at the centre of a lively critical debate about his character and motive. The Elizabethan authorities who defined the proper conduct of children were nervously aware of the fact that the rituals honouring parents could be performed with a false heart, and so the manuals for 'household governance' invariably caution that 'this outward show in vailing of the bonnet, and bowing of the knee or body, is nothing worth, except there be joined therewithal the inward reverence of the mind.'[11] As Hamlet succinctly observes, the observances of filial devotion are 'actions that a man might play' (1.2.84), or perhaps *must* play. But this play-acting is not confined to the rituals of filial deference, for Shakespeare's sons also assume roles like escaped bedlamite or tavern jester that afford rich opportunities for the safely guarded expression of hostility.

One may think of these sons as donning disguises in the protective manner that James C. Scott finds in public performance by members of socially subordinate groups, but there is a key difference.[12] In addition to being a means for sons to disguise their aggression from paternal observation and censure, this role playing also functions as a form of self-deception, a way for them to conceal their emotions from themselves. Because their regal fathers preside in good measure over their minds, these sons scarcely allow themselves to become aware of their disobedient impulses. The best evidence for this self-deception is in, or rather *not* in, the soliloquies they speak. Hal, Hamlet, and Edgar deliver speeches in which they make no explicit reference to their fathers, even though from the context we know that these fathers are very much on their unhappy minds. Although the soliloquy affords these characters the opportunity to speak without concern for external disapproval and although they have good cause to criticize their fathers, they do not directly speak their minds. Indeed, these soliloquies are notable for the speakers' avoidance of reflection about their progenitors and for their corresponding engagement with issues of less than pressing concern. The sons speak as if they are unaware of, or wish to be unaware of, the hostility they feel. But, as we will see, their language betrays them. It is, I believe, impossible to make good sense of these Shakespearean sons without ascribing a measure of internal repression and self-censorship to them.

Filial Ambivalence

To apply a psychological term coined in the early twentieth century to these Elizabethan dramatic characters, we may say that they manifest 'ambivalence,' which can be defined simply as 'The coexistence in one person of contradictory emotions or attitudes (as love and hatred) towards a person or thing' (on-line *OED*). Though the term is modern, the phenomenon can be traced in literature back to the '*Odi et amo*' poem of Catullus, and surely farther still. In current psychological research, ambivalence is a fruitful concept that is being explored in a number of ways, but for understanding Shakespeare's fathers and sons the most useful analytic framework is that of Sigmund Freud.[13] According to Freud, filial ambivalence has shaped many cultural practices because from time immemorial it has been an essential constituent (perhaps *the* essential constituent) of children's attitudes to parents, and especially of sons to fathers.[14] As he remarks of sons in his essay 'Dostoyevsky and Parricide,' 'In addition to the hate which seeks to get rid of the father as a rival, a measure of tenderness for him is also habitually present.'[15] Not only are filial love and hate coexistent for Freud, but they coexist in a specific structure. While the son's love for his father is conscious and conspicuous, his anger is repressed and unconscious: his 'hostility is ... shouted down as it were by an excessive intensification of the affection.'[16] Thus, he observes that even the most devoted sons harbour aggression toward their fathers. When he received the city of Frankfurt's Goethe Prize – Goethe being one of his great masters – Freud remarked that 'Our attitude to fathers and teachers is, after all, an ambivalent one since our reverence for them regularly conceals a component of hostile rebellion.'[17] This division of ambivalence into a latent and a blatant component accords nicely with Shakespeare's representation of sons as divided, with their positive feelings about the father being more conscious and explicit than the negative ones.

Given his impressive knowledge of Shakespeare's plays, it is curious that Freud did not discuss their representation of a phenomenon so central to his thought as filial ambivalence.[18] This silence is all the more surprising in that some of Freud's signature ideas about conflicted sons have correlatives in Shakespeare's characterizations. For example, both the dramatist and the psychoanalyst depict the divided filial attitude toward fathers as difficult for sons to live with. As a result of this difficulty, the phenomenon that Freud calls 'displacement' often occurs in the plays: the son projects his hostile feelings (as Prince Hal does with Falstaff) onto a substitute who can be opposed with less tension and risk than his father. Similarly, in Freud's world as well as that of characters like Hal and Hamlet, the energies of repressed filial hostility are sometimes released through tendentious jokes that simultaneously cloak and express aggression.[19]

One can speculate on Freud's silence concerning this understanding that he shares with Shakespeare. A plausible Freudian interpretation is that, in an act of filial ambivalence of his own, Freud repressed his awareness of his great debt to Shakespeare's originative work. (Perhaps Freud was able explicitly to locate the Oedipal complex in *Hamlet* without pre-empting his own claim to intellectual precedence because he stressed that Shakespeare was not conscious of its presence in the play.) This interpretation would accord with some curious aspects of Freud's relationship to Shakespeare, such as his late-life belief that the plays were written by someone other than the man from Stratford.[20] More importantly, it supports the sceptical view of a recent commentator that 'psychoanalysis "works" in reading Shakespeare precisely to the extent that it was shaped by doing so.'[21] Whatever the source of Freud's silence may be, it is certainly the case that Shakespeare's depiction of the characters discussed in the chapters to follow anticipates some key aspects of the psychoanalyst's understanding of the father-son relationship.

But, despite the element of truth in Harold Bloom's provocative formula that 'Shakespeare is the inventor of psychoanalysis; Freud, its codifier,' the psychoanalyst remains useful for explicating the dramatist's fathers and sons.[22] Precisely because of its frequent resonance with the plays, or more precisely its reflection of them, Freud's work sometimes casts an oblique but clarifying light on Shakespeare's depictions. The most important of these connections is not, as Freud himself thought, the Oedipal complex.[23] Rather, it is a motif in boys' dreams that Freud discusses without noting its recurrent appearance and central importance in Shakespeare's plays: filial rescue.

Rescue and Revenge

A defining if rarely discussed feature of Shakespeare's depiction of ambivalent sons is their rescue of their fathers. At the risk of their own lives, these sons either save their fathers from sudden death on the battlefield or (if he has died) attempt to rescue the paternal name and legacy. The frequency of these filial rescues is especially revealing because either they do not appear in Shakespeare's sources or, if they do, they figure less importantly than in the plays. The earliest instance occurs in *1 Henry VI*, when young John Talbot refuses to desert his aged father, even though the two of them are surrounded by a sea of French soldiers; after Lord John Talbot has been wounded, young John bravely rescues him from his attackers. Similarly, in *1 Henry IV* the King is on the verge of being killed at the battle of Shrewsbury, when Prince Hal intervenes and drives off the raging Douglas. Late in *King Lear* the scenario plays itself out once again when Edgar, armed with only a cudgel, saves his blind, helpless father from Oswald's sword. In other plays, when the death of the father has made physical rescue impossible, sons like Hamlet and Laertes engage in highly vocal attempts to rescue the father's reputation or to avenge his death. These rescue scenes, which usually occur near the ends of plays, would seem to provide decisive evidence for a sanguine interpretation of the father-son relationship in which the son's rescue signals his filial piety and the achievement of a full reconciliation with his father. It is not surprising that a recent biographer of Shakespeare has observed that the plays are informed by 'the rending, moving Tudor theme of the love and fealty due a parent.'[24]

On the face of things, no act could be less ambivalent, less hedged or conflicted, than the son's life-risking rescue of his father. But a more complex filial attitude can be glimpsed behind the theatrically thrilling deliverance. A suggestive comment is a brief observation by Freud that makes no reference to Shakespeare. In a discussion of the dreams that boys have of saving their fathers, Freud postulates that the 'rescue-*motif*' has its origin not in filial piety but in defiance born of the constant reminder of indebtedness:

> When a child hears that he *owes his life* to his parents, or that his mother *gave him life*, his feelings of tenderness unite with impulses which strive at power and independence, and they generate the wish to return this gift to the parents and to repay them with one of equal value. It is as

though the boy's defiance were to make him say: 'I want nothing from my father; I will give him back all I have cost him.' He then forms the phantasy of *rescuing his father from danger and saving his life*; in this way he puts his account square with him ... In its application to a boy's father it is the defiant meaning in the idea of rescuing which is by far the most important.[25]

The idea that filial rescue can be a form of aggression and even constitute a kind of revenge resonates with the plays, even after we remind ourselves that they depict brave sons who save their fathers on the battlefield, not analysands who merely fantasize about doing so. Especially for the student of *1 Henry IV*, with its depiction of a father-king saved by his rebellious but debt-obsessed eldest son, there is a *frisson* in Freud's conception of rescue as a defiant (but concealed) settling of accounts, a form of payback.

Though there are subtle hints of filial aggression in the rescue scenes, the clearest evidence for the hostility of sons occurs not during the rescues but immediately afterwards. When versions of these rescues occur in Shakespeare's sources, they are followed by unambiguous acts of inter-generational reconciliation. But in the plays the opposite happens: after having risked his life to save his father, the apparently dutiful son proceeds to avenge himself (in a devious way) against that same father. It is as if the son compensates for the rescue by a reprisal, undoing what he had done. A quick inventory of these revenges, which are discussed in detail in the chapters to follow, must suffice to make the point. In *1 Henry VI*, young John Talbot first rescues his wounded father and then abandons him on the battlefield, dying and alone, in order to mount a solo attack on the French. A similar situation occurs near the end of *King Lear*; soon after having saved his blinded father, Edgar leaves him alone on the battlefield as he pursues his trial by combat with his brother Edmund. More unobtrusive, but perhaps also more aggressive, is Prince Hal's intervention in the final scene of *1 Henry IV* to save the life of the Douglas, the rebel from whose attack he had rescued his father only moments earlier. When Hal rescues the captured rebel from his father, he effectively undoes the earlier scene. As with so many father-son motifs, the richest example of the revenge of the good son occurs in *Hamlet*. In what is virtually his last breath, Hamlet obliquely strikes at his father by naming Fortinbras as the new king of Denmark. In effect, Hamlet is rejecting his patrimony; he not only surrenders the lands that the elder

Hamlet had risked his life to win from the elder Fortinbras but also for-feits the Danish kingdom itself to the son of his father's enemy. For these sons, as for the Black Prince in the probably Shakespearean play *Edward III*, the cloak of chivalry covers an act of aggression that cannot be owned.[26]

The Pressure of Historical Context

As suggestive as Freudian ideas about sons can be, they must not be allowed to obscure the historical and cultural contexts of the plays. Though Freud sometimes spoke as if it were a universal state equally present at all times, filial ambivalence is rooted in time and place, and thus one wants to know how the specific pressures of Shakespeare's England nourished and inflected it. With regard to Freud's *aperçu* about aggression in filial rescue, we can see the difference that history makes. In Freud's formulation, the essential scene occurs on the stage of the nuclear family, where parents beget guilt-ridden resentment by reminding their children that they have brought them into being. But in Elizabethan England the burden of filial obligation was heavier and more pervasive, articulated not only by the parents who had been good enough to create their children but also by a chorus of public voices in the discourses of church, state, and school. In Shakespeare's England, a child – and especially a boy – could hardly avoid having the religious and civic duty of filial rescue drummed into him.

In innumerable catechisms expounding the Fifth Commandment – 'Honour thy father and thy mother' – religious authorities insisted on the necessity of children coming to the aid of their parents. Thus, in his authorized catechism, the Reverend Alexander Nowell explicates the commandment by insisting that the true honouring of parents extends well beyond mere obedience to include 'saving, helping, and defend-ing them, and also finding & relieving them if ever they be in need.'[27] As the forceful piling up of gerunds suggests, there can be no end to the sacrifices that children owe their parents. More explicitly demand-ing is Robert Cleaver's *A Godlie Forme of Householde Government* (1598), where 'honour thy parents' is taken to mean that, 'if need require,' children must 'give their lives for them: remembering that they are their parents' goods and possessions, and that they owe to them even their own selves & all that they are able to do, yea, and more than they are able.'[28] Try as hard as they may, children cannot repay their parents for the gift of life – but try they must.

Figure 1 Aeneas Rescuing His Father Anchises, from Geffrey Whitney, *A Choice of Emblemes* (1586), ed. John Manning (Menston: Scolar Press, 1989), 163

Not surprisingly, this inculcation of filial indebtedness found a touchstone in the famous scene in Virgil's *Aeneid* in which Aeneas rescues his aged father Anchises from the burning ruins of Troy (2.634–744). But Elizabethans gave the exemplum an inflection of their own. In the most influential classical interpretation, the Roman moral philosopher Seneca had understood the scene as a competition in generosity between father and son, with Aeneas dutifully vanquishing his father by fully discharging the debt he owed him as his progenitor.[29] In Elizabethan culture, Aeneas remained a great example of filial duty, but the notion of a son discharging his debt to his father and virtuously overcoming him (which is reminiscent of Freud's analysis of rescue dreams) did not accord with official views. In a widely distributed Renaissance woodcut, the scene is represented so as to stress the painful difficulty of the rescue (see fig. 1). In the strain of Aeneas's body and in his gasping mouth, we see the burden of filial sacrifice more than the triumph of a son. The verses accompanying the woodcut hammer out the Elizabethan lesson that

> sons must careful be and kind,
> For to relieve their parents in distress:
> And during life that duty should them bind
> To reverence them, that God their days may bless.[30]

The ancients may glorify him as a pious hero, but here Aeneas is simply a good, 'careful' son who will be blessed by God because he honours his father by rescuing him, a duty that binds every son.

As catechisms and the emblem indicate, in Shakespeare's England the obligation of filial rescue was inculcated into sons in a far more systematic and more coercive form than in Freud's Vienna. Elizabethan sons are exhorted to save their fathers, even at the cost of sacrificing their own lives, but also forcefully reminded that the act of rescuing one's father from death is merely a minimal, insufficient repayment for his supreme gift of life. What an Elizabethan son owes his father is not only, in Prince Hal's terse phrase, a 'debt ... never promised,' but also one that is never payable. This is a world in which sons are hectored to perform a duty that entails the sacrifice of individuality and perhaps of life itself, a duty which perhaps few sons can completely reject or unequivocally accept. It is small wonder that, while sons in the plays feelingly acknowledge the debt they owe their fathers, they bridle against the forfeiture of autonomy that is an explicit condition of that debt.

To appreciate the contextual resonance of Shakespeare's rescue scenes, to say nothing of his larger depiction of the father-son relationship, history must be invoked. We need to supplement Freud's psychoanalytic interpretation of rescue fantasies with an understanding not only of the Elizabethan prescription of filial duties but also of the youthful energies of the time that resisted (and in part provoked) this repression. To that end, chapter 1 examines the social and religious context that informs Shakespeare's representation of fathers and sons, locating the ambivalent attitude toward paternal authority in the uneasy confluence of two powerful currents of thought – one demanding the unconditional obedience and obligation of sons, the other asserting, or at least acknowledging, the value of filial talents and autonomy.

In the final chapter, this Elizabethan context of patriarchal dominance and filial ambivalence will be brought directly to bear on the relationship of William Shakespeare and his father, John Shakespeare. In effect, this concluding chapter will create a second historical bookend to complement the survey of Elizabethan attitudes in chapter 1, with the analytical chapters on single plays standing in the middle. Thus, the broad cultural sweep of the first chapter eventually leads to the sharp focus on a single historical father and son in the last. One virtue of deferring biographical interpretation until the end is that it allows the plays to be approached as coherent fictional worlds that make sense without recourse to the private life of the author, and of course these plays are abundantly challenging without the extra difficulty of speculating about what they may have meant to the man who wrote them. A second benefit of this deferral is that the recurrent patterns identified in the analyses of individual plays can be advanced as possible reflections of the author's personal experience, insofar as that notably elusive experience can be determined. But, attractive as it is, biographical speculation must wait upon the evidence that history and textuality afford.

1 Paternal Authority and Filial Autonomy in Shakespeare's England

Placing Shakespeare's depiction of fathers and sons in its historical context is not straightforward because the nature of that context is itself the subject of debate. In 1977 Lawrence Stone's weighty but stylishly provocative study, *The Family, Sex and Marriage in England 1500–1800*, initiated a major controversy about affective relations in the early modern family. Stone argues that from roughly 1580 to 1640 the norm in English families was a pernicious form of patriarchy in which the father became a 'legalized petty tyrant within the home.'[1] In large brush strokes, Stone connects the burgeoning of paternal authority in the nuclear family to the decline of the medieval kinship-based, extended family and to the reinforcement provided by two concomitant developments in church and state: the rise of Protestantism and of the authoritarian nation state. What emerges from the book is a dismal and sometimes lurid picture of despotic patriarchal rule, in which children were the numbed recipients of a good deal of violence and manipulation in the name of discipline and obedience. For family relationships, the net result was a 'general psychological atmosphere of distance, manipulation and deference' in which 'evidence of close bonding between parents and children' is rare, being 'hard, but not impossible, to document.'[2]

Stone's book detonated an avalanche of dissent from historians taking issue with its emphasis on the endemic coldness ('psychic numbing') and generally bad feeling within the early modern family. Indeed, one such study has as its subtitle 'The Loving Family in Old Europe.'[3] Drawing on letters and journals from family archives in England and the Continent, these revisionist historians have amassed a considerable body of evidence to illustrate the commonness of the 'close bonding between parents and children' that Stone said was so difficult to document.[4] A central concern of these historians has been to challenge Stone's view of the early modern father as a petty, emotionally removed tyrant; much evidence has been adduced of fathers fully engaged in the emotional life of their families, sensitive to the needs of living children and deeply mourning those who had died. Moreover, the very concept of patriarchy has been shown to have had a religious dimension stressing the tender, nurturing aspects of the father's role.[5]

Although most historians of the family now agree that this evidence undermines Stone's alleged norm of a brutal patriarchal tyranny, we should be wary of replacing the stereotype of the despotic father with the equally misleading stereotype of a kinder, gentler patriarch devoted to the tender nurture of his domestic flock. Even when a father's authority was worn lightly, it carried great weight. And it was not always worn lightly, especially among the gentry and aristocracy, where the transfer of land through primogeniture was an overriding paternal concern. When fathers deemed a child to be irrevocably disobedient with regard to a prospective marriage partner or another crucial issue, through the Statute of Wills (1540) they had legal recourse to the drastic punishment of disinheritance, or at least the compelling threat of it.

In a propertied family, the degree of a father's emotional distance from his children was likely to vary according to gender and birth order. Precisely because they were excluded from the privileges and responsibilities of patriarchy, daughters were 'often a source of delight to their fathers and of all their children the ones they were readiest to indulge.'[6] For similar reasons, many heads of families, including the head of the royal family, King James, found it easier to develop an openly affectionate relationship with their younger sons than with their heirs. Indeed, the relationship of James to his (presumptive) heir, Prince Henry, was so frosty that, after the Prince's sudden death, many people thought his father had poisoned him.[7] Usually the eldest son was the recipient of the lion's share of paternal control and censoriousness as well as wealth and land, for he was destined to bear the responsibility for managing the next generation of the family's fortunes. An only son or eldest son was inevitably a patriarch-in-training, to be treated with austere discipline. In a very revealing comment, William Cecil, Lord Burghley, who has been called the 'archetypal father' of Elizabethan England, matter-of-factly remarked of his troubled heir Thomas that 'I never showed any fatherly fancy to him, but in teaching and correcting.'[8]

In light of the historians' debate, it is clear that Shakespeare's plays do not provide a balanced picture of the full range of contemporary family relationships, especially with regard to fathers and sons.[9] Not only do the plays focus on the relatively small, propertied social stratum in which differences between fathers and sons were most likely to occur, but they also stress the sons most likely to have been emotionally distanced from their fathers, the patrilineal heirs. Moreover, Shakespeare's plays often emphasize the isolation of the prime son by removing younger male siblings that appear in his sources.[10] By the same token, the frequent absence of mothers in the plays' families removes a figure who might be expected to mediate between demanding father and resistant son, as Elizabethan mothers often did and as mothers do when Shakespeare adds them to the father-son dyad.[11] These characteristics point to a representation of fathers and sons that is darker than the model of the 'Loving Family in Old Europe' but also considerably more nuanced than the model of the despotic patriarch.

The central phenomenon – for the present study – of filial ambivalence is not discussed by the historians advocating for either position. This is not surprising, since its origin was not in either of the discrete opposing realities documented by historians, but rather in the intersection of the two. Underpinning ambivalent attitudes toward fathers is a collision of two fields of force. One was prescriptive and cautionary, stressing the unquestioning obedience of sons to the unquestionable authority of fathers; this pervasive attitude was drummed into Shakespeare's generation by the mutually reinforcing catechisms of church and state, bolstered by various legal sanctions, and enacted in the rituals of everyday life. The opposing force had its origin in the energies of sons who resisted their fathers by seeking autonomous action and a measure of self-definition. While the first impulse preached the imitation and even replication of the father, the second militated for the expressiveness and independence of the son. Both of these attitudes were powerful, and they jostled in the minds of many young men. Few Elizabethan sons could have escaped entirely the concerted inculcation of deference, and few could have been totally oblivious to the call of ambition and autonomy. While, *pace* Freud, sons in all historical periods may feel ambivalence toward the fathers who both support and control them, in Shakespeare's time the polarities of feeling were intensified by the sharp opposition between the indoctrination of filial deference and the unprecedented surge of filial creativity. After anatomizing the lesson of deference and its many manifestations, we will examine the forms of resistance that Elizabethan sons developed in response to it.

Father and Subordinate Son: Political and Religious Analogies

In the first volume of his autobiography (1966), the socialist man-of-letters Kingsley Martin recalled how his father, a Nonconformist Victorian preacher, rewrote the Ten Commandments to express his contrarian principles. For his Fifth Commandment, the staunchly anti-Calvinist minister retained the biblical 'Honour thy father and thy mother' but added an ameliorative codicil of his own: 'Respect the individuality and independence of thy children.'[12] Three centuries earlier, however, not even the most radical of dissenting Elizabethan clergymen would have questioned the strictly hierarchical nature of the family. Even on the verge of the English Civil War, when rebellious sects proliferated, interpretations of the Fifth Commandment retained the traditional emphasis on unqualified filial obedience.[13] It was only at the end of the seventeenth century, with the advent of conceptions of political reciprocity and contractual obligation, that John Locke could declare that 'he that would have his Son have a Respect for him, and his Orders, must himself have a great Reverence for his Son.'[14]

In Shakespeare's England, the notion of a father revering a son was conceivable only in the context of radical inversion, the world turned upside down. The dominant theological construction of parental superiority posited an analogy between the parent-child relationship and the relation of God to man. One of the fountainheads of English Protestant thought, William Tyndale's *The Obedience of a Christian Man* (1528), interpreted the Fifth Commandment's 'Honour thy father and thy mother' by stressing that 'Our fathers and mothers are to us in God's stead.'[15] It follows, then, that the proper attitude of children to their parents should be very like religious veneration, and Tyndale specified that the proper honouring 'is not to be understood in bowing the knee, and putting off the cap only, but that thou love them with all thine heart; and fear and dread them, and wait on their commandments; and seek their worship, pleasure, will and profit in all things; and give thy life for them, counting them worthy of all honour; remembering that thou art their good and possession, and that thou owest unto them thine own self, and all thou art able, yea, and more than thou art able to do.'[16] As the insistently repeated 'all' suggests, nothing less than complete, unequivocal self-sacrifice can be acceptable to parents who, like God, expect their charges to 'wait on their commandments.' In this austere formulation, the difference between parent and child is not a matter of degree but of kind; they are separated not only by years but by different places on a spiritual hierarchy. Children can no more repay their manifold debts to their parents than sinful man can win redemption without divine grace.

We should be careful, however, not to lift Tyndale's powerful formulation out of context, for to do so would be to misrepresent not only his treatise as a whole but also the thinking of the age. Even the most severe espousers of hierarchical obedience (like Tyndale) recognized that superiors owe duties to their inferiors, and later in the treatise he qualifies his absolutist stance with a section on the duties of parents to children. Interestingly, Tyndale's treatment of parental responsibilities includes some psychologically astute advice that is predicated on the *difference* between parents and God: 'Let the fathers and mothers mark how they themselves were disposed at all ages; and by experience of their own infirmities help their children, and keep them from occasions.'[17] Although proper Christian parents are placed *in loco Dei*, they had best not act as deities over and above their children. When Tyndale cautions 'Let not the fathers and mothers always take the utmost of their authority of their children,' his careful phrasing reveals an awareness of the potential dangers attending the discipline that good and godly parents must maintain.[18]

We see the excess that Tyndale warned of when, at the beginning of *A Midsummer Night's Dream*, Duke Theseus exhorts young Hermia to defer to her father's marital preferences for her:

> To you your father should be as a god;
> One that compos'd your beauties; yea, and one
> To whom you are but as a form in wax,
> By him imprinted, and within his power,
> To leave the figure, or disfigure it.   *MND*:1.1.47–51

Though these lines have occasionally been read as evidence of Shakespeare's supposed belief in paternal authority, their insistence on the unconstrained power of fathers to 'disfigure' children is quite excessive even by sixteenth-century standards.[19] Aggrieved fathers might occasionally feel nostalgia for the Roman law of *patria potestas* – by which progenitors were justified in killing children who defied them – but in early modern England this violent exercise of paternal power was always perceived as unnatural and even un-Christian.[20]

While it is unlikely that many early modern children confused their fathers with the deity (Hermia does not do so for a moment), there were occasions on which the connection between the two could be almost palpable. In England the most pervasive of these was a venerable domestic ritual in which the father played a priest-like role. In the morning and in the evening, as well as on special occasions such as parting before a journey, children were to beseech their parents for their blessing. The ritual called for the child to kneel before the parent, and for the parent to place his or her hands on the child's head and then to invoke God's blessing. The parental blessing was beginning to be looked upon as old-fashioned in Shakespeare's time, having already disappeared on the Continent, and, as the historian Ralph Houlbrooke has noted, 'With the gradual decline of the formal blessing there disappeared the most potent ritual expression of the direct link between divine and parental authority.'[21]

In the course of the sixteenth century the analogy of the father to God gradually underwent a transformation and took on a political shape: the father in the family is like the ruler in the state. Tellingly, the chapter in Tyndale's *Obedience of a Christian Man* that sets out paternal duties is headed 'The Office of a Father, and how he should rule.'[22] The correspondence between the microcosm of the family and the macrocosm of the body politic, which can be traced back at least as far as Aristotle, was advanced in early modern Europe with a zeal that sometimes obscured its figurative nature. In Shakespeare's time it was extremely difficult to think about the father's role in the family without also thinking about the maintenance of public, political order. In the official discourses of the age and in much imaginative literature as well, references to fathers often invoke the figure of the highest political ruler of the land, and vice versa. In John Donne's lament on the decay of political and social order, the analogy is precisely and succinctly drawn:

Tis all in pieces, all coherence gone;
All just supply, and all Relation.
Prince, Subject, Father, Son are things forgot.[23]

 In the religious literature of Reformation England, the family father is almost invariably associated with civil figures of authority. One of the most important English Protestant bibles, the Geneva Bible of 1560, makes a revealing marginal comment on the Fifth Commandment, glossing 'father' (not 'father and mother') with the comment 'By the which is meant all that have authority over us.'[24] In its imposition of political terms on family relationships, this gloss is entirely typical of orthodox Elizabethan thinking. After an exhaustive study of Tudor and Stuart religious commentaries, Gordon Schochet noted that 'without exception ... whenever the Decalogue was discussed, political duty was extracted from the Fifth Commandment.'[25] Religious catechisms, which were designed to shape young Elizabethan minds through godly rote learning, routinely applied this metaphorical sense of 'father' to the whole range of figures of male authority, including magistrates, clergymen, schoolteachers, and masters of trades.[26] To 'honour thy father,' then, is to be obedient to the reverend men who ruled not only Elizabethan families but also the various corporations of this gerontocracy in which age and authority walked hand in hand.[27] Of course, the presence of a superbly competent woman on the throne did create a tacit note of dissonance, but this anomaly disappeared with the accession in 1603 of the insistently patriarchal James I, a ruler who was literally the father of a family (including sons).

 A primary consequence of the father-king analogy was that it served as a vehicle to exalt obedience as the *sine qua non* of family life. For political authorities, it was tempting to depict the father as a king whose word was law, and hence 'Obedience was seen as the principal duty of children and it was instilled in them by all the religious, emotional and social pressures available.'[28] An early example of this tendency was the lumbering six-part 'Homily against Disobedience and Wilful Rebellion' that Elizabethan authorities added to the collection of official homilies to be delivered as sermons in every parish in the land. Written by officials shaken by the Northern Rebellion of 1569, this homily argues that, in response to Satan's primal sin of rebellion against divine authority, God 'not only ordained that in families and households the wife should be obedient unto her husband, the children unto their parents, the servants unto their masters: but also ... he by his Holy Word did constitute and ordain in cities and countries several and special governors and rulers, unto whom the residue of his people should be obedient.'[29] The clear intent is to identify proper order in the kingdom with proper order in the family, the essence of both being obedience. The identification of ruler and father meant that it was a very short step to conceive of filial disobedience as a form of *lèse majesté* or even as the crime of 'petty treason.' Richard Helgerson concluded his fine discussion of sixteenth-century parental authority by remarking, 'No wonder then if a young man felt that in disobeying his father he was disobeying the governing powers of the universe and of his own being.'[30]

In the often hyperbolic idiom of church Reformers, any act of filial resistance could be identified as a form of parricide; thus Bartholomaeus Battus declared a disobedient son to be a 'cruel murtherer of his Parents.'[31] Since filial disobedience was represented as being so extremely heinous, the actual crime of parricide became virtually unspeakable and unimaginable.[32] Indeed, the murder of fathers by their sons was rarely depicted in the literature of the age. Even in Marlowe's plays, where one senses a good deal of animus toward fathers, the act of parricide is conjured up by allusions to classical mythology rather than shown on stage.[33] When parricide does occur in early modern plays, the father and son are apt to belong to nationalities or races beyond the pale of natural (that is, Christian and English) relations. In the anonymous tragedy that bears his name, the cruel Turk Selimus has his father the king poisoned and then usurps his kingdom.[34] When parricide occurs in European settings, the unnaturalness of the deed is often emphasized by making the perpetrator an illegitimate son.[35]

Shakespeare never depicts the act of parricide and, with one exception, does not get closer to the deed than references that appear in several visions of universal chaos. In *Troilus and Cressida*, Ulysses warns about the loss of degree by imagining a disordered world in which 'Strength should be lord of imbecility, / And the rude son should strike his father dead' (1.3.114–15), and a similar image occurs in *Timon of Athens* when the embittered Timon curses Athens by conjuring up a state of chaos that includes parricide:

> Son of sixteen,
> Pluck the lin'd crutch from thy old limping sire,
> With it beat out his brains!   4.1.13–15

The closest Shakespeare comes to representing the act of parricide is a curious scene in *3 Henry VI* (2.5) in which a soldier discovers that the man whom he has just killed (offstage) is in fact his father. When he recognizes his victim, the son's grief is eloquently allusive: 'Pardon me, God, I knew not what I did! / And pardon, father, for I knew not thee!' (2.5.69–70). Not only is the parricide inadvertent, but it is also distanced by not being shown onstage and by the high degree of formalization in the entire scene. Indeed, in an allegorical symmetry, this son bearing his father's corpse – an ironic inversion of Aeneas carrying his father from Troy – is followed immediately (in the stage direction's words) by a *'father that hath kill'd his son.'* Once again, the victorious soldier discovers the terrible identity of his victim, exclaiming, 'Ah, no, no, no, it is mine only son!' (2.5.83). Significantly, neither pair of fathers and sons has names, and so the detached, allegorical nature of the scene is foregrounded. For sons to kill fathers, and fathers sons, is the essence of civil war. As often in the discourse of early modern England, parricide takes on a political dimension, becoming 'a vivid and accessible figuring of the sin a subject commits in rising against his prince.'[36]

Any ideology that discourages parricide must be attractive to fathers with adolescent sons, but the analogy of father as king demands a price for the protection it bestows. As the household ruler, the father assumes a quasi-political responsibility to maintain obedience and deference, if necessary at the cost of personal feeling. (Mothers were also, vis-à-vis children, in a position of rule, but among men there was a widespread acceptance of the stereotype that women were apt to be 'cockering mothers' who inadvertently encouraged vice in their children by failing to reprimand them for their faults.)[37] Insistent on the pre-eminent need for obedience, Elizabethan authorities often counselled fathers that their paternal duty included the repression of displays of fondness for their children, and especially for their sons. In the first Elizabethan blank-verse tragedy, a horrific civil war ensues when King Gorboduc allows his 'tender love' toward his sons to cloud his judgment. (Gorboduc's queen is more foolishly partial than he, and her excessive love for their elder son leads her to murder the younger one.) In *Gorboduc* a pervasive image pattern of flaming destruction alludes to the fiery disaster that ensued when Apollo handed over the reins of his sun chariot to his headstrong son Phaeton, and the Chorus draws the appropriate, turgid moral:

Oft tender mind that leads the partial eye
Of erring parents in their children's love
Destroys the wrongly loved child thereby.[38]

The Elizabethan ruling class was determined not to make the doting Gorboduc's mistake. Just as God chasteneth whom he loveth, so a good father should enforce severe discipline on a cherished son.[39]

In theory, the association of fathers with authority figures benefited both members of the analogy, placing a crown on the often-beleaguered family father while representing civic fathers as loving and protective of their charges. A special concern was the attempt to make the severe political authority of the ruler more palatable by associating it with supposedly natural family order. In Alexander Nowell's catechism, when the teacher asks the pupil why magistrates and other superiors are called by the names of parents, the response is that the human mind is 'puffed with pride and loath to be under others' commandment' and that parents represent 'that authority which of all other is naturally least grudged at.'[40] This emphasis allows the state to be represented as a family ruled by a firm but benign father in accordance with supposedly timeless norms. While the analogy of father and king served (in theory) to domesticate and naturalize political power, it often had (in practice) a deleterious effect within the family: it imposed political hierarchy on affective relationships, investing the family father with the stern, impersonal sanctions of the state. It is usually with regard to the subordination of wives that modern scholars have studied 'the consequences for private life that it was informed by a political construct,' but the emotional consequences for parent and child (and especially father and son) could be equally noxious.[41]

Needless to say, this ideal of austere, autocratic fatherhood could have painful effects on sons, but it is useful to recall that, as it was predicated on the concealment of private feelings, it could also wound fathers. If patriarchal values led sons to repress anger, they also led fathers to repress affection. Praising the importance of open discourse between father and son, Michel de Montaigne recounts how the Marshal de Monluc suffered 'infinite displeasure and heart's-sorrow' after the sudden death of his son,

> inasmuch as [Monluc] had never communicated and opened himself unto him; for with his austere humour and continual endeavouring to hold a grim-stern-fatherly gravity over him, he had lost the means perfectly to find and thoroughly to know his son, and so to manifest unto him the extreme affection he bare him, and the worthy judgement he

made of his virtue. Alas (was he wont to say) the poor lad saw never any-thing in me, but a severe-surly-countenance, full of disdain … I have forced and tormented my self to maintain this vain mask, and have utterly lost the pleasure of his conversation, and therewithal his good will.[42]

This moving passage draws as sharply as possible the internal conflict between 'grim-stern-fatherly gravity' and expressions of intimacy, but to a lesser degree the tension can be found in many fathers. Sir Henry Sidney, for instance, was usually formal, even stern, in his correspondence with his eldest son Philip, but in a letter to Lord Burghley he felt free to declare that, 'For my boy, I confess if I might have every week a boy, I should never love none like him.'[43]

Shakespeare's plays depict the problem of entangled public and private realms in the ritual of the paternal blessing, an action that manifests the doubleness of the father's role.[44] On the one hand, the ritual may express the tender, protective concern of the father, as he calls down the blessings of God upon his kneeling child. On the other hand, the father may be demonstrating his authority by compelling his son to kneel before him. The parental blessing is clearly most complicated when, in a recurring situation in Shakespeare's plays, a child kneels before a man who is both father and king, thus rendering the traditional analogy literally true and making filial love and political duty difficult, if not impossible, to separate.[45] As Shakespeare shows most clearly in *King Lear*, a play in which kneeling is a central action, the political conception of the paternal role can inflict pain on fathers as well their progeny.

Filial Debt and Imitation

The analogy of family organization to political hierarchy helped to foster the defining of filial responsibilities in quasi-legal terms as the discharging of duties and debts. (Elizabethans often spelled 'duty' as 'duety,' being aware that a duty involved paying something due.) Of course, financial indebtedness was an unhappy reality for every son, and begging letters from sons to fathers make up a significant body of Elizabethan correspondence.[46] But this monetary debt was only a part of the overarching obligation noted in the introduction: that children were forever indebted to their parents for their very existence. A volume titled *A Discourse for Parents Honour and Authoritie* draws for

children the inevitable, guilt-inducing lesson: 'As for us, be we never
so obsequious and dutiful to them [parents], yet shall we come short
of that measure of thankfulness which we owe them.'[47] Conversely, for
a son to deny his indebtedness to his parents, and especially his father,
was to reveal an unnatural mind that was capable of anything. In the
anonymous tragedy *Selimus*, when the evil title character contemplates
overthrowing his father the king, he derides the concept of filial debt:
'Is he my father? Why, I am his son. / I owe no more to him than he to
me.'[48]

The most unremitting insistence on the immensity of filial debt came
from preachers and catechists, but often fathers themselves found the
notion a means to enforce their will. A case in point is a letter written
by Baldassare Castiglione, the author of *The Courtier*, to his eleven-
year-old son, Camillo. The elder Castiglione begins by reminding him
that 'it is ordained, alike by Nature and the laws of man, that we reverence our parents next to God,' and then he moves into the language
of indebtedness: 'And you may be said to owe me an especial debt,
since I have remained content with one son, and have been unwilling
to share either my fortune or my love with another. You are bound,
therefore, to pay me this filial duty, lest I should repent of my resolution. And, although I have no doubt that you recognize this, I wish you
to understand that I do not regard this duty lightly, as other parents
often do, but I exact it from you as my due.'[49] After this gravely coercive prologue, the rightful payment that Castiglione exacts as his due
turns out to be almost anticlimactic: 'This debt you will best discharge
by looking upon the admirable teacher whom your friends have given
you, in the light of a father, and by obeying his voice as if it were my
own.' It is easy, however, to imagine the paternal insistence on filial
debt being put to less benign purposes, as it sometimes is in Shakespeare's plays.

Among the debts that Elizabethan sons were thought (and taught)
to owe their fathers, the duty of imitation was paramount. In the
Renaissance, the concept of imitation was central to education and to
literary culture, and when Elizabethan patriarchs exhorted their male
progeny to use them as models of virtue, they were themselves following venerable precedents, as they well knew. Marcus Tullius
Cicero's *De officiis* (On Public Duties), which had a kind of scriptural
authority among the humanists, argued that the fulfilling of duties is
the core of the ethical life, with one's duty to one's father being second
only to one's fatherland.[50] Addressing his son and namesake, Marcus,

Cicero praised himself rather fulsomely; he justified his immodesty by invoking the doctrine of imitation: 'I may boast to you, my son Marcus; for to you belong the inheritance of that glory of mine and the duty of imitating my deeds.'[51] The greater the father's noble bequest, the greater the son's onus of emulation.

As in so many other aspects of the father-son relationship, the burden of imitation fell heaviest on the son who would succeed his father. In the anonymous tragedy *Locrine*, for example, the dying King Brutus speaks as both father and ruler when he calls Locrine ('the eldest of my sons') to his deathbed and exhorts him, and him alone, to 'imitate thy agèd father's steps.'[52] The ideal son was a figure like King James's son Prince Charles, of whom the Venetian ambassador reported: 'His chief endeavour is to have no other aim than to second his father, to follow him and do his pleasure and not to move except as his father does.'[53] This compulsion to imitate the father (which did not stand Charles in good stead upon his elevation to the throne) exacerbates what is already an inherent doubleness in Elizabethan father-son relationships. On the one hand, the son is the father's legitimate successor, the guarantor of his line, the extension into the future of his identity and authority. On the other hand, the very fact that the son is his father's successor means that he will someday supplant and in effect usurp his progenitor. The King is dead, long live the King. Montaigne, who was uncommonly sensitive to the problems faced by elder sons, decried the difficulties that primogeniture imposed on both fathers and their heirs; speaking as a father, he declared that 'Since in sober truth things are so ordered that children can only have their being and live their lives at the expense of our being and of our lives, we ought not to undertake to be fathers if that frightens us.'[54]

From one orthodox perspective, it was hardly necessary to instruct a young man to imitate his father because the two figures were already joined by a natural, organic bond that resulted in something like a shared identity. This idea lies behind the common Renaissance trope that the son is a mirror in whom the father is reflected and perpetuated, an idea hinted at in the double portrait of the elder and younger Walter Raleghs. Similarly, in his double portrait of John Godsalve and his son Thomas, Hans Holbein literalizes the conceit of the son as an extension of his father. Not only are the two faces strikingly similar, but the bodies overlap so as to compose a single mass; since father and son wear identical fur-trimmed robes, it is difficult to determine where

one leaves off and the other begins.[55] Thus, in an elemental consolation, fathers saw themselves living on in their sons. In a narrative in Sir
Philip Sidney's *Arcadia* that Shakespeare would transform for the sub-
plot of *King Lear*, the Gloucester-figure declares of his loyal son that 'I
needed envy no father for the chief comfort of mortality, to leave
another one's-self after me' (Bullough 7:404).

The idea of a common nature shared between fathers and sons was
widespread in Shakespeare's time, as an incident involving Philip
Sidney indicates. At the Elizabethan court, Sidney taunted the Earl of
Ormonde, who had taken issue with his father's, Sir Henry Sidney's,
administration of Ireland. Ormonde, however, refused to seek redress
against the younger Sidney because, he is reported to have said, 'he
will accept no quarrels from a gentleman that is bound by nature to
defend his father's causes.'[56] 'Bound by nature' suggests that the
young Sidney was compelled by a debt of blood and instinct to
support his father, as if his dutiful action could not be held against him
because it had been predetermined. A similar assumption about filial
bonds being naturally compelling is made by the Ghost of Hamlet's
father when – in response to Hamlet's 'Speak, I am bound to hear' – he
retorts, 'So art thou to revenge, when thou shalt hear' (1.5.6–7). But in
the case of the Ghost, as we shall see, the assumption proves to be
wishful thinking.

Notwithstanding the reassurance provided by the concept of natural
bonds, many Elizabethan fathers took pains to shape their sons, so far
as possible, into a replica of themselves. For many firstborn Elizabethan sons, this process of being fashioned into the image of their
fathers began with their christening, as often they received the first
name that was also their father's. A recent study indicates that from
the middle of the sixteenth century to the end of the seventeenth there
was 'an unhesitating upward course of the rise in the proportion of
eldest children named after a parent.'[57] Though the incidence of
shared names for parent and child increased for both sexes, the desire
to stress patrilineal succession resulted in a difference with regard to
frequency: boys were two to three times more likely to be named after
a parent than were girls. Shakespeare's plays reflect this tendency
toward male name-sharing, and indeed, eldest sons with names different from their fathers are in the distinct minority. For every Laertes
(son of Polonius), there is both a Hamlet (son of Hamlet) and a Fortinbras (son of Fortinbras). After sons of the elite were sent off to
grammar school or university, often at a surprisingly early age, they

received letters from home exhorting them to virtue and stressing the duty to imitate their fathers and forefathers.[58] In a letter in *Gargantua and Pantagruel*, Rabelais captures the mix of pride, exhortation, and guilt-tripping that characterizes these missives. For the most part, Gargantua is an admirable figure, and there is no questioning his affection for his son, but it is chilling how quickly his tone segues from cordiality to coercion. After thanking God for the gift to be able 'to behold my hoary old age flowering again in your youth,' he reminds Pantagruel that what truly matters is the continuance not of the body but of the family name, lest it become 'bastardized and degenerate.' After a quick reminder that he has 'spared no expense' in Pantagruel's education, Gargantua characterizes his own life in plaintive terms calculated to put pressure on him: 'I might seem to have desired nothing but to leave you, after my death, as a mirror representing the person of me your father, and if not as excellent and in every way as I wish you, at least desirous of being so.'[59]

Sir Philip Sidney was well schooled in the offices of filial duty, as we have seen, and chief among the lessons he learned was the obligation to imitate his virtuous ancestors.[60] In a letter to the eleven-year-old Philip, Sir Henry Sidney delivered a double-barreled exhortation, stressing the need to imitate both sides of his family. First he says, 'Remember, my son the noble blood you are descended of by your mother's side; and think that only by virtuous life and good action you may be an ornament to that illustrious family.' Then, he (rather sternly) admonishes Philip to be as light-hearted as he himself is: 'give your self to be merry, for you degenerate from your father if you find not your self most able in wit and body to do any thing when you be most merry.'[61] To 'degenerate' is to fall away from the ancestral stock, a charge that fathers level at sons in Shakespeare, most memorably when King Henry accuses Prince Hal of being cravenly obsequious to Hotspur and thus showing 'how much thou art degenerate' (*1H4*:3.2.128). The only way for the son to avoid degeneration (and its attendant suggestion of bastardy) was of course through vigorous imitation, as the painting of the two Walter Raleghs reminds us.

For sons the burden of imitation began early but was by no means limited to childhood. Indeed, for a properly trained son the work of imitation was never done, for even after the father's death his obligations continued unabated, sometimes decreed by manipulative testamentary clauses or magnified by guilt. A truly reverent son would not only devote himself to his living father, but after his progenitor's death he would strive to incorporate him into his own life. What seems to be asked of the son (though of course never explicitly spelled out) is to be willing to be possessed by the spirit of his father. In his treatise on *Domesticall Duties*, the Puritan minister William Gouge declared that a dutiful child should endeavour to embody the virtues of a deceased parent, 'For when they who knew the parents behold the like good qualities and actions in their children, they will thereby be put in mind of the parties deceased, and say, Oh how such parents yet live! behold a lively, and living Image of them.'[62] Sons in Shakespeare need not believe in purgatory or spirit-possession in order for the injunctions of dead fathers to sound clearly in their ears.

As one would expect, for some Elizabethan sons the duty to shape themselves in their father's image served to deny, or at least to delay, their realization of their true talents. Such a person was Sir Francis Bacon, a man who was hardly deficient in ego and scarcely an under-achiever. His father, Sir Nicholas Bacon, was a most impressive figure: a brilliant lawyer, Lord Keeper of the Great Seal under Elizabeth for many years, a pillar of the Puritan community, and a prose stylist praised by Roger Ascham as one of the greatest in the realm. Sir Nicholas died when Francis was eighteen, and the son spent the greater part of his life attempting to imitate his father's career in law and politics, though he was (as he came to realize) by disposition unfit for the work.[63] Ironically, Bacon's self-denying reverence for his father 'made him especially sympathetic to any doctrine that stressed the rights of parents over children,' and thus he supported the idea that the killing of a parent by a child was like the killing of a king by a subject and therefore to be punished as 'petty treason.' To compound the mordant ironies, Bacon delivered a legal opinion defending the power of fathers to disinherit children, even though his own father had 'failed to keep his pledge to provide for him in his will.' Nor did Bacon give up his father's ghost easily. Some thirty years after the death of Sir Nicholas, his ever-dutiful son perused a manuscript of William Camden's *Annals of Queen Elizabeth*, found comments on his father that he deemed unworthy, and successfully pressured the histo-rian to incorporate in the published text interpolations he had written 'for my father's honour.' As Bacon and his generation had been taught, there were no proper limits to filial duty.

In the plays that are the focus of this study, Shakespeare's depictions of fathers and sons highlight the duty of filial imitation, imposed explicitly by fathers or intuited by sons. In the most forceful example of a father spelling out the behaviour he expects to be replicated, King Henry accuses Prince Hal of failing to imitate his own political machinations and instead following in the footsteps of the hapless Richard II, whom he deposed (1H4:3.2.29–128). But here and elsewhere this paternal coercion fails to be successful; these sons rarely act out the roles their fathers have written for them, being especially wary of the danger of losing autonomy by imitating their fathers. For these sons imitation becomes not a form of deference but rather an instrument of resistance, as figures like Hamlet and Prince Hal mimic the speech and action of their fathers in ironic, often parodic ways. They turn their imitation inside out, putting the father's lesson to work in ways calculated to discomfort him. In this twisting and transforming of paternal fiat, Shakespeare's sons contrive in their ambivalent way to reconcile their sense of duty with their anger at being made to act out the paternal script.

Filial Resistance and Autonomy

In *The Family and Family Relationships*, Rosemary O'Day makes a useful distinction between the 'prescriptive' and the 'descriptive' family, the first being the view of the family advanced by authoritative, external agencies, the second being the reality experienced by actual members of families. In a warning relevant to our study, she cautions against the impulse to 'treat *prescriptive* sources as though they were *descriptive*.'[64] Buttressed by the law court and the pulpit, the hierarchical view of father and son was certainly the official understanding of Elizabethan England. But it did not go unchallenged. For simplicity of exposition, we can divide the resistance into two distinct forms, one in the realm of ideas and education, the other in the world of work and the quotidian search for sustenance, where the vast majority of English youth had to make their way. In addition to their common emphasis on the freedom of the young, these forms of resistance shared an avoidance of direct confrontation with the patriarchal powers of the day. It would, for instance, be a mistake to read Thomas Nashe's vivid evocation of open conflict between the generations as fact rather than fantasy: 'The Ancients, they oppose themselves against the younger, and suppress them, and keep them down all that they may. The young men, they call them dotards, and swell, and rage, and with many oaths swear on the other side they will not be kept under by such cullions, but go good and near to out-shoulder them.'[65] Given the deferential attitudes inculcated by church and state, as well as the sanctions fathers could bring to bear, it seems unlikely that many young men called their elders and betters 'cullions' (literally 'testicles' and figuratively 'base fellows') to their faces; even the most rebellious sons were likely to harbour some ambivalence, or at least to disguise their desire to 'out-shoulder' their fathers.[66]

Though patriarchal values were rarely attacked in a direct, systematic way, some pointed criticisms can be found, especially in translations of Italian and French writers. It would, for instance, be hard to match in an English author the undisguised animus toward fathers that Girolamo Cardano expressed in his philosophical consolation on death. Cardano begins a discussion of filial grief by citing the biblical injunction to honour one's father and mother but suddenly veers onto a subversive track. Addressing children, he remarks that 'reverence and respect towards the father doth chiefly hinder thee, or altogether let [obstruct] thee' with regard to 'the desire of glory' and the pursuit of rule and wisdom. Then he remarks bitterly that 'The authority of fathers containeth in it somewhat more than service, and hindereth the execution of great things, be it in wars, learning or administration of the common wealth: for all things having evil success are imputed to the son, & all good to the father.'[67] Cardano was something of a polymath, being a noted mathematician and astrologist as well as a philosopher, and the most outspoken criticisms of paternal authority came from people like him who were loath to allow their creative autonomy to be stifled.

Insofar as there is a common philosophy underlying the resistance to unqualified filial deference, it derives in good part from the theory and practice of humanist education. This pedagogical program was articulated by schoolmasters who argued that truly 'liberal education' was predicated on the liberty of students and that the compelled obedience of young men amounted to a tyrannical limitation of human potential, for it denied freedom of choice. Thus, in a declamation on the early humanist education of boys, Erasmus attacked the reliance on corporal punishment in schools, arguing that the imposition of discipline through fear reduced students to servility. True education, according to Erasmus, should be liberal in that it frees the mind and encourages liberty. A father should be the opposite of a slave master: 'A master can exert his authority only through compulsion, but a father who appeals to his son's sense of decency and liberality can gradually build up in him a spontaneous capacity for moral conduct which is untainted by any motive of fear.'[68] Similarly, in his important essay 'Of the Affection of Fathers to Their Children,' Montaigne blasted learning that was based on mere force and authority: 'I utterly condemn all manner of violence in the education of a young spirit, brought up to honour and liberty. There is a kind of slavishness in churlish-rigour and servility in compulsion; and I hold, that *that which cannot be compassed by reason, wisdom and discretion, can never be attained by force and constraint.*'[69]

It would of course be misleading to see the Elizabethan schoolroom as a site where paternal authority was actively subverted and filial rebellion advocated. Teachers were an integral part of the structure of authority, and we recall that Elizabethan catechisms often included them in the catalogue of 'civil fathers' whom children were compelled to honour.[70] Also, the humanists' pedagogical method stressed the concept of imitation, as children were trained by modelling their writing on the great exemplars of the classical past, and imitation of authors could look like the imitation of fathers advocated in arguments for filial deference. Ben Jonson, who was a stellar product of this system, came to acknowledge in his later years the dangers of servile imitation and authoritarianism, noting that 'Greatness of name, in the Father, oft-times helps not forth, but o'erwhelms the Son: they stand too near one another. The shadow kills the growth.'[71]

Certainly, the humanist emphasis on free will and on rational choice helped to shape ideas of what a dignified life for a young person might consist of. Thus, in George Pettie's translation of Guazzo's *Civile Conversazione*, an interlocutor rails against fathers who thrust their children into religious houses, 'which is nothing else, but to withstand the will of God, and to take from their children that free choice which he of his divine goodness hath promised them.'[72] Moreover, humanist pedagogy posited that a child has a natural aptitude (*ingenium*) which it is the responsibility of teachers and parents to recognize and cultivate.[73] Treatises on pedagogy often criticized fathers who, being oblivious to their sons' true natures and talents, selfishly attempt to force them into inappropriate careers. Implicitly or explicitly, the assumption is that society as a whole will benefit from the realization of children's aptitudes, and thus Erasmus declares, 'For human happiness depends mainly on this, that everyone should wholly apply himself to that for which he is naturally fitted.'[74] This new respect for filial predisposition is one cause of what one historian has called the 'real but partial and very gradual relaxation among the propertied classes of parental control over the choice of marriage partners and callings' during Shakespeare's lifetime.[75]

With the coming of the Reformation, the humanist emphasis on free choice and the fulfilment of inborn talent found a parallel in the Protestant conception of a particular calling or vocation that was God's intention for the individual to take up. Like the humanist idea of a way of life (*genus vitae*) suitable to one's gifts, this idea of an inwardly received spiritual calling tended to diminish the importance of parental approval. The traditional Lutheran and Calvinist position had been to emphasize the absolute authority of parents to determine children's callings, but by the end of the sixteenth century the humanist emphasis on the importance of a child's particular gifts began to complicate the doctrine.[76] In his *Treatise of the Vocations, or Callings of Men*, the popular Calvinist theologian William Perkins discusses not only the general spiritual calling imposed by God but also the particular societal calling to be taken up by a child. While declaring that 'it is the duty of parents to make choice of fit callings' for children, he adds that in order to judge this fitness the parents 'must observe two things in them: first, their inclination; secondly, their natural gifts.'[77] William Gouge expands on Perkins when, in discussing 'parents' care in choosing a fit calling for their children,' he emphasizes the importance of recognizing 'a child's best *ability*' and excoriates parents who 'train up children which have a great inclination to learning, and are very fit thereunto, in some other trade, which, after many years spent therein, they are forced to leave.'[78] So, while he stipulates that the decision is for the parent to make, he also appears tacitly to acknowledge the fact that legitimate needs may compel an otherwise dutiful child to renounce the vocation chosen for him. In Shakespeare's plays, as we will see, the incompatibility between a father's imposed vocation and a son's natural inclination is a recurrent problem.

Important as the framework of humanist thinking was for shaping educated opinion, at the heart of filial resistance was simply the energetic insubordination of young people.[79] It seems likely, indeed, that deference and obedience were promulgated so vigorously precisely because youth were prone to resist the prescriptions of their elders.[80] If every son were a willing Aeneas, devoted to his father and eager to carry him on his back, there would have been no need to exhort the youth of England to emulate the Trojan's pious heroism. Indeed, an anxiety about the vitality of traditional and supposedly natural values surfaces at the end of the poem accompanying the woodcut of Aeneas's rescue of Anchises (see fig. 1, p. 12). We are informed that, in addition to praising filial devotion, the picture 'reprehends ten thousand to their shame, / Who oft despise the stock whereof they came.'[81] That these ten thousand sons repeatedly ('oft') scorn their parents suggests a note of hyperbole, but the acute concern had some basis in social and demographic reality. Underlying the concern about deference was real cause for alarm: in the middle of the sixteenth century between 30 and 40 per cent of the population was under sixteen years of age.[82] It must have seemed to authorities that there were simply not enough domestic and civic fathers to police England's potentially wayward children.

Sometimes the resistance to fathers took violent forms, including even parricide. Thus, Shakespeare's occupation of New Place in Stratford was unexpectedly delayed because, after the deal had closed, the seller was lethally poisoned by his eldest son, who was duly convicted and hanged.[83] But for most sons the better part of valour was discretion, and insubordination took the form of withdrawal rather than confrontation, flight rather than fight. When there was a danger of open conflict with his father, a son was well advised to walk away rather than risk a conflict he could not win. The scholar and polemicist Gabriel Harvey recalls following the counsel of prudence when he was sharply chastised at dinner: 'My father began to chide and square with me at the table. I presently, and doing my duty, rise from the board, saying only "I pray you, good father, pray for me and I will pray for you."'[84] For every son who, like Wat Ralegh in the anecdote, chose to 'box about' in response to a paternal reproach, there were no doubt innumerable Gabriel Harveys.

The agency and expressive freedom of Elizabethan sons were curtailed with the greatest severity in the father's august presence; so long as the son stood cap in hand before his progenitor, the observances of obedience were tightly scripted. The possibilities for liberty lay in removing oneself from the stifling paternal presence. Some sons seized the possibility of joining military expeditions, and those who were away from home often looked for reasons to remain away. When Walter Bagot lost patience with his eldest son Lewis's prolonged absence, Lewis responded that 'he had been a long time in London because he lived there more contented than at home.'[85]

As social historians have noted, 'Adolescents were the most rest-less, the most untrammelled of the population, and the most evi-dently on the move,' and for parish authorities, not surprisingly, 'the most persistent nuisance were young runaways.'[86] Though there had long been a tradition of children going out for household service (mainly young women) and apprenticeship (mainly young men), sometimes far from home, that practice was intensified by immigra-tion to London from places as far away as the wilds of Yorkshire.[87] An historian calculates that 'approximately one-half of the young men who began apprenticeships in sixteenth-century London simply abandoned their training at some point during their service' – as Prince Hal tempted Francis to do.[88] It would appear that often chil-dren did not seek their parents' permission before leaving home or breaking apprenticeships, and so in a discussion of filial disobedience William Gouge fulminated against 'the practice of such children as travel, and seek their fortunes (as they speak) without consent of parents, like the *Prodigal child*.'[89]

Icarus and the Prodigal Son Transformed

The waywardness of youth helps to account for the fact that two great Elizabethan exempla of filial insubordination, the biblical Prodigal Son and the mythological Icarus, were figures who abandoned their places by their fathers' sides in order to undertake journeys of self-realiza-tion. After demanding his inheritance from his father, the Prodigal Son 'took his journey into a far country, and there he wasted his goods with riotous living' (Luke 15:13). After severe privation, he returns to his father, confesses his unworthiness, and is joyfully accepted. By con-trast, the desire of young Icarus to go his own way proves to be tragic. Upon donning the waxen wings his father Daedalus made for him, Icarus disregards his father's warning; leaving him behind, Icarus flies too close to the sun and plummets into the sea.[90] Since, in their differ-ent ways, both of these assertions of filial independence proved to be failures, the stories were seized upon by authorities to warn youth of the dangers of disobedience. In a sermon that contrived to blend the two figures by noting that the Prodigal Son's goods 'melt like wax before the heat of the Sun,' Samuel Gardiner declared that disobedient children are 'always of a gadding spirit, they are never well, but when they are ranging, and their feet stand upon thorns until they be gone out of their parents' house.'[91]

In Shakespeare's England, the Prodigal Son and Icarus underwent a transformation in which they ceased to be exclusively cautionary tales. Proud young writers like Thomas Nashe, who asserted that 'the vein which I have ... is of my own begetting, and calls no man father in England but my self,' were not inclined to accept the entirely negative depiction of father-deniers like Icarus and the Prodigal Son.[92] The orthodox interpretation of the stories was often questioned or simply ignored by a generation of writers that had found something to celebrate in solo flight and filial truancy. In these transformations the balance of sympathies shifted, as the fathers became increasingly tyrannical and the sons attractively rebellious. But the stories never became completely detached from their traditional cautionary moorings, and in this they represent the ambivalence of the age.

In late sixteenth-century England the revolt of the Prodigal Son became increasingly sympathetic among critics of the status quo. Throughout the first half of the century, writers employed the parable in a straightforward, didactic fashion, using it as the basis for countless morality plays about the need for Youth to eschew Worldliness and submit to Wise Counsel. But, with the supplanting of morality plays by the secular drama of the new repertory companies in London, the Prodigal Son began to be depicted in more complicated and often subversive ways. In a key shift, the parable is often rewritten to fit the plot of New Comedy, and the prodigality of the son's desires begins to look distinctly positive because it is contrasted to the grasping avarice of the father. A moral treatise called *A Display of Dutie* could declare that 'by God's justice, the prodigal son doth scorn the careful sighs of his covetous father.'[93] Indeed, in the private, coterie theatres of the early seventeenth century, 'hostile attitudes toward the form and morals of the traditional Prodigal Son play seem to have been something of a hit.'[94] A parallel, if less subtle, subversion of the parable is apparent in the fact that it often appeared as the subject of wall furnishings in Elizabethan taverns and alehouses.[95] (Falstaff recommends to Mistress Quickly that she acquire for her walls a 'pretty slight drollery, or the story of the Prodigal' [2*H*4:2.1.144–5].) Presumably the depictions of the Prodigal Son's 'riotous living' that graced these establishments were not intended to exhort customers to honour their fathers and to reduce their alcohol intake. The subversive treatment of the Prodigal Son and his father complicates Shakespeare's *1 Henry IV*, where the tavern clearly provides a more attractive environment for the prodigal prince than the court maintained by his usurping father, the King.

Even more strikingly than the Prodigal Son parable, the Icarus myth underwent a kind of transformative journey in the sixteenth century, starting out as a warning against filial excess but becoming for many a celebration of youthful desire. In the moralized interpretations of Ovid in pre-humanistic Europe, the story of Icarus had represented the danger of disobeying God's paternal law. This cautionary view persists in Arthur Golding's Tudor translation in which Icarus is no longer Ovid's innocent boy 'led by a desire for the open sky,' but rather a symbol of overweening pride, being 'Of fond desire to fly to Heaven, above his bounds.'[96] But increasingly a new note is heard first on the Continent and then in Elizabethan England, as poets begin to adopt the over-reaching Icarus as a fellow-traveller, 'an example of noble courage ill-fated but motivated by an understandable, and even admirable, ambition for a great goal.'[97] Both the old and the new attitudes toward Icarus are apparent in the emblem and explanatory poem from Geffrey Whitney's *A Choice of Emblemes* (see fig. 2). As the title ('*In astrologos*') indicates and the accompanying poem expounds, Icarus is identified as a symbol of intellectual pride and improper surveillance of God's secrets. But the depiction of him in his naked beauty, falling Satan-like from the sky, is more attractive and heroic than the moralistic view allows, evoking tragic sublimity as well as cautionary restraint.

Even Sir Philip Sidney and Sir Francis Bacon, two contemporaries of Shakespeare whom I have cited as examples of filial deference, found something to admire in the flight of Icarus. Throughout the *Defence of Poetry* Sidney sings the praises of Aeneas, who is a kind of anti-Icarus in his dutiful bearing of the heavy burden of his father.[98] But Sidney's glorification of Aeneas does not preclude an ambivalent attraction to Icarus. Despite his being carefully trained in filial obedience and despite his warm respect for his father, Sidney (like many in his generation) was irritated by the restraints imposed by his elders.[99] If Aeneas's rescue of his father speaks to Sidney's conscious commitment to his duty, the supremely unburdened figure of Icarus informs his celebration of the 'high flying liberty of conceit proper to the poet, [which] did seem to have some divine force in it.'[100] In the *Defence of Poetry*, Sidney imaginatively releases a poet-Icarus who soars up to perilous and barely imaginable heights; but, instead of crashing, this Icarus returns to safety at his father's side, though perhaps not without some chafing.[101]

Figure 2 Icarus Falling from the Sky, from Geffrey Whitney, *A Choice of Emblemes* (1586), ed. John Manning (Menston: Scolar Press, 1989), 28

Even dutiful, well-grounded sons like Sir Francis Bacon, who once opined that the mind needs weights instead of wings, could feel a tug of exhilaration when contemplating Icarus.[102] Francis was ever obedient to the gravely stoical Sir Nicholas Bacon, whose personal motto – *Mediocria firma* ('moderate things are steadfast') – sounds like a quotation from Daedalus's warning to Icarus about flying neither too high nor too low.[103] But in the younger Bacon's *The Wisdom of the Ancients*, a collection of heavily allegorized readings of Greek myths, the interpretation of Icarus contains an unexpected ambivalence. Bacon begins in a traditional way by associating Icarus with 'the pride of youthful alacrity' and the sin of excess, but then he undertakes a little Icarian flight of his own when he ponders the relative merits of excess and of defect (which he associates with age): 'For sins of defect are justly accounted worse than sins of excess; because in excess there is something of magnanimity – something, like the flight of a bird, that holds kindred with heaven; whereas defect creeps on the ground like a reptile.'[104]

Like Sidney and Bacon, Shakespeare had to reconcile his possession of great creative gifts with an upbringing that stressed filial imitation and indebtedness. And like them, he may well have entertained ambivalent feelings toward the rule of fathers. Shakespeare, however, is unlike Sidney and Bacon in one crucial regard: instead of merely experiencing the dilemma of the ambivalent son and expressing it in a symptomatic way, he depicts and explores it in his art. One means he uses to do so is by associating the mythical icons of good and bad filial behaviour with the same son. Often these contrary associations occur in conjunction with Shakespeare's depictions of sons who rescue and then reproach their fathers. This complex imaging is apparent in the next chapter, which examines Shakespeare's first sustained treatment of a father and a son, Lord John Talbot and his son John Talbot in *1 Henry VI*. In a key passage, the young John is depicted as a pious Aeneas rescuing his father on the battlefield but also as a wayward Icarus who deserts his father. The presence of both frames of reference suggests that young John Talbot (and his successors) harbour within themselves conflicting impulses toward their fathers, as some of Shakespeare's creative contemporaries did with regard to their progenitors.

2 *Henry VI, Part One*: Prototypical Beginnings – The Two John Talbots

In *Part One* of *Henry VI*, one of Shakespeare's earliest plays, we encounter a depiction of a father and son – Lord John Talbot and young John Talbot – that anticipates in uncanny detail his accomplished handling of the relationship. As in plays to come, the father is an imposing figure past his prime and becoming increasingly vulnerable, while his son is coming of age and hoping to prove himself. Although the two John Talbots espouse the same commitment to family honour, they are soon engaged in a muted conflict, as Lord John attempts to impose his will and young John resists him. In this deferential but stubborn denial of paternal command, we see the first appearance in the plays of what will become a recurrent figure, the ambivalent son. Young John Talbot expresses his filial dividedness in a sequence of actions that serves as a model for many of Shakespeare's sons-to-come: combining the piety of Aeneas with the restlessness of Icarus and the Prodigal Son, he conducts a heroic rescue of his father and immediately leaves him behind. In the persons of the two John Talbots, at the outset of his career, Shakespeare is already exploring the tensions between the deferential commitments and personal imperatives that being an Elizabethan son could entail.

If the relationship of the two John Talbots points toward future plays, the response to it by critics also prefigures things to come. The usual tendency of critics to underestimate the complexity of Shakespeare's sons is exacerbated by the common assumption that in these early history plays Shakespeare is not much interested in characterization: 'personality is invariably subordinated to what can be called theme.'[1] In this view, family relationships are presented in terms of the venerable Elizabethan analogy between the ordered family and the ordered kingdom, and thus a monograph concerning Shakespeare's histories entitled *The Family and the State* declares that 'The family in the *Henry VI* trilogy has no independent role ... it functions almost entirely as a commentary on the causes and consequences of political disorder.'[2] Since it is presented in the context of a growing factionalism in England that will soon lead to the outbreak of the War of the Roses, the depiction of the two Talbots is usually interpreted as the representation of an exemplary father and son. But, important as they are, these public and political concerns are not the whole story of fathers *and* sons in these plays. What the political interpretations do not take account of, because they do not value it, is the emotional experience of sons. While the obligations and privileges of patriarchy may be the whole story for fathers, they cannot be for sons.

This purportedly historical interpretation is itself ahistorical because, following the voices of Elizabethan authority, it assumes an idealized father-son relationship based on the lack of discrepancy between public and private concerns. But the relationships of fathers and sons could be troubled with private differences, even if there was agreement on large public and political ones. Shakespeare may have surmised that a shared commitment to family unity and to patrimonial lineage could create deep, if concealed, rifts between father and son. Modern historians of the family corroborate the potential for conflict. In his fine study entitled *Patriarchy and Families of Privilege in Fifteenth-Century England*, Joel T. Rosenthal notes that 'Just because father and son were engaged in a common enterprise is no compelling argument for sustained interpersonal cooperation. While the common goal may have been implicitly endorsed, the enterprise neither needed nor necessarily received complete harmony between the participants.'[3] And of course Elizabethan writers were aware of potential conflicts between father and son, especially with regard to a central topic for the Talbots, the pursuit of martial honour. It would seem that a mutual commitment to chivalry could entail a degree of (presumably healthy) familial rivalry. Thus, in a contemporary study of honour, John Ferne praises 'young Gentlemen of fore-spent times' who 'did contend in a commendable emulation to excel the worthiness of their ancestors.'[4] As Coppélia Kahn has noted, with regard to Elizabethan sons 'emulation' is a complex term, as it includes the old meaning of 'imitation' but also can carry more modern and pejorative meanings of competitiveness and envy.[5] In Ferne's account, the place of these young men is still more delicate, as they felt compelled to challenge the deeds of their elders 'lest they ... incur the judgement of [being called] a bastard or degenerated brood.'[6] An honourable son must contend with his elders, but in the right way.

Perhaps the best contextual evidence for thinking that Shakespeare wished to explore a doubleness in young John's relationship with his father stems from his handling of his chronicle sources. Revealingly, he revises his historical sources for the play in two opposing directions: he magnifies both the unity of father and son and the differences between them. Thus, he highlights the oneness of the relationship by inventing not one but two rescues on the battlefield: first the father saves his son, and then the son returns the favour. But Shakespeare also revises in the contrary direction, inventing many details that suggest resistance and even aggression on the part of the son. Thus, the final image of a father and son joined in noble death is openly celebrated and also subtly questioned.

Two John Talbots as One

By any reckoning, the three consecutive scenes (4.5, 4.6, 4.7) depicting the heroic deaths of the two John Talbots are central to *1 Henry VI* and designed to be 'the emotional high point of the play.'[7] Unlike the rest of the play, these scenes are cast in rhyming couplets and convey a heightened, formal feeling, suggesting that the two Talbots are exemplary, larger-than-life figures. Clearly this is a father-son relationship fraught with symbolic significances. Lord Talbot is himself a kind of archetypal father, for by act 4 he is the last living representative of the older generation of English heroes who had conquered France with Henry V. The play opens with the funeral of the great Henry, and the ongoing action is punctuated by the deaths of Henry's aged brothers-in-arms. From the outset, Lord Talbot is represented as the cynosure of chivalric values (valour, honour, loyalty) that are being destroyed by corrosive forces both in England and in France.[8] Given the fact that Lord Talbot has sent for his son John in order to teach him the ways of war in France, the relationship of father and son takes on a larger social significance, for young John must internalize these chivalric and familial values if they are to survive time's tooth. But of course there will be no future for young John or for the Talbot family. To make this termination as absolute and poignant as possible, Shakespeare revises his sources by deleting young John's siblings (including an illegitimate brother) and thus making him an only son.[9] The death of the two John Talbots, then, marks the tragic end of the dynastic line as well as the extinction of the chivalry that the father incarnates and the son has recently mastered.[10]

The pathos of the Talbot scenes is heightened by the isolation in which the father and son find themselves. As the brisk scenes leading up to young John's arrival in 4.5 indicate, Lord Talbot is trapped within Bordeaux and is essentially alone. Though he has sent word of his dire circumstances to other English commanders in the field, none of them comes to his rescue, preoccupied as they are with squabbling with each other. When young John arrives, he represents (pathetically) the only reinforcement that his father will receive. The isolation of father and son is intensified by the fact that we see no English soldiers with them until both are mortally wounded. In effect, they are an army of two. Betrayed by the English commanders who should support them and surrounded by untold numbers of French soldiers who would destroy them, the elder and the younger John Talbot stand together on the battlefield, a study in unity-in-isolation.

What is most moving about the Talbots is the frequently signposted suggestion that the closer they come to death, the more fully they are united as one. By contrast, in Shakespeare's principal source for the play, Edward Hall's *The Union of the Two Noble and Illustrious Families of Lancaster and York*, the brief account conveys little if any sense of a union of father and son. If the idea is present at all, it is only vaguely implicit in the father's counselling his 'entirely and well-beloved son' (Bullough 3:73) to flee from the French and in his son's refusal to do so. As a necessary precondition for the unity he suggests, Shakespeare changes the name that Hall had given to the younger Talbot. In Hall's chronicle, this figure is referred to as 'the Earl of Lisle,' which implies his independence from and lordly equivalence to his father (late in life the elder Talbot had been named Earl of Shrewsbury). Not only does Shakespeare strip his title from him but he also restores his Christian name of John to him. And, by having the elder Talbot identify himself (in a challenge to the French) as 'English John Talbot' (4.2.3), he reminds the audience that father and son share a given as well as a family name. Even more than with other same-named fathers and sons in Shakespeare, the common name hints at the subsuming of the two men's identities into a single, corporate one. The pervasive suggestion of an exemplary unity of the two Talbots becomes unmistakable at several points, most obviously when young John refuses to leave his father on the battlefield, declaring that 'No more can I be severed from your side / Than can yourself yourself in twain divide' (4.5.48–9). The care with which Shakespeare is working out the theme of shared identity is apparent in the mirroring effect created by the back-to-back placement of 'yourself yourself.'

The intimations of father-son unity are physically acted out in the actions of the Talbots on the battlefield. In Hall's sketchy account of the battle, most of the descriptive detail concerns the extremely unchivalric means by which the French contrive to kill Lord Talbot: they 'first shot him through the thigh with a handgun, and slew his horse, & cowardly killed him lying on the ground.' As for the young Talbot, Hall merely says that 'with him [Lord Talbot], there died manfully his son' (Bullough 3:73). In a major addition to his sources, Shakespeare invents two actions that convey the mutuality of father and son. In a symmetrical reciprocity, the Talbots save each other from certain death at the hands of the French, with the elder Talbot first rescuing the younger and then with the younger giving what he had received.

These mutual rescues represent the culmination of a motif developed throughout the play. In the careful lead-up to the Talbot scenes, Shakespeare stresses the failure of the English to rescue Lord Talbot from the French, in contrast to the earlier scene (2.2) in which his men rush in to save him from the predatory Countess of Auvergne. Desperately searching for reinforcements, the loyal Sir William Lucy declares that Talbot 'looks for rescue' (4.4.19) and fears that 'Too late comes rescue' (4.4.42). Significantly, young John enters the stage (and the play) only a few lines after this lament; in place of the withheld armies of the fractious English lords, this solitary neophyte comes to the rescue.

As it happens, young John himself soon needs to be rescued. At the beginning of 4.6, the stage direction reads: '*Alarum. Excursions, wherein Talbot's son [JOHN] is hemm'd about, and* TALBOT *rescues him*.' As the most recent Arden editor speculates, this action was likely staged as a 'spectacular fight,' with Lord Talbot intervening to save his untutored but quickly learning son from the three veteran French warriors who have surrounded him.[11] After a debate in which young John insists on remaining to fight, the next scene opens with Lord Talbot entering with the assistance of a servant. We learn from the wounded Lord that he has just been rescued (offstage) by his son: after the elder Talbot had been brought to his knees by the French, young John drove them off, becoming his father's 'angry guardant' (4.7.9). The sense of inter-generational exchange is supported by a number of very significant details. For instance, Lord Talbot declares that, when he saw his youthful son's prowess on the battlefield, he was invigorated by his son's example, his own 'leaden age' being 'Quicken'd with youthful spleen' (4.6.12–13). And we may assume that, in an example of a father's chivalric behaviour being modelled by an aspiring son, young John's rescue of his father has been inspired by his father's earlier rescue of him. Each figure partakes of the qualities of the figure whom he saves, and the mutuality of these rescues seems to transform their earlier debates about the merits of staying and leaving. It can be argued that, when words give way to deeds, father and son are one.

When it (very quickly) comes time for the Talbots to die, these suggestions of shared identity are expressed in ways that no sentient theatre-goer could easily miss. Thus, after having been separated from him on the battlefield, Lord Talbot enquires about his son by asking 'Where is my other life? mine own is gone' (4.7.1). In his last words, Lord Talbot characterizes the two of them as 'Coupled in bonds of perpetuity' as they fly side by side to heavenly fame. And the death scene is transformed into a final emblematic stage picture in which we see the young Talbot lying dead in his dying father's arms. As many critics have noted, this tableau of the father and son who have rescued each other serves as the first of a pair of symbolic bookends, the second being the scene near the end of the trilogy (3H6:2.5) in which we see a son who has killed his father and a father who has killed his son. Given this heightened presentation, it is easy to see why critical commentary has assented to Lord Talbot's prompting and lifted the two Talbots into 'the lither sky' (4.7.21) above the ruck of human complexity.[12]

Rescues and the Gap between Father and Son

This celebrated unity of father and son is, however, at best only a partial truth. Unlike the unnamed father-killing son and son-killing father of *Henry VI, Part 3*, the Talbots are not mere abstractions; critics caught up in expounding their emblematic unity have missed a vital dimension of the play. As will quickly become apparent, my foregoing account of the unity of the pair has neglected a good deal of evidence that points to distance and conflict between this father and son. Though of course Lord Talbot does not acknowledge the fact, the story

of the Talbots is also a story of the tension between the paternal assertion of control and the filial desire for autonomy. At the same time that
Shakespeare is transforming his chronicle source material to emphasize the element of father-son unity, he also transforms that material in
the opposite direction, stressing the conflict between the generations,
and especially the filial resistance to paternal commands. It is useful to
think of the emphasis on unity generating a countervailing, subversive
impulse. In his depiction of the Talbots, Shakespeare is on double business bound.

Ironically, the first evidence of the differences between the two
Talbots comes from the dialogue in which young John states his
reasons for refusing to abandon his father. In Hall's chronicle, young
John is not argumentative and is given no rationale for disagreeing
with his father. Hall wishes to affirm the traditional hierarchy of paternal superiority, and so his young Talbot comes across as a model of
filial obedience that is above all 'natural.' Thus, in response to Lord
Talbot's counsel that he depart from the field and save himself, 'the son
had answered that it was neither honest nor natural for him, to leave
his father in the extreme jeopardy of his life, and that he would taste of
that draught, which his father and Parent should assay and begin'
(Bullough, 3:73). After the Lord Talbot advises flight a second time,
Hall stresses still more heavily the instinctual naturalness of the young
Talbot's response: 'But nature so wrought in the son, that neither desire
of life, nor thought of security could withdraw or pluck him from his
natural father' (Bullough, 3:73). The son's only concern is an instinct to
sacrifice himself for his quasi-divine 'father and Parent.' Sir Philip
Sidney, that great admirer of Aeneas's filial devotion, praised the
young Talbot of the chronicles because he 'chose rather manifest death
than to abandon his father.'[13] This heavy stress on the natural devotion
of young John allows the chronicler to slide over a potentially embarrassing fact: that the son's insistence on remaining with his father is
itself an act of disobedience.

By contrast, Shakespeare's young John Talbot has a mind of his own,
as Lord Talbot discovers to his surprise. In Shakespeare, the elder
Talbot cannot possibly know his son very well, for the dramatist
invents the illuminating detail – conveyed by an English lord – that
'This seven years did not Talbot see his son' (4.3.37). Assuming that his
son is still the pliant youth whom he knew as a child, Lord Talbot ends
his first speech to his 'dear boy' with the peremptory command,
'Come, dally not, be gone' (4.5.11). It is as if he cannot imagine that his

son would dare to disagree. As he says in his first lines, 'I did send for thee / To tutor thee in stratagems of war' (4.5.1–2). Now, seeing that the military situation has darkened, he has decided summarily to send him away, and he adds a further denial of filial agency: 'I'll direct thee how thou shalt escape' (4.5.10).

But this young man has a lively sense of his separate identity and circumstances, to say nothing of a gift for argument and even clever casuistry. In a witty series of exchanges, young John repeatedly caps the points his father makes:

> Tal.   Fly, to revenge my death, if I be slain.
> John. He that flies so will ne'er return again.
> Tal.   If we both stay, we both are sure to die.
> John. Then let me stay, and, father, do you fly.   4.5.18–21

In the abstract, it is plausible to think that this joining of paternal and filial lines into generationally rhymed couplets is a sign of spiritual union, as their minds can be said to be rhyming together. But the dominant effect of the snappy stichomythia, rhymes notwithstanding, is to convey the differences between them. While it is true that young John is attempting to save his father's life, there is something cheekily irreverent in his 'father, do *you* fly' (italics added).[14] What is remarkable about this debate (and surely not anticipated by Lord Talbot) is how effectively his son counters paternal persuasions and stands up for himself.

In his initial response to his father, who has urged him to save the Talbot name, young John Talbot cleverly invokes his claim to the name as a means of defending his resistance to his father:

> Is my name Talbot? and am I your son?
> And shall I fly? O, if you love my mother,
> Dishonor not her honorable name
> To make a bastard and a slave of me!   4.5.12–15

Revealingly, young John makes his argument about the common family name while employing a profusion of first-person-singular pronouns ('I,' 'me,' 'my'). And in his second line he somewhat surprisingly adduces 'my mother' in order to argue for his own legitimacy and freedom of choice. (Usually it is fathers who raise the spectre of bastardy to coerce recalcitrant sons.) Young John's main concern would seem to be not so much his mother's 'honorable name' as the danger of his being transformed into 'a bastard and a slave.' The second of these terms is especially revealing, for 'slave' unobtrusively moves the debate beyond bloodlines and legitimacy to raise the issue of autonomy.

Despite the emphasis on shared name and shared blood, the unity of Shakespeare's two Talbots is deeply asymmetrical, for it places a much heavier burden on the son than the father. As happens even in exemplary families, the constraints of unity generate difference. From the outset, the differences between the Talbots are as important as their similarities, as each understands the exigencies of a shared code of fame and honour according to his own lights. Lord Talbot, who is secure in his personal fame as a warrior and aware of his impending death, thinks of honour in terms of the perpetuation of the family name, while young Talbot insists on his need to establish himself by securing his own honour. Instead of accepting a corporate family honour, young Talbot distinguishes between 'mine' and 'yours': 'Flight cannot stain the honor you have won, / But mine it will, that no exploit have done' (4.5.26–7).

The verbal debate between the Talbots reaches its climax in lines that contain an important stage action. In rejecting his father's plea (originally a command) that he flee in order to continue the family name, John Talbot kneels before him to make a plea of his own: 'Here on my knee I beg mortality / Rather than life preserv'd with infamy' (4.5.32–3). Young Talbot kneels to seek his father's blessing, in the central Elizabethan ritual of filial subordination, when he seems to sense how dangerously close he is to outright disobedience, and so he abases himself in an attempt to gain his father's agreement. Lord Talbot's response, however, is conditional: 'Upon my blessing I command thee go' (4.5.36). The *OED* uses this line to illustrate that 'upon' can mean 'on condition of' (*prep*.11.h), and so Lord Talbot is in effect saying that he will bless his son, but only if young John obeys his command to leave.[15] Without missing a beat, John indicates that he will obey the command, but only if it means the opposite of what his father intends:

John. To fight I will, but not to fly the foe.
Tal. Part of thy father may be sav'd in thee.
John. No part of him but will be shame in me.   4.5.37–9

Very quickly, Lord Talbot tries another tack: playing on his son's guilt. But, once again, John Talbot's response is strong and his resistance unequivocal: to save himself by fleeing would indeed keep alive a part of the father, but a part that, he says, 'will be shame in me.' Unity begins to look like contamination.

Even the mutual rescues that father and son perform for each other are not as straightforwardly chivalric as my earlier account of the action suggested. Indeed, both heroic rescues are qualified by being exploited for advantage, as if a price tag were quickly attached after the event. Immediately after Lord John rescues his son, his first words to young John set the ambivalent tone of tender paternal solicitude and crass ownership: 'Pause, and take thy breath; / I gave thee life, and rescu'd thee from death' (4.6.4–5).[16] Young John's response is to acknowledge how much his father has given him, especially the double debt of life he owes his father:

> O, twice my father, twice am I thy son!
> The life thou gav'st me first was lost and done,
> Till with thy warlike sword, despite of fate,
> To my determin'd time thou gav'st new date.   4.6.6–9

In traditional Elizabethan formulations, as we have seen, for a son the very fact of being alive constitutes an unpayable debt to his father, and now by dint of having been rescued by his father young John feels he owes that infinite debt twofold.

Lord Talbot's immediate response is to attempt to turn to his own advantage his son's gratitude for having been given so much. In one of the longest speeches in the play, Talbot contrives to show solicitude for young John in such a way as to remind him of his youthfulness and vulnerability. Not only does he address him as 'boy' three times, but he adroitly uses his concern for young John's weakness as a prologue to a restatement of his old tune. That young John needed to be rescued, he implies, indicates that he should allow himself to be sent away from combat:

>   Speak, thy father's care:
> Art thou not weary, John? How dost thou fare?
> Will thou yet leave the battle, boy, and fly,
> Now thou art seal'd the son of chivalry?   4.6.26–9

In the lines that follow, Lord Talbot repeats many of the reasons he had given young John to flee in the previous scene, and it has been hypothesized that this repetition represents a textual flaw, 4.6 being a first draft that Shakespeare supposedly intended to replace with 4.5.[17] This hypothesis, however, misses the dramatic point: Talbot is repeating himself because he is seizing on the indebtedness created by his rescue to complete the unfinished business of sending his 'boy' away.[18]

When young John responds to this speech, there is reason to think that he feels used and belittled by his father's manipulations. John's first lines express a steely anger that we have not heard before, an anger that is expressly directed not at the French but at his father: 'The sword of Orleance hath not made me smart; / These words of yours draw life-blood from my heart' (4.6.42–3). A few lines earlier, Lord Talbot had (rather gratuitously) reminded his son that the bastard Orleance had drawn blood from John, blood that he, as John's lordly father, had avenged. The first line, then, throws back into Lord Talbot's face the narrative of paternal rescue – John says in effect that the real wound to his dignity is the one given to him by his father. Were he to do his father's bidding, he says, he would be like 'the peasant boys of France, / To be shame's scorn and subject of mischance' (4.6.48–9). His powerful monosyllables ('Then talk no more of flight, it is no boot' [4.6.52]) make it clear that he will countenance no more manipulation from his father, and the Talbots exit to engage in the battle that will afford young John the opportunity to rescue his father.

Rather than being shown onstage (as the earlier rescue was), young John's ensuing rescue of Lord Talbot is recounted by his father in a fascinating speech that begins with his being saved and ends with his being left behind:

> Where is my other life? mine own is gone,
> O, where's young Talbot? where is valiant John?
> Triumphant Death, smear'd with captivity,
> Young Talbot's valor makes me smile at thee.
> When he perceiv'd me shrink and on my knee,
> His bloody sword he brandish'd over me,
> And like a hungry lion did commence
> Rough deeds of rage and stern impatience;
> But when my angry guardant stood alone,
> Tend'ring my ruin and assail'd of none,

> Dizzy-ey'd fury and great rage of heart
> Suddenly made him from my side to start
> Into the clust'ring battle of the French;
> And in that sea of blood my boy did drench
> His overmounting spirit; and there died
> My Icarus, my blossom, in his pride.   4.7.1–16

Divided into two equal sections by the 'But' at its centre, the speech associates young John Talbot with two antithetical Elizabethan archetypes of sons: the dutiful Aeneas-figure of the beginning gradually morphing into the overreaching Icarus of the final line.

In the first half of the little narrative, young John Talbot plays the role of pious Aeneas to his father's Anchises as he courageously rescues Lord Talbot, who has been reduced (like Troy) to 'ruin.' (John Talbot's earlier refusal to 'flee' from his father calls to mind the lines accompanying Geffrey Whitney's emblem of Aeneas: 'No fire, nor sword, his valiant heart could fear, / To flee away, without his father dear.')[19] If, however, the story of the Talbots were simply a tale of heroic father-son unity, then the passage should end at line 8, with no reference to young John's abandonment of his father and disastrous solo flight. In Shakespeare's sources there is no reference to young John's rescue of his father, but just as significantly there is also no reference to John's leaving his father's side, and (perhaps because they are committed to the union of father and son) most critics make no mention of John's abandonment of his wounded father.[20] If young Talbot is like Aeneas, he is an Aeneas who saves his father but then sets down the paternal burden so he can return to Troy, to fight and die.

Lord Talbot's account makes it very clear that young John's attack against the French had no immediate provocation: his son was 'Tend'ring my ruin and assail'd of none.' Much less clear, however, is young John's motive for the attack, a problem that is compounded by his silence (he does not speak again in the play).[21] A number of details suggest that John Talbot's leaving his father's side is metaphorically a birth and, more literally, an assertion of independence and a coming of age.[22] This rising of the son is accompanied, as often proves to be the case in Shakespeare, by the precipitous decline of the father. Though in the previous scene Lord Talbot rescued his hapless son from no fewer than three imposing French warriors, he is suddenly reduced to being '*old* TALBOT' (4.7., *s.d.*). The reversal of roles was foreshadowed when, at their first meeting, Lord Talbot expresses the hope to his son

> That Talbot's name might be in thee reviv'd,
> When sapless age and weak unable limbs
> Should bring thy father to his drooping chair.   4.5.3–5

On the battlefield, the father has been reduced to helplessness, and he has begun to 'shrink' in more ways than one, calling to mind the 'shrunk shank' of Jacques's sixth age of man (*AYLI* 2.7.161). And the submissive posture of his father ('on his knee') recalls the earlier scene when it was young Talbot who kneeled, seeking his father's blessing. Coppélia Kahn, one of few commentators to read the speech with appropriate care, speaks of how it suggests John Talbot's 'ambivalence as a son,' and she shrewdly observes that, had his solo attack been successful, 'it would have redounded to his glory alone.'[23] Young John Talbot's (momentary) achievement of autonomy is suggested by the powerful phrase that ushers in the Icarian half of the speech: he 'stood alone.' John Talbot's first act of filial independence is to insist on remaining with his father, and his second is to abandon him.

There is reason to think, however, that young John's leaving his father's side is not simply a step in a natural process of maturation but also part of a bitter payment of a filial 'debt never promised.' Even before young Talbot leaves his father, there are curious suggestions of filial aggression in the account of the rescue. On a first reading, Lord Talbot's lines describing young Talbot's rescue of him sound, oddly enough, as if his son is attacking rather than saving him: 'When he perceiv'd me shrink and on my knee, / His bloody sword he brandish'd over me.' In common Elizabethan usage, to brandish a sword over someone is to threaten him.[24] As there is no mention of the French enemy for another five lines, the sword-brandishing invites us to imagine a scene in which young Talbot takes advantage of his father's recumbent position to press an attack upon him. For an instant, there is a suggestion that the rescue has become an assault.[25] Of course, we quickly realize that young John's ensuing 'rough deeds of rage' are committed against the French rather than his father, and so we assume that our first interpretation was mistaken. But the ominous phrasing may suggest a moment of fear on the helpless Lord

Talbot's part, as if he were unsure of where his son's brandished sword might fall. That Lord Talbot is in the posture of a submissive son ('on my knee') may remind us that, in the very act of rescuing his father, young John Talbot has usurped him as a man and a warrior. As the narrator observes in Donald Barthelme's *The Dead Father*, 'When you have rescued a father from whatever terrible threat menaces him, then you feel, for a moment, that you are the father and he is not. For a moment.'[26]

In the lines immediately following the image of the brandished sword, two curious phrases appear that deepen the suggestion of filial aggression in Lord John's narrative. They occur in the lines just before young John's leaving: 'when *my angry guardant* stood alone, / *Tend'ring my ruin* and assail'd of none' (emphases added). There is a hint of oxymoron in 'my angry guardant' that points to more than young John's being irate at the French from whom he guards his father. Given the fact that a short while earlier he has himself expressed anger toward his father's claim to superiority, and that he may now be angry precisely because he is reduced to the duty of guarding his father, the phrase indicates Lord Talbot's perception of threat. The element of oxymoron is more arresting in the phrase that describes young John as 'tend'ring my ruin,' a problematic locution that is almost always glossed by editors so as to remove the suggestion that young John Talbot may be taking care to further his father's ruin.[27] (A typical gloss is that of the *Riverside Shakespeare*, which offers 'anxiously protecting me in my fall.') Of course, the words *can* carry this innocent meaning, but if Shakespeare wished it to be the only significance he could easily have avoided all hint of ambiguity by simply writing 'tend'ring me in my ruin.' Taken together, these three phrases suggest a riddling doubleness that pervades the scene and that is certainly felt by Lord Talbot. The Talbots' physical combat with the French, and even their commitment to die together, cannot be separated from their conflict with each other.

Daedalus, Icarus, and the Two Talbots

Shakespeare's primary vehicle for conveying the complexity of the Talbots' relationship is the encompassing myth of Icarus and Daedalus. Indeed, the resonances between the story of the Talbots and Ovid's brief narrative are so rich as to suggest that Icarus and Daedalus provide an informing model for Shakespeare's representa-

tion of the English pair.[28] Certainly, *1 Henry VI* evokes the mythological father and son long before their names appear in the text. Clearly
the incarceration of Daedalus and Icarus in the labyrinth on the island
of Crete shapes Shakespeare's imagining of the entrapment of the two
Talbots by the 'sea' of French forces that surround them. The parallel
is emphasized by the labyrinth imagery that the French general uses to
inform Lord Talbot that he is trapped:

> If thou retire, the Dolphin, well appointed,
> Stands with the snares of war to tangle thee.
> On either hand thee there are squadrons pitch'd,
> To wall thee from the liberty of flight.   4.2.21–4

Of course, 'the liberty of flight' punningly alludes to 'flight' as both
escape from the battlefield and the winged flight of Daedalus and
Icarus. Throughout the Talbot scenes, Shakespeare plays on 'flight' in
this double sense, putting a twist on all of the Icarus allusions. Thus,
young John can be said to be Icarus-like because he refuses to obey his
father, but with regard to 'flight' he is also the opposite of Icarus. Since
Lord Talbot repeatedly exhorts him to 'fly' (flee) from the battlefield,
young John is an Icarus who disobeys by refusing to 'fly' rather than
by insisting on flying too high.[29]

To suggest the complex interactions between the two John Talbots,
Shakespeare draws upon the Elizabethan ambivalence toward this
volatile myth. As noted in chapter 1, in medieval Europe the Icarus
and Daedalus story usually had been put to use as a warning against
the vainglory of filial revolt, but in the late sixteenth century it was
increasingly employed to celebrate feats of audacity and the brave
transcendence of restrictive norms. The most obvious note of ambivalence comes at the end of the speech in which Lord Talbot describes his
son's fatal attack on the French:

> And in that sea of blood my boy did drench
> His overmounting spirit; and there died
> My Icarus, my blossom, in his pride.   4.7.14–16

Perhaps for good reason, critics are divided on Lord Talbot's attitude to
his fallen son. The orthodox association of Icarus with Luciferian arrogance seems to be conveyed by 'overmounting spirit' and especially by
'pride,' but on the other hand these words could carry positive conno-

tations (at the end of the previous scene Lord Talbot had exhorted his son to fight by saying 'let's die in pride' [4.6.57]).[30] Thoughtful commentators have discovered both criticism and praise of young John in Lord Talbot's words, and both are probably right.[31] No amount of critical cleverness can make 'my blossom' pejorative or completely expunge pejorative overtones from a fall attributed to 'pride.'

The many allusions to the Daedalus and Icarus story also illuminate and complicate the significance of young John's dereliction of his father. Just as Ovid mitigates Icarus's disobedience by stressing how he was fatally 'drawn by a desire for the sky,'[32] so Lord Talbot attempts to exonerate his son for his solo flight by ascribing it to uncontrollable impulses that 'Suddenly *made him* from my side to start' (italics added). Lord Talbot's stress on the phrase 'from my side' characterizes this desertion with a word that echoes throughout the three Talbot scenes. The play as a whole is much concerned with taking and leaving *sides* (a word appearing more frequently in *1 Henry VI* than in any other Shakespeare play),[33] and for the Talbots the crucial 'side' is the father's. Indeed, when he first articulates his insistence to remain on the battlefield, John Talbot speaks as if parting from his father were a physical impossibility: 'No more can I be severed from your side / Than can yourself yourself in twain divide' (4.5.48–9). In his response, Lord Talbot accepts his son's argument and echoes his phrasing: 'Come, side by side, together live and die, / And soul with soul from France to heaven fly' (4.5.54–5). In the next scene, in which father and son repeat their debate about the latter's leaving, Lord Talbot reiterates the emphasis on his 'side,' this time making the allusion to Daedalus and Icarus explicit:

> Then follow thou thy desp'rate sire of Crete,
> Thou Icarus; thy life to me is sweet.
> If thou wilt fight, fight by thy father's side,
> And commendable prov'd, let's die in pride.   4.6.54–7

Lord Talbot's invoking of the myth is of course ironic, for just as Icarus disregards his father's advice to fly in tandem, so young Talbot will not heed the paternal behest to fight and die side by side.

Notwithstanding these complications, one thing seems clear: young Talbot's attack on the French is also in effect a desertion of his helpless father. Once again the scene resonates with Ovid's account, which says that Icarus 'deserted his leader' (*deseruitque ducem*). But there is a telling difference, for unlike the masterful Daedalus, Lord Talbot is a leader who is wounded and at the mercy of his enemies. Young John's desertion, then, seems much more aggressive than that of Icarus, and there is a suggestion that the desertion is in fact an undoing of the just-accomplished rescue. In a curiously similar scenario in *King Lear*, Edgar (disguised as Tom o'Bedlam) first rescues his blinded father from a man who attempts to murder him, and then he unceremoniously leaves him, alone, on the battlefield in order to pursue his own business of revenge (*KL*:5.2.1–4).

Shakespeare's appropriation of Ovid's myth has one more important facet, the motif of the son's being schooled in what one translator terms 'that fatal apprenticeship' to imitate his father.[34] Just as Daedalus 'encourages the boy to follow, instructs him in the fatal art of flight,' so too Lord Talbot summons young John to France so that he can be tutored in war.[35] Not only is Icarus's lethal flight made possible by his father's inventiveness and careful instruction, but in his (prohibited) flying too high the son is modelling himself on a rule-breaking father who 'sets his mind at work upon unknown arts, and changes the laws of nature.'[36] Similarly, young John Talbot's very commitment to imitating his father's honour is what leads him to disobey (with fatal consequences) his father's command to leave. And when he deserts his father's side, 'the great rage' and 'fury' that motivate him are reminiscent of the uncontrolled passions that earlier had characterized his father's martial conduct. It is in a Talbot-like manner that young John leaves Lord John. In the plays to come, sons like Prince Hal, Hamlet, and Edgar will consciously employ imitations of their fathers to gain revenge against them.

The Father as Tomb and Epitaph

Given the differences in perspective between father and son, it is ironic that at the end it is Lord Talbot who tells his now voiceless son's story, and tells it in such a way as to reinscribe the very unity of son and father that young John had resisted. Immediately after having characterized young Talbot as an Icarus who left his Daedalus to fly a mission of his own, Lord Talbot reinvokes and rewrites the myth to create a highly idealized image of father and son flying in eternal concord:

> Thou antic Death, which laugh'st us here to scorn,
> Anon, from thy insulting tyranny,
> Coupled in bonds of perpetuity,
> Two Talbots, winged through the lither sky,
> In thy despite shall scape mortality.   4.7.18–22

Linking these lines to the consolatory rhetoric of humanist funeral orations, David Riggs notes that 'the Talbots discover that the ideal figured by their heroic "name" is too pure for sublunary existence.'[37] There is no evidence, however, to indicate that *both* John Talbots have made this discovery. Though the speech masks as choric statement, it is first and foremost an expression of Lord Talbot, who now speaks as if young Talbot's solo Icarian flight had not happened. In rhetorical terms at least, Lord Talbot has contrived to bring his son back to his side again. And his rhetoric is forceful enough to induce most readers, including even careful readers, to accept what he says and to forget the more complex reality of young John's desertion.[38] If, as appears to be the case, young John's intention on the battlefield had been to break away from and even to punish his father by establishing a separate identity for himself, the ending endorsed by Lord John could scarcely be more ironic. In this light, the 'bonds of perpetuity' in which father and son are 'coupled' sound suspiciously like permanent shackles. Perhaps in death Lord Talbot has imposed on an unwilling son the shared unity of purpose that he could not in life.

Though the magniloquence of his consolatory sentiments tends to obscure the fact, there is a rather disconcerting absence of grief on the part of Lord Talbot. This is a speech that can move audiences and readers to tears, but Talbot sheds none.[39] Apart from urging him to defy death, Talbot has nothing to say to the son apparently dying in his arms, nothing to lament or atone for. One might expect Lord Talbot to show a degree of remorse, as he had summoned his son to what turned out to be a slaughterhouse, but the father's mind creates public images rather than expressing private feelings, and away from the battlefield he can scarcely know his son at all. From a son's viewpoint, Lord Talbot (like Daedalus) has a good deal to answer for. As Richard Duke of Gloucester nastily but pointedly asserts:

> Why, what a peevish fool was that of Crete
> That taught his son the office of a fowl!
> And yet, for all his wings, the fool was drown'd.   *3H6*:5.6.18

But Ovid's Daedalus, unlike Lord Talbot, shows tender solicitude for his son. Not only does Daedalus weep as he fashions the fatal wings with trembling hands, but later he is painfully aware of his responsibility for his son's fall, despite the care he took to instruct and warn him. At the close of the story, after repeatedly calling for his lost son, Daedalus sees the feathers scattered on the water and 'curses his skill' (*devovitque suas artes*). Talbot has no such moment of awareness.

The pervasive doubleness of the Talbots' relationship, its uneasy linking of both union and separation, of deference and defiance, is epitomized in Lord Talbot's dying couplet: 'Soldiers, adieu! I have what I would have, / Now my old arms are young John Talbot's grave' (4.7.31–2). These lines proclaim the ultimate union of father and son in noble death, as Lord Talbot bids farewell to his soldiers in order to join spirits with his heroic son; as one critic has noted, the icon of a son held in the 'benevolent circle of a father's arms' recalls earlier scenes in the play in which protective arms surround dying heroes.[40] But there is something unbenevolent and self-interested in what Talbot 'would have.' If they are protective, his encircling arms are also confining, as if the father has defined himself as the outer limit of his son's possibilities, becoming not only his begetter but also his tomb. This tableau, which can be read as both outwardly heroic and inwardly ironic, is an appropriate final emblem for a father-and-son relationship that has been characterized by its ironies and ambivalences.[41] Once again, the differences between Lord Talbot and Daedalus are instructive, for Daedalus pointedly does not attempt to subsume his dead son – he buries him on an island to which he gives his son's name, a name different from his own.

The trope of the father as tomb has its grisly origins in classical tragedy's scenes of fathers consuming their sons. In his *De officiis*, Cicero quotes a line from Attius's lost tragedy *Atreus* in which it is said of Thyestes (after he has unwittingly dined on his sons) that 'The father is himself his children's tomb.'[42] Similarly, in Ovid's telling of the Philomel myth, Tereus – another father who should have declined the meat course – 'calls himself his son's most wretched tomb' (*vocat bustum miserabile nati*) after being fed his boy Itys.[43] This idea of (usually male) parents as tombs of their offspring is also hinted at in Shakespeare's first two tragedies, *Titus Andronicus* and *Romeo and Juliet*, where family crypts symbolize not only the unity of the family but also the imposition on the living of patriarchal imperatives that spell death.

As Michael Neill notes, the family sepulchre becomes the 'emblem of a pride so consuming that it devours its own progeny.'[44] There is a further parallel between the final moments of these tragedies and the ending of the Talbot story. Just as Lord Talbot attributes to his recently deceased son values that young John may well have been resisting, so Titus Andronicus attributes his own values to his mute daughter Lavinia after he has killed her, and old Capulet vows to build a golden statue in honour of Romeo and Juliet that seems distinctly inappropriate to the values of the young lovers.[45] In all three instances, the father who misinterprets the values of his child is in some degree responsible for the death but does not acknowledge the fact.

The dark side of the father being the son's tomb is obliquely but powerfully insinuated in yet another of the play's tellingly oxymoronic phrases. When the Duke of Burgundy looks upon the bodies of the two John Talbots, he declares of the young John Talbot that

> Doubtless he would have made a noble knight.
> See where he lies inhearsed in the arms
> Of the most bloody nurser of his harms!   4.7.44–6

The problem is whether 'his harms' means the harms done *by* John or *to* John. Like most editions, the *Riverside Shakespeare* neglects to acknowledge the ambiguity, simply glossing 'nurser of his harms' as 'fosterer of his power to injure (the French).'[46] This timid interpretation tacitly disambiguates the line and thus discourages readers from considering a suggestion that is at least equally plausible: the elder John Talbot is the source of his son's bloody wounds. As we have seen, this suggestion of the father's violence against his son resonates with a good deal of the scene, especially since 'bloody nurser' chimes with the ambiguous 'angry guardant' phrase and since it immediately follows the line about the young Talbot being 'inhearsed' in his father's arms. Moreover, 'bloody nurser' (the adjective is important) reminds us of how the tableau of Talbot holding his son is a twisted patriarchal version of the *pietà*, with the dead Christ's mother being replaced by the warrior father and with milk being replaced by blood.[47]

The French Connections:
Joan of Arc and the Master Gunner's Boy

As I noted earlier, the two Talbots are isolated from their English peers on the battlefield, and their relationship as father and son seems separate from the rest of the play, too. They are the only father and son whom we see together among the English – such sons as Henry VI and Richard Plantagenet are fatherless and much the worse for it. There are, however, two quite relevant relationships among the French characters, one between a father and a son and the other between a father and a daughter. These two parent-child pairs – Joan of Arc and her shepherd father as well as the Master Gunner of Orleance and his Boy – are revealing because they reflect a greater degree of authorial freedom than does the self-consciously honourable depiction of the chivalric Talbots. They are French, after all, and, as Simon Shepherd has noted, Elizabethan dramatists usually projected their depictions of crimes against fathers onto foreign cultures.[48] The social distance separating these lower-class French families from the nobility creates another disparity (young John scornfully distinguishes himself from the 'peasant boys of France' [4.6.48]). In *their* language, feeling is not formalized in rhyming couplets, nor is motive concealed within the high resonances of classical myth. In both these relationships we see a degree of open rebellion against paternal control that is quite different from the more surreptitious and refined resistance of the young Talbot. But these two French rebellions are not equally open. In line with the gender difference suggested in chapter 1, Joan's negative response to her father is considerably more forthright than that of the Gunner's Boy (to say nothing of young John Talbot's).

Many critics have stressed that throughout the play Joan and Lord Talbot are counterpointed as mighty opposites, the champions of France and England and the representatives of differing, gendered attitudes to history.[49] But the play links Joan in a more complicated way with the young John Talbot, especially near the end. The key scene (5.4) occurs after the Talbots' deaths, when Joan has been captured by the English and is sentenced to be burnt as a witch. In a situation that recalls the meeting of the Talbots in the previous act, Joan's peasant father suddenly appears at the English camp in a maladroit attempt to rescue her. But she will have none of it (or him). After he movingly declares, 'Ah, Joan, sweet daughter Joan, I'll die with thee' (recalling the Talbots' arm-in-arm deaths), she retorts:

Decrepit miser! base ignoble wretch!
I am descended of a gentler blood.
Thou art no father nor no friend of mine.   5.4.7–9

This Marlovian denial of origins (in *Doctor Faustus* Pride declares 'I disdain to have any parents') places Joan among the 'ten thousand' in

Whitney's emblem of Aeneas carrying Anchises 'Who oft despise the stock whereof they came.'[50] But, as is usually the case in Shakespeare, the dramatic situation is more complex than the commonplaces allow. While there is no reason to question the shepherd's good intentions, there is something demeaning to Joan in his attempt to rescue her. Every child knows the humiliation of being the recipient of a parent's unwelcome public solicitude, and with the appearance of her clownish father all of Joan's pretensions and ambitions are in danger of collapsing.

The rupture between daughter and father becomes complete when the greatly forbearing shepherd becomes enraged by her refusal to kneel to him (another echo of the Talbot scenes) and suddenly switches from promising a blessing to hurling a curse: 'Now cursed be the time / Of thy nativity!' (5.4.26–7). In a chilling reversal of his earlier willingness to die with her, he exits exhorting the English to be cruel: 'O, burn her, burn her! hanging is too good' (5.4.33). Unlike the Talbots, who rescue each other and then die together (more or less), this parent and child grotesquely consign each other to their enemies. And other contrasts with the Talbots proliferate, especially with regard to illegitimacy. In place of the Talbots' emphasis on legitimacy and pure blood, the stigma of bastardy arises in a number of ways, including references to Joan's birth outside wedlock and her claim to be carrying the child of any one of a number of noble Frenchmen.

This contrast between the two families (and especially between good English son and wicked French daughter) is so striking that it is tempting to construe the differences as absolute. And indeed it is *de rigueur* for critics to locate their arguments for the exemplary unity of the Talbots within the framework of a systematic opposition to the fractious French parent and child.[51] But the force of this contrast between good English John and bad French Joan may serve to occlude the many intimations of tensions between the Talbots. While young John Talbot is obviously unlike Joan in that he does not engage in outright defiance of his father, he certainly does not represent the unqualified filial sacrifice of self that the absolute contrast with Joan demands. This technique of creating contrasts so obvious that they blind the eye to more subtle and more basic similarities becomes a central device in Shakespeare's later plays, and especially in those that focus on father-son relationships. Again and again, we will meet pairs of sons who are contrasted in black and white terms (the loyal vs the rebellious son, or the legitimate vs the illegitimate son, or the vengeful vs the philosophical son) but who in fact prove to be rather similar in their attitudes toward their fathers. The son who rescues the father and the son who attacks him are brothers in ways that run deeper than family affiliation. And sometimes the same son engages in both chivalric rescue and covert attack, as Prince Hal at Shrewsbury Field will follow in the footsteps of young John Talbot at Bordeaux.

The brief exchange between the Master Gunner and his Boy occurs so early in the play (1.4.1–22) that, unlike the obvious juxtaposition of Joan and her father with the Talbots, it has rarely been linked to the Talbots' battlefield heroics.[52] But this vignette is extremely rich, with important implications for the Talbots as well as for Shakespeare's ongoing exploration of the father-son relationship.[53] While the appearance of Joan's father is Shakespeare's invention, the exchange between the Gunner and his Boy is like the Talbot scenes in that it has its origin in Hall's chronicle. But once again Shakespeare transforms what he finds by adding a darker element to the father and son of his source. According to Hall's account, at the siege of Orleance the great Earl of Salisbury was killed by a clever and very unchivalrous French stratagem. The master gunner of Orleance trains a cannon on an observation post frequented by the English leaders and then patiently waits for them to show themselves. The ambush occurs according to plan, but with a twist that appears to have interested Shakespeare. When the English finally come within gunshot, the master gunner is taking his dinner break, and so it is his son who actually touches off the fatal shot: 'the son of the Master gunner ... took his match, as his father had taught him, which was gone down to dinner, and fired the gun' (Bullough, 3:73). For Hall, Salisbury's death signals the irreversible decline of England's military supremacy in France, and the son's firing of the gun emphasizes the absolute supersession of the traditional arts of combat by modern firearms – a mere youngster can bring down the flower of chivalry.

Shakespeare follows Hall's account in specifying that the gunner's son fires the lethal shot in the absence of his father, but he complicates the story by providing what the chronicler does not: an exchange between the Master Gunner and his Boy that defines the shot as an act of disobedience. In Shakespeare the emphasis shifts from the supplanting of chivalry by technology to the rivalry between the gunners *père et fils* and then to the usurpation of father by son. In effect, Shakespeare is transforming Hall's little anecdote into a quotidian version of the Daedalus and Icarus myth: a father teaches his craft to his son, who employs it to disobey and surpass his father. But tragic myth is subverted as the boy escapes scot-free.

Beginning with its dismissive initial word, Shakespeare's depiction deftly conveys the Master Gunner's insistence on his authority and the Boy's resistance to it:

> M. Gun.   Sirrah, thou know'st how Orleance is besieg'd,
> And how the English have the suburbs won.
> Boy.   Father, I know, and oft have shot at them.
> Howe'er unfortunate I miss'd my aim.
> M. Gun.   But now thou shalt not. Be thou rul'd by me.
> Chief master gunner am I of this town,
> Something I must do to procure me grace.   1.4.1–7

The Boy's 'Father, I know' suggests many a son's impatience with paternal explanations of the obvious, and he seems to take undisguised pride in the fact that 'oft' he has shot at the enemy, even if he has not been successful. Though critics have sometimes interpreted it as an assurance to his son that this time he will be successful and not miss, the Master Gunner's blunt 'But now thou shalt not' is prohibitive rather than supportive.[54] An obstreperous son is being brought to heel: 'Be thou rul'd by me.'

Unexpectedly, the father's response quickly modulates from sharp, quasi-biblical commandments to rather plaintive self-definition. While 'Chief master gunner am I of this town' may at first sound like a vaunt (as if Hall's Master Gunner has given himself a promotion), the next line abruptly reveals the father's anxiety about living up to his title. Like Charles, the court wrestler in As You Like It, who feels he must maim his opponents because 'I wrastle for my credit' (1.1.126–7), the Master Gunner knows the cost of failing to sustain the role that defines him. His note of desperation – 'Something I must do to procure me grace' – reveals a Master Gunner who is himself under the gun. In this light, his rather demeaning assertion of authority over his son begins to look like an attempt to reassure himself of his importance. His superiors may doubt him, but there is still someone he can give orders to.

The father's petulant vulnerability may also derive from frustration and exhaustion, for he declares that

> even these three days have I watch'd
> If I could see them.

Now do thou watch, for I can stay no longer.
If thou spy'st any, run and bring me word,
And thou shalt find me at the Governor's. *Exit.*   1.4.16–20

The odd half-line ('If I could see them') is particularly expressive, for the truncation suggests that the father has reached the limit of his endurance. What follows suddenly is the Master Gunner's commission of his fractious son to relieve him; his claim to absolute authority is compromised by the reality of his dependency. It is significant that, unlike Hall's father-gunner, who has merely absented himself for dinner, Shakespeare's figure seems to suffer from physical and spiritual inanition. There is a clear suggestion of a generational changing of the guard in the terms with which he deputizes his son: 'Now do thou watch, for I can stay no longer.' But, in spite of his weakness and his dependence on his son, the Master Gunner is not willing to relinquish control, and so he stipulates that, if the English appear, his Boy should not shoot but rather 'run and bring me word.' When he exits, he vanishes from the play.

Shakespeare's reworking of the incident not only turns the father into an authoritarian figure but it also (not coincidentally) transforms the son into a rebel. In Hall, there is no paternal prohibition of filial shooting, and the fact that the son fires the gun 'as his father had taught him' suggests that he is acting dutifully. Shakespeare's Boy, however, disregards the command to hold his fire and fetch his father. As the Master Gunner exits, his son remains on stage to exclaim, 'Father, I warrant you, take you no care, / I'll never trouble you, if I may spy them' (1.4.21–2). While the first line (probably spoken when the father is still within hearing) appears to be reassuring, the second is so cleverly ironic as to have deceived some critics.[55] The Boy presents his resolve to flout his father's command in terms of mock filial solicitude – he won't 'trouble' his weary father's sleep by (obediently) reporting to him.[56] When Salisbury and the English captains soon appear within gunshot, the Boy seizes the prohibited opportunity to act alone: '*Enter the* BOY *with a linstock.*' The great Salisbury is struck down according to plan, but the Master Gunner has been deprived of the 'grace' that he sought to procure for himself. Shakespeare has transformed this little episode from Hall into a powerful representation of the rivalry between fathers and sons.

Though psychoanalytical critics have passed over the scene without comment, it implies a primal, Oedipal story.[57] What could be more patly and patently Freudian than a conflict between father and son focused on the issue of who discharges the family ordnance? Every father is a Master Gunner until decrepitude and filial energy depose him, every son a Boy until he defies his father and pulls the trigger. A full-blown Freudian interpretation could go a step farther, perhaps a step too far, by seeing the wounding of the venerable Salisbury (he loses an eye) as a symbolic castration of the displaced Master Gunner. But these psychoanalytical tropes may distract attention from what is most important in the scene, the sense that father and son are both caught up in their own particular needs and that an eerie distance separates them. Though cast in the form of dialogue, the speeches of father and son involve little communication, and indeed they seem mainly expressions of self-absorption, as if each is in his own world. After the Master Gunner delivers his commandment, he exits without bothering to acknowledge (or perhaps even to listen to) his son's response. And the Boy expresses his masked defiance only after his father has disappeared.

Like Joan and her father, the Master Gunner and his Boy have the double virtue (or perhaps lack of virtue) of being French and of being commoners, and so Shakespeare can represent them without being constrained by the decorum that should characterize noble English fathers and their sons. Yet, despite the obvious difference between chivalry and artillery, the underlying human issues for the two Talbots and the two gunners are not so very dissimilar. One thing they have in common is a crucial absence: neither relationship involves the 'natural,' instinctual obedience of son to father that Hall (and orthodox Elizabethan thinking) postulates. Indeed, both relationships reveal the shared story of a son's resistance to a failing but still authoritarian father's imposition of his will. In their very different ways, each son follows a course of his own choosing, a course intended to establish his autonomy without directly defying the father. And in both instances, the newly found autonomy of the son dovetails with the sudden decline of the father, as both the Master Gunner and Lord Talbot quickly lose their force and (in their different ways) fail to live up to the martial reputations that have defined them and sustained their authority.

But of course Shakespeare depicts these two relationships in very different ways, and the filial resistance to paternal control is markedly more emphatic with the French than the English pair. Perhaps the best way to understand the different emotional valences of these two relationships is to think about the story of the Talbots as a kind of subli-mated, dream version of the quotidian rivalry between the Master Gunner and his Boy. In the persons of the noble Talbots, the unedify-ing story of a son's mocking rejection of his waning father has been decked out in classical mythology, cadenced in heroic rhyming cou-plets, and structured as tragedy. But at its core it remains the same story.

The future representations of fathers and sons in Shakespeare's canon can be seen as a creative negotiation between these impulses, an oscillation between the heroic postures of the Talbots and the demotic struggle within the Gunner family, always containing ele-ments of both. The tragic deaths of John Talbot and his only son mark the end of the family line, as the play repeatedly stresses, but in the context of Shakespeare's career they represent a most fruitful begin-ning. Though he dies childless, young John proves to be a prolific pro-genitor, the forebear of many sons to follow, most notably Prince Hal, Hamlet, and Edgar. Like their prototype, these deeply ambivalent sons will resist the stories fabricated by their revered fathers and attempt to create their own. But, unlike young John Talbot, they will have the last word.

3 *Richard II*: Patrilineal Inheritance and the Generation Gap

In the history plays following *1 Henry VI*, the father-son relationship continues to loom so large as to suggest that it was central to Shakespeare's understanding of historical continuity. Elizabethans often conceived of history in genealogical terms, and from this perspective the relationship of father and son (especially eldest son) was crucial, for the legal and economic continuity of families was maintained through this patrilineal bond. The continuance of great families depended on the patrimony being inherited by a son, who in turn could bestow it on a son of his own. As the fate of the John Talbots in *1 Henry VI* illustrates, the exclusive emphasis on the male line of inheritance greatly increased the likelihood of genealogical default, and a lack of male inheritors was one of the causes contributing to the widespread Elizabethan anxiety about what Lawrence Stone has termed 'the crisis of the aristocracy.' In an appendix starkly titled 'Biological Failure, 1559–1641,' Stone's tabulation indicates that over that period fully two-thirds of the great aristocratic families either failed altogether in the male line or (less disastrously) failed to maintain direct descent (that is, from father to son or to grandson).[1] As the sixteenth century and Elizabeth's long reign drew to their close, the continuance of aristocratic families was increasingly perceived to be a precarious triumph over the vicissitudes of time.

While concerns about patrimony and (male) succession appear in all of Shakespeare's histories, they have an insistent prominence in *Richard II*, the opening play in his second tetralogy (*Richard II*, *1 Henry IV*, *2 Henry IV*, and *Henry V*). Genealogical concerns are everywhere implicit in this story of the overthrow of a childless monarch by his cousin, and they are also the subject of a number of long set speeches.

The most notable formulation occurs early in the play, when the Duchess of Gloucester criticizes her brother-in-law John of Gaunt for his failure to avenge the death of his brother (and her husband). The murdered Duke of Gloucester was one of seven sons of the patriarchal Edward III, and the Duchess evokes the primal unity of these sons first as vessels containing the father's 'sacred blood,' and then as branches of a genealogical tree of Jesse:

> Edward's seven sons, whereof thyself art one,
> Were as seven vials of his sacred blood,
> Or seven fair branches springing from one root.   1.2.11–13

When she proceeds to challenge Gaunt to avenge his brother's death, the Duchess strikingly stresses the shared identity of the family's males:

> Ah, Gaunt, his blood was thine! That bed, that womb,
> That mettle, that self mould, that fashioned thee
> Made him a man; and though thou livest and breathest,
> Yet art thou slain in him. Thou dost consent
> In some large measure to thy father's death,
> In that thou seest thy wretched brother die,
> Who was the model of thy father's life.   1.2.22–8

These sons are so much images and extensions of their father, she argues, that to allow a brother to die is to agree to the father's death, perhaps even to participate in it. In this view, the extension of males through the generations is in essence a transmission of an unchanging paternal identity.[2]

Despite the Duchess of Gloucester's argument for the organic unity of male progenitor and progeny, a quiet irony pervades *Richard II*: while patriarchal values celebrate unbroken patrilineal descent as the guarantor of aristocratic status and property, the actual relationships between fathers and sons are at best conflicted and at worst severely alienated. Much more so than in *1 Henry VI*, there is a powerful discrepancy between the corporate bonds linking male generations and the temperamental differences separating them. Ironically, one of the forces driving fathers and sons apart is their very sense of being deeply related to, or even inseparable from, each other. To the extent that fathers and sons see themselves as sharing a common identity, as

many Elizabethan commentators said they did, a set of special problems is created. The closer they perceive themselves to be, the more
each becomes a comment on and potential embarrassment for the
other; the images of themselves that fathers and sons perceive in each
other can threaten as well as reassure. In *Richard II*, sons often refuse to
see themselves in their fathers, while fathers apprehend an unwelcome reflection of themselves in their truant sons. This play that
begins with hieratic images of cross-generational male identity (articulated by a woman) ends with a father pleading with the King that his
son be put to death.

Prodigal Sons and the Prodigal Sun King

In *Richard II* the politics of the kingdom cannot be separated from the
politics of generational strife within families, and especially within one
extended family. Each of the play's three central pairs of fathers and
sons (the deceased Black Prince and his son King Richard; John of
Gaunt and his son Henry Bullingbrook; the Duke of York and his son
the Duke of Aumerle) represents two generations within the same
extended family, as the three fathers are brothers and thus the sons are
first cousins. Taken together, these pairs of fathers and sons constitute
a broad division of generational identities that cuts across and
becomes entangled with the larger political issues of the realm.

It is primarily through the lens of generational difference that
Richard II depicts what prove to be the troubled relations between
fathers and sons.[3] Shakespeare's emphasis on the contrast between the
young and the old represents a subtle and pervasive transformation of
the play's historical materials. Holinshed's account of Richard's reign,
the play's primary source, conveys very little sense of collective generational identities, and nothing like the vast division in years and
spirit that separates young and old in *Richard II*.[4] While the play's generation of fathers and uncles is stricken with debility and indecision,
their sons and nephews are full of passionate, but frustrated, intensity.
The modifiers 'old' and 'young,' which are volleyed back and forth as
terms of abuse, carry stereotypical Elizabethan associations, with the
old men complaining that the young are hot, and the young in turn
dismissing the aged as frigid. While the old men repeatedly attempt to
lecture the young into a sense of duty, the young disregard these platitudes and, with some bows toward deference, proceed on their own
way.

In *Richard II*, the two generations seem to live in different worlds, as the aged are oriented to the past and the youth engaged in plans to shape the future. Early in the play the three main representatives of the older generation (John of Gaunt, the Duke of York, and their sister-in-law the Duchess of Gloucester) all deliver nostalgic speeches in which they harshly contrast the present with an idealized past, with Gaunt conjuring up in his deathbed oration a timeless prelapsarian England.[5] These figures are painfully aware of being the remnants of a bygone age, as their physical decrepitude reminds them; later York speaks of his arm as being 'prisoner to the palsy' (2.3.104), which prevents him from taking action against his disobedient nephew Bullingbrook. In addition to its physical ailments, the older generation – or at least the men in it – suffers from a moral paralysis that stems from severely compromised values.[6] While Gaunt and York are committed in principle to a view in which the king is God's vice-regent, an anointed figure through whom the divine will makes itself known, they are flummoxed by the obvious moral deficiencies of the brash young man who sits on the throne and is responsible for the death of one of their brothers.

When they watched *Richard II*, Elizabethan audiences probably felt a sense of immediacy because the play depicts the gap between generations in ways that chimed with contemporary realities. In a ground-breaking historical study, Anthony Esler characterized the relationship between the older and younger Elizabethan generations as a conflict between chilly moderation and ardent aspiration; against the cautious opportunism and hypocritical platitudes of their fathers, many sons pursued ambition, personal honour, and decisive action.[7] In Elizabethan England, as in Shakespeare's play, a generation of extremely successful men deplored their sons as undisciplined and dangerously inclined to be prodigal with the hard-won inheritance that would some day be theirs. This moral disapprobation of prodigality had some basis in current economic realities, for the finances of many aristocratic families were stretched dangerously thin in the 1590s, and a taste for what was called the 'bravery' of conspicuous consumption was common, or at least feared to be common, among young noblemen.[8]

Richard II explores these contemporary attitudes in that its fathers see their sons as prodigals eager to waste the assets their forebears have laboriously accumulated. Thus, York complains of Aumerle that 'he shall spend mine honor with his shame, / As thriftless sons their scraping fathers' gold' (5.3.67–8), and the freshly crowned King Henry will ask for information about his 'unthrifty son' (5.3.1). Even the Gardener joins the chorus as he orders his helper to

> Go bind thou up young dangling apricocks,
> Which like unruly children make their sire
> Stoop with oppression of their prodigal weight.   3.4.29–31

In discussing the Prodigal Son motif in the play, critics have tended to accept it at face value and thus to emphasize the unworthiness of sons.[9] As we saw in chapter 1, however, the Prodigal story was open to contending interpretations in Elizabethan England, with many writers playing mischievous variations on it. In *Richard II*, as in later plays, Shakespeare complicates the moral of the story by representing the claims of fathers as less than compelling. Certainly, the fathers in the play are nowhere near as generous and forgiving as the father in the parable, as York's homicidal raging against his son in act 5 illustrates. And, by the time the play concludes, there is reason to question the value of the older generation's patrimony, perhaps even good cause to reject it.

At the outset, one salient fact ensures that the play's representations of the male generations will not conform to conventional ideas: by age and especially by temperament King Richard is very much a member of the younger generation.[10] Not only is he young but there is a strong suggestion that, in the biggest incongruity of all, King Richard is himself a prodigal son. Repeatedly, Richard's failings are imaged in terms of squandered legacy and economic waste. In a crowning display of feckless disrespect, upon hearing of Gaunt's death Richard seizes upon his estate to finance his Irish wars. Moreover, as the barons complain, the kingdom has been leased out to support the king's luxuries, and in one of his last speeches Gaunt castigates Richard by saying, 'Landlord of England art thou now, not king' (2.1.113). One would expect Richard, as king of England, to be chastising the youth of the realm for irresponsibility, but instead he is on the receiving end of such rebukes. Given the insistence of Richard's behaviour, more is involved in his prodigality than simply youthful self-indulgence and extravagant squandering of the realm's resources.

According to the analogous hierarchies of polity and family that were widely inculcated in Shakespeare's time, Richard as king of the realm and *pater patriae* should be the father of a domestic family as well. But, though married, he is strikingly without family. Not only does he have no children, but there is no indication that he misses them or wishes for them. The great Elizabethan trope of children as the extension of the parent through time, a trope that is crucial in the genealogically minded world of the play, holds no interest for Richard. In one of the play's major ironies, Richard has no respect for the patrilineal system of which he is the visible symbol and upon which his reign (to say nothing of his life) depends.

Richard's unkingly apathy toward reproducing himself is of a piece with his total lack of positive emotional connection with the previous generation. Indeed, Richard is remarkable for the blatant disrespect and downright aggression he shows toward the brothers of his father. If we can believe the explicit charge of the Duchess of Gloucester, which is hinted at by many other characters in the play, Richard has been responsible for the murder of his uncle the Duke of Gloucester. And he seems scarcely less antipathetic to John of Gaunt, the older and more critical of his two remaining uncles. At the outset of the play, Richard mischievously places Gaunt in the very awkward situation of passing judgment on his own son. Later, when he hears that Gaunt is on his deathbed, Richard quips, 'Pray God we may make haste and come too late!' (1.4.64), and he proceeds to reject Gaunt's dying advice with shocking disrespect. After Gaunt dies, Richard immediately mounts a final attack on his uncle, cavalierly claiming all of his land and wealth as his own and thus effectively disinheriting Gaunt's son Bullingbrook.

In the first two acts of the play, much of the generational theme is carried by the conflict between Gaunt and Richard, which at times seems like an emblematic debate between Age and Youth. The most explicit opposition between uncle and nephew occurs in 2.1, the scene in which Gaunt delivers his eloquent deathbed oration about England. Here familial and political hierarchies are at loggerheads, in that Richard is simultaneously an authoritative king berating a rebellious subject and a rebellious nephew berating his authoritative uncle. Gaunt, by the same token, is both a loyal counsellor doing his duty to his sovereign and an uncle who has taken umbrage at his nephew's lack of respect. This collision of polity and family is apparent in the scene's opening lines, in which the dying Gaunt asks York, 'Will the *King* come, that I may breathe my last / In wholesome counsel to his unstayed *youth*?' (italics added, 2.1.1–2). And Gaunt proceeds to contrast himself to facile counsellors whom 'youth and ease' have taught to flatter (2.10.10). For his part, York worries that Richard will not listen because 'the open ear of youth' always heeds lascivious promptings and newfangled fashions. Indeed, when Richard arrives he does not hear Gaunt out, interrupting his uncle's 'frozen admonition' and dismissing its author as 'A lunatic lean-witted fool, / Presuming on an ague's privilege' (2.10.115–17). After Gaunt says he wants to die since it is meaningless to live without love and honour, Richard counters on a remarkably childish and peevish note: 'And let them die that age and sullens have' (2.10.139). When, a few lines later, news is brought to him of Gaunt's death, Richard responds with a clever parody of what he deems a laughably obsolete world view:

> The ripest fruit first falls, and so doth he;
> His time is spent, our pilgrimage must be.
> So much for that.   2.10.153–5

What is most puzzling about Richard, given the thematic prominence of the father-son bond in the play, is that he almost never mentions his legendary father, Edward the Black Prince. Richard refers to his father only twice in the play, both times indirectly and fleetingly. One reference occurs in the opening scene, when Richard slights his degree of relationship to his cousin Bullingbrook by characterizing him as being 'but my father's brother's son' (1.1.117). The second reference is more interesting, being a quick acknowledgment that is part of Richard's attack on his father's brother, John of Gaunt. Richard declares:

> Now by my seat's right royal majesty,
> Wert thou not brother to great Edward's son,
> This tongue that runs so roundly in thy head
> Should run thy head from thy unreverent shoulders.   2.1.120–3

This reference to his father the Black Prince as 'great Edward's son' is a clever periphrasis; not only does it reduce his father to the status of a presumably not-great son and deny him his proper name, but it also helps to distance the fact that Gaunt is Richard's uncle. He will deny his family relationships as best he can. Richard's failure (or refusal) to acknowledge his male progenitors eventually helps to damn him when he is in the process of being usurped by Bullingbrook. As one critic notes, when Richard is in danger of losing his throne, 'It is truly remarkable that he never once affirms his right to the crown by calling on his lineage and ancestry.'[11] Even though his claims are specious, Bullingbrook will not make Richard's mistake.

As the son of the heroic Black Prince and the grandson of the great Edward III, Richard has a noble past that in patriarchal theory should inspire him to deeds of martial emulation. As a marginal gloss declares in John Ferne's Elizabethan treatise on heraldry and family honour, 'The noble actions of the ancestors provoketh the son to imitate the same.'[12] But just the opposite happens. Richard finds this patrimony oppressive, and quite apart from the fact that they chastise him for his youthful negligence, he resists his uncles as reminders of his father's heroic past. In Holinshed's chronicle, Shakespeare would have read passages in which Richard's uncles make severely critical comparisons between him and his father.[13] Similarly, in *Richard II* York stresses Richard's physical resemblance to his father ('that young and princely gentleman' [2.1.175]), but then criticizes him for his failure to live up to paternal standards:

> His face thou hast, for even so look'd he,
> Accomplish'd with the number of thy hours;
> But when he frowned it was against the French,
> And not against his friends.   2.1.176–9

After a quick glance at Richard's prodigality (his father 'Did win what he did spend' [2.1.180]), York tacitly criticizes Richard's involvement in his uncle Gloucester's death by stressing that the Black Prince's 'hands were guilty of no kinred blood, / But bloody with the enemies of his kin' (2.1.182–3). Richard's response is mockingly disingenuous: 'Why, uncle, what's the matter?' (2.1.186).

In the middle of the play, however, Richard does have one moment when he comes close to admitting the difference between himself and his noble ancestors. When Bullingbrook confronts him at Flint Castle and imperiously requests him to come down from the walls, Richard exclaims: 'Down, down I come, like glist'ring Phaëton, / Wanting the manage of unruly jades' (3.3.178–9). Earlier Richard had associated his kingship with the sun, but now he identifies himself as the ambitious son of the sun king, too weak to control the wild energies of his father's horses. In the moralizing conduct literature of the time, Phaeton appeared as a symbol of 'youthful willfulness,' because Apollo had begged him not to take out the sun-chariot (much as York warns Richard not to seize Gaunt's lands).[14] But whatever confession of inadequacy may be implied, Richard's main emphasis seems to be one of self-dramatization and self-aggrandisement, as 'glist'ring' (rather than 'flaming') suggests.

Psychological interpretations of Richard's rejection of his father and uncles vary, ranging from an obvious diagnosis of extreme narcissism to the inference of an unresolved Oedipal rivalry resulting in unconscious parricidal wishes.[15] Regardless of its putative origin, the distance Richard maintains from his forebears has disastrous consequences for his kingship, leading to his fatal seizure of the patrimony of the deceased John of Gaunt.[16] Revealingly, Richard persists despite York's forceful and heartfelt warning about the dangers of his action:

> Did not the one deserve to have an heir?
> Is not his heir a well-deserving son?
> Take Herford's rights away, and take from Time
> His charters and his customary rights;
> Let not to-morrow then ensue to-day;
> Be not thyself; for how art thou a king
> But by fair sequence and succession?   2.1.193–9

Of course 'fair sequence and succession' are exactly what Richard does not want to think about: for him the former is an embarrassment and the latter an impossibility. York's 'Be not thyself' will echo through the rest of the play; in a foreshadowing of Hamlet, Richard will ponder what his – and any man's – essential selfhood is.

In effect, Richard becomes a kind of generational anomaly, the sole member of an ambiguous inter-generation located between his senescent, once-heroic uncles (whom he mocks as antiquated) and his lustily fractious cousin Bullingbrook (whose energies threaten him). Being neither a father nor a son, nor a brother, Richard is curiously detached not only from family relationships but also from the society that he rules. His only family relationship is with his wife, but the play for the most part keeps them separate. In this world of tight kinship relations, there are no human beings in whom he can see a reflection of himself, and he shatters the mirror in which he sees himself.

Richard becomes progressively isolated as the action unfolds; his ultimate and symbolically appropriate destination is the solitary prison cell in which he finds himself at the end. Poignantly, given his radical disconnectedness, in his last long soliloquy he attempts to populate an imaginative world with a generation of thoughts. It is the closest this pathetic king will come to being the father of his country. In this long and strained speech, Richard creates a world more ordered than the one in which he finds himself, and in this regard he may remind us of his antagonist and antitype at the beginning of the play, John of Gaunt. Despite their obvious differences, Gaunt's deathbed speech about England as an island garden and Richard's deathbed speech about his isolated prison cell have deep similarities. In his desire to lose himself in words, and in his fascination with the nearness of death, Richard has suddenly joined the generation that he had earlier mocked. The whirligig of time has brought in its revenges.

The Deferential Usurpations of Bullingbrook

Richard, a king who does not believe in the values that legitimize his rule, has a curious counterpart (and mirror image) in the cousin who usurps him, one who professes respect for the values that he proceeds coldly to violate. Understandably, criticism has tended to position Richard and Bullingbrook as polar opposites, especially with regard to the former's actionless words and the latter's wordless actions. But their similarities are crucial, beginning with the fact that they are cousins belonging to the same age group, and indeed the histories say they were born in the same year. This generational kinship manifests itself in their key similarity, a common resistance to the authority of their fathers and uncles. Shakespeare calls attention to this shared defiance of authority in a number of ways, such as by constructing two parallel scenes (2.1 and 2.3) that depict first Richard and then Bullingbrook rejecting the sensible, quietist counsel of their uncle, York.

Of course, these two cousins express their rejections of paternal and avuncular authority in very different fashions: Richard being prodigally free with his contempt and Bullingbrook very controlled. Since he is king, Richard does not have to worry about deferring to the authority of his elders, and his father is long gone. Bullingbrook, however, is quite careful about concealing his disrespect for his father, and indeed he often adverts to the importance of his honourable legacy. Thus, when he is confronting Mowbray, Bullingbrook swears by 'the glorious worth of my descent' that he will conquer him (1.1.107), and he makes several speeches that articulate a quite conspicuous filial piety. But, as his actions reveal, Bullingbrook is not as deferential as he says he is, and there is often a note of defiance in his attitude toward the offices of filial obedience.[17] The relationship of Henry Bullingbrook and his father John of Gaunt – hidden and elusive, one thing on the play's surface and something else just beneath it – signals the direction that Shakespeare will be taking in future plays.

Despite his outspokenness in the opening scene, Bullingbrook is a master of politic indirection and dissimulation; there is good reason to think he is challenging Mowbray in order to mount an oblique attack on Richard himself. The unspoken undercurrents of accusation are further complicated by the participation of John of Gaunt in the proceedings (in Holinshed there is no indication that Gaunt is present). Interestingly, the play opens with Richard questioning Gaunt about what he has been able to learn of his son's motives, before Bullingbrook and Mowbray enter to argue their cases, and Gaunt reports, guardedly, on the results of his attempts to 'sift' his son. This suggests a Polonius-like attempt at interrogation on Gaunt's part, an action that would not dispose his son to place trust in him, and it supports the likelihood that Bullingbrook is mounting an attack against his father as well as the King.

When Bullingbrook refuses to obey his father it is impossible to define exactly whom he is defying:

> *Gaunt.*   To be a make-peace shall become my age.
> Throw down, my son, the Duke of Norfolk's gage.
> *K. Rich.*   And, Norfolk, throw down his.
> *Gaunt.*   When, Harry? when?
> Obedience bids I should not bid again.
> *K. Rich.*   Norfolk, throw down, we bid, there is no boot.   1.1.160–5

When Gaunt invokes the force of 'obedience,' the term has a twofold application of submissiveness to both himself and to the King, whose wish for the contretemps to end is clear. Even though (or perhaps because) he acts in concert with the King, Gaunt is unable to command the obedience of his fractious son. By refusing to heed the command but also remaining silent, Bullingbrook expresses his defiance without indicating at whom it is directed; he could be flouting either his father or the king who first gave the order, or perhaps both of them. This may be the opening gambit in a move to usurp the authority of his king, or of his father, or both.

After Mowbray delivers a proud speech in which he refuses to shame himself in the name of duty (a sentiment we may suspect Bullingbrook shares), the King turns to Bullingbrook, urging him to begin the gauntlet exchange. In a comment directed at no one and everyone, Gaunt's son finally speaks:

> O, God defend my soul from such deep sin!
> Shall I seem crestfallen in my father's sight?
> Or with pale beggar-fear impeach my height
> Before this outdar'd dastard? Ere my tongue
> Shall wound my honor with such feeble wrong,
> Or sound so base a parley, my teeth shall tear
> The slavish motive of recanting fear.   1.1.187–93

Clearly, these lines are disrespectful to the King, as they dismiss his desired reconciliation as a 'sin,' and at first glance they may appear to honour John of Gaunt in their expressed concern about 'seem[ing] crestfallen in my father's sight.' But, as Sharon Cadman Seelig points out, the lines also convey 'a sense of pride verging on rivalry, for it is precisely in his father's sight – or in comparison with his father – that the son must assert his potency.'[18] Moreover, one may be suspicious of a filial deference that comes, with no apology, so soon after having defied his father's command. As young John Talbot had been, Bulling-brook seems more worried about protecting his own honour than his father's. Revealingly, immediately after his reference to 'my father's sight,' he drops all paternal reference and instead invokes 'my height' and then 'my honour,' his truer concerns. When he disdains 'slavish' talk and 'recanting fear,' he is insisting on his defiance of both Mowbray and his elders.

A similar shift from invocation of father to celebration of self occurs in Bullingbrook's address to Gaunt before his imminent trial by combat with Mowbray, a speech that on the surface appears to be the exact antithesis of Richard's disregard of patrimony:

> O thou, the earthly author of my blood,
> Whose youthful spirit, in me regenerate,
> Doth with a twofold vigor lift me up
> To reach at victory above my head,
> Add proof unto mine armor with thy prayers,
> And with thy blessings steel my lance's point,

That it may enter Mowbray's waxen coat,
And furbish new the name of John a' Gaunt,
Even in the lusty havior of his son.   1.3.69–77

Though Bullingbrook begins by expressing what one critic calls a 'scrupulous piety,' his emphasis quickly shifts as the speech unfolds.[19] After acknowledging his progenitor, he characterizes the relations between the two of them as a supportive exchange in which the 'youthful spirit' of the aged father invigorates the son and in turn the son's vigorous deeds will renew the fame of the father and of the family line. (The exchange recalls the mutual rescues of the two John Talbots in *1 Henry VI*.) But, despite the opening invocation, Bullingbrook's emphasis is not on the efficacy of paternal prayer and blessing but rather on his own 'lusty havior.' In this context, to 'furbish new' means 'to brush or clean up (anything faded or soiled),' which suggests that his father has been remiss in maintaining the family's honour.[20]

It would appear, however, that Gaunt soon gets his own back. After the king decides to abort the trial by combat that would establish which disputant is guilty, he calls together his council (including Gaunt) for a quick consultation. After the sentence of twin banishments has been announced and Gaunt has complained about the harshness of his son's sentence, Richard reminds him that he himself had participated in the discussion and approved of the 'party-verdict.' Gaunt's plaintive response reveals his mixed feelings:

You urg'd me as a judge, but I had rather
You would have bid me argue like a father.
O, had't been a stranger, not my child,
To smooth his fault I should have been more mild.   1.3.237–40

Though he begins by claiming that he would have been more lenient if he had been asked to speak 'like a father,' he quickly contradicts himself by acknowledging that he would have been more lenient if he had *not* been related to Bullingbrook.[21] The implication is that Gaunt cannot 'argue like a father,' for what he cares most about (and perhaps sacrifices his son for) is his image as a just counsellor. He has sought to avoid a 'partial slander,' the charge of favouritism, and as a consequence he says he has 'my own life destroyed.'[22] Gaunt's attempt to shift the blame to his colleagues is unconvincing: 'Alas, I look'd when some of you should say / I was too strict to make mine own away' (1.3.243–4). Ironically, these lines recall Bullingbrook's earlier speech about seeming crestfallen in his father's sight; both father and son reveal more concern about personal honour and humiliation than about the other's well-being, ostensibly the subject of both speeches.

Given his father's participation in the verdict of banishment, it is small wonder that Bullingbrook maintains his distance in the lines leading up to their parting. The exchange between father and son takes the form of a repeated pattern: first Gaunt delivers a traditional consolation for exile and then Bullingbrook rejects it as being merely a false naming of an intrinsically sad experience.[23] Once again, we may wonder whether Gaunt is not more concerned with his own feelings than his son's, and perhaps the consolations serve to assuage his own guilt rather than his son's sorrow. Bullingbrook seems to suspect as much, as he angrily knocks down each of the conventional arguments that his father erects. Bullingbrook's most revealing response is his rejection of Gaunt's point that the unhappiness of the exile will prove to be merely a foil to set off the jewel of his return home:

Must I not serve a long apprenticehood
To foreign passages, and in the end,
Having my freedom, boast of nothing else
But that I was a journeyman to grief? 1.3.271–4

Bullingbrook bitterly identifies himself – cutting across class lines – with an ordinary, frustrated Elizabethan youth: after serving a long apprenticeship (usually seven years), he gains his freedom and privileges, but only to remain a 'journeyman' (literally, one who works for a daily wage), a mere hireling at the trade of grief.[24]

In their parting exchange – the last words they will speak – one can hear an unarticulated but still audible anger in Bullingbrook's words. When Gaunt urges, 'Come, come, my son, I'll bring thee on thy way; / Had I thy youth and cause, I would not stay,' he seems rather eager to rid himself of his inconsolable and thus guilt-inducing son. Pointedly, Bullingbrook responds in kind (and with a Hamlet-like twist of kin) by ignoring his father and addressing a metaphorical mother: 'Then England's ground, farewell, sweet soil, adieu; / My mother, and my nurse, that bears me yet!' (1.3.304–7).

When Bullingbrook returns in defiance of his banishment, his double attitude to his recently deceased father is quite apparent. Once again, his actions belie his formal pronouncements. When he invades England, Bullingbrook presents his return as an act of filial deference, in that he returns in the name of his family and especially his great father. He is careful, for instance, to use many family relationship words when he resists the authority of York, Richard's delegated regent in his absence. Upon meeting York, Bullingbrook kneels and addresses him as 'My noble uncle' and 'My gracious uncle' (twice). After York's 'Uncle me no uncles' response, Bullingbrook insists on an even closer bond, stressing the unity of shared familial blood:

> You are my father, for methinks in you
> I see old Gaunt alive. O then, my father,
> Will you permit that I shall stand condemn'd.   2.3.117–19

This remark echoes how, two scenes earlier, York had claimed to see in Richard's face *his* father. Stressing family bonds again, a few lines later Bullingbrook reminds York that 'You have a son, Aumerle' (2.3.125) and that, in a similar situation, Gaunt would have come to his nephew's aid. No one invokes family ties more readily than Bullingbrook, when such talk is advantageous to his situation.

Although Bullingbrook invades England with the declared purpose of recovering his patrimony, his action quickly becomes a rebellion not only against the King but also against his father and his father's ideal of loyalty to God's viceregent on earth. Despite his invocation of Gaunt at strategic moments, Bullingbrook shows no evidence of an emotional response to his death. As a form of filial rescue, Bullingbrook's return to England is unlike that of other Shakespearean sons, being devoted to saving his father's estate rather than his life or his memory. It is a critical commonplace that Bullingbrook is a Machiavellian figure, but proper attention has not been paid to a passage in *The Prince* that makes an incisive comment on the young man's relation to his father. In the chapter in which Machiavelli argues that it is better to be feared than loved, he tartly remarks that the prince 'must abstain from the property of others, because men forget the death of a father more quickly than the loss of a patrimony.'[25] Once his patrimony is recovered ('I come but for mine own') and eventually augmented by that of the royal line itself, Bullingbrook does not refer to his father again, either in this play or in the two *Henry IV* plays that follow.[26]

Guilty Fathers at the Close

Act 5 of *Richard II* is both an ending and a beginning – an ending because it depicts the murder of the deposed Richard and a beginning because the former Henry Bullingbrook now rules as King Henry IV. To complicate matters, many motifs in act 5 have equivalents in act 1, which serves to suggest that the new political dispensation in England is not so very different from the old. For example, at the beginning Richard banishes Mowbray, who had apparently carried out the murder of the Duke of Gloucester at his behest, and at the end Henry banishes Piers Exton for having killed, at his urging, Richard. Of particular interest is a renewed emphasis on the connections between fathers and sons, a theme especially important in the first two acts. This revisiting pervades the whole of 5.2 and 5.3 and is focused on two families: that of the Duke of York, his wife, and their son Aumerle, and that of King Henry and his son Prince Hal. These late scenes return repeatedly to the issue of fathers being reflected in their sons, an idea that Richard had resisted and that the ascendant Bullingbrook had emphasized when it suited him. Now, at the end of the play, Shakespeare emphasizes the deep unease that can arise between fathers and sons when they fear a public recognition of their shared identity. In a cross-generational pairing, Shakespeare depicts a father (York) who cannot tolerate the existence of a son who reflects badly on his loyalty and a son (Prince Hal) who is apparently troubled by his likeness to his usurping father.

The scenes with the York family are extremely interesting because of the presence of the Duchess, who is York's wife and Aumerle's mother. She is the first mother to appear in the play, and her presence creates a grouping fairly rare in Shakespeare, for it constitutes one of the few depictions of a more or less intact nuclear family (i.e., a child and both parents) in his plays.[27] In this case, Shakespeare's provision of a mother for Aumerle is especially interesting in that it represents his improvement on history. The story of York's discovery of Aumerle's conspiracy against the newly crowned King Henry appeared in Hall and (with minor changes) in Holinshed, but these chronicles make no reference to Aumerle's mother being present, and for good reason. Holinshed noted that in 1394 (six years before the conspiracy) Isabel, Duchess of York and the mother of Aumerle, died.[28]

By creating a living mother for Aumerle, Shakespeare was able to depict the York family as a triangle involving two common Elizabethan gender types, the disciplinarian father and the overprotective 'cockering mother.' Accepting these stereotypes as reality, one contemporary treatise on parental and filial responsibilities observed that 'a child hath given unto him a father and a mother ... that the severity of the father may be somewhat mitigated by the levity of the mother.'[29] And there is historical evidence to indicate that these stereotypes had some basis in the actual behaviour of parents. As we saw in chapter 1, with varying degrees of tactfulness mothers sometimes intervened on behalf of sons when their husbands threatened to punish and even disinherit them.[30] But Shakespeare differentiates between these figures in an extreme way that verges on caricature and comedy. When the Duchess learns of Aumerle's participation in a conspiracy to murder the newly crowned King Henry, her sole concern is saving the life of her son. In stark contrast, the Duke is possessed with the need for his son to be punished to the hilt for the capital offence of treason. The Duchess recognizes only the private, affective dimension of the parental relationship, and the Duke recognizes only its public, political dimension.

The response of the Duchess is the simpler of the two and requires little explication. Before the entrance of Aumerle, the Duke and Duchess are in harmony as they talk about their sympathy for the deposed and humiliated Richard, and York has interrupted his own narrative by weeping for the deposed King. When Aumerle enters, the Duchess describes him as '*my* son Aumerle' (italics added; 5.2.41), and the singular pronoun points toward their different attitudes, especially since York corrects her by insisting on a political reality: their son has been stripped of his title and must now be called Rutland. She ignores him, however, exclaiming 'Welcome, my son!' (5.2.46). She will underscore her rejection of York's politic advice by continuing (three times in all) to refer to her son as 'Aumerle.'[31] Throughout the play many people fail to heed York's advice, but no one does so with the splendid contempt of the Duchess. For better or worse, the vicissitudes of the public world will not change her private relationship with *her* son. Aumerle may have been on the verge of becoming a king killer, but the Duchess pleads with York by invoking the natural impossibility of future childbirth: 'Have we more sons? or are we like to have? / Is not my teeming date drunk up with time?' (5.2.90–1).

The Duchess's untroubled affection for Aumerle casts in high relief the Duke's sudden explosion of anger. There are so many possible and plausible causes of York's rage that a kind of overdetermination seems to be at work, as if we were watching an encyclopaedia of paternal grievances. The lack of salutations between father and son – and probably a lack of filial kneeling as well – may reflect the fact that they have been estranged for some time. Before this scene they have not exchanged a word in the play, even though they have appeared onstage together in a number of scenes.[32] The probable cause of this distance, we infer, is that Aumerle has been one of Richard's favourites and, like his king, has been a sharp-tongued mocker of the ceremonies valued by York and the older generation. When, for instance, York criticizes Richard for surrounding himself with parasites and flatterers, he is presumably including his son in the broadside.[33] Interestingly, this emphasis on the distance between father and son is Shakespeare's; the playwright passes over in silence Holinshed's observation that York and Aumerle retired together to their ancestral home at Langley after Richard seized Gaunt's inheritance.[34]

But the fact of a prior antagonism does not explain the violence of York's diatribe against Aumerle. Nor, I think, does the heinousness of the regicide planned by Aumerle and his associates account for it. For one thing, York becomes angry at Aumerle before he learns of the plot. Even though Aumerle attempts to be deferential when evading his father's demands to see the suspicious seal, York very quickly comes to a boil. After addressing Aumerle with a sarcastic 'sir' (5.2.63), York shifts to the term that Elizabethan fathers used to cut their sons down to size: 'Boy, let me see the writing' (5.2.70). This contemptuous address should remind us of York's similar but less intense dressing-down of Bullingbrook for returning to England illegally: 'Why, foolish boy, the King is left behind, / And in my loyal bosom lies his power' (2.3.97–8).[35] We may wonder whether, in part, York's anger is the outrage felt by an aged father whose authority has been defied by his son. The violent tirades of disregarded fathers like Titus in *Titus Andronicus*, old Capulet in *Romeo and Juliet*, and especially Gloucester in *King Lear* quickly come to mind, suggesting that York may feel that *he*, as well as the new King, is in danger of being usurped by Aumerle.

Since York conceives of his relationship with his son in public terms, we should examine his political situation at the time of his discovering Aumerle's conspiracy, a situation that Shakespeare has richly dramatized. When Aumerle first enters, York is explaining to the Duchess that their son has become his legal charge: 'I am in parliament pledge for his truth / And lasting fealty to the new-made king' (5.2.44–5). Clearly, Aumerle's behaviour is York's responsibility and, for better or worse, will reflect on him. And it reflects on him in one more unsettling way: Aumerle's conspiracy upsets the uneasy accommodation that York has made with a new and (for him) unpalatable political reality. Actually, this process of accommodation began when York merely chastised Bullingbrook for returning to England without the King's permission. In that scene (2.3), York began by roundly condemning his nephew for insubordination but wound up inviting him to spend the night in his castle. Later, in the deposition scene, York appears to be acting as Bullingbrook's emissary to Richard and to take it upon himself (he is the first to do so) to declare Bullingbrook king.

York's contradictions are clear at the beginning of 5.2, when he breaks into tears while narrating to his wife the 'gentle sorrow' with which Richard comported himself when 'dust was thrown upon his sacred head' (5.2.30). York can maintain his own ideological composure only by dint of a sudden, unconvincing assertion of divine providence:

> But heaven hath a hand in these events,
> To whose high will we bound our calm contents.
> To Bullingbrook are we sworn subjects now,
> Whose state and honor I for aye allow. 5.2.37–40

York's hurried discovery of heaven's 'hand in these events' sounds like an attempt to remove his own fingerprints from view, as Hamlet will also attempt to do in *his* act 5, and the strained nature of his assumed placidity is apparent in the supposedly 'calm contents' that he must nevertheless 'bound' to God's will. His reference to the newly crowned king as merely 'Bullingbrook' indicates his emotional allegiance to the past, and the awkwardness of the pun in the final line (recalling the 'eye for an eye' of Mosaic justice) suggests that he is less than fully committed to a regime which he feels he must 'allow.' It is immediately following these lines that the Duchess announces the approach of Aumerle, whose conspiracy will blow the lid off York's pretence to 'calm contents.' This context provides plenty of evidence for Norman Rabkin's view that York is turning on Aumerle 'the anger of a father who has reluctantly made his decision against a large part of his own moral being to support a principle in which he only half believes, and now finds his son actively engaged in supporting the position he has reluctantly ruled out for himself.'[36]

It is only in the following scene, after Aumerle, York, and the Duchess (in that order) have ridden to the King at Windsor Castle, that the full strangeness of York's rage becomes clear. At this point the actual threat of regicide has passed, but York's anger does not diminish, and if anything it becomes even more incandescent. When Aumerle and the Duchess beg Henry's pardon, York goes on his knee to exclaim to the King, 'Ill mayst thou thrive if thou grant any grace!' (5.3.99). He seems to be wishing misfortune upon Henry should he allow Aumerle to continue living; the suggestion is that he is more dedicated to the destruction of his son than to the preservation of the King.

York's most striking lines occur after the King has expressed his willingness to pardon Aumerle since the father's 'abundant goodness' serves to remove the blot from his 'digressing son' (5.3.65–6). Far from accepting this exoneration of Aumerle, York intensifies his vehement insistence that his son be put to death:

So shall my virtue be his vice's bawd,
An' he shall spend mine honor with his shame,
As thriftless sons their scraping fathers' gold.
Mine honor lives when his dishonor dies,
Or my sham'd life in his dishonor lies:
Thou kill'st me in his life; giving him breath,
The traitor lives, the true man's put to death.   5.3.67–73

As the author of an early psychoanalytic study incisively remarked, this 'is rather the speech of a perishing man trying desperately to save himself than the speech of a devoted servant trying to save the life of a master no longer imperilled.'[37] York's speech is particularly unsettling because it inverts a traditional idea of patrimony: that after his death the father lives on in his son. Here, however, is a kind of zero-sum equation: the continued life of the son entails the spiritual death of the father. The simplicity of York's last line, in which his son becomes 'the traitor' and himself 'the true man,' indicates how inadequate these moral terms are to characterize behaviour in this new political world.

At its deepest level, York's volcanic outrage stems from his seeing himself reflected in the mirror of his devious son. As we have seen, Elizabethan commentators often insisted that the shameful behaviour of sons was a direct reflection on their fathers, the apple not falling far from the tree.[38] In addition to this tendency to attribute filial faults to progenitors, there was a belief especially relevant to the situation of York and Aumerle: that the predisposition to treason was passed from father to son. York's fear that Aumerle reflects his own wavering loyalties explains why the Duchess's defence of her son backfires when she asks York, 'Is he not like thee? is he not thine own?' (5.2.94). For York, the problem is precisely that his son *is* like him. In Berger's phrasing, 'Aumerle may be doing what York would have liked to do had he the will and means and courage to do it.'[39] After she denies what she mistakenly thinks is York's charge of bastardy, the Duchess unwittingly twists the knife by trying to reassure him that

> He is as like thee as a man may be,
> Not like to me, or any of my kin,
> And yet I love him.   5.2.108–10

Another unintended twist of the knife occurs when she asks York, 'Wilt thou not hide the trespass of thine own?' (5.2.89). While the Duchess clearly intends 'the trespass of thine own' to refer to Aumerle's crime, the phrase may serve to remind York of *his* trespass. In York's response to Aumerle, then, we see a dark side of patrimony in which the son comes to represent the impulses that the father does not want to see or to acknowledge in himself. York's response is the stuff of Nietzsche's anxiety-inducing epigram: 'What the father hath hid cometh out in the son, and often have I found the son a father's revealed secret.'[40]

Since they immediately follow the established overthrow of Richard and since they deal with a plot to kill the new king, we should think of the Aumerle scenes as also being about usurpation. Indeed, King Henry may be tacitly acknowledging the parallel when he accedes to the Duchess's pleas for mercy: 'I pardon him as God shall pardon me' (5.3.131). Not only does Aumerle fail to overthrow the King, but in the process he loses his autonomy as an adult as well. By the end of the Windsor scene, the Aumerle who as recently as act 4 showed considerable resolve in facing down the many charges made against him by rivals has ceased to be an independent agent. In the presence of his parents, he is reduced to silence, and the Duchess has to tell her 'transgressing boy' (5.3.96) what to do. In the final line of the scene, the

Duchess leads him offstage, declaring 'Come, my old son, I pray God make thee new' (5.3.146). While in her words there may be, as a critic has suggested, an echo of the Book of Common Prayer's baptismal service and thus 'a muted Resurrection note,' there is no evidence to indicate that Aumerle is celebrating his rebirth.[41] He remains passive and silent, and he seems more a victim of lost identity than a recipient of a new life. From this angle he begins to look like his cousin and former master, a usurped figure who is no longer capable of knowing who he is.

The theme of fathers and sons reflecting on each other, and especially reflecting on each other's problematic legitimacy, resonates with a brief scene that Shakespeare inserts into the middle of the York family's domestic and political chaos. In his first words spoken as king in the play (spoken, significantly, just before the squabbling Yorks arrive at his doorstep), Henry IV wonders about the whereabouts of 'my unthrifty son' (5.3.1). This mention of the figure who will become Prince Hal in *1 Henry IV* is conspicuously *not* prepared for – there has been no reference in the play to Bullingbrook's being married, much less to his having a son. And the shock is increased by the fact that this quickly fledged son is already old enough (as the King complains) to frequent taverns and engage in highway robbery. To this point, most of the chronological references in the play have concerned short units of time, and according to Holinshed's chronology of events, less than two years have passed since the banishment of the 'young Bullingbrook' with which the play began. As John Sutherland noted, it is as if the plot has leapt into the chronological equivalent of *Star Trek*'s 'warp speed,' with Henry suddenly having aged and produced a son who has immediately come of age.[42] Clearly, part of Shakespeare's strategy involves introducing (offstage) a grown-up Prince Hal at the end of *Richard II* to prepare for his central presence in *1 Henry IV*.

But there is a poignant thematic consideration as well, for the sudden reference to Prince Hal creates a notional third, younger generation of adults in the play. This allows Shakespeare to begin the play depicting Bullingbrook as a lusty son eager to challenge his father and to end it depicting him as a father of a son old enough to challenge him; the scene places King Henry in the position of the paternal authorities, including his father, whom he had rebelled against earlier. As Elizabethans were fond of observing, 'our children will deal with us, as we deal with our parents.'[43] Moreover, as *1 Henry IV* will demonstrate, the relationship between Hal and his father recreates some of the tensions that had estranged Bullingbrook from *his* father, John of Gaunt. Like his father before him, but in still more indirect, unstated ways, Hal will display an ambivalence toward paternal authority. Of course, Hal finds himself facing an ethical dilemma that Bullingbrook did not have to contend with: the awareness that his father has usurped the crown that he will now be compelled to wear.

In the King's opening reference to Hal, we can see a close connection with York's shamed alienation from his son:

> Can no man tell me of my unthrifty son?
> 'Tis full three months since I did see him last.
> If any plague hang over us, 'tis he.   5.3.1–3

What hangs over the speech is not the plague but rather the parallel relationship of York and Aumerle. Not only does the King's question occur in the middle of the Aumerle subplot with its stress on generational difference and filial rebellion, but his criticism of his 'unthrifty son' is interrupted by the sudden arrival of York's 'digressing son' (5.3.66) to plead for mercy (which Henry is willing to give, it being easier to forgive his uncle's son than his own). Earlier York had called Bullingbrook 'foolish boy' (2.3.97) when he invaded England, and now the former Bullingbrook criticizes his son as a 'young wanton and effeminate boy' (5.3.10).

King Henry's uneasy question about the Prince recalls York's animus toward Aumerle, for the Prince's actions, like Aumerle's, involve a violation of filial obedience. Moreover, the responses of the fathers suffer from a similar strain; in both cases the son's actions threaten the father's fragile posture of legitimacy. The King's reference to a retributive 'plague' is very telling, for it alludes to the divine 'Armies of pestilence' (3.3.87) that Richard threatened him with and also to the long and vivid prophecy of ruin that the Bishop of Carlisle delivered when the then-Bullingbrook announced that 'In God's name I'll ascend the regal throne' (4.1.113). Seen in this light, the King's comments would seem to say more about his own guilt than his son's crimes. Interestingly, Carlisle's prophecy had warned against civil war, with emphasis on divisions within the family (struggles of 'kin with kin and kind with kind'), and he had concluded by exhorting Henry to desist from deposing Richard, 'Lest child, child's children, cry against you "woe!"' (4.1.141, 149).

There is good reason to think that Prince Hal's removal to the taverns is indeed his (characteristically oblique) means of crying woe against his father. Shakespeare's suggestion, which he will develop in *1 Henry IV*, is that Prince Hal's misbehaviour is not (as Henry fears) a visitation of divine displeasure but rather the Prince's means of creating an unmistakable distance between his father and himself, and also between his father's seizure of the throne and his own presumably legitimate accession to it in the future. If one thinks of Prince Hal's removal to Eastcheap as a rejection of his father, the King's remark that "Tis full three months since I did see him last' is very suggestive, perhaps implying that Hal left the court immediately after participating in his father's coronation.[44] When the father ascends, the son decamps.

The lines that prefigure most clearly Shakespeare's conception of an ambivalent Hal in *1 Henry IV* are those spoken to the King by 'Percy,' who conveys Hal's plans concerning the upcoming joust at Oxford:

> His answer was, he would unto the stews,
> And from the common'st creature pluck a glove
> And wear it as a favor, and with that
> He would unhorse the lustiest challenger.   5.3.16–19

Hal's intent to wear a common prostitute's glove as a chivalric favour shows his contempt for the spectacle of display and, by extension, for its occasion, the visit of the new king. Perhaps he is suggesting that this chivalry is merely a form of prostitution, a meretricious glorification of an illegitimate, usurped authority. We recall that another disillusioned son, Aumerle, planned to make a considerably blunter statement about dubious royal authority at these same jousts on the 'triumph day' at Oxford (5.2.66) – by murdering the King.

But mockery is not the whole story, for Hal also signals his intent to participate in the jousts and indeed to be victorious. In the annual tilts celebrating her Accession Day, Queen Elizabeth always appointed a champion to meet the various challengers, and Hal seems to be arrogating a similar role to himself when he swears to 'unhorse the lustiest challenger.' The lines bespeak Hal's dividedness, as he indicates his awareness of the falseness of the proceedings but nevertheless commits himself to participating and winning. At Shrewsbury Field, Hal's prophetic vaunt will be realized; the clear-eyed prince will defeat the challenge to his father's (and, eventually, his own) throne. There is a poignant irony as well as prophecy in the passage, for in the battle that concludes *Part One* of *Henry IV*, the 'lustiest challenger' will prove to be Harry Hotspur, the very 'Percy' who is relaying Hal's words – his own death warrant – to the King.

4 *Henry IV, Part One*:
'Deep Defiance' and the Rebel Prince

A troublesome discrepancy runs through much of the critical writing on *1 Henry IV*. While praising the play for its richness and many points of view, critics have usually endorsed a fairly simple interpretation of its central character, Prince Hal. In this view, the play is about the maturation (or education, or reformation) of the Prince. The most influential exposition of this view was formulated in John Dover Wilson's *The Fortunes of Falstaff* (1943), which begins by associating Prince Hal with the prodigal sons of Tudor morality plays and then refines upon that model in a chapter entitled 'The Prince Grows Up.' According to Wilson, Hal undergoes a gradual maturation rather than the sudden conversion of the biblical Prodigal Son, but the trajectory remains the same: Hal has left his father's court for the unruly life of the taverns, but he learns to reject the world of subversive temptation (represented by Falstaff), commits himself to honour and chivalry by conquering Hotspur, and arrives at maturity. This basic template has accommodated readings from a number of different approaches. In numerous psychoanalytical studies, the arc of Hal's learning process remains essentially the same as in Wilson's formulation, though the critical language changes. We learn that in Hal Shakespeare 'describes the characteristic course of the development of the male' (with emphasis on the overcoming of parricidal tendencies), or that Hal represents 'the story of the education and emotional life of an adolescent' (with emphasis on the formation of mature ego ideals).[1] And, in an anthropological approach, Hal learns to differentiate himself from others while successfully integrating their positive qualities, thus resulting in 'the progress of Prince Hal from riotous adolescent to mature man and king.'[2]

Critics have found this interpretation of Prince Hal's growth to maturity in *Part One* of *Henry IV* so satisfying that they have identified the same pattern in the other plays in which he appears. Beginning with Wilson himself, many critics have discovered in the second part of *Henry IV* a pattern of maturation similar to that in the first part, one in which Hal runs essentially the same course again but this time with regard to civic rather than personal, public rather than private, challenges. This duplication of the pattern, however, created a problem: since Hal had supposedly already reached maturity in *Part One*, it is not clear why his second progress to maturation (or 'education,' as it was sometimes called) is not simply redundant. Whereupon, some critics took the additional step of maintaining that in *Part Two* Shakespeare was essentially 'turning back the clock' by depicting Prince Hal as if the events in *Part One* had not happened.[3] Not to be outdone, one critic has discovered that in *Henry V* – Hal having finally become king – Shakespeare 'has decided to dramatize again the maturation of a ruler.'[4] After reviewing this chorus of approval of Hal's growing up, it is tempting to exclaim, 'O monstrous! But one half-pennyworth of youthful rebellion to this intolerable deal of maturation.'

The problem with this critical focus on Hal's growing up is that it is a pattern that critics have substituted for, or at least imposed on the rich complexities of the text. Foremost among the complications that the model ignores are the personal and political differences that separate Hal from his father, at the end no less than at the beginning of *Part One*. Virtually all of these interpretations end with an emphasis on (as Wilson phrases it in one of his subheadings) 'The Reconciliation between Father and Son,' an event that supposedly reveals Hal's achieved maturity. But the critics' recourse to this reconciliation has not been very critical. In general, it is unclear why reconciliation with his father is necessarily the mark of a son's maturity, and in this play the idea of reconciliation is supported by the text only if one does not read very carefully. Though the first two times Hal and his father appear on stage together (3.2 and 5.4) have often been characterized as reconciliations, in both instances father and son remain at cross purposes, with the prince obliquely expressing his disapproval of the king.

The more aware critics are of the events of *Richard II* and especially the usurpation of Richard, the more likely they are to discard the maturation model and to see the unresolved tensions between Henry IV and Hal.[5] *Part One* of *Henry IV* flows directly from the ending of *Richard II*, for its subject is the consequences of Henry Bullingbrook's seizure of Richard's throne, one of which is its effect on the newly minted Prince Henry. Among much else, the play explores the dilemma of a young man upon whom greatness has been thrust in the form of a sudden and apparently unsought elevation to a new role, Prince of Wales. When Henry Bullingbrook usurped his cousin Richard II, he was also undermining the autonomy of his own son in that he forced a new title and identity upon him. The effects of Henry's usurpation are twofold: in the great world of national politics, it leads to the rebellion of the Percy clan (who had supported him in his rise), and in the little world of family politics, it leads to the much more subtle and repressed rebellion of the prince. In a brilliant gambit, King Henry will resolve both his problems at the same time by using the threat of the Percy rebellion to bring his son to heel and by using his son as his primary instrument for bringing down the Percys.

In King Henry and Prince Hal Shakespeare closely examines, and for the first time, the relationship between a reigning king and his heir. As we might guess from the problems of sons and fathers in his earlier plays, including the friction between Henry Bullingbrook and his father in *Richard II*, the relationship does not prove to be an easy one. As in *Richard II*, the generational differences between father and son are greatly compounded by political and ethical differences, in this case the ambiguous status of a father who is both a king and a usurper. On the one hand, a king for a father literalizes the father-as-ruler trope and invests him with the most commanding degree of authority a father could have. On the other hand, this enormous paternal authority is severely qualified by the fact that the regal father has snatched the throne and thus lacks the moral legitimacy that should underwrite his paternal and political office. For a moral person to serve as prime inheritor under such a figure is to suffer a divided allegiance: to be alienated (in some degree) like the rebels who attempt to overthrow the king but also to be, even more than his father's henchmen, committed to protecting him. Whether he likes it or not, Hal is inevitably his father's successor, and his life depends on maintaining his father's success, tainted though it may be.

The Prince in Eastcheap

It is only by paying the closest attention to what Hal says and does that we can begin to discern the underlying tensions in this secretive young man, who is in many ways the prototype for an even more elusive, ambivalent prince, Hamlet.[6] Though Hal is not as puzzling as Hamlet, at the centre of Shakespeare's characterization of the young English prince is a question: why does he leave his father's court for the taverns of London? Or rather, why *has he left*, since the first reference to Hal in the tetralogy (late in *Richard II*) reveals that he is already "mongst the taverns' in London (*R2*:5.3.5). We are not allowed to see Hal before he leaves, nor do we ever hear an account of his leaving. To be sure, early in *I Henry IV* Hal does give a soliloquy in which he seems to be explaining his presence in Eastcheap to himself, but this is after the fact and smacks (as we will see) of special pleading. In its offstage opacity, Hal's removal from his father to Eastcheap is like young John Talbot's leaving his father on the battlefield to attack the French, which is reported rather than shown (*1H6*:4.7.9–16). There is a key difference, however, as John Talbot's story comes to an end with this crucial, unseen action, while Hal's departure marks his beginning. In terms of the audience's perception, Hal does not exist until he leaves his father's court. Since the Prince's story opens with a question mark, interpretations of that decisive earlier action must be based on inferences derived from (or at least consistent with) what we actually see and hear.

Given the dubious but widespread assumption that Hal's story is one of a young man growing up, it is not surprising that many critics have followed John Dover Wilson's lead and interpreted his withdrawal to Eastcheap as a form of adolescent pleasure-seeking that links him with the Prodigal Son.[7] But if we compare Shakespeare's Hal to his counterpart in the anonymous pre-Shakespearean play called *The Famous Victories of Henry the Fifth*, which clearly draws on the Prodigal Son parable, we can see how little Prince Hal conforms to type. Elizabethan audiences would have been familiar with a folklore tradition that depicted the prince as a roisterer and a hellraiser, a wayward son so insolent that he staged various highway robberies and struck the Lord Chief Justice in the face. This material was gathered into the *Famous Victories*, which depicts a hard-drinking prince who is good with his fists and even harbours explicit parricidal desires. In one of that play's key scenes, the prince enters his father's chamber with a dagger in his hand but suddenly has an attack of conscience and begs his father's pardon in words borrowed from the Prodigal Son parable.[8] Compared to that seriously fractious but ultimately repentant figure, Shakespeare's prince maintains an ambivalent detachment from his Eastcheap companions, including Falstaff.

Though Hal participates in combats of wit and other forms of jesting with Falstaff, he seems always to be on the edge of the festivity, withholding his full engagement and biding his time. Unlike most Elizabethan depictions of the Prodigal, he shows no interest in women, and it is not clear that he ever actually takes a drink.

Despite the King's 'unthrifty son' reference at the end of *Richard II*, Hal proves to be more nearly an anti-prodigal than a prodigal. Far from stealing and living riotously on the proceeds, as the Prince of the *Famous Victories* does, Hal is obsessed throughout the play with the paying of debts, those of other people as well as his own.[9] Not only does he assiduously return the money he steals from the King's Exchequer, but he also pays Falstaff's bar bills 'with advantage' (2.4.547–8). (One attraction of Falstaff to the Prince is that Hal feels he owes him no debts.) Hal's emphasis on making good on liabilities extends beyond the realm of financial indebtedness: it seems to be at the centre of his sense of ethical conduct. On the battlefield, for instance, he will punningly remind his stout companion that 'thou owest God a death' (5.1.126), a debt that Falstaff is not willing to pay before it is called in. Clearly, Hal's insistence on paying debts sets him apart from his father, who is accused by the Percys of breaking his commitments to them and who, more seriously, has stolen the entire kingdom from its rightful owner. With regard to this larger debt, there is a poignant limit to Hal's ability to repay: he can pay back the victims of Falstaff's thefts and make good on his bar bills, but to whom can his father's stolen crown be returned?

Related to his fiscal and moral responsibility is Hal's quite unprodigal attitude toward time, always a factor in the paying of debts. Unlike Richard II's famous wasting of time and reciprocal wasting of himself, Hal seems always to have a sharp awareness of what the time is and what the hour calls for. In his opening banter with Falstaff, the prince is both amused and angered by the gratuitousness of Falstaff's question, 'Now, Hal, what time of day is it, lad?' (1.2.1). Even after a long night of theft and game playing, Hal knows the time well enough to correct the sheriff who wishes him 'Good night' when it is past midnight (2.4.523–4). Alert as he is about the present time, the prince's orientation is always toward the coming time, the future, when he will become king of the realm.[10] Far from being self-indulgent, Hal seems by nature to be self-denying and acutely aware of his responsibilities, a young man who is worried about the debts he owes and the duty that awaits him.[11]

In response to the difficulties with seeing Hal as simply a pleasure-seeking prodigal led astray by Falstaff, some critics have gone to the opposite extreme and pictured him as a ruthless Machiavellian politician who travels to Eastcheap as a public relations ploy, thus creating a wastrel's image that he can reject when the time is ripe for him to look good. Not the least of the attractions of this view is that Hal articulates it himself. In his only soliloquy in the play (1.2.195–217), he looks at life in Eastcheap so askance and so coldly that defenders of the Prodigal Son thesis have had to resort to the desperate expedient of saying that the speech exists merely as a choric reassurance to the audience that Hal will reform and that it reveals nothing of his character.[12] Hal says in effect that he has quite deliberately taken on the role of the Prodigal so that onlookers will be amazed when he throws it off and reveals his true self beneath the costume:

> And like bright metal on a sullen ground,
> My reformation, glitt'ring o'er my fault,
> Shall show more goodly and attract more eyes
> Than that which hath no foil to set it off.
> I'll so offend, to make offense a skill,
> Redeeming time when men think least I will.   1.2.212–17

In this soliloquy Hal refers to Falstaff and his other Eastcheap companions with a muted disgust, as they become 'base, contagious clouds' (1.2.198) that would smother the excellence of the sun (son), Hal's image for himself. His strategy, he says, is to 'falsify men's hopes' (1.2.211), which can refer to the expectations of onlookers or to the desires of his companions, both scenarios involving his gimlet-eyed manipulation of those who depend upon him.

Although this speech fires a final torpedo into the simple Prodigal Son scenario, it would be wrong to accept it as evidence of Hal's Machiavellian political cynicism or his total revulsion toward Eastcheap. We should think twice about taking at face value a speech so full of images of misleading appearances. Precisely because it *is* deeply revelatory about Hal, the speech is complex and even contradictory. Despite its scorn for Hal's Eastcheap companions, this soliloquy does not cancel out the interpretation of Hal as a young man in search of pleasure. It smacks of Hal's protesting too much (another trait he shares with Hamlet), as his intention seems to be to convince himself that he does not enjoy Eastcheap and does not belong there.

He tells himself that he is in Eastcheap, but not of it. The immediate context of the speech is revealing, for against Hal's protestations Poins has managed to talk him into participating in a theft, and now Hal is explaining his conduct to himself. In Dr Johnson's shrewd analysis, Hal's soliloquy 'exhibits a natural picture of a great mind offering excuses to itself, and palliating those follies which it can neither justify nor forsake.'[13]

Beneath its confident rhythms and strikingly simple opposition of sun and cloud, the speech is full of contradictions. Oddly, Hal's justification of himself for being cleverly strategic is couched in natural imagery that implicitly denies agency to the sun with which he identifies. The Prince says that he is being sun-like in that he 'doth permit the base contagious clouds / To smother up his beauty' (1.2.198–9), but of course the sun grants no such permission, and neither can the clouds be 'contagious' since they never come close to the sun. Besides, the image of permitting oneself to be smothered up is rather different from the reality of Hal's having chosen to go to Eastcheap (and to remain there). Though he is scarcely a wholehearted, prodigal participant in the world of Eastcheap, Hal is not as elementally different from it as his imagery implies; he appears to be denying the limited but real degree of pleasure that he takes among the base contagious clouds. In Sheldon Zitner's succinct formulation, 'If Hal is not of the tavern, neither is he wholly of the court.'[14] Although the King may think that Hal is a Prodigal Son and the Prince may think that he is a clever Machiavellian, neither label suffices.

There is a third, more compelling explanation of Hal's presence in Eastcheap, one which is usually overlooked by critics: that he has left the court not for a prodigal's pleasure or for a politician's profit, but rather to put some distance between himself and his father. This move on Hal's part would seem to be both principled and aggressive: principled in that it indicates his disapproval of his father's seizure of the crown from Richard and aggressive in that he refuses to play the role of Prince of Wales in the conventional, regime-strengthening way that a questionably legitimate king would wish from his eldest son. As we have seen, Hal is not mentioned in *Richard II* until after Henry has become king, and so we are not allowed even a glimpse of Hal's attitude toward the deed. But there is reason to think that Shakespeare's Hal would not have found his father's usurpation of Richard very edifying, partly because Richard was Bullingbrook's first cousin as well as his king.[15] More to the point is the fact that Shakespeare in *1 Henry IV* emphasizes Hal's responsibility and dutifulness, qualities that do not chime well with the crime of usurpation. And we do know that Hal considers the death of Richard a crime, even though he does not directly say as much in *1 Henry IV*. Two plays later, in *Henry V*, Hal finally reveals his feelings when he prays on the evening of Agincourt:

> Not to-day, O Lord,
> O, not to-day, think not upon the fault
> My father made in compassing the crown!   *H5:4.1.292–4*

Hal's guilty unease is vividly suggested by the repeated 'not' as well as the slippage from the largely forthright 'fault' to the euphemistic 'compassing' (rather than stealing or snatching) the crown, as if the act of naming the 'fault' activates the impulse to ameliorate or deny it.

One virtue of this interpretation of Hal's removal from court is that it is consistent with the intriguing hints about Hal that Shakespeare makes at the end of *Richard II* to prepare his audience for the appearance of the Prince in *1 Henry IV*. It certainly fits with the suggestion that Hal absented himself from his father's presence immediately after the coronation ceremony, and, most important, it illuminates the lines describing Hal's intentions at the Oxford joust, especially his subversive vaunt that he will wear a common whore's glove as a favour. Moreover, as noted in the previous chapter, the context in which the King first refers to Hal is replete with allusions to deep divisions between fathers and sons.

If Hal's motive for leaving the court is largely to dissociate himself from the King, then the difference between his behaviour and that of the Prodigal Son comes into still sharper focus. The parable opens with the Prodigal asking his compliant father to 'give me the portion of the goods that falleth to me,' but the Prince does just the opposite. By leaving the court for Eastcheap, Hal is refusing his patrimony instead of claiming it.[16] This denial of inheritance must be related to the fact that his father seized the crown from Richard and subsequently had him murdered. Unlike the Prodigal Son's dissolute waste of his portion from his good father, Hal's refusal of *his* father's ill-gotten estate becomes a principled act. Of course, it is also merely a temporary solution. Unlike the Prodigal in the biblical parable, who travels to a 'far off country' to enjoy himself, Hal retires only to Eastcheap – he knows he will be called by his father, and he knows he will answer the call.

The best-known argument for Hal's rejection of his father is unfortunately flawed. In a frequently reprinted essay titled 'Prince Hal's Conflict,' Ernst Kris begins by making very forcefully the central point about Hal's removal to Eastcheap: 'The Prince has dissociated himself from the court that his father won by treason. In silent protest he has turned to the tavern rather than to participate in regicide.'[17] But Kris, a noted psychoanalyst, is apparently uncomfortable with a motive that is primarily moral, and so he soon weakens and perhaps erases his incisive point by saying of the removal to Eastcheap that Hal 'avoids contamination with regicide because the impulse to regicide (parricide) is alive in his unconscious.'[18] In defence of the argument about parricide, Kris resorts to the feeble claim that Hal and Hotspur 'form a unit' and that 'Hotspur's rebellion represents also Prince Hal's unconscious parricidal impulses.' While in dream interpretation it may be valid to read one figure as a displacement of another, in a play with such complex, sharply individuated characters as Hal and Hotspur the recourse to displacement seems simplistic. If Hotspur's rebellion represents anyone's parricidal impulses, they must be Hotspur's. Though Kris cites no textual evidence for the key idea of Hal's 'silent protest,' he tantalizingly says that it 'would be easy to demonstrate from metaphors and puns alone.'[19]

Reading the Hidden Hal: Silences, Slips, and Jests

The argument that the Prince has left the court in order to distance himself from his father's illegitimate rule invites an obvious criticism: that Hal never directly voices disapproval of Henry. Unlike his openly parricidal namesake in the *Famous Victories*, Hal does not brandish a dagger in the royal presence; indeed he never even speaks daggers at his father. There is in fact plenty of evidence for Hal's hostility toward the King, but it is always expressed obliquely. When the thief Gadshill speaks of his association with 'nobility and tranquility, burgomasters and great oney'rs, such as can hold in, such as will strike sooner than speak' (2.1.75–8), what he does not say is that no one can 'hold in' better than Hal. The prince's manner of complaisant ease seems calculated to hide the matters that trouble him. His instinctively cautious orientation to the world can be seen in the warning he gives to Poins before the robbery of Falstaff – 'Stand close' (2.2.3) – and in his strategy for handling the papers taken from Falstaff's pocket – 'keep close' (2.4.542). Indeed, Hal is so adept at keeping his feelings inside his doublet that he does not understand them himself. In this regard, as in many others, Hal serves as a rough draft for Hamlet.

Hal's silence about his father is at the centre of the play's strong thematic emphasis on the unspoken and the unspeakable. At the court of King Henry, history is what cannot be spoken. In the opening scene, the issue is raised with specific reference to atrocities perpetrated on the English dead,

> Upon whose dead corpse' there was such misuse,
> Such beastly shameless transformation,
> By those Welshwomen done as may not be
> Without much shame retold or spoken of.   1.1.43–6

Like so much else in the play, these lines have an oblique application that is more resonant than the one intended by the speaker. There is an even more unspeakable 'shameless transformation' for which castrating Welshwomen cannot be blamed: the transformation of Henry Bullingbrook from subject to king. Indeed, this latter metamorphosis has proven to be unmentionable at exactly this moment in the play, since the King has concluded an oration on the horrors of civil war without any reference to his role in bringing it about. Given the King's insistent silence, the members of his court are scarcely likely to raise the issue of usurpation, though it is palpably in the air. When Worcester, two scenes later, dares to remind the King of how he helped to place him on the throne, he is summarily dismissed.

The most notable exception to this pervasive censorship is Harry Hotspur. If he is often more attractive than Hal, one reason is his insistence on speaking his mind to his elders and betters. A favourite Hotspurian proverb is 'tell truth and shame the devil,' which in his squabble with Glendower he employs three times in only five lines (3.1.57–61). And in the face of the King's quite evident displeasure, Hotspur launches into long, spirited narratives defending his retention of prisoners and asserting the loyalty of Mortimer, who had been designated as heir presumptive by Richard. After the King departs, Hotspur amusingly imagines himself shouting 'Mortimer' in the sleeping King's ear and even training a starling to repeat 'Mortimer' endlessly to plague him. Hotspur's truth telling is most admirable when he reminds his father (Northumberland) and uncle (Worcester) of their former complicity with the King:

Shall it for shame be spoken in these days,
Or fill up chronicles in time to come,
That men of your nobility and power
Did gage them both in an unjust behalf
(As both of you – God pardon it! – have done)
To put down Richard, that sweet lovely rose,
And plant this thorn, this canker, Bullingbrook?   1.3.170–6

Though Hotspur is inclined to exonerate himself from the usurpation, his indictment of his elders has outspoken moral force behind it.

The son of Bullingbrook will never speak with such frankness and freedom. Nothing could be more unlike Prince Hal than Hotspur's declaration that 'I will ease my heart, / Albeit I make a hazard of my head' (1.3.127–8). Hal never falls prey to the impulse to ease his heart; it is appropriate that he has no love interest, and he retains his head (in every sense) at the play's end. In his desire to let sleeping dogs lie, Hal closely resembles his father, and indeed the King and Prince treat the usurpation as a kind of nasty family secret, to be mentioned only in whispers and in code.[20] Among his high-spirited Eastcheap companions, Hal is always vigilant to prevent the story of the recent past from surfacing, and he is careful to steer the conversation away from direct criticism of his father. While Falstaff's language is full of seductive invitations to criticize the King, Hal always resists them, sometimes icily challenging Falstaff to explain what he means. Thus, when Falstaff says Hal will have Majesty but not Grace when he becomes king, Hal twice demands that he explain himself (1.2.19, 22). But of course Falstaff, true to the spirit of the times, evades spelling out the fact of King Henry's usurpation.

Unlike his feckless namesake in the *Famous Victories*, who frequently grouses about his father in the company of his new friends, Hal declines to speak his mind to Falstaff and his other companions. One can understand his caution. But the Prince's disciplined refusal to break his silence about his father extends beyond his Eastcheap companions. Indeed, it extends to his father himself, as Hal never mentions Henry's usurpation in his presence. Since his father is after all the king, Hal's face-to-face deference is understandable. What is, however, especially disconcerting is that Hal refrains from criticizing his father even within the privacy of his own mind. There is self-censorship at work, as Hal cannot allow himself the painful freedom of thinking directly about his father's – and thus perhaps his own – political illegitimacy. Though it is spoken to Falstaff, Hal's first speech in the play is applicable to himself: 'thou hast forgotten to demand that truly which thou wouldest truly know' (1.2.4–5).

Oddly enough, the most significant of Hal's silences is at the centre of his only extended soliloquy in *Part One* (1.2), a speech as important for what it does not say as for what it does. What is perhaps most interesting about the speech is that Hal does not pose any questions about himself, even though (as we have seen) the soliloquy has been triggered by his unease about joining in a robbery. Instead, he adopts a stance of knowingness of others ('I know you all'), while resolutely refusing to explore his own motives. This is a soliloquy in which, instead of expressing his feelings, Hal stands outside himself, imagining what it would be like to be a spectator watching himself perform the role of Prodigal Son, and so he stresses the clouds that obscure and the foils that beautify but never addresses the issue of who he is.

The most notable silence in the soliloquy is the lack of reference to his father's usurpation and thus to his own dubious legitimacy as crown prince and future king. But it is not quite right to say that Hal is entirely silent about his father, even though he apparently wishes to be. In a classic Freudian slip (that psychoanalytic commentators seem invariably to have missed), a telltale expression of repressed anger does escape from Hal. I refer to the single line that deviates from the stress on appearance and reality in this otherwise fluently organized speech:

So when this loose behavior I throw off
And pay the debt I never promised,
By how much better than my word I am.   1.2.208–10 (italics added)

Momentarily, while contemplating throwing off his disguise of prodigality, Hal allows a glimpse of his embittered attitude to his father, with the intensive 'never' suggesting righteous indignation. According to an Elizabethan proverb, 'Promise is debt,' but Hal has incurred the debt without having made a promise.[21] The 'debt' must refer to the role of Prince of Wales and Hal's eventual assumption of the throne, and clearly he is not happy about having this greatness thrust upon himself, presumably without his compliance.[22] As we have seen, Elizabethan authorities stressed the infinite debt of life that every child owed to his or her parents. But in addition to that univer-

sal filial obligation, Hal owes his father the debt of having been elevated to the office of Prince of Wales and of eventually becoming King.
Throughout the play, the language of legal and financial indebtedness
is Hal's most persistent and personal strain of imagery, and here it contrasts sharply with the speech's pervasive reference to costumes, role
playing, and glittering shows.

As commentators have often noted, many of Hal's images in this
soliloquy will be echoed later by the King when he castigates Hal for
profligacy on his return to court (3.2.29–91). Indeed, virtually all of
Hal's images of politic manoeuvre have a close equivalent in his
father's language, as both speeches 'dwell on the proper management
of one's political visibility and the importance of avoiding overexpo-
sure.'[23] In the theatre, one perceives the similarities (if at all) in terms
of the King's echoing his son's earlier comments, but upon reflection
one may wonder who is echoing whom. (In *Hamlet* there is a similar
instance of a son's speech being followed by paternal speech that
reveals the source of the former: soon after young Hamlet's first soliloquy, we hear the ghost of the elder Hamlet apply many of the same
images and ideas to Gertrude that Hamlet had used.) Since in language acquisition 'like father, like son' makes more sense than 'like
son, like father,' a large irony comes into focus: that Hal is using his
father's language of political strategy to explain to himself why he has
defied his father's wishes. Part of Hal's problem is that he is too much
his father's son to be able to articulate his sense of being used by his
father, or to construct an alternative explanation of his conduct.

As the slip in the 'I know you all' soliloquy indicates, Hal's vigilance
in repressing his filial displeasure is not perfect. It is in Hal's jests that
his self-censorship is most lax, as is prefigured at the close of *Richard II*
by his mocking joke of wearing a common prostitute's glove for a
favour at the royal joust. There is rich evidence to suggest that for Hal,
as will also prove true for Hamlet, the royal road to repressed emotion
and buried understanding is through joking.[24] For *1 Henry IV* (and
perhaps for *Hamlet* as well), Freud's most illuminating concept is not
the Oedipal complex but rather his analysis of wit as a vehicle for
expressing unconscious aggression. Though Freud does not mention
Hal, many of his observations are relevant to him, such as his point
that tendentious jokes make it possible to criticize persons in exalted
positions who claim to represent authority. The joke represents a rebellion against that authority, a liberation from its pressure.[25] It is through
Hal's jests that we can best see what is on his mind; he is never more

serious than when he is joking, if one sees to the bottom of the joke. In the complex play of similarity and difference that defines father and son, Hal's predilection for jests marks his greatest individuation from his dour, businesslike father. For him, to joke is to distance himself from the King.

Not surprisingly, the King often figures tacitly in Hal's jests, as in the first scene with the Prince and his companions in Eastcheap. After Poins jokes that Falstaff has sold his soul to the devil for a snack of wine and capon, the following exchange occurs:

> *Prince.* Sir John stands to his word, the devil shall have his bargain,
> for he was never yet a breaker of proverbs. He will give the devil his due.
> *Poins.* Then art thou damn'd for keeping thy word with the devil.
> *Prince.* Else he had been damn'd for cozening the devil.   1.2.117–23

It is Hal, revealingly, who makes the paradoxical observation about Falstaff's being inevitably damned, regardless of whether he breaks or does not break his deal with the devil. (Once again, Hal's introduction of the issue of indebtedness points toward the engagement of his deeper feelings.) Presumably, the idea occurs to Hal because he sees his own situation as a double bind similar to the one he constructs for Falstaff. Behind the joke, then, Hal reveals a poignant awareness of having been placed in an impossible dilemma: that he is damned if he supports his usurping father, and damned if he betrays him. In the role-playing scene in the tavern, Hal (speaking in his father's voice) will describe Falstaff as 'that old white-bearded Sathan' (2.4.463), but Hal's tacit identification of the desire to flee his father as 'cozening the devil' reveals another candidate for the role of Satan, one whom he cannot name.

It is through a much more elaborate jape, this time an extended practical joke, that Hal most fully voices his frustration and anger about the quandary he has been placed in. While waiting in the Boar's Head Tavern for Falstaff to return from robbing and being robbed at Gadshill, Hal invents a practical joke to play on Francis the drawer. Poins repeatedly calls for Francis from another room, but Hal persistently engages him in conversation and thus prevents him from serving his customer. As a result, Francis is stupefied and reduced to calling 'Anon, anon' to Poins – 'Right away.' As is his wont, Hal is working so indirectly that he appears not to be conscious of what he is doing. Certainly, Poins doesn't understand what is going on, for he later asks Hal what he meant by 'this jest of the drawer' (and does not receive a straight answer). For the most part, directors and editors of *1 Henry IV* have seen no more in the joke than Poins has, for it is routinely trivialized or even cut from productions, and some of the best scholarly editions have missed the point.[26]

This joke played on Francis makes good sense only if it is read as an oblique expression of Hal's unarticulated misgivings about his father. With whatever degree of awareness, Hal places Francis in the same unpleasant situation that he himself has been placed in. (Sheldon Zitner cleverly characterized Hal's earlier 'I know you all' soliloquy as *his* 'Anon, anon' speech.)[27] Hal hints at the substitution when he tells Poins that he can call the drawers by their Christian names, 'as Tom, Dick, and Francis' (instead of the proverbial Tom, Dick, and *Harry*). Like Hal, Francis is tugged at in two directions at once; his conversation with a man he admires (he has just given Hal a pennyworth of sugar) is interrupted by an insistent call for him to fulfil his duty and serve his master. The scene is virtually an allegorical representation of Hal's divided allegiances, or of a division between duty and desire. An instruction for the actors to get it right is embedded in an authorial stage direction: '*Here they both call him; the drawer stands amazed, not knowing which way to go.*' Immediately following this stage direction, the Vintner appears and issues a peremptory order to Francis: 'What, stand'st thou still, and hear'st such a calling? Look to the guests within' (2.4.80–1). The relevance to Hal's immediate situation could hardly be greater, for he, too, has been of more than one mind about 'which way to go,' and the issue of heeding a 'calling' or vocation has paralysed him. Just as the authoritative command of the Vintner resolves Francis's dilemma by removing the unpleasant responsibility of choosing his direction, so too will Hal's tuggings and misgivings be resolved by his father's command to report for duty.[28] Later in this same scene, an emissary from the King will arrive with Hal's marching orders: 'you must to the court in the morning' (334–5).

What is most interesting about the joke is its oblique suggestiveness. In Hal's attitude to Francis, one can begin to tease out his feelings about his own situation and his father. His perception of a shared situation with Francis shapes his conflicted response, as he both mocks his drawer-double and also shows some sympathy for him.[29] Hal's mockery of Francis conveys an attempt to convince himself that the two of them are not really similar, that Francis is merely a marginally human tool totally bereft of language. As Hal exclaims to Poins after-wards, 'His industry is up stairs and down stairs, his eloquence the parcel of a reckoning' (2.4.99–101). Ironically, these dismissive terms have a precise application to Hal himself, as 'up stairs and down stairs' points to Hal's vacillation between the court and Eastcheap, and 'his eloquence the parcel of a reckoning' is a perfect description of Hal's own predilection for using the language of indebtedness in his most powerfully felt moments.[30] And so throughout the scene Hal deliber-ately talks over Francis's head, happily confusing this creature who is so eager to please him.

In the midst of this mockery, however, Hal seems to realize the deeply sad situation in which Francis is trapped, and in which he himself is of course also trapped.[31] Upon learning that Francis has five years of apprenticeship to serve, Hal declares: 'Five year! by'r lady, a long lease for the clinking of pewter. But, Francis, darest thou be so valiant as to play the coward with thy indenture, and show it a fair pair of heels and run from it?' (2.4.45–8). When Hal speaks of being 'so valiant as to play the coward,' he is doing more than confusing Francis with wanton paradox, for the terms apply perfectly well to Hal's having 'run from' the court to Eastcheap. For Hal to continue to flout the court and his father would be an act of considerable bravery, but at the same time it would be cowardly, revealing an inability to face up to duty and to pay the debt owed to one's father (exploitative though he may be). Alternatively, if what Hal might 'run from' is the impend-ing war with the Percys, a similar paradox obtains: there can be cow-ardice in entering into combat thoughtlessly and great bravery in prin-cipled resistance to war.

As we might expect, Hal's most cryptic lines to Francis are also his most deeply felt. In lines that most editors dismiss as nonsense, Hal evokes the bleak alternatives awaiting Francis (and himself): 'Why then your brown bastard is your only drink! for look you, Francis, your white canvas doublet will sully. In Barbary, sir, it cannot come to so much' (2.4.73–5). If Francis does not seize the valiantly cowardly action of running away, then a life of sordid abjection will be the inevitable consequence.[32] As Hal had remarked of Falstaff's deal with the devil, so he suggests that Francis is damned if he does and damned if he doesn't. The image of the 'white canvas doublet' becoming sullied poignantly evokes the remorseless besmirching of innocence – it is as close as Hal comes to the imagery of Hamlet ('too, too sullied flesh'). But running away to the exotic but dangerously lawless Barbary coast is hardly an attractive alternative. Indeed, a pathetic innocent like Francis would be lucky to make it to the coast of England, as he would be easy prey for predators like Falstaff, who complacently lists 'revolted tapsters' among the conscripts whom he will lead into the thick of battle as cannon fodder (4.2.29).

Hal's lines about Francis's lack of alternatives reveal his unspoken understanding of his own situation as well as the drawer's. He and Francis are a kind of 'doublet' in the sense of being paired figures, for in his menial serving role as Prince of Wales Hal will also be sullied. Indeed, his lines make a more trenchant comment on himself than on Francis, for being a waiter is not morally degrading, unlike being heir to a stolen, bloodstained throne. And the hint of a staining illegitimacy in the cheap, adulterated wine known as 'brown bastard' says much more about Hal (the son of an illegitimate monarch) than Francis. From the King's opening charge that 'riot and dishonor stain the brow / Of my young Harry' (1.1.85–6), the play has been full of references to stains, blemishes, and the pitch that doth defile, but none is more indelible than this sullying which Hal shares, and does not share, with Francis.

Given his intimation of a common apprenticeship with Francis, it is not surprising that the Prince would also perceive a likeness in the masters they serve. Hal's spirited excoriation of the Vintner conveys his repressed animus against the hypocritical king:

> *Prince.* Wilt thou rob this leathern-jerkin, crystal-button, not-pated,
> agate-ring, puke-stocking, caddis-garter, smooth-tongue, Spanish
> pouch –
> *Francis.* O Lord, sir, who do you mean?   2.4.69–72

Francis asks exactly the right question (which Hal disregards), and the answer must be something like 'All exploitative, patriarchal authority, but with special reference to the King.' Hal's Rabelaisian cataloguing of the accoutrements of this smug, bourgeois Vintner makes an oblique comment on a king who repeatedly comments on ruling the realm as 'business.'[33] (It is plausible that Shakespeare intended the part of the Vintner to be doubled with that of the King, and certainly his stage comportment should be reminiscent of Henry's.) When the Vintner immediately appears, as if conjured up by Hal's description of him, he commands Francis with an irate authority that soon will be echoed in the King's dispatch of *his* delinquent apprentice: 'What, stand'st thou still, and hear'st such a calling?' (2.4.80–1).

Revealing as it is, Hal's playing with Francis serves as a warm-up for the climactic jesting with Falstaff that will occupy the rest of this great scene. If Francis serves Hal as a mirror, Falstaff functions (as many commentators have noted) as an alternative father for Hal. For a few moments in the tavern, this surrogacy becomes explicit, as Hal asks Falstaff to 'stand for my father' (2.4.376), but for the most part it is implied and elusive. The traditional interpretation is to contrast Falstaff and the King, and certainly the indulgent playfulness of Falstaff could hardly be more unlike Hal's father's severe criticism. We can imagine Hal turning to Falstaff for some of the same reasons that the young James Boswell sought in London to replace his disapproving father, the dour and demanding laird of Auchinleck, with the affable, appreciative figure of Dr Johnson.[34] But we should be wary of sentimentalizing this relationship; Falstaff has designs on Hal no less than his father does, and he represents more to Hal than simply a Carnival substitution for the King's Lent.

Despite the rather obvious, ingratiating contrasts to Henry that he provides, what makes Falstaff most valuable to Hal is his resemblance to the King. Both men are, in their different theatres of operation, thieves, and the designation of 'father ruffian' (2.4.454) applies to both. While Falstaff steals 'the king's exchequer' on Gadshill, the King has made off with the entire kingdom, and both wish to use Hal to legitimize and protect their thievery. In this parallel, Falstaff is a far more transparent and literal offender than is the King, which means that he is also an easier target for reproach and exposure. Unlike the unassailable father/King, Falstaff demands no respect; he is the reprobate father who can be directly impugned. From their first exchange onwards, Hal showers ambivalent abuse on Falstaff in a streaming jocularity broken by frequent gleams of flint. The usefulness of Falstaff to Hal becomes apparent when we consider which aspects of this ample target he chooses to derogate. Though Hal never misses an opportunity to taunt Falstaff for his girth, he takes particular pleasure in denouncing him for his pretence of innocence, his lies and hypocrisy, his shameless presentation of himself as something he is not. Thus Hal accuses Falstaff of exactly those flaws that he sees, but cannot criticize, in his father.

Throughout the tavern scene (2.4), the King is an unseen presence in Hal and Falstaff's games, though occasionally he is conjured up in the dialogue, as when Falstaff provocatively claims to Hal that (during the robbery) 'I knew ye as well as he that made ye' (2.4.267–8). And for a moment or two the person of the King assumes distorted shapes onstage as Falstaff and Hal take turns playing him to the other's prince. But for the most part the King is a shadowy figure behind Hal's attempts to expose Falstaff's impostures, while Falstaff employs his wit and charm to evade these charges. In his nimble reinventions of himself (and of reality), the portly Falstaff is evasion personified. For his part, Hal is both amused and offended by the old man's ability to dance away from shame. Hal's interest in trapping Falstaff in his lies appears to grow as he ponders his own return to the court; the closer Hal comes to returning to his father, the stronger becomes his impulse to mock Falstaff as a surrogate for him. There is real fervour in Hal's drawn-out jest to trap Falstaff in 2.4, with the Prince demanding, 'What trick? what device? what starting-hole? canst thou now find out to hide thee from this open and apparent shame?' (2.4.262–4).

Since Falstaff's pretence to virtue does not appear to be an adequate reason for the Prince to be so angry (especially since everyone, including Falstaff, knows what the truth is), we can only assume that Hal is trying to get something off his chest. A particularly telling revelation of Hal's inner state of mind is the phrase he uses to declare that he is through with Falstaff's evasions: 'I'll be no longer guilty of this sin' (2.4.241). In the first place, it is not clear why Hal should feel 'guilty' about Falstaff's twisting of the truth, since he is in the process of vigorously attacking Jack's credibility. Moreover, it seems an unfunny exaggeration on Hal's part to speak of Falstaff's lies as 'sin.' But it is easy to see how Hal can feel guilty about condoning his father's heinous crimes of usurpation and murder, crimes that he will participate in as inheritor of the crown.

Hal's veiled references to the King are most poignant in his final words to Falstaff in the play. In response to Falstaff's ridiculous claim that he killed Hotspur, Hal says to his companion: 'For my part, if a lie may do thee grace, / I'll gild it with the happiest terms I have' (5.4.157–8). There is more reason for Hal to be angry now than in the après-robbery party at Eastcheap; after all, Falstaff is now stealing from Hal. But Hal's lines express the very antithesis of his aggressive truth telling against Falstaff in 2.4, and one may wonder why. The traditional critical comment is that by now Hal has internalized true honour and has matured, so he does not care who gets the credit for slaying Hotspur. But this interpretation misses the most interesting aspect of Hal's words to Falstaff: that they would be much more appropriately spoken to his father. Since his return to the court, and especially since his insistent identification of himself as Prince of Wales on the battlefield, Hal has been gilding the lie of his father's claim to legitimacy. (Hal's interest in his early soliloquy on making himself look good to onlookers has given way to his burnishing the appearance of his father's regime.) To gild Falstaff's lie as well as his father's is perhaps a way for Hal to balance his moral accounts, for he may realize that his companion's lie is, finally, minuscule and harmless compared to his father's.

The Return of the (Not So) Prodigal Son

The first meeting of Hal and his father, which is the centre of the play (3.2) and the fulcrum on which its action turns, is usually called the 'reconciliation scene' in the critical literature. In performance the element of reconciliation is usually stressed, as a description in the influential 'French's Acting Version' indicates: 'the scene rings to its close on the notes of inspired chivalry and the glorious union of father and son in reconciliation and in arms.'[35] But a quick glance at the scene's primary sources in Holinshed's chronicle and in the anonymous *Famous Victories* will indicate how mistakenly the label has been applied to Shakespeare's scene. As is his wont, Shakespeare complicates the idealized father-son relationship that he finds in his sources. In Holinshed (as in the *Famous Victories'* version of the same scene and also in the reconciliation of the Prodigal Son parable), the son comes to the father of his own volition, and the chronicle's prince pays his respects in the prescribed Elizabethan protocol: 'The prince kneeling down before his father said: Most redoubted and sovereign lord and father, I am at this time come to your presence as your liege man, and as your natural son, in all things to be at your commandment' (Bullough 4:194). Not only is Holinshed's prince perfectly deferential, but he also acknowledges his twofold obligation to the man who is both his 'sovereign lord and father,' and thus he identifies himself doubly as 'liege man, and as your natural son.' Obedience in the state and the family are one, with the state taking precedence. As does the father in the Prodigal Son parable, Holinshed's King Henry embraces the kneeling prince, kisses him, and sheds tears. (In the parallel scene in *Famous Victories* there is still more sentiment, with plentiful sighs and weeping on the part of both father and son.) Holinshed's summary, like his scene, is unequivocal: 'Thus were the father and the son reconciled' (Bullough 4:195).

In reworking the scene, Shakespeare adds a good deal of salt to his sources, with the Prince and King remaining at a hostile distance from each other. In the corresponding scenes in Holinshed and the *Famous Victories*, the King is so 'grievously diseased' (Bullough 4:194) that the Prince feels pity for him and quickly repents of his prodigal ways. But in Shakespeare the King is in full control of himself and of his son, as his long, vigorous reprimands indicate. To be sure, critics have occasionally described Hal as having the upper hand and 'letting his father talk himself out,' but the language indicates that the King seizes the offensive and retains it.[36] This stiff, formalized scene stresses the triumph of what Elizabethans called the civil father over the natural father. Upon entering, the King dismisses his advisors, saying that 'the Prince of Wales [not 'my son'] and I must have some private conference' (3.2.1), and their attitude toward each other is largely formal. Whether or not a throne is present, and whether or not the King sits on it, and whether or not Hal kneels to him – none of this is specified in the Quarto or Folio stage directions – a sense of unease pervades the atmosphere. Instead of acknowledging his usurpation of the throne, the King refers euphemistically to being punished by God 'For some displeasing service I have done' (3.2.5). Hal *could* spell out what the king's 'displeasing service' was, and he *could* add that Henry is now demanding a deeply 'displeasing service' to be done by himself as prince. But instead Hal responds in kind by conceding that, among the many false allegations brought against him, he may need pardon 'for some things true' (3.2.26). The father and son are, as it were, joined in a common isolation by their inability to name what they have done. This situation will become increasingly familiar in Shakespeare's future plays: a coming together of a father and son that remains a staying apart.[37]

The King speaks first, of course, demanding that the Prince account for his failure to behave properly, and we are not allowed to forget that, to use Falstaff's apposite phrases, Hal has returned not 'by instinct' but rather 'upon compulsion' (2.4 passim). It is surprising how unprepared Hal seems to be for this interview, even though in Eastcheap he has been rehearsing for it, both in his politic soliloquy and in his interlude with Falstaff. It is as if, in the august presence of his king and father, Hal's glib script evaporates into thin air. While Hal's facile soliloquy had ended with the easy reassurance that 'I'll so offend, to make offense a skill' (1.2.216), this tortuous speech begins with his awkward wish that he 'could / Quit all offenses':

> So please your Majesty, I would I could
> Quit all offenses with as clear excuse
> As well as I am doubtless I can purge
> Myself of many I am charg'd withal.   3.2.18–21

Unlike the imagined populace in the Prince's soliloquy, the King is quite undazzled by his son's supposed reformation, and so Hal pleads that

> I may for some things true, wherein my youth
> Hath faulty wand'red and irregular,
> Find pardon on my true submission.   3.2.26–8

There is an awkward doubleness about Hal's convoluted language, like a radio receiving two stations at once, one broadcasting a confession and the other an exculpation. The contrast with the Prodigal Son's simple self-abasement ('Father, I have sinned against heaven, and before thee, and am no more worthy to be called thy son') could hardly be greater, especially since in Shakespeare it is the father who insists on his son's unworthiness.[38]

If Hal hopes that ending with 'pardon on my true submission' will satisfy his father, he is sorely mistaken, for in three words Henry dismisses everything Hal has said: 'God pardon thee!' (3.2.29). The implication is clearly, '*I* won't.' What the King *will* do is continue to expatiate (in the longest speech in the play) on the cleverness with which he manipulated the public gaze while unseating Richard. Unbeknownst to the King, his speech is rife with ironies, one of which is that his son has already used some of the same images that Henry is now using to prove his own superiority. Morever, like many a successful Elizabethan father, the King complacently assumes that his way is best, and so he prefers Hotspur to Hal on the grounds that Hotspur is following in his footsteps. But Henry's usurpation has thrown into chaos the kingdom that he gained, and inevitably Hotspur's imitation of the King's ambition, if successful, would involve usurping him and having him killed. In addition to all of this, the King is of course wrong in his assumption that, in character, Hotspur is more like him than Hal is. In saying these things, Henry is opening himself to the kind of deadly riposte that Hal frequently inflicts on Falstaff, but the Prince is too subdued to voice any of these ironies.

When Hal does respond, it is because the King has finally paused, saying that his eye, which 'hath desir'd to see thee more,' is now about to 'blind itself with foolish tenderness' (3.2.89, 91). Hal seizes the opportunity to make a second attempt at placating his father, but this time he offers no excuses about the past, saying simply: 'I shall here- after, my thrice-gracious lord, / Be more myself' (3.2.92–3). The words of his protestation are a family locution. Unbeknownst to Hal, the King had vowed to 'be myself' (1.3.5) when he defied the Percy family at court earlier in the play. To make the echoing of father and son still more complicated, only a minute or two in stage time before the King's vow to 'be myself,' Hal in his soliloquy had spoken of the time when he (imaging himself as the sun) will 'please again to be himself' (1.2.200). It is disturbing that both father and son can conceive of their actions as stemming from a source that is not their true self (and thus not to be blamed on the self). But there is a difference. When the King threatens to be himself, he specifies what that 'self' is: 'Mighty and to be fear'd' (1.3.6). But when Hal asserts that 'I shall ... Be more myself' there is no telling what he means. Since the King is interested not in Hal's being himself but rather in his playing the role of prince, he com- pletely ignores his son's protestation. As if his son had not spoken, King Henry continues with his cautionary lesson about the fall of Richard. To increase the pressure on Hal, he plays his Hotspur card, likening Hotspur to himself and Hal to the hapless Richard. Moreover, he praises Hotspur because he threatens to seize the crown, even though he is 'of no right, nor color like to right' (3.2.100). Once again, there is ample opportunity for Hal to comment on his father's obvi- ously faulty logic and on the evil consequences of his usurpation, but he does not avail himself of it.

After praising Hotspur's victory over the Douglas, to which we will return later, the King concludes with a biting mockery of Hal's lack of manliness and family pride:

> Thou that art like enough, through vassal fear,
> Base inclination, and the start of spleen,
> To fight against me under Percy's pay,
> To dog his heels and curtsy at his frowns,
> To show how much thou art degenerate.   3.2.124–8

Whether or not the Henry had this conclusion in mind from the begin- ning, he has brilliantly succeeded in batting down Hal's defences and rousing his indignation. Without explicitly urging Hal to do so, he has led him to a simple commitment: by killing Hotspur, Hal can prove his worthiness to his father and his ancestral line, can prove he is not 'degenerate.'

The King has reduced to abject silence the witty Prince who excels at quick retorts to Falstaff's provocations. But, finally, the taunt of degeneracy sets Hal off, as it was designed to do, and the Prince explodes into cold fury:

> I will redeem all this on Percy's head,
> And in the closing of some glorious day
> Be bold to tell you that I am your son,
> When I will wear a garment all of blood,
> And stain my favors in a bloody mask,
> Which wash'd away shall scour my shame with it.   3.2.132–7

These lines are a desperate recasting of Hal's glib soliloquy in act 1. In place of his envisioned quest to 'redeem the time,' he now commits himself to a redemption that is violent, even murderous. Hal's 'garment all of blood' and his 'bloody mask' become a dark transformation of the 'foul and ugly mists / Of vapors' (1.2.202–3) that he imagined wrapping himself in so as to amaze onlookers when he threw them off. In the soliloquy, Hal thought he could win over his imagined audience merely by discarding a disguise, but now he is driven to invent a magical purification in which blood will stain, disguise, and ultimately serve to cleanse his features.

While Hal's rage is directed explicitly at Hotspur, there is an undercurrent of anger at his father, who has successfully denied his son's independence, humiliated him, and trained him on Hotspur. Not without irony, Hal declares that he will prove he is his father's son by wearing the blood of a rival he has killed; he will become a true son, he may imply, by re-enacting his father's crime. Thus, the exact nature of the 'shame' that Hal feels he must scour away is deeply ambiguous: is it the shame of being perceived by his father as a wastrel, or is it the shame of his father's bloody usurpation of Richard, or is it the shame of buckling under his father's pressure and agreeing to do his bidding?

The question of whether Hal is like or unlike his father generates ironies throughout the scene, reaching a terrible climax in the Prince's final lines:

Percy is but my factor, good my lord,
To engross up glorious deeds on my behalf;
And I will call him to so strict account
That he shall render every glory up,
Yea, even the slightest worship of his time,
Or I will tear the reckoning from his heart.   3.2.147–52

Once again, as in his early soliloquy, Hal articulates his intentions in imagery that derives from his father. To the king who sees the rule of England as a business, Hal speaks in insistently economic terms: Hotspur is merely a 'factor' or business agent who acts on his master's behalf and has no claim to the wealth he accumulates. The most trenchant irony is that Hal not only agrees to defend his father's usurped crown, but also that Hal's commitment reflects his father's crime in gaining it. Hal will destroy Hotspur as his father destroyed Richard: by usurping his counterpart's identity and taking his honours. There is a further twist: in the process of declaring that Hotspur will become his compliant factor, in effect Hal surrenders himself, factor-like, to the cause of *his* master, the King. In this scene in which the King insists that Hal must account for himself, Hal promises to call his enemy 'to so strict account / That he shall render every glory up' (3.2.149–50).

Hal's Rescue of, and Revenge upon, His Father

It is easy, too easy, to read acts 4 and 5 as if they fully realize and harmonize the reconciliation of father and son that supposedly had begun in Hal's return to court (3.2). If actions are taken at face value (always dangerous in this play of masks and counterfeiting), then the fullness of this reconciling and unifying can hardly be doubted. Certainly it is true that Hal fights bravely at Shrewsbury, even though he is wounded, and that he saves his father from certain death at the hands of the Douglas. Also, there can be no doubt that, despite Falstaff's preposterous claims, Hal does defeat Hotspur in single combat, just as he had promised his father. Moreover, at the close of the play Hal does free his enemy the Douglas, an act invariably taken by critics to indicate his true arrival at magnanimity and chivalry. Thus we can speak of Hal's acceptance of his father and of himself, and we can identify a process of learning in which he has resolved the difficulties that earlier troubled him. But this pattern of princely growth and reconciliation, like the other patterns of the play, is more apparent than real. When each of these events is examined carefully, it becomes clear that Hal's differences with his father are anything but resolved.

The cornerstone for the argument that Hal and his father are reconciled is of course his rescue of Henry at Shrewsbury Field. As no such rescue was mentioned in Holinshed or other chronicles and as it appeared (briefly) only in Samuel Daniel's poem *The Civile Warres*, Shakespeare was not compelled by his audience's expectations of historical fact to include it.[39] Nor was he compelled in his account to include details that may seem to point to an imminent reconciliation between father and son:

> *They fight; the king being in danger, enter* PRINCE OF WALES.
> *Prince.* Hold up thy head, vile Scot, or thou art like
> Never to hold it up again! The spirits
> Of valiant Shirley, Stafford, Blunt are in my arms.
> It is the Prince of Wales that threatens thee,
> Who never promiseth but he means to pay.
> *They fight: Douglas flieth.*   5.4.39–43

By claiming to incorporate within himself the spirits of comrades slain by Douglas, Hal identifies himself with his father the King's cause, as he does by identifying himself as 'the Prince of Wales' for the first time, thus affirming his identity as heir apparent.[40] Moreover, the last line seems to turn his early, angry reference to the 'debt I never promised' into something positive.

But the immediately ensuing dialogue between father and son – the first occasion for 'private conference' (3.2.2) since their original meeting – presents good reason to think that the rescue has not resolved their differences and has even exacerbated them:

> *King.* Stay and breathe a while.
> Thou hast redeem'd thy lost opinion,
> And show'd thou make'st some tender of my life
> In this fair rescue thou hast brought to me.   5.4.47–50

The King's words about his 'fair rescue' are distinctly cold and grudging in their gratitude, as his customary financial language indicates. For Hal merely to have 'redeem'd [his] lost opinion' suggests that he has done no more than make good on a previous default, and the financial meaning of 'tender' reduces Hal's heroic rescue to the status of a barely repaid ('*some* tender') debt.[41] Very clearly, the King's language implies the idea inculcated by Elizabethan authorities: that children are bound, at a bare minimum, to rescue their parents from all danger.[42]

Given his sensitivity to questions of indebtedness, and especially to the debt he says he never promised his father, one might expect Hal to be displeased with his father's calculation of repayment. And he is:

> *Prince.* O God, they did me too much injury
> That ever said I heark'ned for your death.
> If it were so, I might have let alone
> The insulting hand of Douglas over you,
> Which would have been as speedy in your end
> As all the poisonous potions in the world,
> And sav'd the treacherous labor of your son.
> *King.* Make up to Clifton, I'll to Sir Nicholas Gawsey. *Exit.* 5.4.51–8

Hal's first lines are reminiscent of his attempts at self-justification in the earlier, humiliating audience scene (3.2), but this time he seizes the advantage. Instead of minimizing his deed as an expression of due deference, he disclaims the desire to kill the King (as if the issue were still in doubt), and then with oblique but unmistakable hostility he reminds his father of how powerless he (the King) was. By emphasizing the danger posed by 'the insulting hand of Douglas over you,' the Prince is himself insulting his father anew. And he compounds the insult by quite gratuitously suggesting that he had indeed contemplated the too laborious process of poisoning his father.[43] After Hal finishes, the King is clearly eager for their exchange – which he had asked for – to be over, and he quickly leaves without acknowledging that Hal had spoken. To characterize Hal's response as a 'putting to rest any Oedipal fears on the part of his father' is to specify what Hal pointedly does *not* do.[44]

The exit of the King is followed immediately by the entrance of Hotspur, and Hal's resentment shifts from his father to the target designated by him, just as in 3.2 the King had transferred Hal's rage from himself to Hotspur. Hal's quickly ensuing victory over Hotspur has usually been interpreted as a cementing of his relationship with his father, unequivocal evidence that a full reconciliation has been effected. For instance, Franz Alexander's influential psychoanalytic critique interprets Hal's victory over Hotspur as his victory over the parricidal rebel within himself: 'In killing Hotspur, the arch-enemy of his father, he overcomes his own aggressions against his parent.'[45] But, like much psychoanalytic commentary, this reading seems excessively abstract and detached from the particular contours of Hal's emotional experience. Indeed, it seems more plausible to argue just the opposite: since he has clearly been used by the King to kill his arch-enemy, Hal has more reason to feel anger at Henry when the deed is done. Thanks to his father's manipulation, this is the debt that Hal *has* promised.

Though Hotspur's death is the Prince's great victory in the play, there is reason to think (and especially for Hal to think) that it is at best a pyrrhic, self-destructive victory. When Hal kills Hotspur, he kills a figure who is in many ways an alter ego, almost a brother. Not only do they share a common Christian name, but they also share the burden of being named after their fathers. Of many situational parallels between the two young warriors, the most important is the fact that both have been used by their conniving elders. From their first appearance in 1.3, there is tension between Hotspur and the two men he most respects, his father Northumberland and uncle Worcester. In part, the differences between youth and age are comic, as the old men wait for Hotspur's rant against the King to run its course. But there is also a very serious difference, as Hotspur condemns them for aiding Henry's overthrow of an anointed king. Indeed, some critics have divined so much animus against his father on Hotspur's part that they have interpreted Hotspur's rebellion against the King as a displacement of this Oedipal hostility.[46] It is more illuminating, however, to stress that a considerable distance opens up between the interests of Hotspur and his exploitative mentors, and that in their different ways both of them betray him. Northumberland prudently stays away from the conclusive battle at Shrewsbury (the Induction to the second part of *Henry IV* describes him as being 'crafty-sick' [l. 37]), while urging Hotspur onward. Worse yet, on purely self-interested grounds Worcester deviously conceals from Hotspur the King's offer of clemency; Worcester knows that the King might well pardon the 'hare-brain'd Hotspur' (5.2.19) but would never pardon *him*. So, while these wily greybeards pretend to chastise Hotspur for his hotheadedness, they shrewdly manipulate it for their own ends. As recent editors of the play have noted, 'That a naive Hotspur should regard the ... King as a "vile politician" (1.3.238) and fail to notice how his own father and uncle "train him on" (5.2.21) is one of the tragic ironies of the play.'[47]

There is poignancy in the spectacle of the two young Harrys, who in age and station are more like each other than like anyone else in the play, fighting to the death. It is difficult to ascertain how much Hal knows of Hotspur's having been manipulated by his elders and thus how much he knows about his own similarity to him. But certainly he feels no jubilation upon killing Hotspur, and his speech over Hotspur's corpse expresses a good deal of (guarded) respect. Earlier Hal had saved his father and then launched a verbal attack against him; now he kills Hotspur and then proceeds to praise him. So long as Hotspur lived as his martial rival, there was no time for moral reflection on Hal's part, no leisure to think about young men fighting for the dubious claims of their elders. After Hotspur's death, however, Hal cannot push out of his mind his guilt for having killed him at the behest of, and for the benefit of, his father. As we have seen, he is happy enough for Falstaff to take credit for the deed.

The best evidence for Prince Hal's continuing hostility toward his father is so adroitly concealed by the Prince that it appears never to have been explicated by commentators.[48] The crucial action is his freeing of the Douglas at the end of the play. In Holinshed, it is the King who commands that the Douglas be 'frankly and freely delivered' (Bullough 4:191) for his valiantness, but in Shakespeare the deliverance is Hal's idea. The traditional, virtually the only, critical interpretation has been that Hal's freeing of the Douglas reveals the Prince's exemplary chivalry, especially his 'native magnanimity' and 'real nobility.'[49] But a number of details make this interpretation unconvincing. It is odd, for instance, that upon setting the Douglas free the Prince calls him 'The noble Scot' (5.5.17), but then proceeds to recount how, having

> fled with the rest,
> And falling from a hill, he was so bruis'd
> That the pursuers took him.   5.5.20–2

Even if the audience does not know Holinshed's specification that the bruise was in fact a ruptured testicle (he 'brake one of his cullions'), the Douglas does not sound conspicuously noble. We recall that when Hal had confronted him on the battlefield, he called him not 'noble Scot' but 'vile Scot' (5.4.39). Seymour Connor, one of the few critics to have noticed these problems, conjectured that there must have been some stage business in the early performances which would have justified Hal's suddenly positive attitude toward the Douglas. And so the critic conjures up a wordless act of chivalry on the Douglas's part for which the stage directions have disappeared from the text: earlier the Scot had honourably refrained from joining Hotspur in a two-on-one attack against Hal, and now Hal returns the favour by freeing him.[50]

Rather than inventing improbable stage business to demonstrate why the Douglas *merits* the generosity of his erstwhile enemy, it is more profitable to concentrate on why Hal *chooses* to free the Scot. The key is that only a few minutes of stage time earlier the Douglas had come very close to killing the King, being prevented only by Hal's timely intervention. Hal's freeing of the Douglas, then, is effectively an undoing of his earlier rescue. Quite apart from questions of nobility and chivalry, Hal is giving another life to the only man who held his 'insulting hand' (5.4.54) over the proud King, thus adding a second insult of his own.[51] When Hal explains that

> His [Douglas's] valors shown upon our crests to-day
> Have taught us how to cherish such high deeds
> Even in the bosom of our adversaries   5.5.29–31

the suggestion is that one of the 'high deeds' most cherished by the Prince is the attack upon the crest of his father.[52] Revealingly, there is a characteristic element of trickery and game playing on Hal's part, as he poses his request to his father in misleading terms: 'I beseech your grace / I may *dispose* of him' (5.5.23–4, italics added).[53] Presumably the King assumes that Hal will 'dispose' of Douglas in a lethal manner, Worcester and Vernon having just been sent 'to the death.' For the first time in the play, he gives his son his unqualified approval: 'With all my heart' (5.5.24).

If we recall an earlier scene, we can be reasonably sure that Hal's freeing of the Douglas conceals hostility toward his father. The crucial evidence appears in 3.2, when Hal and the King first meet in the play, and it involves an incident Shakespeare added to the historical record. In the course of browbeating Hal, the King stresses how Hotspur conquered Douglas and then set him free to become a partner in rebellion:

> Thrice hath this Hotspur, Mars in swathling clothes,
> This infant warrior, in his enterprises

Discomfited great Douglas, ta'en him once,
Enlarg'd him and made a friend of him,
To fill the mouth of deep defiance up,
And shake the peace and safety of our throne.   3.2.112–17

From Hal's perspective, the irony of his freeing the Douglas could not be more exquisite. In the course of berating Hal for not being like Hotspur, the King had praised Hotspur for conquering and then freeing the Douglas, thus making an ally of him to threaten the 'safety' of the throne. With mock dutifulness, Hal has played the Hotspur role that his father has assigned him, including even a bit of discreet throne shaking. Hal's irony is even more appropriate in light of the King's comment that Hotspur freed the Douglas 'To fill the mouth of deep defiance up.' By dint of freeing this same Scot, Hal is sounding his own 'deep defiance' of his father, deep in the sense of being repressed and cleverly hidden.[54] Since the King cannot be sure if he is being defied or not, we may think of the freeing of the Douglas as Hal's last and best jest.

Speaking primarily of Prince Hal, the Oxford editor of *1 Henry IV* has remarked that 'The form of the play is ... one of conflict successfully resolved.'[55] And a monograph on family and political order in the histories notes that 'Shrewsbury establishes the forces of order as dominant in the kingdom, and its final moment is this public symbol of unity, a king and his crown prince, reconciled and victorious.'[56] To be sure, the final scene does in some ways have the feel of a positive resolution, primarily because the decisive battle has been fought and won by those onstage. As we have seen, most critics have found in Hal's progress through the play a pattern of education and maturation, and a military victory could be seen to complete the pattern. But there is, I think, an important sense in which nothing is resolved at the end, either for the King or (more significantly) for Hal.[57] The King's political problems remain, and so he must dispatch troops to new battlefields with 'dearest speed' (5.5.36). And the ethical problems that led Hal to flee to Eastcheap just as surely remain. But there is nothing for 'son Harry' (the Prince of Wales) to do but to accompany his father in the attack on Wales.

This brief final scene, in which Hal frees the Douglas, opens and closes with chilling words spoken by the King. Henry's first words, 'Thus ever did rebellion find rebuke' (5.5.1), are of course breathtaking in their regal hypocrisy. The word 'rebuke' may remind us also of the

King's dressing-down of Hal in their first interview, and thus we realize that he has put down not one but two rebellions in the course of the play. Equally pointedly, the King's couplet that closes the scene and the play has ironic implications for Hal: 'And since this business so fair is done, / Let us not leave till all our own be won' (5.5.43–4). One can imagine Hal wincing when the illegitimate king talks of winning 'our own,' because it is clear that the winning of what is supposedly the King's involves a loss for Hal.[58] Eventually, it is true, he will succeed his father to the throne and inherit his takings, but only at the cost of having ceded a good part of himself.

5 *Henry IV, Part Two:*
The Prince Becomes the King
(with a Note on *Henry V*)

Part Two of *Henry IV* has never been as popular or critically acclaimed as *Part One*, but not for the reason a person unacquainted with the play might expect. Instead of the repetitiveness and lack of inspiration that characterize most sequels, *Part Two* is perhaps too surprisingly inventive, too different from its celebrated predecessor. Though the action is continuous with that of *1 Henry IV* – it begins with messengers bringing news of the battle of Shrewsbury to the Earl of Northumberland in the north of England – everything is changed. Suddenly old age, disease, and exhaustion have overtaken the pulsing world of the first part. Even Hotspur suffers from retroactive enervation, with a messenger describing him as 'Rend'ring faint quittance, wearied and outbreath'd' at Shrewsbury (1.1.108), a state we did not see in the earlier play. Nor is his conqueror in much better shape; Prince Hal's first words declare that, 'Before God, I am exceeding weary' (2.2.1). The exhaustion of the younger generation is matched by the sudden incidence of advanced age and disease in the older. Falstaff, who had been remarkably robust in *Part One*, begins to act his age; his first words in *Part Two* inquire about the results of his urinalysis: 'what says the doctor to my water?' (1.2.1). Equally unexpectedly, the King is a shadow of the man who had engaged with the Douglas at Shrewsbury Field; his delayed first appearance is, according to the stage direction, *'in his night-gown, alone'* (*s.d.* at 3.1.1), and he proceeds to lament the insomnia that prevents his head from resting easy. These transformations are shocking, partly because they cannot be accounted for entirely by natural processes of change. Perhaps the best way to understand them is as symbolic manifestations of the sick state of England; Richard II's prophecies about England's horrific future seem to have come true, especially with regard to disease and civil war.[1]

Clearly, the problem of succession to the throne is central, since the usurpation of Richard by Henry Bullingbrook/Henry IV violently disrupted legitimate inheritance. Succession is also important in a second, less moral and symbolic, regard: it seems anticlimactic for Hal to remain subjected to his father after winning the victory at Shrewsbury for him. In this connection, the very title of the play may be relevant; it suggests another of the same rather than a truly new beginning, and this reflects the situation that Hal finds himself in.[2] Regardless of the misgivings he may have felt in *Part One* about the prospect of ascending his father's tainted throne, Hal now seems to be ready for the opportunity and essentially at loose ends until it offers itself.

In *Part Two*, the relationship of Henry IV and Prince Hal is harder to place than it was in *Part One*, as it is the only father-son relationship in the play. Apart from two early scenes in which Northumberland responds to the announcement of his son's death, that illuminating foil, Hotspur, is missing from the play. Northumberland's response to the death does, however, provide a parallel for assessing King Henry's paternal dealings that flatters neither father. Northumberland, we recall, had decided to claim sickness and to sit out the battle of Shrewsbury, effectively betraying Hotspur. Upon hearing the news of Hotspur's death in *Part Two*, Northumberland breaks out into a long declamation (1.1.136–60) in which he claims to be 'enrag'd with grief' but makes no specific reference to his son at all. As Robert B. Pierce puts it, 'Hearing of Hotspur's death, he starts to vow revenge, but drifts into a fascinated vision of chaos' in which his son is quite forgotten.[3] In startlingly blunt and damning language, one of the Earl's counsellors tries to call him to his senses by saying 'It was your presurmise / That in the dole of blows your son might drop' (1.1.168–9).[4] It is against the backdrop of Northumberland's callously self-involved response to Hotspur's death that we see the reversed situation in which a son responds to the decline and death of his father.

In addition to removing a foil to the Prince (fathers outnumber sons in the play), *Part Two* challenges interpretation by refusing to give a narrative shape to the interaction between Hal and the King. There is of course plenty of ambiguity surrounding the King and Prince in *Part One*, and throughout that play appearances are often misleading, but at least there is a clear narrative arc in which Hal withdraws from court, returns on his father's demand, and then rescues him in combat. In *2 Henry IV*, however, Hal does almost nothing – his most decisive actions are taking his father's crown and banishing Falstaff at the end.

One familiar theme missing from the play is the ambivalent action of filial rescue. (The issue of rescue arises only when, in her kerfuffle with Falstaff and Bardolph, the Hostess cries out, 'Good people, bring a rescue or two' [2.1.56]). There is no opportunity for the Prince to save his father, perhaps because in this play the enemies that Henry faces – disease and death – are insurmountable opponents. The closest the Prince can come to rescuing his father is to swear to do battle with the entire world to retain the crown that he will inherit from him. The story of King and Prince is played out in a single, extended scene, the only one in which the two Henrys directly interact. Significantly, that scene centres on the King's deathbed.

One of the central issues of the sequel is Prince Hal's pressing need to sort out and simplify his feelings. To prepare himself for the succession, Hal must – to put matters bluntly – find a way to connect himself with his father, to accept him as progenitor and himself as lineal successor. And he must do this in spite of what he knows about his father. Not surprisingly, then, all of his interactions with the King are marked by a sense of strain, a sense that what he says is a denial of, or perhaps a hopeful attempt to ameliorate, what he actually feels. (In this predilection for protesting too much, as in much else, Hal becomes a prominent stepping stone on Shakespeare's way to Hamlet.) Ultimately, Hal attempts to simplify his untidy filial feelings by directing them at diametrically opposed father substitutes; his acknowledgeable emotions are channelled toward the upstanding Lord Chief Justice, a respectable if lifeless figure, and his anger is directed at Falstaff, who continues to attract the darker filial emotions that cannot be acknowledged. In a play deeply interested in doubles and the doubling of identities, this duplication of surrogate fathers represents Hal's attempt to split the King/Father into distinct, manageable public and private entities.[5]

The Reformed Prince Returns to Eastcheap

A question has bedevilled criticism of the play: if the critical consensus is to be accepted that the King and Prince are reconciled at the end of *Part One*, how can sense be made of the plot of *Part Two*, which begins with their being at loggerheads – again – and ends with a second reconciliation scene at the King's deathbed? From this perspective, during the course of these two plays, the Prince has grown up, or been educated, or undergone a reformation, not once but twice. Inevitably, *Part Two* begins to look like a curious redundancy, a re-reformation.[6]

To deny this redundancy, some critics have resorted to a desperate explanation: that with regard to Hal's reformation, *Part Two* begins as if *Part One* had not happened. As Harold Jenkins's frequently reprinted article titled 'The Structural Problem in Shakespeare's *Henry the Fourth*' phrases it, 'In the two parts of *Henry IV* there are not two princely reformations but two versions of a single reformation. And they are mutually exclusive.'[7] Or, as another critic puts it, at the beginning of *Part Two* 'The clock is simply turned back and all is begun again.'[8] But the idea of turning back the clock at the beginning of *Part Two* is, in my view, wrong-headed. In the first place, it is premised on an impossibility, for it asks us to unknow what we already know. Moreover, the very thought of undoing the past runs counter to the play's emphasis on the terrible, irreversible shaping power of Time. And in terms of dramatic design, the argument that the audience is expected to forget about *Part One* is questionable; *Part Two* not only makes many explicit references to events that happened in *Part One* but also offers enough scene-for-scene counterpointing to suggest the analogy of a diptych.[9] In a cogent critique of the turning-back-the-clock theory, Sherman Hawkins wondered, 'if he [Shakespeare] wants us to forget Part 1, why these detailed parallels that so constantly recall it?'[10] Only a curiously selective amnesia would require us to forget about the interactions of Hal and his father in *Part One* while inviting us to recall, say, the death of Hotspur.

It is preferable to see the injunction that *Part One* be forgotten as an attempt to solve a non-existent problem. There is a problem with reduplication in *Part Two* only if, as a commentator of the clock-turning persuasion claims, at the end of *Part One* Hal is '[f]ully reconciled with his father' and 'seems to have set the issue between them completely at rest.'[11] But, as the previous chapter demonstrated, this view fails to notice Hal's veiled animosity toward his father throughout *Part One*, an attitude which persists beyond the filial rescue at Shrewsbury and culminates in his outwardly chivalrous but inwardly vengeful release of his father's near-killer, the Douglas. There is no need to worry about the reconciliation of the Prince and King being repeated in *2 Henry IV* because it did not happen in *1 Henry IV*. Indeed, there is reason to question whether father and son are 'fully reconciled' even at the end of *Part Two*, though they certainly achieve a new level of understanding.

In this play of surprises, appropriately introduced by Rumor, nothing is more unexpected than Hal's curiously delayed first entrance (2.2), which takes place not at court but in Eastcheap, the old stomping ground of Hal and his present companion Poins.[12] Even if one is aware of the undertone of conflict between King and Prince at the end of *1 Henry IV*, Hal's appearance with a dissolute comrade is hardly expected after his battlefield heroics, especially since the King's last words to him are, 'Myself and you, son Harry, will towards Wales / To fight with Glendower' (*1H4*:5.5.39–40). It is an added fillip that Hal's companion is Poins instead of Falstaff, who had come onstage with him in his first appearance in *Part One* and who (unlike Poins) accompanied him to Shrewsbury Field at the end. In an odd balancing act, Hal has removed himself from the ambit of his father the King, as he had at the beginning of *Part One*, but he has also removed himself from the man whom he had adopted in the earlier play as his counter-father.

Like much of what he says in the play, Hal's opening exchange with Poins reveals a subtle mix of conflicting attitudes – what seems at first to be a relaxed familiarity quickly gives way to a venting of open contempt for his companion. The central vocabulary of the conversation, as Erich Auerbach noted in *Mimesis* more than half a century ago, is language designating high and low status. But Auerbach neglects to mention the nasty tone of the exchange (he speaks of Hal's 'wittily charming impertinence') because his study celebrates the blending of the high and low in Western literary culture. What the scene emphasizes, however, is the growing distance between the self-consciously elevated Hal and the common Poins.[13] In a sense nothing has changed from *Part One*, when everyone in Eastcheap knew that Hal was the heir apparent and thus a creature of a finer water. But in a deeper sense everything has changed. Certainly, Hal looks upon himself and Eastcheap differently, perhaps because he has distinguished himself in combat and perhaps because, since his father is seriously ill, he feels himself much closer to occupying the throne. It is as if Hal himself is wondering why he has returned to the 'small beer' of Eastcheap.

The Prince proceeds to blame his return to this now manifestly unworthy milieu on his companions and on the tyranny of public opinion, a rationale familiar from his self-justifying soliloquy early in *Part One*. But, unlike the buoyancy of the soliloquy, a sourness now prevails. The uneasy distance between Hal and Poins is already apparent in the latter's opening remark that 'I had thought weariness durst not have attach'd one of so high blood' (2.2.2–3). In response, albeit with shadings of self-critical irony, Hal refers twice to 'my greatness' (2.2.5, 12), as if he is reminding Poins (and himself) of a crucial reality. Before many lines have been spoken, Hal will be openly contemptuous of his former friend, disparaging 'wits of no higher breeding than thine' (2.2.35–6).

All pretence to badinage disappears when Poins retorts to Hal's disrespect by criticizing him for talking idly: 'Tell me how many good young princes would do so, their fathers being so sick as yours at this time is' (2.2.29–31). An obvious response to this thrust would be for Hal to challenge the hypocrisy of Poins's pretence to concern about the King, but instead he feels the need, as he will throughout the play, to justify himself. Clearly, Hal is stung by this reproach: 'Marry, I tell thee it is not meet that I should be sad, now my father is sick, albeit I could tell to thee – as to one it pleases me, for fault of a better, to call my friend – I could be sad, and sad indeed too' (39–43). When Poins dismisses this claim to filial concern, Hal protests more strongly, declaring that 'my heart bleeds inwardly that my father is so sick, and keeping such vile company as thou art hath in reason taken from me all ostentation of sorrow' (2.2.48–50). There is, of course, a problem with Hal's justification because it blames Poins for the choice that he himself has made to return to 'vile company' rather than to his father's court. In their emphasis on blaming others for his own actions, Hal's arguments are similar to the soliloquy about the sun and clouds that he delivered in *Part One* to justify to himself his presence in Eastcheap. That soliloquy, we recall, echoed many turns of phrase of his father, and his justification of himself to Poins continues the process. Hal's dismissive phrase 'such vile company as thou art' echoes his father's rebuke of him in *Part One*, when he accused Hal of being more like Richard than himself: 'For thou hast lost thy princely privilege / With vile participation' (1H4:3.2.86–7).[14] In an attempt to defend the sincerity of his feeling for his father, Hal makes use of a humiliating argument that his father had used against him.

Perhaps reflecting an indecent haste to usher Hal toward reformation, many critics have tended to take him at his word in this scene, misrepresenting him in the process. Thus, John Dover Wilson declares that the scene with Poins 'exhibits [Hal] as completely grown up, chafing at the worthlessness and uselessness of his companions, and with the ties of real affection that bind him to his dying father dragging at his heartstrings.'[15] But if Hal has arrived at maturity and is indeed chafing at the worthlessness of Poins, the question naturally arises: why has the Prince sought such a low fellow out? This thought may have occurred to Hal as well, which would help to account for his note of sour self-contempt. In *Part One*, he justified his presence by seeing himself as the sun that shines on baser realms; now, he sees himself as being on the same, vile level as those (like Poins) he had earlier scorned: 'Well, thus we play fools with the time, and the spirits of the wise sit in the clouds and mock us' (2.2.142–4). He realizes that he should not be with Poins and is not comfortable with him, and yet there is at least a shadow of companionship, or would be if Poins did not voice the Prince's own misgivings. One can only think that Hal still feels at least some of the ambivalence that he felt in *Part One* toward both the court and Eastcheap, though the attraction of the latter has clearly begun to fail.

The key question about this exchange is what it reveals of Hal's feelings toward his father. The inclination of most criticism has been to take Hal at his word and thus to criticize Poins because he 'uses Henry IV's illness as a weapon in the battle of wits, oblivious to the sincerity of Hal's grief.'[16] While there is no reason to deny a degree of sincerity to this expression of grief, there is equally no reason to deny the presence of less acceptable (to Hal) feelings. When Hal refers to having lost the 'ostentation of sorrow' (2.2.50) his words remind one of Prince Hamlet, who – when attesting to the sincerity of his grief for his dead father – says 'I have that within which passes show' (*H*:1.2.85). What one sees on the outside does not comport with what is inside them, Hal and Hamlet declare. But in both cases the vehemence of the son's denial raises questions about how well he knows what it is that resides within himself. There is a distinct possibility that Hal's lethargy and melancholia have less to do with his father's sickness than with the fact he is not yet dead. Hal's comment to Poins that 'I am exceeding weary' is uncannily echoed and perhaps explained by his dying father when he greets his son with the dry comment, 'I stay too long by thee, I weary thee' (4.5.93).

When Hal and Poins attempt to undo, or at least paper over, the deep insults they have exchanged, the means they choose recalls the corresponding scene in *Part One*. In the earlier scene (*1H4*:1.2), Hal had expressed his resistance to participating in a robbery, and Poins had drawn him aside to suggest the trick of robbing Falstaff and then confronting him with his lies. In a futile attempt to replay this once-exhilarating game and perhaps regain a semblance of their old camaraderie,

Hal and Poins once again fabricate a trick to play on Falstaff in the same setting as before, the Boar's Head Tavern in Eastcheap. But the glorious fooling of the previous scene is not to be recaptured; this time, the jest is feeble and ill-defined. When Hal and Poins disguise themselves as drawers so they can observe the 'true colors' of Falstaff, the game scarcely amounts to a shadow of the searchingly imaginative fooling of the Boar's Head scene in *Part One*. Since Hal and Poins are in effect attempting to lessen the distance between themselves by turning on Falstaff, it is no surprise that a disturbing note of nastiness quickly obtrudes, with Poins making the chilling suggestion, 'Let's beat him before his whore' (2.4.257).[17]

When the Prince steps forward to reveal himself, Falstaff's first comment sets the tone that will follow: 'Ha? A bastard son of the King's?' (2.4.283). In addition to suggesting a criticism of the legitimacy of the entire royal family, King included, the implication is that no honourable son would comport himself as Hal does. But before the unpleasantly concerted attack of Hal and Poins, Falstaff is reduced to repeating in a desperately unfunny way, 'No abuse, no abuse.' The contagion of ill feeling quickly spreads, with Falstaff resorting to demeaning – one after another – Doll Tearsheet, Mistress Quickly, and Bardolph. Hal and Poins are mocking Falstaff in an attempt to restore their relationship with each other, and Falstaff in turn attempts to avoid their abuse by finding a scapegoat who can be a common target for all of them. When, as in the corresponding scene in *Part One*, a knock at the door calls Hal away to duty, the Prince senses a kind of relief: 'By heaven, Poins, I feel me much to blame / So idly to profane the precious time' (2.4.361–2), and his only words to Falstaff are a curt farewell: 'Falstaff, good night.' He will not see Falstaff again until he is crowned, when the witty reprobate will serve as scapegoat in a more obvious and troubling manner.

The Crown Changes Hands Again, and Again

Despite Hal's insistence that his heart bleeds inwardly for his father, he does not visit the declining King until act 4, when it is very nearly too late. The long scene at the King's deathbed, which the *Riverside* edition conventionally but probably erroneously divides into two (4.4 and 4.5), is probably the most sustained and subtle depiction of a father and son in all of Shakespeare.[18] Its central event, Hal's carrying away of the crown when he thinks his father is deceased, was not Shakespeare's invention: both Holinshed's chronicle and the anonymous play, *The Famous Victories of Henry the Fifth*, contain a corresponding scene in which the Prince leaves with the crown, only to be called back when the King awakes and finds it missing. But, as is usual in his depictions of fathers and sons, Shakespeare complicates and darkens his sources.

In Holinshed and *Famous Victories*, the King and Prince are depicted as having become fully reconciled before the crown incident, and in both works the Prince's thinking his father dead and taking the crown are not intended to raise questions about motive. Holinshed's version is simplicity itself. When the sick King's vital signs disappeared, his caretakers thought him to be dead and accordingly 'covered his face with a linen cloth' before they left the room (Bullough 4:277). The rest is brisk narration: 'The Prince his son being hereof advertised, entered into the chamber, took away the crown, and departed.' In *Famous Victories*, the dying King shows his faith in Hal by insisting, before he falls asleep, that his lords honour his last will and testament, which stipulates that Hal will duly inherit the crown. After Hal tearfully expresses heartfelt grief upon finding his father (apparently) dead and carries off his crown, the awakened King does not blame the Prince (as he does in Shakespeare) but rather worries, 'No doubt 'tis some vile traitor that hath done it to deprive my son.'[19] Later, to be sure, there is a brief moment of tension in *Famous Victories* when the King questions the Prince's celerity in taking the crown, but Hal responds so plausibly that Henry immediately accedes and even hands the crown to him for his keeping. Thus, both chronicle and chronicle play are careful to depict the Prince's premature taking of the crown as an embarrassing mistake rather than an expression of excessive ambition or of parricidal wishes.

Shakespeare's scene, however, is deeply ambiguous, as befits a king and prince who (unlike their literary prototypes) have certainly not reconciled their earlier differences: Hal apparently cannot make himself return to the court, and the King is deeply troubled by Hal's failure to put Eastcheap behind him. When Henry asks his son Thomas about his brother's whereabouts, Thomas says that Hal 'dines in London' (4.4.51) in the company of 'Poins, and other his continual followers' (4.4.53), and this provokes Henry to lament what he fears will become of the apparently incorrigible Hal when he ascends the throne. While conceding that Hal is 'the noble image of my youth' (4.4.55), the King dreads the consequences of his future rule. He launches into a vision of the chaos that will descend on England after his death, when the Prince's 'headstrong riot hath no curb, / When rage and hot blood are his counsellors' (4.4.62–3). Given his disapproval, fear, and guilt, the King will not be inclined to believe Hal's excuses when his crown soon disappears.

In the ensuing crown scene, the King is relatively easy to read, while Hal's behaviour and words raise many questions. It is impossible to know Hal's immediate motives, partly because Shakespeare does not provide a scene in which the Prince gives his reasons for deciding (finally) to visit his father. Has he come to see his father to pay his final respects before death, or to be at hand to claim the crown when death comes? All we know is that, after having dined with Poins and company, Hal suddenly and unexpectedly appears at court. We may surmise that Hal is ill at ease and perhaps feeling guilty, as he makes a cold and awkward joke upon arriving; when he sees his brother, Thomas of Clarence, weeping, Hal quips: 'How now, rain within doors, and none abroad?' (4.5.9–10). And when Hal hears of his father's decline after receiving the good news of the rebels' surrender to Prince John, his tone seems drily detached: 'If he be sick with joy, he'll recover without physic' (4.5.14–15).

The scene in which Hal sits alone with his sleeping father is quietly ambiguous, as the emphasis slides back and forth from Henry as king to Henry as father. We are observing a son's deathbed watch over his father as a labour of love, and we also see a prince waiting for the crown to devolve upon him. In this most intimate of settings, a setting in which even a repressed son might speak freely to his unconscious father, Hal maintains his attitude of detachment – his first words are spoken to the crown that lies on the pillow next to the King, his 'bed-fellow.' Clearly, Hal seems more engaged with the crown than with his father, and so he meditates for eleven lines on the sorrows that this 'polished perturbation' creates. As Harold Goddard noted in what remains the most detailed and perceptive analysis of the scene, Hal's 'address to the crown is half over before he discovers the supposed death of his father.'[20] Suggestively, Hal's meditation on the burden of the crown recalls in many ways the sleep-deprived soliloquy spoken by the King in his first appearance (3.1.4–31). Hal may be more engaged with the crown than with his father, but in a way that shows he is his father's son.

It is only after the long apostrophe to the crown that Hal moves from abstractions to the minutely particular. Upon noticing a feather that he thinks would stir if his father were breathing, he speaks words that subtly reveal his divided concerns:

> My gracious lord! my father!
> This sleep is sound indeed, this is a sleep
> That from this golden rigol hath divorc'd
> So many English kings. Thy due from me
> Is tears and heavy sorrows of the blood,
> Which nature, love, and filial tenderness
> Shall, O dear father, pay thee plenteously.
> My due from thee is this imperial crown,
> Which as immediate from thy place and blood,
> Derives itself to me. [*Puts on the crown.*] Lo where it sits ...   4.5.34–43

After the sudden burst of feeling in 'My gracious lord! my father!' – where 'father' has more force than the formal 'lord' – Hal quickly clamps down on his emotions. (In its quick shift from spontaneous feeling to consciously ethical consideration, there is a clear parallel between this speech and his remarks in the similar situation in *Part One* when he thinks that Falstaff is dead [*1H4*:5.4.102–10].) Using his most characteristic imagery, which reaches all the way back to 'the debt I never promised' in *Part One*, Hal moves into a scrupulous settling of accounts ('Thy due from me' and 'My due from thee'). Though a critic has remarked that Hal's words 'balance filial sorrow and consciousness of inheritance,' that balancing is more rhetoric than reality, more formula than feeling.[21] While his nicely parsed expression of sorrow is self-conscious in its itemization of decorous dutifulness ('nature, love, and filial tenderness'), his sense of what is due to himself is more 'immediate.' As Anthony Dawson acutely observes, 'Instead of expressing grief directly, he talks of what is due from him, what he will pay in the future.'[22] There is no reason to doubt that Hal does, or at least *will*, sorrow for his father, for Warwick soon tells the awakened King that he found the Prince 'in the next room, / Washing with kindly tears his gentle cheeks' (4.5.82–3). But Hal's first impulse is to take the crown.

A telling difference between this scene and its simple antecedents in Holinshed and *Famous Victories* is the fact that Shakespeare's Prince places the crown on his head. In Holinshed we are told that the Prince 'took away the crown,' with no reference to self-coronation, and in *Famous Victories* a good deal is made of the fact that the Prince does not

don the crown.[23] The taking of the crown can be convincingly justified
as a careful, protective measure (as the Prince Henrys of the sources
justify it) only so long as it does not touch the Prince's head. Thus,
taking Hal at his word, John Dover Wilson feels compelled to invent
some extremely improbable stage business: Hal 'falls to his knees by
the dead man, as he supposes him to be, and remains a moment in
prayer before walking out of the room, shaken with sobs and as in a
dream; the crown, now forgotten, still upon his head.'[24] This fails to
convince because after Hal crowns himself his language is anything
but dreamlike or shaken. Indeed, there is an element of iron resolve:

> Lo where it sits,
> Which God shall guard; and put the world's whole strength
> Into one giant arm, it shall not force
> This lineal honor from me. This from thee
> Will I to mine leave, as 'tis left to me.   *Exit.*   4.5.43–7

The force of Hal's declaration, spoken in private but with a firmness
appropriate for a public occasion, reflects his suppression of the fact
that he knows so well: the crown is a 'lineal honor' only in the limited
sense that it was his father's and now he holds it in his hand. Hal
remains in the ambiguous position of being, in Robert Watson's
phrase, 'a lineal heir to an unlineal throne.'[25] He leaves the stage,
crown on head, with this fiercely resolute claim to possession ringing
in his ears.

For the King, Hal's taking of the crown is a bad dream come true, a
confirmation of his worst fears about sons in general and Hal in particular. When the King asks, 'Is he so hasty that he doth suppose / My
sleep my death?' (4.5.60–1), he raises a lucid, not easily refutable, question about Hal's motives. But this pointed question quickly gives way
to an angry, self-pitying tirade at the selfish violence of sons against
their 'foolish over-careful fathers,' lines that look backward to *Richard II*
and forward to *King Lear*. In these lines, a guilty acknowledgment of his
own crimes slips out in the attack on his son's. Thus, when he laments
'How quickly nature falls into revolt / When gold becomes her object!'
(4.5.65–6), the word 'revolt' has special relevance to his own rebellion
against Richard, and his vilification of sons for their wasteful expenditure of their fathers' wealth includes the unnecessary, and thus revealing, euphemism that the gold is 'strange-achieved' (4.5.71), much like
Richard's crown. The stolen crown has been stolen again.

When Hal returns with the crown, the scene is strongly reminiscent of the first meeting of father and son in *1 Henry IV*. As in the earlier scene, the King dismisses the attendant lords so that the Prince can account for himself in private, and, once again, Hal begins by making a futile attempt to justify himself. When the Prince says 'I never thought to hear you speak again,' the King brushes aside the excuse with a shrewd analysis of unconscious motive: 'Thy wish was father, Harry, to that thought' (4.5.91–2). The King speaks at considerable length, as he had earlier, but now his tone is quite different; he sounds more like a petitioner than the absolute authority of *Part One*. Instead of praising himself for his successful usurpation of King Richard and contrasting Hal's 'degenerate' behaviour with his own, Henry speaks in the pathetically self-pitying accents of Richard. Thus, he makes many references to his grave, to worms, and to the mocking of form, and he allows himself a plea for affection that in *Part One* he was far too proud to have made: 'Thy life did manifest thou lov'dst me not, / And thou wilt have me die assur'd of it' (4.5.104–5). As was the case with Richard's tragic speeches, there is an obvious contradiction between the helplessness the King ascribes to himself and the fact that he monopolizes the discourse at very great length (forty-five lines); as with Richard, we hear a desperately self-dramatizing rhetoric that stems from a premonition of the end of the self.

The King's speech to Hal is the culmination of a series of associations that Shakespeare has been drawing in *Part Two* between Henry and the king he usurped, Richard. Thus, like his predecessor, Henry suffers in fretful isolation, is unable to sleep, calls for music, and, most pathetically, fixates on the crown as the symbol of his identity. These associations between Henry and Richard are important, for they are part of a great irony that shadows the entire scene: as we watch Hal carry away his father's crown, we are reminded of Henry's previous seizure of that same crown from his cousin. Not only is the father's crime committed again by the son, but now the father has become the victim. The emotional ambiguities are rich, for the King can see himself as both the perpetrator and victim of the crime. In *Part One*, the father had chastised his son for imitating Richard rather than himself, and in *Part Two* the son has paid his father the compliment of imitation, but at his father's cost.

Hal's taking of the crown poses ambiguities of a political as well as a personal nature. From a political perspective, the central issue is whether Hal's self-crowning represents a new beginning or a continuation of his father's illegitimate reign. Critics who see Henry V as Shakespeare's depiction of the ideal king argue that Hal's action is morally positive in that he 'does not initially receive the crown from the hand of the usurper.'[26] Similarly, another critic argues that 'Because Hal's possession of the crown must be seen to be "plain and right," Shakespeare devises a scene, which ... shows Hal symbolically stealing the crown of England from his father rather than receiving it at his hands.'[27] But this argument that the theft of the crown from a usurper legitimizes the thief's claim to it seems strained. To steal a crown twice does not remove its tarnish. To be sure, in Eastcheap Hal only pretended to be a thief, playing at robbing the King's Exchequer instead of stealing the entire kingdom as his father had done, but after his return to court the difference between him and his father begins to blur, especially with regard to Hal's taking of Hotspur's honours. In his dying words, Hotspur makes a serious accusation of Hal: 'O Harry, thou hast robb'd me of my youth' (1H4:5.4.77). This accusation has more truth than Hotspur can know, as Hal has pledged to his father to usurp Hotspur's fame by taking his titles and deeds from him.[28]

When he responds to his father's charge, which is a mere shadow of his powerful denunciation of Hal in the comparable scene in *Part One*, the Prince's tone is far more forceful than earlier. Once again, Hal begins by asking for his father's pardon, but in place of his earlier, muddied apology he now pays his father/king the traditional, expected form of filial deference that he apparently withheld in *Part One*: he kneels before him. There is, however, something self-conscious in Hal's characterization of his gesture:

> If I affect it [the crown] more
> Than as your honor and as your renown,
> Let me no more from this obedience rise,
> Which my most inward true and duteous spirit
> Teacheth this prostrate and exterior bending.   4.5.144–8

It is as if Hal is recalling and denying the oft-expressed worries of Elizabethan moralists that the 'prostrate and exterior bending' of a son's knee may disguise a heart that is not truly honouring the father.[29] Even Hal's specification that his spirit '[t]eacheth' this obedient kneeling to his body seems strained in its stiff deliberation, as if he needs to insist on 'most inward true and duteous' motivation. In this protestation of a decent deference in which the outward expresses the inward, there is more than a touch of Hamlet. When Hal develops yet another 'If let me' formulation three lines later, the ambiguities multiply: 'If I do feign, / O, let me in my present wildness die' (4.5.151–2).

The problem with Hal's speech recounting his actions is simply that it does not square with what we saw and heard when he thought he saw his father lying dead next to the crown. In the first place, Hal's description of himself as 'thinking you dead, / And dead almost, my liege, to think you were' (4.5.155–6) is not supported by the fluent lines that Hal actually spoke over his father's body. Moreover, the implication in his supposed recounting that he immediately sensed his father was dead when he entered the room is not borne out by his earlier words.[30] The discrepancies are clearer still when Hal recounts what he supposedly said to the crown. The crucial difference is that he recasts his original, meditative invocation of the crown as 'polish'd perturbation! golden care!' (4.5.23) into a defiant accusation of it for having killed his father. He placed it on his own head, he says,

> To try with it, as with an enemy
> That had before my face murdered my father,
> The quarrel of a true inheritor.   4.5.166–8

Hal has recast his original comments into the most acceptable form possible, in which the taking of the crown becomes a selfless picking up of a gauntlet on behalf of his father. (Revealingly, Hal speaks as if the problem is the crown itself rather than his father's usurpation of it.) In a plausible psychoanalytic interpretation, Hal 'shifts the parricidal impulse from himself to the crown: It is not I but the crown who kills my father.'[31]

Hal's most revealing lines come at the end of his speech, after his declaration that he took up the crown in the spirit of '[t]he quarrel of a true inheritor':

> But if it did infect my blood with joy,
> Or swell my thoughts to any strain of pride,
> If any rebel or vain spirit of mine
> Did with the least affection of a welcome
> Give entertainment to the might of it,
> Let God for ever keep it from my head,
> And make me as the poorest vassal is
> That doth with awe and terror kneel to it!   4.5.169–76

This strained assertion of complete innocence (*any, any, least*) is a study in protesting too much. These climactic lines comprise the third and by far the most elaborate of a series of 'if ... let' constructions:

1 *If* I affect it more ... let me no more from this obedience rise
2 *If* I do feign ... let me no more live to show
3 *If* it did infect my blood with joy – or swell my thoughts – or if any vain spirit of mine even welcomed it ... Let God for ever keep it from my head.

Beyond their echoing of Falstaff's rhetoric of evasion in *Part One*, Hal's insistent need to return to these 'ifs' is very revealing.[32] At this point in the scene it is Hal himself, not his father, who is raising the questions about what he truly affects, whether he feigns, whether he welcomes his father's death, and so on. The suggestion is that through these conditionals (which he implies are contrary to fact) Hal is denying what he has felt, and perhaps still does.[33] There is not much virtue apparent in these *Ifs*.

Though the reader or spectator may have misgivings about Hal's speech, his father does not. The King's response is more positive and less guarded than ever before:

O my son,
God put it in thy mind to take it [the crown] hence,
That thou mightst win the more thy father's love,
Pleading so wisely in excuse of it!   4.5.177–80

Entirely in character, the King attributes Hal's devious behaviour to God, asserting that the apparent crime was simply a means for Hal to ingratiate himself more fully; the King's extenuation of Hal is curiously similar to Hal's self-extenuation in his 'I know you all' soliloquy in *Part One*. The ability to excuse oneself wisely is valued by father and son. In his indirect way the King seems to be acknowledging his approval of, and perhaps even his love for, his son, though we note that his reference to 'thy father's love' is, like Hal's earlier reference to his own 'filial love,' a standing outside the emotion that is claimed. The grounds for the King's love are strange: his son has become a convincing talker. The King does not say that he believes what he has heard, and indeed he seems happy to observe how compellingly devious his son has been.[34] He is applauding a great performance, and in this he sees his son as a true successor to himself.

These lines are followed by a long discourse in which the King largely acknowledges the fact of his usurpation and the problems it has caused; also, he advises Hal on how to proceed as king. Clearly, the Prince listens carefully to this advice, for many of his subsequent actions seem cut from his father's cloth.[35] Thus, the King's advice to 'busy giddy minds / With foreign quarrels' (4.5.213–14) would seem to be the germ of Hal's invasion of France, and Henry's banishment of Falstaff and the rest accords nicely with his father's proud claim to have 'cut ... off' his former friends. Whatever misgivings Hal may continue to have about his father's 'purchase' of the crown, and from *Henry V* we know that he continues to have them, he does not reject his father's political strategies.

Despite the new degree of understanding between father and son, it is not convincing to characterize their relationship at the end of the deathbed scene in wholly positive terms. Early in the twentieth century, the estimable A.C. Bradley could speak of the 'beautiful scenes of reconciliation and affection between his father and him [Hal],' but a closer, less sentimental examination makes this interpretation untenable.[36] An adequate assessment of their relationship at Henry's death needs to be more balanced and qualified, along the lines of Robert Ornstein's remark that 'if Henry does not find a loving son, he sees in Hal his true inheritor, one who is as nimble at kneeling and quick at seizing a crown as he was in his own youth – one to whom he can confide his innermost thoughts.'[37] If it does make sense to talk of a final 'reconciliation' of the two Henrys, what we see is a very significant diminishment, rather than a disappearance, of the distance separating them.

After the King's guilty, euphemistic cry – 'How I came by the crown, O God forgive' (4.5.218) – Hal formulates a brisk affirmation that is in part consolation for his father and in part justification for himself:

> My gracious liege,
> You won it, wore it, kept it, gave it me;
> Then plain and right must my possession be,
> Which I with more than with a common pain
> 'Gainst all the world will rightfully maintain.   4.5.220–4

Cast as two sets of rhyming couplets, closure on top of closure, these lines move from the past to the future, from the passive inheritance of the lineal inheritor (like Richard) to the defiant struggle to retain the inheritance for one's progeny (unlike Richard). These lines recall Henry's praise of Hotspur (at Hal's expense) in their interview in *Part One*:

> He hath more worthy interest to the state
> Than thou the shadow of succession.
> For of no right, nor color like to right,
> He doth fill fields with harness in the realm.   *1H4*:3.2.98–101

Now, at Henry's deathbed, Hal has become a son who is no longer a shadowy successor. Not only will he 'fill fields with harness,' but also he will continue to insist on his right to the crown he grasps.

A Father Created and a Father Destroyed

Between the end of act 4 and the beginning of act 5, King Henry IV dies, and in the final act we see the new King's decisions as a coming-to-terms with that death. Two actions of Henry V are especially relevant to the death of his father: his elevation of the upright Lord Chief Justice (5.2) and his banishment of the not-so-upright Falstaff in the closing lines of the play (5.5). In what has proven to be a foundational analysis, John Dover Wilson discussed these two characters as derivations from the allegorical morality-play tradition in which moral abstractions are set upon the stage, with the figure of Falstaff who stands for 'Riot and Misrule' and with the Lord Chief Justice as 'the official representative of the Rule of Law.'[38] There can be no question but that Shakespeare places these two figures in careful opposition from their first meeting (1.2) onward and that in very explicit terms they represent conflicting attitudes to law and much else. But, in a less allegorical vein, it is useful to examine how the new King Henry's treatment of these two figures relates to the recent death of his father, especially since in *Part One* Falstaff clearly played the role of father figure for Hal and in *Part Two* the newly crowned Henry explicitly addresses the Lord Chief Justice as 'father.' By insisting on the differences between these two figures, the hitherto ambivalent Prince licenses himself to act with a severe simplicity.

Being nameless and transparent, with no private dimension, the Lord Chief Justice is much easier for the new King Henry (and perhaps for Shakespeare as well) to reduce to an abstraction than is the more substantial Falstaff. The Lord Chief Justice is drawn from the legend of the madcap prince and especially from its dramatization in the anonymous *Famous Victories*, where the Prince is imprisoned after he '*giveth him* [the Lord Chief Justice] *a box on the ear*' (*s.d.*) for insisting on the execution of one of his thieving companions.[39] Neither this blow nor the ensuing imprisonment is depicted in Shakespeare's *Henry IV* plays, though early in *Part Two* Falstaff's page refers to both when he sees the Lord Chief Justice approaching: 'Sir, here comes the nobleman that committed the prince for striking him about Bardolph' (1.2.55–6). And in the acrimonious and extended exchange that follows, Falstaff is happy to remind the Justice of his recent humiliation at the hands of the Prince: 'For the box of the year [*sic*] that the Prince gave you, he gave it like a rude prince, and you took it like a sensible lord' (1.2.194–6).

Though it drops the dramatization of the ear-boxing, *2 Henry IV* makes more of the Lord Chief Justice than the *Famous Victories* had done. Not only does he appear in more scenes, but also his relationship with the new King has a deeper dimension. In both plays, the Lord Chief Justice fears what will happen to him when his erstwhile adversary ascends the throne, and in both he defends himself by identifying himself with King Henry IV, but the new King's response differs in each play. In *Famous Victories*, when he sends the Prince to prison, the Lord Chief Justice justifies the action by saying 'in striking me in this place you greatly abuse me, and not me only but also your father whose lively person here in this place I do represent.'[40] This is traditional legal doctrine, and the play makes no more of the connection between Henry IV and the Lord Chief Justice. Thus, after the Prince becomes King in the *Famous Victories*, he rewards the worried Lord Chief Justice in straightforward terms, saying 'you, that would not spare me, I think will not spare another.'[41]

After the two early scenes with Falstaff, Shakespeare's Lord Chief Justice does not appear again until 5.2, where we see him expressing his fears about the revenge that the new King Henry may exact for having been imprisoned. (Here the inverted parallel with Falstaff is sharp: while the Lord Chief Justice expects to be punished because he called down the law on the Prince in the past, Falstaff hopes to be rewarded because he broke the law with the Prince in the past – both men will be surprised.) When the new King confronts him, it looks as if the Lord Chief Justice's fears are well founded, for Henry asks him,

How might a prince of my great hopes forget
So great indignities you laid upon me?
What, rate, rebuke, and roughly send to prison
Th'immediate heir of England!   5.2.68–71

By dint of an eloquent response to the King, the Lord Chief Justice avoids punishment. (The scene can be staged as Henry's trick on a frightened magistrate whom he has already decided to reward, but there appears to be no evidence for this interpretation in the text.) Like his counterpart in the *Famous Victories*, the Lord Chief Justice defends himself by arguing that he punished Henry in his role as legal surrogate for the Prince's father: 'I then did use the person of your father, / The image of his power lay then in me' (5.2.73–4).

But the Lord Chief Justice goes beyond his predecessor in the source by emphasizing the relevance of fathers and sons. In words that recall Henry IV's criticisms of Hal, he asks the new king to imagine having a scapegrace son who would 'set your decrees at nought' and 'mock your workings in a second body' (5.2.85, 90). And he creates a hypothetical situation:

Be now the father and propose a son,
Hear your own dignity so much profan'd,
See your most dreadful laws so loosely slighted,
Behold yourself so by a son disdained;
And then imagine me taking your part,
And in your power soft silencing your son.   5.2.92–7

This language is reminiscent of the role-playing scene (2.4) of Hal and Falstaff in *Part One*, and thus the phrase 'imagine me taking your part' has a double meaning: not only 'taking your side in the argument' but also 'standing in for you in your role.' The Lord Chief Justice is expressing his willingness to play the role of civic father, and indirectly he is asking Henry to imagine himself in the situation of his father, a king troubled by a law-breaking son.

The appeal to Hal's imagination seems to work, as he states his support by conjuring up a hypothetical male heir like his previous self and by recalling the words his father had spoken in praise of the Lord Chief Justice's initial decision to arrest him:

And I do wish your honors may increase,
Till you do live to see a son of mine

Offend you and obey you, as I did.
So shall I live to speak my father's words:
'Happy am I, that have a man so bold,
That dares do justice on my proper son.'   5.2.104–9

In the upright company of the Lord Chief Justice, Hal can quote his father without hesitation or embarrassment. It is as if, for a moment, he takes his father's side against himself, realizing that he must now do as his father had done if he is to have a 'proper son.'

Unlike his counterpart in the *Famous Victories*, who does not identify the Lord Chief Justice with his father, Hal in *2 Henry IV* is extremely insistent on the connection. After committing the sword of justice to the Lord Chief Justice, which is reminiscent of his returning the crown to his father, Henry warms to the topic of surrogate fatherhood:

You shall be as a father to my youth,
My voice shall sound as you do prompt mine ear,
And I will stoop and humble my intents
To your well-practic'd wise directions.   5.2.118–21

Later, speaking of the need for noble counsel in the state, Hal returns to the association of the Lord Chief Justice with his father, saying 'you, father, shall have foremost hand' (5.2.140) in the future.

There are likely several reasons why Hal seizes on the opportunity to place himself in a filial relationship with the Lord Chief Justice. Surely one of them is that in the process he is in effect begetting or recreating his own father. Though he is placing himself in what in the abstract is a position of deference and obedience, he is doing so from a position of power. Interestingly, the interchange with the Lord Chief Justice recalls the scene in *1 Henry IV* (3.1) in which Hal was called to account by his father, but this time the tables are turned, and it is the Lord Chief Justice who has to justify himself to Hal as King. The implication is that the Lord Chief Justice will serve as a father only so long as it suits the new King Henry's needs. (Despite Hal's commitment to placing himself under his guidance, the Lord Chief Justice does not appear in *Henry V*, perhaps having already served his purpose.)

A major part of the attraction (to Hal) of the Lord Chief Justice must be the fact that he is clearly honest, lawful, and true to his office, none of which was true of Henry IV.[42] Thus, Hal can create, as it were, a more proper progenitor for himself, a progenitor whose purity allows his son to be at ease in his new identity as ruler. A related benefit of this new father is that Hal's connection with this nameless functionary is exclusively public and institutional; unlike his relationship with his real father, there is nothing personal – no repressed anger, no inherited guilt, and (best of all) no debt. For the new King, the Lord Chief Justice provides a sanitized and simplified version of his father.

It is revealing that, immediately after Hal affirms to the Lord Chief Justice that 'You shall be as a father to my youth' (5.2.118), he rather unexpectedly reveals his ambivalent relationship to his biological father:

> And, princes all, believe me, I beseech you,
> My father is gone wild into his grave;
> For in his tomb lie my affections,
> And with his spirits sadly I survive,
> To mock the expectation of the world.   5.2.122–6

Unlike Henry's lucid, straightforward praise of the Lord Chief Justice, these complex lines require interpretation. In the gloss of one recent editor, Hal is saying: 'My wildness is now in my father's tomb, because I have buried my passions ("affections") at his death,' and according to another, 'Henry V proclaims that he has buried his riotous behaviour with the body of his father.'[43] Similarly, a third critic has pointed out that Hal expresses a reciprocity between himself and his father, as he gives him his 'affections' and survives by incorporating his father's 'spirits.'[44] These interpretations are useful, but they do not take sufficient account of Hal's most forceful and arresting line: 'My father is gone wild into his grave.' (The poet John Berryman declared that a play containing this line 'cannot be negligible.')[45] This blunt statement suggests that his father is damned (see the OED for 'wild') because of his ambition and usurpation of the throne, but no sooner does Hal speak it than he transforms what he has said, turning the statement into a burying of his own 'affections' rather than his father's. True to his long-standing filial ambivalence, the speech trembles between scapegoating and assimilating his father.

There is yet another reason for Hal's adoption of the Lord Chief Justice as his father, for the Justice is a surrogate not only for the King's biological father but also for his old surrogate father, Falstaff. The King's confirmation of the Lord Chief Justice signals the imminent decline of Falstaff, and his very public commitment to the rule of law represented by the Lord Chief Justice indicates quite unequivocally that Falstaff's hopes for preferment will be dashed. If anything, the banishment of Falstaff is even more inevitable than it already seemed when the Prince had responded to Falstaff's 'banish plump Jack, and banish all the world' with his cold 'I do, I will' (*1H4*:2.4.479–81). Indeed, in his first appearance in *2 Henry IV* Falstaff is quickly confronted by the Lord Chief Justice, who is stolidly unyielding in his criticism and in his refusal to be amused. These are not figures who can peaceably coexist. And to make matters worse for Falstaff, some of the Lord Chief Justice's criticisms of him are reminiscent of Prince Hal's in *Part One*, such as the magistrate's insistence that Falstaff pay the Hostess the debt he owes her (2.1.118–19). When Falstaff and his friends saddle up to ride to London, with Falstaff declaring 'woe to my Lord Chief Justice' (5.3.138), we see a group of self-deluded men about to run helter-skelter into a stone wall.

Though it comes as a devastating surprise to Falstaff, his banishment by Hal has been a project in the making since the beginning of *Part One*. But, since the Prince's mixed attitudes toward Falstaff mirror his feelings about his father, it has been an ambivalent project, an inevitability postponed as long as possible. From his first appearance with Falstaff Hal has told himself that it is only a matter of time until he leaves him behind. But how much time? In his portentous soliloquy in *Part One*, Hal begins by saying that he will 'a while uphold / The unyok'd humor of your idleness' (1.2.195–6) but that casual 'a while' becomes increasingly important. We notice that, even after his commitment to banish Falstaff in the Boar's Head Tavern in *Part One*, Hal still brings him along when his father calls him to war. And in *Part Two*, even though Hal's attitude continues to sour, he does not decisively sever the tie. Thus, Hal finishes his single unpleasant conversation with his old companion with a curt, ominous 'Falstaff, good night' (*2H4*:2.4.366), but without creating a clear break. In addition to whatever residue of good feeling remains in the Prince, there is a second, less sentimental cause for continuance: so long as his father remains alive, Hal seems to need Falstaff as a (very heavy) counterweight and irritant to the King.[46] But after the old Henry's death and the new Henry's adoption of the Lord Chief Justice as a replacement for both Falstaff and Henry IV, the witty scoundrel's days are numbered.

Still, it is Falstaff who precipitates the crisis. When he bursts into the presence of the newly crowned King, for the first time in the play we see onstage the triangulation of Hal/Henry, the Lord Chief Justice, and Falstaff:

Fal.	God save thy Grace, King Hal! My royal Hal!
Pist.	The heavens thee guard and keep, most royal imp of fame!
Fal.	God save thee, my sweet boy!
King.	My Lord Chief Justice, speak to that vain man.
Ch. Just.	Have you your wits? know you what 'tis you speak?
Fal.	My King, my Jove! I speak to thee, my heart! 5.5.41–6

To maintain decorum and perhaps to protect Falstaff from his folly, Henry attempts to interpose the Lord Chief Justice between himself and his former companion, but Falstaff refuses to acknowledge his old opponent and insists on the significance of his personal relationship with the King. Indecorous as they are, Falstaff's spirited interjections indicate real, if desperate, affection, with the very phrase 'King Hal' revealing the impossibility of the relationship that he wishes for.

When the King addresses Falstaff, as he must, he takes several tacks, first denying any knowledge of him, then admitting to a dreamlike knowledge, and finally acknowledging that he was a companion:

> I know thee not, old man, fall to thy prayers.
> How ill white hairs becomes a fool and jester!
> I have long dreamt of such a kind of man,
> So surfeit-swell'd, so old, and so profane;
> But being awak'd, I do despise my dream.
> Make less thy body (hence) and more thy grace,
> Leave gormandizing, know the grave doth gape
> For thee thrice wider than for other men.
> Reply not to me with a fool-born jest,
> Presume not that I am the thing I was,
> For God doth know, so shall the world perceive,
> That I have turn'd away my former self;
> So will I those that kept me company.   5.5.47–59

In the King's emphasis on the signs of Falstaff's age, we recall the Lord Chief Justice's scornful description of his decrepitude early in the play. When his emphasis shifts to Falstaff's corpulence, the memory of jokes past seems to creep into the denunciation, and when the King declares

'Reply not to me with a fool-born jest' he appears to be cutting off Fal-staff before he can open his mouth.[47] In a final attempt at purification, or at least at the appearance of it, he insists that 'I have turn'd away my former self.' As he did at his father's sickbed, the King resorts to the rhetoric of vehement protestation, and by so doing he attempts to create a new identity through subtraction, as if a denial of relation to Falstaff strengthens his lineal succession to his father.

The remarkably complex play of similarity and difference that has characterized Hal and his father is very much alive in this speech. In the course of rejecting Falstaff as an 'old man' whom he does not know, the new King is imitating an old man whom he has known very well, and whose name he bears. The ironies multiply because it was apparently Hal's desire to maintain a distance from his father that led to his companionship with Falstaff in the first place, and the new King Henry never acts more like his father than when he ban-ishes Falstaff, his father's erstwhile nemesis. In the long perspective of the tetralogy as a whole, the genealogy of the banishment stretches all the way back to the ending of *Richard II*, when the newly crowned Henry IV hypocritically banished Piers Exton, the man who had killed Richard at his bidding. Now, when the newly crowned Henry V banishes Falstaff in similarly self-righteous tones, the echo is disconcerting. A still more telling connection of the younger with the elder King Henry is an event in *Part One* of *Henry IV*, and once again the parallel flatters neither father nor son. When Henry IV fell out with the Percy family, who had been so instru-mental in his taking the crown from Richard, he provided a model for his son's dismissal of Falstaff. In both cases, the former compan-ions have not lacked for ambition and calculation, and justifications for the two Henrys' decisions can be made in the name of decorum and public order. Nevertheless, an impoverishment of spirit is apparent in both.

For the younger Henry still more than for the older one, the insis-tence on a king's lofty prerogatives involves a real diminishment of his private self. Not only has Henry V inherited the public persona of kingship from his father, with its self-deforming stringencies, but he has also inherited some of the characteristics that had provoked his own filial alienation in *Part One*. Despite his accession to the throne and his new capability to wield an impressive amount of power, this Hal-turned-Henry continues to pay the debt he never promised.

Note: The King and His Father in Henry V

In *Henry V*, the importance of fathers and father figures is greatly diminished. Not only is Henry's father deceased but also his two surrogate father figures are notably missing: Falstaff appears only off-stage, most notably in Mistress Quickly's coarsely poignant narration of his death, and the Lord Chief Justice is not mentioned at all. The closest the play comes to providing yet another father figure for Henry is on the eve of Agincourt, when he chats briefly but affectionately with 'old Sir Thomas Erpingham.' Both Henry IV and Falstaff come to mind when the King says to the genial Erpingham that 'A good soft pillow for that good white head / Were better than a churlish turf of France' (4.1.14–15). But the old man quickly exits, leaving Henry alone to ponder his role as king. As his speeches on the battlefield reveal, King Henry V will replace, or will attempt to replace, the traditionally paternal role of king with a fraternal conception.[48] He will characterize his army as 'we band of brothers' (4.3.60).

Despite the stress on fraternity, Henry's father is a presence in the play, for it is unlikely that the band of English brothers would be in France without Henry IV's deathbed advice to his son: 'Be it thy course to busy giddy minds / With foreign quarrels' (2H4:4.5.213–14). In addition to this unspoken presence, King Henry makes two explicit references to his father that are very revealing, one after he leaves Sir Thomas Erpingham on the eve of Agincourt and the other after his victory the next day. Though the two speeches are totally different in tone, they share a deep similarity: in both utterances Henry acknowledges his father's usurpation and thus says what he could not say – in public or in private – in the two *Henry IV* plays.

The first speech is Henry's fevered prayer in the long night before Agincourt:

> O God of battles, steel my soldiers' hearts,
> Possess them not with fear! Take from them now
> The sense of reck'ning, if th'opposed numbers
> Pluck their hearts from them. Not to-day, O Lord,
> O, not to-day think not upon the fault
> My father made in compassing the crown!   4.1.289–94

Though Henry asks for the 'sense of reck'ning' to be removed from his outnumbered men, a more compelling need is for this sense to be removed from a King who understands morality as debts and reckonings. Hence, in mid-line he transitions from the fear of his men to the fault of his father. (Earlier in the scene, the admirable soldier Michael Williams unknowingly touched Henry's sore conscience when he told the disguised monarch that 'if the cause be not good, the King himself hath a heavy reckoning to make' [4.1.134–5] and then evoked the plight of dying soldiers who cry 'upon the debts they owe' [140].)[49] Movingly and tellingly, Henry acknowledges his father's crime as a thought that must be repressed ('think not upon'), and the force of his own repression is clear in the triple negative that prefaces his naming of the deed. Even so, Henry cannot name the crime without engaging in the characteristic euphemisms of his father: it is the 'fault / My father made in compassing the crown.' After itemizing the benefactions he has commissioned for Richard's body and soul, itself a futile accounting of spiritual investments, Henry ends on a note of desperation that points toward the guiltiness of Claudius in *Hamlet*: 'More will I do; / Though all that I can do is nothing worth' (4.1.302–3).

Unlike the tragic tenor of his strained, self-conscious prayer, Henry's second mention of his father's crime is spoken in prose and is shocking in its apparent triviality. It comes during his courting – if that is the right word – of Katherine, the French Princess, soon after the victory for which he had prayed: 'Now beshrew my father's ambition! he was thinking of civil wars when he got me; therefore was I created with a stubborn outside, with an aspect of iron, that when I come to woo ladies, I fright them' (5.2.224–8). Quite gratuitously, and in comically exaggerated form, Henry says to Katherine what he had been unable to say to anyone – even to himself – in the *Henry IV* plays: that his father was planning rebellion in Henry's youth. For a moment, we can imagine the young Henry's alarm at seeing his father's willingness to risk civil war in order to take the throne. But the phrase 'Now beshrew my father's ambition' reduces moral repugnance to casual annoyance, as if Henry finally *has* reached the mature manhood that his father's death made possible; his lines bespeak a confidence derived from his arrival at autonomous power and his imminent possession of a wife. But even this moment of resolution is not without irony, for the final Chorus will soon remind us that this great champion of 'lineal right' will soon beget the hapless Henry VI, who spells the end of what proves to be a very short line.

6 *Hamlet*: Notes from Underground – Paternal and Filial Subterfuge

Dazzled by its incomparable excellences and puzzlements, critics have often discussed *Hamlet* as if it were a completely unprecedented expression of Shakespeare's creativity. A frequent corollary is a tendency to relate the play to Shakespeare's life (documented or imagined) rather than to his unfolding body of work. Because Shakespeare's father died in 1601, probably a year or so after *Hamlet* was completed, and because the dramatist's only son (who died in 1596) was named Hamnet, many commentators have linked the fathers and sons in *Hamlet* to Shakespeare's putative responses to these deaths in the family. The most noted example of this biographical approach is Freud's argument that the dramatist's revived childhood feelings for his dying father, along with the powerful association of 'Hamnet' and 'Hamlet,' reawakened in him an unresolved Oedipal conflict that found expression in the play and especially in the representation of Hamlet himself.[1] Though Freud's psychoanalytic diagnosis was of course novel, in its emphasis on the formative deaths in Shakespeare's family it belongs (as does Joyce's scintillating treatment in the Scylla and Charybdis episode of *Ulysses*) to a tradition established by late nineteenth-century biographers like Georg Brandes. With many post-Freudian twists, this approach has continued to generate speculative commentary, most recently Stephen Greenblatt's conjecture that the play may reflect Shakespeare's brooding, delayed response to the inadequately solemnized death of young Hamnet.[2]

Suggestive as such possible connections between *Hamlet* and Shakespeare's family life may be, I believe it is more useful to situate the play's fathers and sons in the context of his earlier plays, and especially the histories.[3] In addition to following hard on the heels of

Shakespeare's second tetralogy of histories, *Hamlet* can be seen as the thematic culmination of these plays. In *Hamlet*, as in the histories, the past shapes the present, and in good part it does so through the burden imposed by parents on their children, especially the demands that fathers make upon their sons. The awesome, menacing weight of history is manifested at the very outset by a Ghost who would speak to his son.[4] As in the history plays, in *Hamlet* the differences between the generations are an essential constituent of identity, cutting across differences of nationality and faction. One of the deepest connections between the England of the *Henry IV* plays and the Denmark of *Hamlet* is that in both the older generation uses the younger as instruments to fight its battles and to consummate its revenges. Though there are many connections between Prince Hamlet and the Prince Henry of *Part Two*, in both formal and thematic terms the history play closest to *Hamlet* is *Henry IV, Part One*, and the tragedy can be understood as a realization of the dark potentialities that the earlier play had gestured toward but evaded.

There is a particularly close kinship between Prince Hamlet and Prince Hal, who has been characterized by Bert States as Hamlet's 'older brother.'[5] The parallels between the two princes are remarkable, beginning with the fact that both are trapped in dilemmas created by the previous generation. Hal and Hamlet are commissioned by their regal fathers, after whom they are named, to undertake a violent filial office that demands a dereliction of important parts of themselves. Acutely aware of their duties and yet resistant to paternal edict, these ambivalent sons attempt a momentary escape from their intolerable situation by playing roles and assuming new identities. Both princes are extremely elusive figures. Each manifests a sometimes disconcerting multiplicity of attitudes and emotions, and each operates through indirection and obliquity, so that we understand them (and they understand themselves) only fitfully, through hints and glimpses. Though Hamlet has a wider and more passionate range of emotions than Hal, he shares with his more repressed fellow prince a resistance to paternal edict that he can neither accept nor acknowledge. Hence, what the princes say, and even what they do, is never the whole story. Often their words seem intended for themselves, even when addressed to other people, and their actions sometimes have an inner significance quite different from, or even opposite to, their obvious meaning. Both plays end with the prince undertaking an apparently generous, chivalric action – Hal's freeing of the Douglas and Hamlet's electing Fortinbras as King of Denmark – that can be interpreted as acts of clandestine hostility against an august father who cannot be challenged openly.

Within their common filial ambivalence, however, there is a key difference in degree: Hamlet's impulses both to honour and to resist his father are far more exigent than Hal's. The force of these extremes of Hamlet's filial response can be traced to the greater distance that separates him from his father. While Prince Hal does maintain a geographical and ethical distance, it is relatively easy to bridge; father and son meet on the battlefield to defend their mutual interests. But the Hamlets *père et fils* inhabit quite different worlds, and they did so even before they were separated by the elder Hamlet's death. In making young Hamlet a student, Shakespeare has radically transformed the extant sources of the play; he has removed the Prince from his father's old Norse world of heroic single combat and bloody revenge, placing him in a milieu of sceptical, humanist thinking. The differing worlds of the two Hamlets sharply reflect the two opposing Elizabethan understandings (discussed in chapter 1) of what it means to be a son. Hamlet the warrior father thinks in terms of paternal authority and bounden filial duty, while Hamlet the idealistic student son values autonomy and the freedom to better the mind. Each Hamlet, as we will see, prevents the fulfillment of the other's desires.

The Death of Fathers

For all its similarities to the histories, *Hamlet* places a much greater stress on the impact of paternal deaths on sons. In the histories, the sadness of a father's death is usually mitigated, and sometimes entirely erased, by the prospect of an immediate inheritance, as we suspect is the case with Bullingbrook/King Henry's response to the death of John of Gaunt, and in turn Prince Hal's response to the death of Henry. It is in a history play that a character voices the cynical proverb, 'happy always was it for that son / Whose father for his hoarding went to hell' (3H6:2.2.47–8). But in *Hamlet* variations on the phrase 'a dear father lost' recur throughout the play like a mournful refrain. To be sure, Claudius hypocritically introduces the trope of the 'father lost' as if it is no more than a 'common theme,' a brute, endlessly repeated fact of life. Chastising Hamlet for his excessive 'mourning duties' to his father, Claudius declares:

But you must know your father lost a father,
That father lost, lost his, and the survivor bound
In filial obligation for some term
To do obsequious sorrow.   1.2.89–92

But the still-mourning Hamlet and the soon to be fatherless Laertes give the lie to this vision of paternal loss as numbingly inevitable and choreographed ('bound,' 'for some term'). As if operating through a leverage in which distance increases emotional force, the fathers in *Hamlet* command 'filial obligation' more compellingly in death than in life. And, of course, they command far more guilt as well. When, in response to Gertrude's innocent 'Why seems it so particular with thee,' Hamlet launches into his angry, over-protesting 'Seems, madam? nay, it is, I know not "seems"' speech (1.2.76), we infer that she has accidentally touched a filial anxiety about inadequate love and mourning.

At the outset, all three sons in the younger generation either have lost (Hamlet and Fortinbras) or soon will lose (Laertes) their fathers, and their responses to this primal deprivation go far to shape their lives. Since Hamlet's response is defined against the simpler reactions of Fortinbras and Laertes, let us consider them first. As Fortinbras is largely a cipher and does not appear onstage until the final scene of the play, he can be dealt with briefly. In rough outline, Fortinbras serves as a foil to Hamlet: like Hamlet, he is named after his heroic father the king, and like Hamlet he is under the control of an uncle who has taken the kingship that might conceivably have been his. But the parallels end quickly. In his eagerness for military action, Fortinbras seems to be setting his course by a heroic but defeated father's star. According to Horatio at the beginning of the play, young Fortinbras is dedicated to attempting 'to recover' from Denmark 'those foresaid lands / So by his father lost' (1.1.103–4; cf.1.2.23–4). If Horatio is right, Fortinbras may be attempting – like a number of sons in other plays – a posthumous restoration of the father after whom he is named, a rescue of the family name he shares.

But if he is attempting to recover what his father lost, Fortinbras does the spirit of his father no honour, for in his opportunistic pursuit of his 'vantage' he is denying the oaths of forfeiture in the 'seal'd compact' pledged by the elder Fortinbras.[6] Alternatively, Fortinbras may be living up to being true to name as 'strong-in-arm' and simply venting his martial spirit against a kingdom that appears weakened by the recent death of its king; when his move against Denmark is suppressed by his uncle, the King of Norway, he seems happy enough to turn his attention to Poland. Interestingly, when he seizes the Danish throne at the end of the play, he indirectly alludes to his father but does not pay him the respect of mentioning his name: 'I have some rights, of memory in this kingdom, / Which now to claim my vantage doth invite me' (5.2.389–90).

Unlike the other sons in the play, we see Laertes interacting with his living father, and thus in him the immediate effect of a progenitor's death can be traced in greater detail than in his counterparts. From the outset the key to the relationship between Polonius and Laertes is its highly conventional nature, with both of them hewing close to Elizabethan stereotypes of decorous behaviour for fathers and sons. It is not surprising that, as a trusted, Lord Burghley-like counsellor to the crown, Polonius places great emphasis on the respect that is due his authority and conceives of the father-son relationship in public, institutional terms as a microcosm of order in the state. Appropriately, the first time we see this father and son together they are in the presence of the King and studiously observing the hierarchies of authority. When Claudius asks Laertes what he wants, it is presumably on bended knee that the young man addresses him as 'My dread lord' and attests that 'willingly I came to Denmark / To show my duty in your coronation' (1.2.50, 52–3). Though his destination is Paris and his intentions presumably prodigal, Laertes is no rebel. He kneels to Claudius to seek permission to travel abroad, and Polonius makes it clear that his son has followed due process by first securing paternal permission before approaching the King. Clearly, Laertes' intent is to leave Denmark, and the word 'leave' is used five times, but it always appears as a noun rather than a verb and always means 'authorization,' as in 'your father's leave' (1.2.57). The forms of authority are paramount for this father and son, but not for the silent onlooker whom the King turns to address as 'my cousin Hamlet, and my son' (1.2.64).

On the second and final occasion that we see Polonius and Laertes together, the actual leave-taking of Laertes, the scene is domestic rather than public, and yet the emphasis once again falls on the protocols of duty and deference. In the ritual action that characterizes him, once again Laertes bows to power and authority. After having blessed Laertes and bade him farewell (offstage), Polonius happens upon his son and daughter and seizes the opportunity to bless the kneeling Laertes a second time and to lecture him on the behaviour befitting his station. For good measure, at the end of the speech Polonius adds yet a third blessing. Unlike so many other sons and daughters in Shakespeare, Laertes has no trouble kneeling to paternal authority. Though he may well be impatient to leave, Laertes abides his father's lengthy advice, perhaps recalling the conduct-book admonition that 'Though parents in their speech seem to be long and tedious, yet must children endure it.'[7] Upon departing, Laertes bids his father a farewell that recalls his earlier deference to the King: 'Most humbly do I take my leave, my lord' (1.3.82).

Nowhere is the conventionality of this relationship more apparent than in the parting words that Polonius bestows upon Laertes. Here the language of Polonius – blessing in the form of wise, politic advice – is as public and ritualistic as his son's kneeling. In its facile impersonality, the speech is a source hunter's gold mine and nightmare, one more echo in a series reaching back to ancient Greece and continuing unabated into the many letters of advice that anxious Elizabethan fathers wrote to make their sons prodigal-proof.[8] In many productions the actors playing Laertes and Ophelia exchange sly glances during Polonius's speech, as if to say, 'The old man is at it again.' But it is unlikely that the two of them would be mocking their father's authority, especially since their deference to that authority will help to lead to their deaths. Besides, father and son share a common respect for the wisdom of cliché and proverb; appropriately, the dying Laertes characterizes himself in a saying about folly – 'Why, as a woodcock to mine own springe' (5.2.306) – which had earlier been used by Polonius (1.3.115).[9]

Polonius's lines are full of qualifications and negations, for they articulate a prudential calculus that stresses the risks of interactions with others. Though the thoughts are glibly conventional, they are not simply foolish, and certainly Laertes would have done well to have heeded more carefully the advice to 'Beware / Of entrance to a quarrel' (1.3.65–6). But all of the foregoing lines are reduced to banality by the climactic injunction that Laertes should attend to 'above all':

> To thine own self be true,
> And it must follow, as the night the day,
> Thou canst not then be false to any man.   1.3.78–80

Though the idea of being 'To thine own self true' may connect these lines to Polonius's earlier emphasis on self-protection, the passage transcends questions of risk management and social display in its insistence on being 'true.' Two strands of unintentional irony are germane to the rest of the play, and especially to Hamlet's dilemma. One is the inherent contradiction in a father's charging his kneeling son to be true to himself; while warning Laertes about the danger of listening to other people, Polonius is urging him to incise 'these few precepts in thy memory' (1.3.58). The other irony is that Polonius does not realize he is merely skimming the surface of vast mysteries, including the myriad difficulties of discovering what one's 'own self' may be. Neither Polonius nor Laertes has the slightest intimation that the course of a son's being true to himself may necessitate his refusing to listen to his father.

Laertes' resumption of his Parisian life, like so many hopes of young people in the play, is nipped in the bud, and soon he is called home a second time to bury a father, this time his own. Since he has not shown affection or respect for Polonius beyond the conventional, Laertes responds to his death with a desire for vengeance that is surprisingly passionate and desperate. Even Claudius, that astute judge of character, is not prepared for Laertes' ability to rally an armed force in his quest to 'be reveng'd / Most throughly for my father' (4.5.136–7). Part of being a son in *Hamlet* involves being vulnerable to guilt, and Claudius ensures that Laertes has an adequate amount. As a preface to his plot to murder Hamlet, Claudius abruptly asks,

> Laertes, was your father dear to you?
> Or are you like the painting of a sorrow,
> A face without a heart?   4.7.107–9

But of course Laertes was set on revenge before he returned to Denmark, having already 'bought an unction of a mountebank' (4.7.141), and so the question remains: how has this rather placid figure become a single-minded, bloodthirsty avenger?

The death of Polonius removes the anchor of Laertes' inherited values. (Far less young and less conventional men than he have responded to their fathers' deaths similarly; the forty-year old Sigmund Freud declared 'I now feel quite uprooted.')[10] Upon his return, Laertes' very first words to Claudius bespeak, with their childish objurgation, his desperate need for authority: 'O thou vile king, / Give me my father!' (4.5.116–17). It is as if a king, as a kind of superfather, could restore a domestic one. A few lines later Laertes' angry

demand has modulated into a bereft question: 'Where's my father?'
(4.5.129). Given Laertes' predilection for bowing before authority, it is
no surprise that his rebellion against the King is short lived; soon he is
observing the 'divinity [that] doth hedge a king' (4.5.124) and is happy
to comply when Claudius requests, 'Will you be rul'd by me?' (4.7.59).
With disastrous consequences, Claudius *will* give Laertes his father by
assuming that role himself and by directing the young man's angry
gullibility for his own ends. The contrast with Hamlet is plain, for
when Claudius earlier besought the Prince to 'think of us / As of a
father' (1.2.107–8), he was sharply rebuffed.

The connection in Laertes' mind between honourable ritual and
paternal authority is clear in his outburst about his father's death.
When Laertes states his grievances, he surprisingly slides over his
father's murder to fasten on the indecorum of his funeral:

> His means of death, his obscure funeral –
> No trophy, sword, nor hatchment o'er his bones,
> No noble rite nor formal ostentation –
> Cry to be heard, as 'twere from heaven to earth,
> That I must call't in question.   4.5.214–18

There is a notable disjunction between the height of Laertes' passion
('Cry to be heard, as 'twere from heaven to earth') and the fact that a
perceived failure of ceremony has provoked it. His concern with ritual
and propriety is apparent when, in response to Hamlet's tepid apology
for having killed Polonius, Laertes declares that, while he is 'satisfied
in nature,' he cannot risk a reconcilement until he is advised 'by some
elder masters of known honor' (5.2.244, 248). Even as he is engaged in
deceiving Hamlet and preparing to destroy him, Laertes invokes with
apparent sincerity the authority of 'elder masters.' As was true for
Hotspur in *1 Henry IV*, Laertes' credulous commitment to honour
entails a naivety about the motives of his elders; just as Hotspur is
unaware of his father's and uncle's betrayals of him, Laertes does not
dream that Polonius has sent a spy to observe him, and he realizes the
truth about his 'elder master' Claudius only when it is too late.

It is clear that, despite inevitable generational differences, Polonius
and Laertes are possessed of quite similar values, with honour and
decorum being paramount.[11] Father and son alike are concerned with
the proper respect for social surfaces, and thus Polonius's belief that
'the apparel oft proclaims the man' (1.3.72) is matched by Laertes' sub-

sequent anger about the lack of 'formal ostentation' in his father's funeral. It is their concern about honourable appearances and lack of concern for her feelings that accounts for their parallel hectoring of Ophelia about her need to protect herself and her family; their shared assumption of superiority to her and their complacency about male authority in the family are of a piece with their unquestioning obedience to the King. But, notwithstanding their concern about honour, both are only too willing to practise deception, and of course both are killed by Hamlet in the course of acting out their devious plans. If Laertes manages to transcend his father's values and be true to himself, he does so only in his fraternal dying words, when he asks the 'noble Hamlet' to 'Exchange forgiveness with me' (5.2.329).

Hamlet's Filial Ambivalence

Paradoxically, Hamlet both idealizes and resists his father more than the conventional Laertes does, being at once more dependent on and more independent of his father. Whereas Laertes shows little sign of affection for his living father and yet throws his whole being into avenging his death, Hamlet glorifies his father as the best of men and yet, upon learning of his murder, shows little appetite for revenge. Not long after Hamlet foregoes an excellent opportunity to kill Claudius when his uncle is at prayer, Laertes declares to Claudius his willingness 'To cut his [Hamlet's] throat i' th' church' (4.7.126). The contrast between the two as filial avengers could hardly be more pointed. Given Elizabethan conventions about sons' deference to fathers, living and dead, it is easier to understand Laertes' sudden craving for swift revenge than Hamlet's delay and inaction. Hamlet is of course vividly aware of his inability to act, and he attempts to account for it by excoriating himself for such moral deficiencies as cowardice and sloth. But these self-criticisms seem beside the point, or even evasions of more difficult truths.

Despite his volubility, or perhaps because of it, Hamlet's language leaves much unsaid and his motives largely unaccounted for. The interpretive problem has been stated by Anne Barton in judicious terms: 'There are areas in which Hamlet's reason either cannot or refuses to operate, inhibiting factors more potent than mere doubt of the Ghost's veracity. Because he never articulates them even to himself, the audience is impelled to draw conclusions – necessarily tentative – from his speech and behaviour, as though he were not a dramatic character but someone known in real life.'[12] In the twentieth century the single most influential interpretation was the 'real life,' psychoanalytic reading formulated by Freud and elaborated over many years by his biographer, Ernest Jones.[13] Jones begins his widely read monograph, *Hamlet and Oedipus*, with a number of lucid points: that there is a discrepancy between Hamlet's oft-stated eagerness to avenge his father and his agonized failure to do so, that Hamlet does not understand the source of the problem, and that criticism must account for the discrepancy by discovering in Hamlet an unconscious source of repression. The origin of this repression must be, Jones says, an unresolved Oedipal complex deriving from childhood. He argues that Hamlet cannot kill Claudius because Claudius has done what Hamlet as a child wanted to do: he has killed old Hamlet and sexually possessed Gertrude.

Both from a psychoanalytic and a historical perspective, this interpretation fails to convince. One problem is that Hamlet does not repress the feelings that the Oedipal interpretation mandates he should. Whatever forbidden impulses may be safely stowed away in Hamlet's unconscious, a prurient interest in his mother's sexuality is not one of them – he imagines her

> in the rank sweat of an enseamed bed,
> Stew'd in corruption, honeying and making love
> Over the nasty sty!   3.4.92–4[14]

Jones's emphasis on the Oedipal complex stems from his historically questionable assumption about the nature and origin of repression. He errs, I believe, when he assumes that the source of Hamlet's repression must be sexual: 'as the herd unquestionably selects from the "natural" instincts the sexual one on which to lay its heaviest ban, so it is the various psycho-sexual trends that are most often "repressed" by the individual.'[15] But the impulses that the societal 'herd' most heavily bans vary with time and place, and it may well be that the assumption about the centrality of sexual taboos says more about Freud's Vienna and Jones's Toronto than Shakespeare's London. Certainly, Hamlet's most thorough work of repression centres on his ghostly father rather than his carnal mother.[As we have seen, in Elizabethan England the moral prohibition against disobedience to fathers was very strong, and what seems most deeply buried in Hamlet's mind is his awareness of his impulse to disobey the Ghost's command.[16] Much as Prince Hal never directly acknowledges the fact of his father's usurpation of the throne, Hamlet never challenges or even explicitly questions the Ghost's insistence on being revenged. The closest he comes to disobedience is his exclamation against filial duty at the end of the Ghost scene: 'O cursed spite, / That ever I was born to set it right!' (1.5.188–9).[17]

Although Hamlet is never outwardly rebellious, there is a good deal of evidence revealing his resistance to the cry for vengeance. Paradoxically, this resistance is especially apparent in his strongest avowals of revenge, such as his first declaration upon hearing that his father was murdered:

> Haste me to know't, that I with wings as swift
> As meditation, or the thoughts of love,
> May sweep to my revenge.   1.5.29–31

If Hamlet were of a single mind, what he would say would resemble more closely the protagonist's commitment to avenge his father at the beginning of Henry Chettle's *Hamlet*-inflected *Tragedy of Hoffman*: 'And with a heart as air, swift as thought / I'll execute justly in such a cause.'[18] But the very language Hamlet uses to express his commitment to celerity provides evidence for the delay that will ensue. Unlike Chettle's proverbial 'swift as thought,' Hamlet's 'swift / As meditation' is contradictory, since entranced repetition is the essence of meditation as it is of 'thoughts of love.' Not only are meditation and thoughts of love unlikely to conduce to revenge, but it is also discordant for Hamlet to use images of philosophy and love (his previous commitments) to emphasize the alacrity with which he will essay this violent new calling.[19]

Immediately after the Ghost disappears, Hamlet makes another speech that conveys even more strongly the opposite of what he intends. Recalling the Ghost's appeal for him to 'remember me,' the Prince declares:

> Remember thee!
> Ay, thou poor ghost, whiles memory holds a seat
> In this distracted globe. Remember thee!
> Yea, from the table of my memory
> I'll wipe away all trivial fond records,
> All saws of books, all forms, all pressure past

That youth and observation copied there,
That thy commandement all alone shall live
Within the book and volume of my brain,
Unmix'd with baser matter.   1.5.95–104

Once again, Hamlet protests considerably too much, as he elevates the
Ghost's injunction into a Mosaic revelation, a 'commandement.'[20]
Many critics have taken Hamlet at his word, assuming that in his
desire to create a *tabula rasa* he 'wipes away all previous knowledge, all
previous values, and baptises himself as a new man.'[21] And some commentators and directors have even interpreted Hamlet's situation as
an instance of demoniacal possession; in Richard Eyre's 1980 production, Hamlet (Jonathan Pryce) spoke the Ghost's lines as if possessed,
and a critic declares that 'If the old history of Hamlet was a revenge
play, Shakespeare's *Hamlet* is a study in ghost-possession.'[22]

But what Hamlet's lines reveal is not possession but rather the desire
to be possessed. Significantly, it is Hamlet, not the Ghost, who repeatedly insists that this vengeful injunction must supersede 'all' his previous knowledge and live 'all alone' in his brain. The Prince realizes
that, in order to remember the Ghost's 'commandement,' he must first
forget everything he has learned, and thus he is tacitly acknowledging
that it is only by dint of completely obliterating his values and experience that he can remember what he must. Of course, a committed
avenger would have no need to talk about making himself into a
totally new person, but Hamlet senses that avenging his father will
first necessitate a kind of suicide. Hamlet's intimation of a connection
between revenge and suicide will continue to pervade his phrasing
throughout the play, for he senses it is his identity that stands in the
way of doing the deed. Interestingly, in his 'To be or not to be' speech,
commentators have always been puzzled by whether specific lines
refer to taking revenge or committing suicide. But, in light of Hamlet's
avowal to erase himself for revenge, it is better to say both. For Hamlet
these two actions are not alternatives so much as entailments of each
other.

The inner ambivalence that Hamlet attempts to erase in 1.5 pervades
his thinking the next time we see him (2.2). This extended scene, the
longest in the play, supplies eloquent evidence of how unpossessed
Hamlet is, how engaged with the world he remains. Despite his prior
commitment to self-erasure, his detailed recollection of a long speech
from an obscure play indicates that his memory remains impressively

well stocked and ready to hand.[23] The scene culminates with the arrival at court of the touring actors, and from the start it raises many questions about role playing, and especially whether roles are freely chosen and fully embraced. One reason for Hamlet's fascination with actors and acting in this scene is the kinship that he senses with them. It goes without saying that he would not think of himself as playing a role, nor think of actors as his fellows, if he were wholeheartedly committed to revenge. Perhaps he can think of revenge only as theatre.

Especially when Hamlet speaks of the status and the particular dilemma of child actors, we can hear his mind humming underneath the words he speaks. Triggered in part by Rosencrantz's imaging of them as fledgling birds of prey ('an aery of children, little eyases'), Hamlet sees his fate mirrored in that of the boy actors who have usurped the common players and taken their venues. (As a parallel, one might recall in *1 Henry IV* Hal's equally tacit understanding that the situation of Francis the drawer mirrors his own.) Hamlet's fascination is conveyed by a tumble of questions: 'What, are they children? Who maintains 'em? How are they escoted? Will they pursue the quality no longer than they can sing? Will they not say afterwards, if they should grow themselves to common players (as it is most like, if their means are no better), their writers do them wrong, to make them exclaim against their own succession?' (2.2.345–51). Hamlet's question 'Who maintains 'em' reveals his concern about the vulnerable dependence of the young, and he turns from concern for their immediate well-being to thoughts of the future that awaits them. These boys will 'grow themselves to common players,' eventually becoming what they have satirized. Surely Hamlet must be remembering the Ghost's recent 'commandement' when he delivers the strangely resonant opinion that the child actors' 'writers do them wrong, to make them exclaim against their own succession.' This comment reveals Hamlet's sense that he too is a child actor who has been handed a scripted role mandating actions that will blight his future.

Hamlet's mixed feelings about his role manifest themselves more passionately in the narrative speech about Pyrrhus and Priam that he enjoins the First Player to deliver. The intriguing question is why Hamlet calls for this speech: does he intend it to be an inducement or a disincentive to his revenge? Or, to point the question, does the violence inflicted on Priam by the hideously sadistic, subhuman figure of Pyrrhus represent what Claudius did to Hamlet's father, or what Hamlet hopes to do to Claudius? Or both? The speech expresses

Hamlet's ambivalence, since 'Pyrrhus is at once an example of what Hamlet feels he ought to be, and of what he feels he cannot be ... a figure both of the avenging son and of the father's murderer.'[24] From one angle, Pyrrhus's slaughter of Priam, the aged and helpless king of Troy, resembles Claudius's killing of an equally vulnerable king of Denmark. But from another angle, Pyrrhus's killing of Priam points to the revenge that Hamlet hopes to inflict on Claudius. (Moreover, Priam is not an appropriate target for revenge; not only is he pathetically weak, unlike Claudius, but he is the father of the killer of Pyrrhus's father, not the killer himself.) From this welter of possible identifications and partial mirror reflections, one conclusion seems clear: in order to kill Claudius, Hamlet will have to imitate what Pyrrhus did in the narrative and what Claudius did in recent history.[25] To commit revenge is to replicate the act that he seeks to punish, and thus to become what he kills.

Though Hamlet's motives for requesting the Pyrrhus speech may not be clear, his immediate response to it is an unequivocal, instinctive repudiation of violence. In response to the Prince's instruction that the players be 'well bestowed,' Polonius answers with a comment that suggests the ethos of revenge: 'My lord, I will use them according to their desert' (2.2.527–8). Revengers always assume a privileged knowledge of what people have coming to them, and they 'use' people accordingly in their meting out of justice. Hamlet's response to Polonius is in effect the credo of the anti-revenger: 'God's bodkin, man, much better: use every man after his desert, and who shall scape whipping? Use them after your own honor and dignity – the less they deserve, the more merit is in your bounty. Take them in' (2.2.529–33). Every human is morally culpable, he says, and so the best we can do is ascribe to others the virtues to which we aspire. The easy transition from 'God's bodkin' (perhaps an allusion to the consecrated wafer of Holy Communion[26] as well as to a dagger) to the grace that humans can show to each other is moving. The only ethical imperative is to 'Take them in.' And a few lines later, Hamlet heeds his own counsel as he cautions the First Player to respect Polonius ('look you mock him not' [2.2.545–6]). But Hamlet's gracious acceptance of human fallibility does not last for long. As soon as everyone else exits, he launches into a violent soliloquy about what he mistakenly insists is his cowardly failure to commit revenge – thereby administering an undeserved whipping to himself and denying his own 'honor and dignity.' Part of Hamlet's tragedy stems from his failure to acknowledge and to honour his own resistance to revenge, to be true to himself.

It is easier to demonstrate the presence of Hamlet's ambivalence than to ascertain its origin. If we reject the dubious theory of the unresolved Oedipal conflict, we can posit an ethical repugnance for the act of revenge on Hamlet's part, which seems generally plausible but does not sort well with Hamlet's apparent lack of guilt about having killed Polonius. It is more precise to say that Hamlet resists the call for revenge because it denies his idealistic view of man as rational, dignified, and autonomous, a free agent following the dictates of his conscience.[27] Though his meditation on 'What a piece of work is a man, how noble in reason, how infinite in faculties' (2.2.303–4) ends in disenchantment, it is deeply felt. Clearly, Hamlet vests much of this idealism in his view of his deceased father, whom he repeatedly describes (early in the play) as if he were a god among men. But there is a negative side to this elevation of man in the frequent contempt that Hamlet expresses about the debasement of himself and others. A common feature of these diatribes is a charge of slavishness, of a failure to make decisions for oneself, of allowing oneself to become an instrument for someone else to use. The complication for Hamlet is that the very grandeur of this powerful, independent king-father has created dependency and a lack of freedom in those around him, including (as Hamlet suspects) Hamlet himself.

Hamlet's concern with dependency and autonomy surface in his first soliloquy, before he has learned of his father's murder. In a revealing recollection of the dynamics in his family, Hamlet elevates his father and also conveys the awesome power he wielded. The speech begins with the sharp contrast between his father and his uncle in a manoeuvre psychoanalysts describe as 'splitting the image of the father' (into good and evil components):

> So excellent a king, that was to this
> Hyperion to a satyr, so loving to my mother
> That he might not beteem the winds of heaven
> Visit her face too roughly.   1.2.139–42

Hamlet is recalling his father in highly idealized terms, more as king than father and more as god than man. His language calls to mind contemporary formulations of God's love for man, such as the Puritan Arthur Dent's assurance that God 'is most chary and tender over us: he cannot endure the wind should blow upon us.'[28]

As Hamlet continues, however, his tone darkens with the appearance of his mother, and the supposedly ideal relationship of Hamlet's parents quickly begins to appear unhealthy and even parasitical:

> Why, she would hang on him
> As if increase of appetite had grown
> By what it fed on, and yet, within a month –
> Let me not think on't! Frailty, thy name is woman! 1.2.143–6

Gertrude's hanging on old Hamlet reveals her quite literal dependency. While Hamlet presumably intends these lines to indicate how wonderful King Hamlet was (his devoted wife couldn't get enough of him), he seems troubled by his mother's desperate neediness and is eager to gender all weakness as female. Between the lines, however, there is a suggestion that the very excellence of this wind-controlling, sun-god father has created his mother's weakness, and it seems harsh for Hamlet to criticize such a needy figure for remarrying. The implication is that the suicidal Hamlet's railing on his mother's weakness is energized by his refusal to acknowledge his own dependency.[29] As the strained extremes of this speech indicate, Hamlet will not be able easily to reconcile his desire to be autonomous with his strong sense of duty to his glorious father.

With the coming of the wounded, imperious Ghost, Hamlet's dilemma takes its terrible shape. The Ghost employs all the resources of language and self-dramatization – putting to shame the feeble attempts of Polonius two scenes earlier to direct *his* son – to impose his will on Hamlet's. The Ghost denies to Hamlet, the student and thinker, the exercise of his rational choice and thus his spiritual autonomy. Hamlet's problem is pungently defined by Mark Rose: 'It is one of the radical ironies of the tragedy that the same nightmarish figure who takes from Hamlet his freedom should also embody the ideal of man noble in reason and infinite in faculties – the ideal of man, in other words, as free.'[30] And of course this nightmarish figure is also Hamlet's father or (more ambiguously) 'the spirit of his father.' Not surprisingly, this idealized, authoritative figure is beyond the conscious will of Hamlet to criticize. In place of open criticism of the Ghost, often Hamlet's resentment is directed against other, safer figures whom he *can* accuse of manipulating him. Much as Hal attacks Falstaff for the faults possessed by the King, so Hamlet feels free to mock Polonius, who is 'a ludicrous live father in place of the awesome dead one, and therefore a focus for the hatred and resentment that are repressed in the relationship with the real father.'[31]

But Hamlet's scorn is not reserved for the older generation. His demand that his former schoolmate Guildenstern play the recorder is very revealing: 'Why, look you now, how unworthy a thing you make of me! You would play upon me, you would seem to know my stops, you would pluck out the heart of my mystery ... 'Sblood, do you think I am easier to be play'd on than a pipe? Call me what instrument you will, though you fret me, yet you cannot play upon me' (3.2.363–72). Though Hamlet has good reason to be upset at his old friend's betrayal, the feckless Guildenstern is not much of an opponent. It seems likely that much of Hamlet's animus has been displaced on to Guildenstern from more imposing, fatherlike targets, who would include Polonius, Claudius, and especially the Ghost itself.[32] Though all of these figures are attempting to sound Hamlet out, it is pre-eminently the Ghost who is trying to play upon him as an 'instrument' to further its own ends. In part, the lines aimed at Guildenstern are a delayed reaction to the Ghost, the sentiment he should have spoken on the battlements.

Subterranean Action – Hamlet and the Ghost

A long and spirited critical debate has arrived at the sensible conclusion that the Ghost is profoundly ambiguous and perhaps ultimately unknowable. Where it has come from – heaven, hell, or purgatory – is anybody's, and everybody's, guess. What needs to be emphasized is that, though the Ghost cannot be proved to be a devil, there is something rather diabolical in the way it goes to work on Hamlet. When the Ghost appears to Hamlet in 1.5, it may well expect a less than enthusiastic response from him (the father knows his son), and thus it seems determined to overwhelm his resistance. The differences between this scene and its equivalent in *1 Henry IV* (when Hal returns to court and is browbeaten by his father) are revealing, as Henry insults his son's self-respect while the Ghost utilizes all the sanctions – natural and supernatural – of the father as king to play on Hamlet's pity and guilt. When, at the beginning of the scene, Hamlet says 'Speak, I am bound to hear,' the Ghost immediately asserts its authority by cutting him off: 'So art thou to revenge, when thou shalt hear' (1.5.6–7). Here the Ghost's language echoes conventional formulations such as the remonstrance in the 'Homily on Rebellion' reminding the congregation that subjects of kings 'are bounden to obey them.'[33] The stately Ghost is a figure of pathos who carries a truncheon, the symbol of his military and political authority.

Though the Ghost commands Hamlet to 'pity me not,' the speech he launches into is clearly calculated to evoke the greatest pity possible in Hamlet. Using the rhetorical figure of *occupatio* (in which the speaker says he will not discuss a matter but deviously insinuates his view of it), the Ghost says he cannot tell the 'the secrets of my prison house' because the effects on Hamlet would be too terrible:

> I could a tale unfold whose lightest word
> Would harrow up thy soul, freeze thy young blood,
> Make thy two eyes, like stars, start from their spheres. 1.5.15–17

As a study of rhetoric in *Hamlet* has noted, 'From start to finish, the ghost's speech is calculated to excite the kind of horrified pity that leads to rage and vengeance.'[34] Clearly, the Ghost is not taking any chances.

But the Ghost is not content to manipulate Hamlet with this overwhelming appeal to pity. It does unto Hamlet what it says Claudius had done to the elder Hamlet in the orchard: it poisons him through the ear.[35] As Elizabethan fathers were wont to do and as King Henry IV had done unto his Prince, the Ghost contrives to coerce Hamlet through emotional blackmail. With excruciating hesitations, the Ghost awakens and intensifies Hamlet's guilt:

> *Ghost.*   List, list, O, list!
>   If thou didst ever thy dear father love –
> *Hamlet.* O God!
> *Ghost.*   Revenge his foul and most unnatural murder. 1.5.22–5

The Ghost equates filial love with the willingness to commit bloody revenge, a devastating equation that Claudius will express to Laertes after the death of *his* father.[36] Near the end of his speech, the Ghost deepens the wound with a thrice-repeated expletive followed by another compelling conditional: 'O, horrible, O, horrible, most horrible! / If thou hast nature in thee, bear it not' (1.5.80–1). In addition to demanding the unlimited filial duty that Elizabethan fathers assumed to be their prerogative, the Ghost appeals to Hamlet's idealism by including appeals to love and 'nature.' Hamlet cannot question this command without denying everything his father claims to represent.

In the coercive sanctions that it brings to bear, the Ghost's directive to Hamlet is impressively powerful. It is also thoroughly callous. Remarkably, as the Ghost exercises its authority, it shows not the slightest concern for Hamlet. There is perhaps a pretence of regard, but not much more, when the Ghost counsels:

> But, howsomever thou pursues this act,
> Taint not thy mind, nor let thy soul contrive
> Against thy mother aught.   1.5.84–6

Not only is 'this act' a euphemism concealing the Ghost's advocacy of murder, but the warning to 'Taint not thy mind' is so perfunctory and Polonius-like as to be contemptuous. The triviality of the warning stands out sharply when we remember the Ghost's interjection at Hamlet's earlier use of the word 'murther': 'Murther most foul, as in the best it is' (1.5.27). Here the Ghost blandly acknowledges a horrific reality that must inevitably infect the revenger's mind. In this scene, feelings of pity and outrage are clearly at the top of Hamlet's consciousness, as the Ghost had planned, but in retrospect Hamlet cannot but feel he has been treated in a disrespectful manner.

As we have noted, Hamlet's immediate response to the Ghost indicates his unconscious resistance to the insufferable but undeniable command. The pressure on Hamlet is enormous, and an unnerving development begins to take place: he becomes increasingly associated with qualities manifested by the Ghost.[37] Though Hamlet does not obey the Ghost, he becomes more Ghost-like. The earliest and most obvious of these connections comes only a few lines after the 'Remember me' scene. Ophelia seeks comfort from her father, having been 'affrighted' by the way Hamlet came to her:

> Pale as his shirt, his knees knocking each other,
> And with a look so piteous in purport
> As if he had been loosed out of hell
> To speak of horrors – he comes before me.   2.1.78–81

The first thing Hamlet does after having been visited by the Ghost is to visit Ophelia in a similarly pitiful and frightening manner. This replication of the Ghost's coming to Hamlet ('loosed out of hell / To

speak of horrors') vividly suggests the Prince's alienation from the
world of direct, tender emotion, from the world of the living and the
loving. It is as if Hamlet senses that he has been touched by the Ghost
and is in some way infected by the Ghost's bitter, otherworldly
disgust.[38]

The shock of the ghost-like Hamlet, who knows too much, coming
to the unknowing, innocent Ophelia is heightened by our realization
that what is simile for her ('as if he had been loosed out of hell') has
been experienced as literal reality by Hamlet. A similar contrast
between the Ghost-entangled Hamlet and an innocent, unknowing
woman occurs in the scene (3.4) in Gertrude's closet, when Hamlet
sees and hears the Ghost and she does not. The difference between this
scene and the earlier one on the battlements, in which Hamlet's friends
also see the Ghost, suggests he is now interiorizing the figure. Indeed,
Hamlet is not only on speaking terms with the Ghost, but he also is
ready to speak on its behalf, and hence before it can get in a word he
explains why it has come to visit him.

In addition to indicating a troubling family relatedness, we can
think of Hamlet's progressive interiorizing of the Ghost as his means
of dealing with the dangerous, confusing situation that has been
imposed on him. After his appearance to Ophelia, Hamlet's ghostliness has less to do with how he looks than with the way he interacts
with other people; he increasingly deals with them as the Ghost had
dealt with him. Like the Ghost, Hamlet will operate deviously through
concealment and manipulation, going underground.

The theme of concealment is central in *Hamlet*, as it was in *1 Henry
IV*, but with a difference. In the earlier play, the emphasis is primarily
on the concealment of identities and intentions, and so there is much
imagery relating to masks, vizards, assumed names, painted 'colors,'
and counterfeiting, all of them ways of putting on a false front. This
process occurs in *Hamlet* as well, especially with regard to the pervasive concern with role playing and play-acting. But in *Hamlet* this role
playing is part of a larger emphasis on strategies of concealment and
indirection: characters move beyond simple role playing in that they
want to disguise not only their identity but also their agency.[39]
Through the use of surrogates and instrumental intermediaries, the
principal characters wish to conceal the fact that they are actively
involved in bringing about the outcomes they desire. For the most
part, this concealment is controlled by members of the older generation. Thus, Polonius employs Reynaldo to spy on Laertes, and also

uses Ophelia and then Gertrude as means of inducing Hamlet to disburden himself of his secret. Similarly, Claudius first uses Rosencrantz and Guildenstern to plumb Hamlet's mind, and then replaces them with Laertes as his tool to be rid of Hamlet. The Ghost can be seen as doing the same thing in a more sophisticated way, as he slyly enlists Hamlet to be the instrument to carry out his revenge, thus insulating himself from the deed he commissions but scarcely names. In the Ghost we see a frightening intensification of Polonius's disregard for the effects of his scheming, which the courtly patriarch dismisses as 'laying these slight sallies on my son, / As 'twere a thing a little soil'd wi' th' working' (2.1.39–40).

When we look at Hamlet, however, we see a greater degree of concealment altogether. Or, more precisely, we see a greater *depth*. In his plotting, Hamlet works deeper than his opponents, far deeper than the scheming Polonius, Laertes, and Claudius, to say nothing of the hapless Rosencrantz and Guildenstern, whom he will undermine and 'blow at the moon.' Hamlet's descent into concealment is prefigured in and perhaps inspired by the curious stage business that concludes the scene with him and the Ghost (1.5).[40] When Hamlet insists that Horatio and Marcellus swear to secrecy about what they have seen, from underneath the floor the Ghost unexpectedly urges them to 'Swear!' In an odd bit of business that is repeated twice, Hamlet moves his friends across the stage to swear again, and the Ghost follows them, speaking from under their feet. After disrespectfully calling the now subterranean spirit 'boy,' 'truepenny,' and 'this fellow in the cellarage,' Hamlet uses terms that will prove to be thematically suggestive: 'Well said, old mole, canst work i' th' earth so fast? / A worthy pioner!' (1.5.162–3).

Unfortunately, critical commentary on Hamlet's 'old mole ... worthy pioner' lines has been sidetracked by a largely irrelevant issue: whether or not 'old mole' was Elizabethan slang for Satan and thus evidence that Hamlet identifies the Ghost with the devil.[41] More central is the fact that 'mole' and 'pioner' belong to a set of images about burrowing underground that honeycombs the play. Pioners were soldiers who dug entrenchments and tunnels; their most lethal activity was digging 'mines' that enabled explosive charges to be placed underneath enemy fortifications during protracted sieges. In the case of real moles, such tunnelling is what comes naturally, but it could be no less destructive for that – Thomas Nashe speaks of an entire city 'which was undermined and destroyed by moles.'[42] By transference, devious villains could be characterized as moles, and so Antonio prophetically remarks of Bosola in Webster's *The Duchess of Malfi* that 'This mole doth undermine me' (2.3.14).

The imagery of *Hamlet* suggests that, more than in any other play of Shakespeare's, its essential action is occurring out of sight and underground. This descent is foreshadowed in the lines that Hamlet speaks just before the Ghost first appears to him. When Hamlet mentions 'some vicious mole of nature' (1.4.24) that disfigures individuals, he seems to have in mind a blemish on the skin. But four lines later he speaks of its power of 'breaking down the pales and forts of reason' (1.3.28), which suggests the mole-as-pioner action of undermining defensive structures. By the same token, though the Ghost moves from the battlements to underneath the ground, and thence seems (apart from a brief surfacing in Gertrude's closet) to disappear from the play altogether, one cannot be sure that its (unseen) operations have ceased. One reason for the attractiveness of the gravediggers, apart from their ebullient vitality, is that *their* digging is honest work, done in full sight of others.

As Hamlet presumably senses when he addresses the Ghost, he is himself in danger of being undermined by this wraith-like mole and pioner. In literal terms, the Ghost is directly beneath him, and so could cause the earth under him to collapse. But the real threat to Hamlet is an ethical and spiritual undermining. Just as military pioners destroy the foundations of enemy walls, so the Ghost has done its best to undermine Hamlet's instincts and values. As is often the case with Hamlet, his dilemma is laid out in much simpler form in the person of Ophelia. We can see a more domestic but equally destructive version of the undermining of a child in the callous treatment of Ophelia by her father Polonius. By forcing her to question the love between herself and Hamlet ('I do not know, my lord, what I should think,' she says [1.3.104]), Polonius destroys Ophelia's innocence; ironically, his and Laertes' warnings of cankers burrowing in buds and of contagious blastments effectively create a kind of deflowering of her.[43] More explicitly and drastically than in the case of Hamlet, this paternal undermining will lead to Ophelia's self-abandonment and suicidal dereliction of identity.

If the mole and the pioner ominously indicate the dangers that face Hamlet, they point in another direction as well. For they also represent the Ghost-like strategy Hamlet will use to deal with his enemies, including the Ghost itself. Hamlet will turn the weapons of his enemies against them by going underground. For the army undertaking it, mining enemy fortifications was tedious and highly dangerous business, often undertaken as 'the last remedy and policy' when all else failed.[44] Hamlet's turning to mining may indicate a similar desperation on his part. Significantly, his most explicit statement of this strategy occurs immediately after the Ghost visits him for the second time. After the Ghost leaves, Hamlet first applies the image of undermining to his mother. He warns her that, if she refuses to acknowledge her guilt, her evasion

> will but skin and film the ulcerous place,
> Whiles rank corruption, mining all within,
> Infects unseen.   3.4.147–9

Then, remembering that Rosencrantz and Guildenstern are to accompany him to England, he declares (in a passage we will return to) that he will repay their knavery in kind by 'delv[ing] one yard below their mines, / And blow[ing] them at the moon' (3.4.208–9). A standard defence against mining was to dig a countermine, and so Hamlet announces that he will beat his enemies at their own game, undermining them when they are busily working to destroy him.[45]

It is significant that, following Hamlet's talk of stealthy mining and countermining at the end of act 3, he begins to disappear from the play. For the first time he is absent from the stage for three consecutive scenes (4.5 through 4.7) during his voyage to England. Moreover, even when Hamlet is onstage, we sense that he is not entirely present. In place of his earlier penchant for soliloquy, he now engages in colloquy with Horatio and others. Moreover, a suspicious formality shapes his words and actions, as if he is forcing himself to concentrate on surfaces rather than on what is going on beneath them.[46] Hamlet's hidden, mole-like indirection works on several levels. Most obviously, it is a political ploy – an attempt to deceive Claudius and to force him to show his hand. But it is on a deeper level that Hamlet's indirection proves most successful, and this is in his deceiving of himself. Hamlet is trying to keep himself in the dark as he goes to work; more truly than at the beginning of the play, he has 'that within which passes show' (1.2.85), and he does not want to know what it is.

Hamlet's Story

In act 5 Hamlet becomes both ghostlike and Ghost-like. That is, he becomes a wraith-like simulacrum of the remarkably vital person he had once been, a kind of negative image of himself, and he also begins to work underground, as the Ghost has done. Hamlet's most devious and Ghost-like form of manipulation involves, surprisingly, storytelling. The long final scene of the play (5.2) begins and ends with Hamlet's story; at the outset he tells the story to Horatio, and in his dying moments he insists that Horatio tell it after he is gone. There is no equivalent to Hamlet's emphasis on telling his story in any of the extant sources, and one wonders why it is so important to him. Part of the answer is that what Hamlet tells is 'my story' (5.2.349) as opposed to 'his story,' the history of murder and revenge that the Ghost tries to impose on him as the narrative of his life. For Hamlet, to tell his own story is to exercise the creativity and autonomy that the Ghost demands he surrender.[47]

Hamlet's story concerns what happened on board the ship to England, and its narrative events are fairly simple: being unable to sleep, Hamlet slips into the cabin of Rosencrantz and Guildenstern, steals the letter they carry from Claudius, breaks the seal, and discovers a warrant for his immediate execution upon arrival in England. Hamlet responds by forging a new commission (specifying that the bearers be put to sudden death), seals it with his father's signet ring, and replaces the original document with it. On the next day there is an altercation with pirates (about which Hamlet informs Horatio in a letter delivered in 4.6). Hamlet becomes separated from his ship, and Rosencrantz and Guildenstern continue on to England – and to the axe's edge. As we will see, what is crucial to the meaning of Hamlet's story is not what he did but the state of mind in which he did it, and in this regard it is like the play itself.

Though cast in the form of a narrative, Hamlet's story is in effect his spiritual testament, which explains his insistence at the end that it be told. Thus, after speaking just one word of narrative, Hamlet interrupts himself with a series of editorial parentheses to foreground the higher meaning of the tale:

> Rashly –
> And prais'd be rashness for it – let us know
> Our indiscretion sometime serves us well
> When our deep plots do pall, and that should learn us
> There's a divinity that shapes our ends
> Rough-hew them how we will –
> *Hor.* That is most certain.   5.2.6–11

The moral comes before the story and could not be clearer: there is a meaningful, providential shape to life, and 'we' (Hamlet generalizes

his experience before he recounts it) should unthinkingly and spontaneously surrender ourselves to that higher design. In Hamlet's telling
of the story, form embodies eschatology: providence comes first and
human actions follow. The clear implication is that on the ship Hamlet
became the antithesis of his earlier self, favouring 'indiscretion' over
the 'discretion' he had recommended to the players (3.2.17) and acting
impulsively instead of 'thinking too precisely on th'event' (4.4.41).

Though the vast majority of critics has accepted Hamlet's story
uncritically, there are two very significant problems with it, one internal and one contextual. The internal problem is simply that, even in its
own terms, the story does not make very good sense. How indiscreet
and rash *are* Hamlet's actions on the ship? Being unable to sleep, he
slips into the cabin of Rosencrantz and Guildenstern, and in the darkness impulsively happens upon the letter they are carrying? And is it
on account of heavenly ordinance that he happens to have with him
the essential instrument to seal his forgery, his father's signet ring?
Despite his heavy authorial interjection about the value of rashness,
the shipboard Hamlet looks like a person who knows what he is doing,
someone acting more like a calculating cat burglar than a person
beyond conscious control.[48] Indeed, it may be necessary for Hamlet to
stress his rashness before he begins his narrative because there is
nothing in the events themselves that would suggest it. Interestingly,
in one of the play's major sources, Belleforest's *Hystorie of Hamblet*,
rashness and divine providence have nothing to do with Hamlet's
deliverance on the ship. In a passage glossed by the marginal note
'Hamblet's craft to save his life,' we learn that while still at the Danish
court Hamblet 'presently doubted of his voyage' to England, and subsequently when at sea 'the subtle Danish prince' tricked his companions by forging a new document (Bullough 7:102).

Whatever suspicions we may have about the internal coherence of
Hamlet's story are confirmed when we recall his last words to
Gertrude in act 3, scene 4, lines that appear in the second Quarto text
but not the shorter Folio version.[49] In a passage that derives from the
wary Hamblet's interview with his mother in Belleforest (Bullough
7:102), Hamlet suddenly declares to Gertrude that 'I must to England,
you know that?' (3.4.199). Though she has forgotten about the plan,
Hamlet's mind is intently focused on it:

> There's letters seal'd, and my two schoolfellows,
> Whom I will trust as I will adders fang'd,

They bear the mandate, they must sweep my way
And marshal me to knavery. Let it work,
For 'tis the sport to have the enginer
Hoist with his own petar[d], an't shall go hard
But I will delve one yard below their mines,
And blow them at the moon. O, 'tis most sweet
When in one line two crafts directly meet.　　　　　3.4.202–10

Despite the recency of his killing of Polonius and raging at his mother, Hamlet's attention is clearly fixed on the emphatically placed 'letters seal'd' and on the dangerous 'mandate' they contain. The 'marshal me to knavery' phrase is perfectly ambiguous, as the knavery could either be committed upon or by Hamlet, but the subsequent 'I will delve' indicates that he is thinking about taking vengeful action. Given Hamlet's clear-sighted premonition of danger and his intent to undermine his enemies, it is impossible to believe that he could be acting as spontaneously on board the ship as he says he was in his account to Horatio (which of course fails to mention his prior suspicions about the 'letters seal'd'). To be sure, Hamlet's lines to Gertrude do not reveal a specific plan of action, but they do make his later claims for spontaneous rashness unconvincing.[50] In a sense Hamlet himself is hoist with his own petard, for these lines about undermining the plans of Rosencrantz and Guildenstern also serve to undermine his subsequent story to Horatio and blow it at the moon.

If there is reason to doubt Hamlet's story, and I believe there is, then a question immediately arises: why does he not tell the truth to his trusted friend Horatio? The answer is that Hamlet is not consciously fabricating a lie but rather telling Horatio the story that he himself wants to believe, and perhaps does believe, is true. It is precisely because he respects Horatio's integrity that he wishes to convince him, which is tantamount to convincing the moral censor in himself. Besides, all the actions that Hamlet says he performed are real enough. It is his intentions, his thinking, that he misrepresents. His story, then, involves a repressing and willed forgetting of the 'deep plot' he had begun to develop, or perhaps had already developed, in the earlier interview with his mother.[51]

The central point of Hamlet's story is that he is innocent of devious intentions, and thus by telling it he removes himself from the unbearable demands of consciousness and conscience. Instead of being his usual suspicious self, he sees himself as acting without premeditation, a mere instrument through which the Deity can work. Of course, the removal of self from consciousness and conscience is also a removal from responsibility. In a strange turn, Hamlet even implies that his mind is working in a way for which he is not responsible: 'Or [ere] I could make a prologue to my brains, / They had begun the play' (5.2.30–1). He denies any moral responsibility because, in addition to the deviousness of his enemies and his own rashness, heavenly providence is ultimately responsible for what happens on earth. In philosophical terms, Hamlet's argument does not hold water, since 'the praise of impetuous conduct and the confidence in divine providence are ill connected logically,' and one can hardly avoid the suspicion that Hamlet is protesting considerably too much.[52]

Claudius describes Ophelia in her madness as 'Divided from herself' (4.5.85), and the phrase can be applied equally well – if in a more complicated way – to Hamlet in the last act. In the parlance of modern psychology, Hamlet seems to be suffering from a sort of dissociational disorder in which the subject's 'usual self seems not to have access to the recent memories that one would normally expect him to have.'[53] But we need not rely on a modern definition, for in his strained apology to Laertes in the final scene Hamlet comments on the phenomenon himself, even as he is in the act of committing it. After describing himself as 'punish'd / With a sore distraction' (5.2.229–30), Hamlet not very convincingly exculpates himself for having killed Polonius:

> Was't Hamlet wrong'd Laertes? Never Hamlet!
> If Hamlet from himself be ta'en away,
> And when he's not himself does wrong Laertes,
> Then Hamlet does it not, Hamlet denies it.   5.2.233–6

Revealingly, Hamlet unintentionally connects these lines to the motive behind his ship story when he describes his apology to Laertes as 'my disclaiming from a purpos'd evil' (5.2.241).

That Hamlet's tale is predicated on a severe act of repression and dissociation is suggested in its rarely discussed opening lines:

> Sir, in my heart there was a kind of fighting
> That would not let me sleep. Methought I lay
> Worse than the mutines in the bilboes.   5.2.4–6

Although, indeed *because*, it is an apparently descriptive remark, Hamlet's reference to 'mutines in the bilboes' reveals more about his situation than do his more forceful and laboured declarations, including his *credo* (shortly to follow) that 'There's a divinity that shapes our ends, / Rough-hew them how we will.' Hamlet's 'mutines in the bilboes' are apparently rebels who attempted to take over the ship, failed, and are shackled together in the hold, probably awaiting execution upon the return to port.[54] The ship, then, like Hamlet's Denmark and like the Ghost's resting place, is a prison, and Hamlet is a constrained fellow of the mutineers, being 'bound to revenge.' Interestingly, Hamlet does not specify the 'kind of fighting' that took place in his heart; as the prisoners are shoved under the deck, to mutter and toss in the dark, so Hamlet forces out of his consciousness the conflict he would prefer to be unaware of. The shackling of the mutineers suggests, in a conventional Tudor image that Shakespeare had used in *Henry V*, the passions that rational men must subjugate.[55] The inference is that these 'mutines' are analogous to the dark, rebellious feelings that Hamlet must fetter before he can proceed to create his calm, providential tale.[56] Throughout the rest of the play, however, one can catch the sound of telltale groans and the clinking of chains underneath Hamlet's affirmations.

Hamlet, the Ghost, and the Ghost of Hamlet

In both its content and the manner of its telling, Hamlet's tale to Horatio marks an important stage in what could be called his growing ghostliness. There is, for instance, something distinctly wraith-like in his drifting through the darkness of the ship's hold in the dead of night and slipping into the cabins of sleepers. More disconcertingly, in Hamlet's dealing with Horatio there is a lack of forthrightness and of direct engagement that is reminiscent of how the Ghost works in the play. Hamlet's key similarity to the Ghost is rhetorical; his tale to Horatio replicates the manner of the Ghost's tale to himself in 1.5. Like the Ghost's, Hamlet's story gains force through the speaker's manipulation of his hearer's expectations. Indeed, Hamlet begins to prepare Horatio long before he tells his story. In the letter that Horatio receives in 4.6, Hamlet speaks of his rescue by the pirates but does not mention the sealed letter. Instead, in a Ghost-like idiom he makes an alarming request of his friend: 'repair thou to me with as much speed as thou wouldest fly death. I have words to speak in thine ear will make thee dumb, yet are they much too light for the bore of the matter' (4.6.23–6). Just as the Ghost teased Hamlet with the prospect of thinking the unthinkable, so Hamlet promises to speak words to Horatio that will terrify him and yet be less horrific than the unspeakable reality he has experienced. In specifying that the words 'will make thee dumb,' Hamlet recalls the grotesque somatic effects ('harrow up thy soul, freeze thy young blood') that the Ghost attributes to the tale he could tell.

After Hamlet creates these awesome expectations in Horatio, he takes his time before he tells him what happened. Though Hamlet and Horatio are together throughout the entirety of 5.1, Hamlet does not start his promised story until the beginning of the following scene. When Hamlet finally tells Horatio, we notice a change in his manner of address. Earlier in the play, Hamlet had spoken to Horatio, and only to Horatio, with unduplicitous directness, in a 'communication [that] is, compared to everything else in the play, so open, face-to-face, warm and free.'[57] But now Hamlet's procedure is quite deliberate, and he begins with a slow build-up by recounting what he had previously said in the letter: 'So much for this, sir, now shall you see the other – / You do remember all the circumstance' (5.2.1–2). As his newly formal address to Horatio ('sir') indicates here and three lines later, Hamlet now shows a catechist's concentration on getting the response he wants.[58] As he takes Horatio through his story, Hamlet often cues comments and suggests appropriate questions. In Rosenberg's apt characterization, Hamlet is '[h]is father's son' as 'he tells his story masterfully, building suspense through rhetorical questions to climaxes.'[59] The entire narrative is controlled and controlling. It goes without saying that there is a pervasive contradiction between the content and the form of Hamlet's story, as its emphatically designated moral (rashness and indiscretion are best) contravenes the premeditated manner in which it is told.

In addition to the contradiction informing it, a dark irony hangs over Hamlet's story. As we have seen, the narrative is Hamlet's attempt to define himself in morally acceptable terms (to himself) and to remove his father's dread command as a motive for action. The story insists that Hamlet was not plotting on the ship, and thus tacitly it says that he will not be acting as a revenger. Indeed, Hamlet's story is his alternative to the revenge script that the Ghost attempted to impose on him in act 1. The irony crystallizes when we realize that, in telling the story as he does, Hamlet is modelling his behaviour on the Ghost's abusive treatment of him on the ramparts. As Hamlet will insist with great emotion at his death, his tale is 'my story,' but we can see that the Ghost is functioning in effect as its ghostwriter. As in the *Henry IV* plays, a son's desperate attempt to become autonomous involves taking a page from his father's book.

The connection of Hamlet with the Ghost reaches its climax at the end of the play, but it has largely gone unnoticed, as critics have tended to interpret the ending in the providentialist terms that Hamlet conveniently provides when he lectures Horatio on the merits of rough-hewn work, the meaning of fallen sparrows, and the fact that 'the readiness is all' (5.2.222). As a chorus of critics' voices has it, Hamlet has undergone a sea change on the voyage to England and returns as a mature and spiritually enlightened individual. To cite only a few formulations, Hamlet has reached 'a state of psychological harmony'; or he is a 'new man' having 'achieved a sense of his own identity'; or he experiences a 'regeneration' that is the counterpart of his earlier, downward 'transformation.'[60] But the close of the play is more problematic, and certainly Hamlet's behaviour more disturbing, than these interpretations acknowledge. As in the case of the similar misinterpretations of the final scene of *1 Henry IV*, there is an understandable desire on the part of critics to see a completed pattern of maturation in the protagonist, an evolutionary process in which Hal or Hamlet grows into his mature self. But Hal, as we saw in previous chapters, is aware of the cost of becoming his father's creature, and he enacts a subtle revenge against his father's control by freeing the Douglas at the very end of *Part One*. Hamlet's situation is similar to Hal's in that he too is outwardly victorious over his enemies but also embittered about the patriarchal force that impelled him to act in a way he would not have freely chosen.

At first glance, it may appear that by mortally wounding and then poisoning Claudius, Hamlet has avenged his father's murder and thus (finally) discharged the vow he made to the Ghost. But there is no textual evidence to indicate that Hamlet is indeed avenging his father, and some tangible evidence to indicate that he is not. As many people have noted, Hamlet makes no explicit reference to his father when he kills Claudius and instead declares 'Follow my mother' (5.2.327). The Prince's last reference to the elder Hamlet comes 250 lines before his killing of Claudius, and it is to 'my king' rather than 'my father.'[61] The paucity of references to the elder Hamlet is particularly striking, since the Ghost insisted on being remembered and since Hamlet earlier was bitter about how quickly his father had been forgotten at court (3.2.125–35). In the graveyard scene Hamlet's failure to remember his father is brought home by his moving recollection of Yorick, the king's jester. Not only does he speak of Yorick with an affection that had been completely missing from his references to his father, but Hamlet's 'Alas, poor Yorick' (5.1.184) suggests a substitution of this 'fellow of infinite jest' for the Ghost, whom he had earlier addressed with 'Alas, poor ghost' (1.5.4).[62]

Moreover, since a convention of revenge tragedy is that the avenger declares the meaning of the retribution when he commits it, Hamlet's silence is all the more emphatic. Indeed, Hamlet's killing of Claudius could not be more unlike the straightforward revenge of a son for his father at the close of John Marston's contemporary *Antonio's Revenge*. When he stabs his father's murderer, Marston's revenger clearly stipulates 'This for my father's blood' (5.5.75). In Marston there can be no doubt about the murdered father's approval because his Ghost declares, ''Tis done, and now my soul shall sleep in rest. / Sons that revenge their father's blood are blest' (5.5.81–2). In *Hamlet*, however, what Philip Edwards calls 'The Silence of the Ghost' at the close leaves the attitude of the father as well as the son unspecified.[63]

Though Hamlet does not mention either his father or the Ghost at the end, it is clever but not accurate to say that he 'gives up the Ghost.'[64] After the deaths of Gertrude, Claudius, and Laertes, Hamlet's situation comes to resemble very closely the Ghost's at the beginning, and the Prince appears to be aware of the fact. Indeed, there is a very precise parallel between the two situations. Hamlet has expressed in his first soliloquy a willingness to die and perhaps even to take his own life. But the Ghost imposes on him a role that he must play; it tells Hamlet a story about the past that no innocent person knows and urges him to 'Remember me.' Just as Hamlet had earlier mimicked the Ghost's rhetoric in telling his tale to Horatio, he now imitates the Ghost even more closely in his insistence that Horatio remember him by telling his tale and thus communicating the truth that will otherwise be unknown. Indeed, Hamlet speaks as a kind of ghost when he addresses his friend:

> Horatio, I am dead,
> Thou livest. Report me and my cause aright
> To the unsatisfied.   5.2.338–40

As it had when he first told the story to Horatio, Hamlet's rhetoric once again imitates the Ghost's. Like the Ghost, who avers that he 'could a tale unfold' that would be harrowing, Hamlet gestures toward what he might say but cannot: 'Had I but time ... O, I could tell you' (5.2.336–7).[65]

In a twist that Hamlet surely does not expect, for the first time Horatio resists the plan that his friend has for him. Responding to Hamlet's request, Horatio bluntly declares, 'Never believe it; / I am more an antique Roman than a Dane' (5.2.340–1). Whether 'Never believe it' means '*I* will never believe it' or '*you* should never believe it,' Horatio forcefully refuses to play the role of designated mouthpiece that Hamlet has assigned him. In response to this defiance, Hamlet pulls out all the stops, expending a good deal of his remaining energy in a series of sharp, monosyllabic commands: 'As th' art a man, / Give me the cup. Let go! By heaven, I'll ha't!' (5.2.342–3). Hamlet's insistent 'Let go' contradicts the philosophical quietism of the 'let it be' he had pronounced only six lines earlier; throughout this long scene he has spoken as if he had no agency, but now he seizes control with ferocious urgency.[66] Though the Quarto and Folio texts lack a stage direction (a shortcoming not always remedied by modern editors), it is clear the dying Hamlet wrests the cup from Horatio after declaring 'I'll ha't.'

Having prevented Horatio's escape into death, Hamlet sends him on a mission, his language closely echoing the words the Ghost had used to command him:

O God, Horatio, what a wounded name,
Things standing thus unknown, shall I leave behind me!
If thou didst ever hold me in thy heart,
Absent thee from felicity a while,
And in this harsh world draw thy breath in pain
To tell my story.   5.2.344–9

The repetition of the Ghost's 'If thou didst ever thy dear father love' (1.5.23) in 'If thou didst ever hold me in thy heart' is particularly chilling. As the Ghost had practised emotional blackmail on Hamlet, Hamlet now does the same to Horatio. Sometimes noting the echo of the Ghost and sometimes not, a number of critics have attempted to read Hamlet's words as an expression of solicitude for his friend, perhaps even a way to save him from the mortal sin of suicide.[67] But these critical interventions ring hollow. While it is true that he prevents

Horatio from committing self-slaughter, Hamlet seems more concerned with himself than with his friend, and hence he concedes that death by suicide would be 'felicity.' Indeed, the entire passage – and especially Hamlet's injunction to 'in this harsh world draw thy breath in pain' – expresses a shocking indifference to the autonomy and well-being of the devoted Horatio, who is sentenced to remain among the living to tell Hamlet's story. Hamlet has played upon affection to undermine the resolve of the person who cares most about him.

Perhaps Hamlet has a glimmering that his Ghost-like manipulation of Horatio is not worthy of himself, for he immediately acts in a way that cannot make the Ghost happy. In his last and most perplexing action, Hamlet gives his 'dying voice' to advance Fortinbras as the new king of Denmark. Hamlet's action is puzzling on several grounds. Certainly, his 'election' of *anyone* is strange, for it contradicts his quietist commitment to trusting in Providence. Also his declaration that 'I do prophesy th' election lights / On Fortinbras' (5.2.355–6) clangs against his still echoing assertion that 'we defy augury' (5.2.219). And why Fortinbras? Critics' explanations have ranged from political necessity ('there is no princely Dane to rule his kingdom'), to the psychoanalytical-symbolic (Fortinbras is 'Hamlet reborn' since he has been spared the Oedipal conflict that devastated the Prince), and to the weirdly strained ('in his return from the killing-fields of Poland, Fortinbras appears as the figure of old Hamlet *redivivus*, in whom Hamlet can identify the heroic past he idealized').[68] But all of these interpretations ignore the central fact that in act 4, scene 4 (in the second Quarto only) Hamlet had expressed considerable ambivalence toward the mindless militarism of Fortinbras, an example 'gross as earth' of a 'spirit with divine ambition puff'd' (4.4.46, 49).[69]

When we recall that 1 Henry IV ends with a similarly puzzling action by the princely protagonist (Hal's freeing of the Douglas), another interpretation for Hamlet's naming of Fortinbras suggests itself. Just as Prince Hal's ransoming of his former enemy is an outwardly chivalrous action that is really a covert act of aggression against his father, Hamlet's apparently generous choice of Fortinbras is almost certainly – though critics have only rarely seen it as such – an oblique retaliation against his father's Ghost.[70] In electing Fortinbras, young Hamlet is returning to the Norwegian royal family the lands for which old Hamlet had risked his life and killed old Fortinbras. But Hamlet goes further than restoring what the elder Fortinbras lost, for he cedes not only what his father had staked but also the entire Danish kingdom.

Hamlet throws away his entire patrimony. Naming Fortinbras to the throne is Hamlet's conclusive act of revenge in the play, but it is revenge not on behalf of the Ghost but against it. In killing Claudius, Hamlet may have done what the Ghost wanted, and he may even have internalized the Ghost in his own actions, but now on his deathbed he attempts to undo its destructive legacy.

At the beginning of act 5, we are told by the gravedigger of an uncanny coincidence that happened thirty years earlier: Hamlet was born on the very day his father defeated the elder Fortinbras. On that day a patriarch's dream came true for old Hamlet: he conquered a fiefdom and fathered a prince who would rule his possessions after his death. At the end, however, Hamlet walks into his own death and for good measure gives away the kingdom, thereby forfeiting a patrimony too oppressive to bear. For most of the play, Barbara Everett's formulation holds true that '*Hamlet* is the story of a son who must – as the young always must – by living accept an inheritance largely unwanted from the generation of the fathers.'[71] In *dying* as he does, however, Hamlet rejects that inheritance, subtly avenging himself against his father and definitively exclaiming against his own succession.

7 *King Lear*: The Usurpation of Fathers – and of Fathers and Sons

In the great arc of Shakespeare's career, the depiction of fathers and sons in *King Lear* is simultaneously both a climax and an attenuation. Seen in the light of the earlier plays, the depiction of fathers and sons looks to be climactic: it picks up and brings to a new level of intensity familiar motifs. But within *King Lear* itself, the theme – inventive and intense as it is – proves to be less significant than other concerns. In formal terms, Shakespeare's handling of fathers and sons is restricted to a sub-plot, subordinated to the story of King Lear and his daughters. Throughout the play the sub-plot relationships among the Earl of Gloucester and his two sons are sharply counterpointed against those in the main plot, making *King Lear* a play in which it would be manifestly inadequate to discuss fathers and sons without reference to fathers and daughters; the vivid depiction of a father and his sons is enveloped within the play's more moving and more profound examination of a father and his daughters.

The father-son relationships in *King Lear* are all located within a single family: Gloucester and his two sons, the legitimate Edgar and the illegitimate Edmund. Shakespeare has set up two sons as foils before, but this is the first time the foils are brothers (more precisely, half-brothers). In these two father-son relationships we see a sustained study of the shifting dynamics of power between the old and the young. The Earl of Gloucester belongs to a long line of anxious, vulnerable Shakespearean fathers stretching all the way back to the exhausted Master Gunner in *1 Henry VI*. But with a difference. Being of an advanced age, perhaps as old as eighty, Gloucester is intensely aware of his weakness, and his consequent attempt to control his sons quickly leads to disaster. The desperate vulnerability of his old age gives Gloucester's downfall an unprecedented pathos among Shakespeare's fathers; for the first time a father is literally usurped by his son, stripped of his title and his powers. The bastard Edmund represents the extreme of filial insubordination in Shakespeare, and the blinding of Gloucester terribly realizes the abject helplessness that Shakespeare's threatened fathers had been fearing all along. Edgar, the legitimate brother, similarly has antecedents in earlier Shakespearean sons, and especially in the recurrent figure of the ambivalent son who risks his life to rescue his father but also covertly contrives to avenge himself against that same father. Given his father's pathetic weakness, this act of vengeance represents a new extreme in its surreptitious cruelty.

If Gloucester and his sons hark back to plays like *1 Henry VI, 1 Henry IV,* and *Hamlet,* Lear and his daughters point toward plays not yet written. In Shakespeare's forthcoming plays, the relationship of father and daughter will prove to have greater possibilities for spiritual growth and transformation than does that of father and son. In the reconciliation of Lear with Cordelia, the splendidly unambivalent daughter who rescues him more feelingly than any Shakespearean son saves his father, we see the parent-child relationship that most informs the plays to come. *King Lear* not only depicts the usurpation of a father by a son, but it also conducts its own quiet usurpation of what had been a central theme by subordinating father and son to father and daughter.

Bonds and Bondage: The Politics of Fathers and Sons

Never before in Shakespeare has absolute paternal authority proven to be so fragile and fleeting as in the opening scenes of *King Lear*. Not only are King Lear and the Earl of Gloucester brought low, but much to their dismay they are reduced to the status of dependents, becoming in effect the children of their children. The parable of the Prodigal Son is ironically inverted, as fathers are driven from their castles by angry children, forced to confront elemental hardships, and finally harboured by the loyal children whom they had rashly banished.[1] Lear and Gloucester become fathers who are doubly 'child-changed' (4.7.16) – changed *by* their children and also changed *into* children. As Goneril exclaims with jubilant contempt, 'old fools are babes again' (1.3.19). But, despite their common trajectory of precipitous decline, Lear and Gloucester should not be conflated. They personify distinct approaches to the dilemmas of advanced age, including the two primary alternatives for old Elizabethan men vested with patriarchal power: to transfer power before one's death, becoming a 'sojourner' in the house of a dependent (Lear), or to attempt to hang on to everything until the bitter end (Gloucester).[2] There is also a correspondingly different inflection in the paternal anxieties of the two patriarchs; Lear fears primarily the loss of respect and 'ceremonious affection,' while Gloucester fears the loss of his power. Ultimately, the fathers' differing paternal anxieties and strategies may derive from a fundamental and immeasurable difference: the gender of their children. For Lear, his daughters (and especially Cordelia) hold out the promise of a receptive, nurturing love, while Gloucester perceives his sons from the outset as dangerous rivals to his rule.

In the Gloucester sub-plot, Shakespeare returns with new intensity to a familiar concern: the tension between the institutional and the affective, or the public and the private, dimensions of the father-and-son relationship. As their sometimes elaborate denials made clear, early modern advocates of family hierarchy were aware of this troubling doubleness. The Puritan clergyman William Gouge, author of the treatise *Of Domesticall Duties*, describes parental attitudes as a kind of *discordia concors*, emphasizing 'that *authority and affection* which is mixed together in parents. The *authority* of parents requireth *fear* in children: and their *affection, love*. So entire and so ardent is parents' *affection* towards their children, as it would make children too bold and insolent if there were not *authority* mixed therewith to work *fear*: and so supreme and absolute is their *authority* over them, as it would make children like slaves to dread their parents, if a fatherly *affection* were not tempered therewith to breed *love*.'[3] Gouge concludes this elegant exercise by saying that a '*loving-fear* or a *fearing-love*' is the basis of the duties of children. One may question, however, whether such delicate blendings of opposed emotions, such admirably well-tempered parents and children, are as likely to occur in real families as in treatises. Certainly, Shakespeare's plays are considerably less than sanguine about this harmonious coexistence of opposites; there is always tension between the public, political dimension, in which the father is a ruler over the children who must obey him, and the private, affective dimension, in which he simply loves and nourishes his children. In *King Lear* the disparity between institutional and affective exigencies is particularly emphatic, as is to be expected when fathers are the literal rulers of the land as well as the figurative rulers of the family.

Shakespeare's scepticism about the likelihood of the prescribed blending of political authority and domestic affection in fathers is apparent in his transformation of his principal source for the Glouces-ter family story, a brief tale in Sir Philip Sidney's *Arcadia*. Sidney's account of the blinded, dethroned King of Paphlagonia and his two sons – one legitimate and kindly, the other illegitimate and unnaturally cruel – is essentially a moral exemplum. Even though he has been ban-ished by his foolish father, the good son returns to him at great risk and saves him from the bastard brother. The bond between father and son is further idealized by the King's remorse for his rejection of his son and by his attempt to commit suicide so as to make unnecessary his son's dangerous commitment to saving him. Throughout the story Sidney emphasizes a natural bond that joins the son to the father through the private virtue of love and the public virtue of duty. Thus, when the good son enlists two knights to help him defend his father, he addresses them by asking 'if either of you have a father, and feel what duetiful affection is engraffed in a son's heart' (Bullough 7:404). Sidney's common Elizabethan spelling of 'dutiful' as 'duetiful' emphasizes the familiar element of filial indebtedness (what is due the father), and yet this stress on obligation is balanced by the 'affection' that sons feel for their fathers in their heart. The horticultural metaphor of 'engraffed' deepens the sense that the son's affectionate debt is a natural, organic impulse. At the end of Sidney's brief story, this idealized blending of love and duty, affection and indebtedness, is alluded to once again in the father's funeral obsequies, in which we learn that the son 'no less lovingly performed all duties to him dead, than alive' (Bullough 7:407).

Where Sidney's romance idealizes, Shakespeare's tragedy ironizes and historicizes. In *King Lear* the depiction of Gloucester and his sons explores the dark side of the relationship. Indeed, the Gloucester family personifies the problems that Lawrence Stone – in his cele-brated and exaggerated account of patriarchal relations – attributed to the nuclear family of early modern times: an emotional coldness and distancing that derives from the father's insistence on discipline and deference.[4] For Gloucester and his sons, an exclusive concern with the public, political dimension of the relationship has resulted in the atrophy of the personal and affective. This severe imbalance manifests itself in the competition that separates the father from his sons (and they from each other).[5]

In the case of Edmund, the distance from the father is manifested in geographical as well as emotional terms. Gloucester can scarcely know

Edmund, nor does he wish to. In the opening scene he speaks of his younger, illegitimate son as if he were not present, blandly observing to Kent that 'He hath been out nine years, and away he shall again' (1.1.32–3). Editors obscure the evidence for paternal neglect when they gloss Gloucester's pronouncement by referring to the custom of English nobility to send their sons out for service.[6] The legitimate Edgar, we notice, has never been sent away, so Gloucester's readiness to send Edmund out (again) is effectively the first of the play's many banishments. Gloucester's resistance to owning his bastard son is apparent in his evasive response to Kent's question 'Is not this your son, my lord?': 'His breeding, sir, hath been at my charge' (1.1.8–9). Though Gloucester speaks of acceptance ('the whoreson must be acknowledged' [1.1.24]), his language reveals how uneasy he is in the public presence of his illegitimate offspring. To acknowledge Edmund would be to undermine the system of values that Gloucester defines himself in terms of.

More interesting, because more problematic, is the distance separating Gloucester from his lawful son and heir. Clearly, Edgar and Gloucester are not socially alienated: Edgar speaks to Edmund of having spent two hours with his father on the previous night (1.2.155). But there is scarcely a relationship of intimacy and trust between father and son, and it is their mutual suspicion that allows the ridiculously easy success of Edmund's scheme, which is of course predicated on keeping them apart. Gloucester's first reference to Edgar (after his comments on Edmund's illegitimacy) is revealing: 'But I have a son, sir, by order of law, some year elder than this, who yet is no dearer in my account' (1.1.19–21). With its stress on the institutional 'order of law' and its suggestion that paternal feeling is related to financial accounting, the sentence ties together Edgar's legality with Gloucester's lack of affection. As Harry Berger Jr has observed, Edmund's plot allows Gloucester to confirm suspicions about his legitimate successor that he seems eager to entertain.[7] Gloucester's perception is that it is Edgar, his lawful successor, who poses the threat to his authority, and of course every inheritor by primogeniture represents the undoing, as well as the dearest hope, of his progenitor.

Gloucester himself does not realize how narrowly political his relationship to his sons has become, and, indeed, he often speaks of his love for them, but in ironic, inappropriate contexts. Thus, after he has violently condemned Edgar as a villain, Gloucester sees himself as a victimized, perhaps even sacrificial figure, describing himself as 'his father, that so tenderly and entirely loves him' (1.2.96–7). Later, on the heath and in the presence of the disguised Edgar, Gloucester laments that

> I had a son,
> Now outlaw'd from my blood; he sought my life,
> But lately, very late. I lov'd him, friend,
> No father his son dearer.   3.4.166–9

Lear is like Gloucester in that he fails to notice the inconsistency between the cruelty of his actions toward his children and the pity he feels for himself as a victim of their supposed ingratitude. In the scene immediately after he has cursed Goneril by beseeching Nature to 'Dry up in her the organs of increase' (1.4.279), Lear can still describe himself as 'So kind a father!' (1.5.32).

Nowhere are Gloucester's limitations clearer than in his understanding of the 'bond' linking parent and child. The idea of a bond between the generations is richly ambiguous, as it can suggest either a profound spiritual unity, or (with reference to the etymological origin of 'bond' as a manacle or fetter) a binding legal commitment.[8] In orthodox Elizabethan thinking, this 'bond' is often specified to be 'natural,' thereby qualifying the sense of legal constraint with suggestions of the organic and instinctual. An excellent example of this usage occurs in the *True Chronicle Historie of King Leir*, an anonymous play that was in Shakespeare's mind when he was writing *his* version of the story. After the Gallian king has married the banished Cordella and returned with her to France, he worries about her continuing sorrow for her father. She responds to his solicitude by stressing the natural inevitability of her grief:

> O, grieve not you, my Lord, you have no cause:
> Let not my passions move your mind a whit:
> For I am bound by nature, to lament
> For his ill will, that life to me first lent.
> If so the stock be dried with disdain,
> Withered and sere the branch must needs remain.   Bullough 7:367

She begins by characterizing her grief in the conventional terms of filial duty, as she is suffering for a father who 'life to me first lent.' But the botanical analogy that follows shows that she is 'bound by nature' on a deeper level: she partakes of the being of the parent-stock, even if what her father feels toward her is disdain.[9] To be 'bound by nature,' then, is to be nourished by an inner filial mandate that is inseparable from life itself.

In Shakespeare's *King Lear*, the talk of parent-child bonds has an altogether darker, more negative tone. One response of Lear and Gloucester to the shifting ground under their feet is to insist, as Elizabethan authorities often did, on the sanctity and power of the parent-child 'bond' as a means of bolstering a generation under duress.[10] Unlike the passage from the *True Chronicle Historie* quoted above, in *King Lear* the references to familial bonds are more often made by parents than children. And instead of stressing nurture and organic growth, these references emphasize filial duty as compulsory deference and moral obligation. It is as members of a gerontocracy that the fathers understand parent-child bonds in terms of political constraints. When Lear sees Kent in the stocks and realizes that his own authority is melting away, he praises Regan for observing her filial duties better than her sister:

> *Lear.* Thou better know'st
> The offices of nature, bond of childhood,
> Effects of courtesy, dues of gratitude:
> Thy half o' th' kingdom hast thou not forgot,
> Wherein I thee endow'd.
> *Reg.* Good sir, to th' purpose.
> *Lear.* Who put my man i' th' stocks? 2.4.177–82

Revealingly, Lear slides from the philosophical generality of 'offices of nature' to the pressure of the 'bond of childhood,' and then to the blatantly coercive specificity of 'dues of gratitude.' He then proceeds to remind Regan that everything she possesses is owing to him. When she ignores his abstractions and asks what he is driving at, Lear's quick, monosyllabic response suggests that the high-sounding concepts he has invoked have little more than a strategic value for him.

An indirect but still illuminating exposure of the paternal mind-set occurs when Edmund recreates for Gloucester the conversation that had supposedly transpired between himself and the murderous Edgar. Telling Gloucester what he fearfully wants to hear, Edmund declares that Edgar sought to

Persuade me to the murther of your lordship,
But that I told him, the revengive gods
'Gainst parricides did all the thunder bend,
Spoke, with how manifold and strong a bond
The child was bound to th' father ...   2.1.44–8

In these lines the gods stand up for fathers. Though the bond between father and son is said to be 'manifold,' the next line specifies that it is strictly unidirectional, the child being 'bound to th' father' (rather than parent and child bound to each other).

Not long after he has read the forged letter attributed to Edgar, Gloucester places the conflict between fathers and sons in the context of impending apocalypse: 'Love cools, friendship falls off, brothers divide: in cities, mutinies; in countries, discord; in palaces, treason; and the bond crack'd 'twixt son and father' (1.2.106–9). Gloucester's sequencing of chaotic divisions is revealing: he groups the violated father-and-son bond not with the disruptions of affection and family relationship at the beginning of his sequence but rather with the forms of political disorder at the close. For Gloucester, the bond between father and son has more to do with obligation than affection, and he allows his political anxieties to trump his personal feelings for Edgar.

Gloucester's anxiety about his uncertain rule is of course galvanized by the collapse of Lear's authority. In his response to the sudden, chaotic developments in the kingdom, one can hear a breathless consternation:

Kent banish'd thus? and France in choler parted?
And the King gone to-night? Prescrib'd his pow'r,
Confin'd to exhibition?   1.2.23–5

It is revealing that Gloucester makes no reference to Cordelia's recent banishment, as if the fate of a mere daughter is of no great moment in affairs of state. What shakes Gloucester to the core is that the King himself has been limited in power by his children and reduced to living on a pension. Clearly, no father's privileges are safe. In the event, Gloucester proves ridiculously easy for Edmund to manipulate, and we see the beginnings of a pervasive irony: Gloucester's anxiety about losing power leads directly to his usurpation. He is undone by the fear of being undone: 'I would unstate myself to be in a due resolution' (1.2.99–100).

Placing no great faith in his own intrinsic power, Gloucester assumes that his sons want to replace him, and he fears that they have the energy to be successful. When fathers see the relationship in political terms, then turnabout is fair play – the children will see the relationship politically but with the locus of power simply inverted, and so perhaps Edmund's cold scheming against his father and brother is but a reflection of his father's understanding of family politics. From this perspective, Edmund's forged letter is truly a family document in that he ascribes his own ideas to Edgar, and in turn these ideas brilliantly reflect and provoke Gloucester's deepest worries: 'This policy and reverence of age makes the world bitter to the best of our times; keeps our fortunes from us till our oldness cannot relish them. I begin to find an idle and fond bondage in the oppression of aged tyranny, who sways, not as it hath power, but as it is suffer'd' (1.2.46–51). This cynical argument defines the relationship between father and son in strictly political terms ('policy,' 'fortunes,' 'power,' and especially 'tyranny'), with affection and instinct playing no part at all. To respect elders is not an acknowledgment of natural, life-giving bonds but an ignominious acquiescence to 'idle and fond bondage.'

Though Shakespeare derived the outline of the Gloucester family plot from Sidney's *Arcadia*, he did not find in this moral romance the concern with the psychology of paternal anxiety that he explores in Gloucester. It was in the far more sceptical musing on fathers and sons in Montaigne's *Essais* (which had been recently translated into English by John Florio) that Shakespeare found the inner core of his depiction of the Gloucester family. Of particular importance is the essay 'Of the Affection of Fathers to Their Children' (II, viii), which explores the troubled relations between elderly fathers and sons who have come of age.[11] Interestingly, Montaigne does not acknowledge the ethical 'bond of nature' said to link father and son. Indeed, in another essay he blithely remarks that 'There have nations been found, where, by custom, children killed their parents, and others, where parents slew their children.'[12] Rather, he says that, if there is any 'truly-natural law' besides the impulse to self-preservation, it is that fathers love their offspring more than they are loved in return, a variation on the theological idea that 'love flows downward' or 'love descends.'[13] This asymmetry of affection means that fathers should not expect a benign natural impulse to give them their children's love.

Montaigne is especially insightful about how aging fathers can perceive their virile sons as a threat, a constant reminder of impending mortality. (Surely Gloucester's fear of political impotence illuminates his uneasy bravado about the 'good sport' at the conceiving of Edmund.) Speaking on behalf of fathers, Montaigne declares that 'It vexeth and grieveth us when we see them [sons] following us at our heels, supposing they solicit us to be gone' (2:68). Fathers fear that the very order of things prescribes that sons 'cannot indeed, neither be, nor live, but by our being and life' (2:68). Or, as Edmund's more aggressive formula has it, 'The younger rises when the old doth fall' (3.3.25). The perception of life with sons as a competitive, zero-sum game leads fathers to deny economic and spiritual sustenance to their offspring, prolonging an enforced adolescence and dependency. In turn, sons begrudge the well-being of their fathers and seek to hasten their removal. For Montaigne the rational solution is for fathers to step aside (while prudently retaining at least some of their power) when the time comes, thereby allowing sons access to their patrimony when they are most eager and capable.

Especially pertinent to Gloucester is one of Montaigne's examples of helpless paternal anxiety, a once vigorous but now aged man who fears becoming dependent on his family and thus strives to 'preserve his mastery, and to maintain his absoluteness.'[14] But his family and servants manipulate him by playing on his anxieties: 'he frets and consumes himself with cark and care and vigilancy (all which is but a juggling and ground for his [family] to play upon, and cozen him the more)' (2:76). In a Montaignesque moment, Gloucester completely and irrevocably loses control of himself in response to Edmund's shrewd arousal of his deepest anxiety. When Gloucester asks him if he has ever heard Edgar articulate attitudes similar to those expressed in the (forged) letter, Edmund touches the exposed nerve: 'Never, my lord. But I have heard him oft maintain it to be fit that, sons at perfect age and fathers declin'd, the father should be as ward to the son, and the son manage his revenue' (1.2.71–4). Unlike the forged letter, these comments do not insinuate murder, and yet Gloucester responds to them with a greater vehemence. It is as if the very matter-of-fact, domestic possibility of becoming 'ward to his son' is more appalling to Gloucester than death itself. Gloucester's premonition of powerlessness leads to hysterical overreaction and to losing his superiority in the very act of attempting to preserve it. Not only will Gloucester be usurped politically by his illegitimate son, but ultimately he will be usurped in more subtle ways by his legitimate son, in effect becoming what he most feared to be: his child's ward.

Edgar and Edmund – Brothers in Ambivalence

Given its many points of contact with the story of Lear, Sidney's tale of the King of Paphlagonia and his two sons offered Shakespeare a resonant sub-plot for his play. But in one regard it is deeply un-Shakespearean; in its representation of simplified filial attitudes, Sidney's tale differs markedly from Shakespeare's pre-*King Lear* plays. In place of Shakespeare's characteristic emphasis on filial ambivalence, Sidney parcels out to the King of Paphlagonia's sons attitudes that are completely antithetical and unmixed. Not only is the illegitimate son treacherous and unkind, but the legitimate son fulfils to the letter an Elizabethan clergyman's definition of honouring one's parents: 'If the parent be blind, the child must be an eye unto him; if he be lame, he must be a staff to uphold him.'[15] In conduct carefully labelled as 'filial piety' (Bullough 7:406), the good son wishes to sacrifice himself for his father, while the evil son wishes to kill him. Sidney emphasizes the schematic nature of the opposition when he alerts the reader that the story is 'worthy to be remembered for the un-used [i.e., unusual] examples therein, as well of true natural goodness, as of wretched ungratefulness' (Bullough 7:404). In *A Defence of Poetry*, Sidney celebrated the power of the poet to create moving pictures of virtue and vice, and the King of Paphlagonia's sons are two such examples.

At first glance it may appear that in *King Lear* Shakespeare jettisoned his previous fascination with filial ambivalence and embraced Sidney's dichotomized presentation. Certainly, the dramatist retained the actions in Sidney that most clearly demarcate the ethical difference between the sons, as Edmund brings about the usurpation and subsequent blinding of his father, while Edgar ministers to Gloucester in an Aeneas-like fashion, risking his own life to rescue him from certain death.[16] There is no son in Shakespeare who betrays his father more cruelly than Edmund, and no son more conspicuously and heroically dutiful than Edgar. Not surprisingly, many critics have described Edmund and Edgar in black and white, Sidneian terms, stressing that the 'contrast between the two brothers could not be sharper; they appear like back to back pictures of Vice and Virtue in an emblem book.'[17]

Even if Edmund is the most evil of Shakespeare's sons and Edgar arguably the most loyal, each possesses ambivalent feelings that prevent him from becoming either pure good or evil. If there is an absolute antithesis between Edgar and Edmund, it is momentary, existing only at the very beginning of the play when we see Edgar as pitiably naive and Edmund as masterfully Machiavellian – one brother a complete dupe, the other a polished villain. As the action unfolds, however, this opening contrast becomes increasingly attenuated and indistinct.[18] The confusing similarity of their given names, not an issue with Sidney's 'Leonatus' and 'Plexirtus,' begins to be reflected in their actions. There is perhaps a hint of shared identity in the fact that the half-brothers exchange social roles; Gloucester declares Edgar a bastard and banishes him, while he legitimizes Edmund and makes him 'capable' of inheritance.[19] But, disturbingly, it is with regard to their treatment of their father that their similarities begin to come into focus. Edmund's deception and manipulation of his father before the blinding is balanced by Edgar's deception and manipulation of him after it. In more ways than one, Edgar picks up where Edmund leaves off.

The key similarity between Gloucester's two sons is their predilection for role playing and disguises, and once again Shakespeare's revision of Sidney is telling. In the *Arcadia* the theme of playing roles reveals the absolute difference between the brothers. The impulse to play-act is reserved for Sidney's illegitimate son, who masters the arts of deception and subverts his father through 'as much poisonous hypocrisy, desperate fraud, smooth malice, hidden ambition, and smiling envy, as in any living person could be harboured' (Bullough 7:404). True to the prevailing black and white opposition, Sidney's legitimate son manifests 'true natural goodness' and never adopts a disguise, even though he is being hunted by his brother. In Shakespeare, however, the acting/non-acting dichotomy quickly breaks down. Edgar, no less than Edmund, becomes alarmingly adept at disguise and deception. It can be argued that there is an ethical distinction between the brothers' motives for feigning, as Edmund play-acts to promote mischief while Edgar dons a disguise to save his skin, but Edgar discovers a brio in role-playing that clearly exceeds the demands of self-preservation. After declaring that 'Edgar I nothing am' (2.3.21), he dons a succession of disguises: crazed beggar (Tom o'Bedlam), uncouth rustic, helpful gentleman, and finally a nameless challenger to his brother in a trial by combat.

The vigorous role-playing of Edmund and Edgar is a characteristic they share, we recall, with many of Shakespeare's sons in previous plays; so, too, is a closely related phenomenon, their lack of self-knowledge. As with Hal and Hamlet, so it is with Edgar and Edmund:

the adoption of a mask deceives the wearer as well as his intended audience. Neither son is what he wishes to be or thinks he is. Edmund prides himself on being a fully liberated, free-thinking individual, the very opposite of his contemptibly credulous brother and superstitious father, and, obligingly, most commentators have taken him at his word. But in part Edmund's mockery stems from a desire to cauterize feelings that would otherwise render him vulnerable, and his social values are much more similar to his father's than he is willing to acknowledge.[20] It does not sentimentalize Shakespeare's depiction to say that Edmund yearns for the world of withheld family usages that he claims to despise.

Often one hears in Edmund's speeches, as in Hal's and Hamlet's, a line or two that quietly contradicts the vigorous argument he is making. A good example occurs in the middle of his sardonic 'Thou, Nature, art my goddess' (1.2.1) speech:

> Well then,
> Legitimate Edgar, I must have your land.
> Our father's love is to the bastard Edmund
> As to th' legitimate. Fine word, 'legitimate'!   1.2.15–18

The bitter repetition of 'legitimate' does not entirely conceal Edmund's pathetic attempt to assure himself of 'Our father's love,' a phrase in which each word reveals the force of familial relationship. Edmund seems to associate the acquisition of paternal land with the gaining of love, a confusion that Lear had made on a grander scale in the previous scene's division of the kingdom. What Thomas McFarland calls 'Edmund's pathos ... in his exclusion from significant human attention' is memorably expressed in his dying attempt to convince himself he has mattered to someone: 'Yet Edmund was belov'd!' (5.3.240).[21] Whatever else he may be, Edmund is not as simply cruel as his counterpart in Sidney, who is not only responsible for his father's usurpation and blinding but also appears with sadistic relish to have performed the deeds himself.[22]

If Edmund represents a humanizing of the wickedness of the illegitimate son in Sidney, Edgar represents a symmetrical amelioration of the legitimate son's virtue. Indeed, they are mirror images of each other; despite his evil, Edmund lets slip his need for his father's love, while Edgar's virtuous deeds conceal filial feelings of a negative cast. If Edmund thinks he is more villainous than he actually is, Edgar sees himself as less aggressive than he proves to be. If Edmund fails to take account of the ways he is like his father, Edgar refuses to see the ways in which he is actually punishing his father. We can see the half-brothers, then, as twin studies in the repression of filial feeling, with Edgar attempting to repress his anger toward his father and Edmund attempting to repress his need for his father's love.

Though in recent years there has been a salutary turn toward locating darker motives in Edgar than he expresses in deed and statement, these studies have failed to notice that he belongs to an unfolding series of ambivalent Shakespearean sons.[23] We can see Hal, Hamlet, and Edgar as a progression in which the son assumes increasingly complex disguises in order to release more deeply repressed emotions toward his progenitor. Primary among these inadequately acknowledged feelings is anger. Like Hal and Hamlet, Edgar never expresses indignation toward his father in his own voice, but one often detects in his theatrical ranting the presence of filial animus.[24] Edgar's anger is unmistakable when, outside the hovel, he sees his father for the first time since his banishment. When Gloucester suddenly appears out of the darkness, carrying a torch, Edgar's immediate response is mordant: 'This is the foul fiend Flibbertigibbet; he begins at curfew, and walks till the first cock; he gives the web and the pin, squinies the eye, and makes the hare-lip; mildews the white wheat, and hurts the poor creature of earth' (3.4.115–19). While there may be a note of mockery in the name Flibbertigibbet, there is nothing funny about what Edgar says of his doings. A restless prowler in the night, he is the enemy of the young, causing birth defects, blighting the promise of healthy growth, and in general 'hurt[ing] the poor creature of earth.' Driven into the darkness, Edgar has transformed his frightened father, who has ventured into the storm to aid Lear, into a demonic spirit.

Edgar's disguise as an escaped Bedlamite who thinks he is possessed by an evil spirit is brilliantly functional, for it allows him to express and perhaps exorcise emotions that he wishes to see as foreign to his proper identity as a son who observes the Fifth Commandment and says 'Obey thy parents, keep thy word's justice' (3.4.80–1). Thus, when Gloucester asks Edgar-as-Tom o'Bedlam his name, his son identifies himself as 'Poor Tom' and characterizes himself as one who 'in the fury of his heart, when the foul fiend rages, eats cow-dung for sallets; swallows the old rat and the ditch-dog' (3.4.131–3). After Gloucester disregards Tom's tale of woe and expresses instead a concern about the decorum of a beggar being in the presence of the

King, Edgar's response is a bitter indictment of social hierarchy in general and of his status-obsessed father in particular: 'The prince of darkness is a gentleman' (3.4.14). It is immediately after this thrust that Gloucester, speaking more wisely than he knows, declares that 'Our flesh and blood, my lord, is grown so vild / That it doth hate what gets it' (3.4.145–6).

It is typical of Edgar's Hamlet-like repression that his most aggressive act against his father is not an act at all but rather a refusal to act. A decisive moment in the relationship of Edgar and Gloucester comes when, soon after his father's blinding, Edgar hears him cry out,

> O dear son Edgar,
> The food of thy abused father's wrath!
> Might I but live to see thee in my touch,
> I'ld say I had eyes again.   4.1.21–4

Given Gloucester's earlier evasions and non-committal remarks about one son being 'no dearer' than the other, there is remarkable emotional force in 'O dear son Edgar.' To touch his son would be to be made whole again. Edgar's response to this poignant plea is to remain in disguise and to declare in an aside, 'O gods! Who is't can say, "I am at the worst"? / I am worse than e'er I was' (4.1.25–6). Despite its philosophical tenor, Edgar's comment seems unduly self-concerned, for it is in his power to rescue his father from feeling *his* worst simply by identifying himself. It is difficult not to read an element of anger into Edgar's refusal to do for his father what only he can do. For reasons we can only surmise, he is much more moved by the plight of Lear than of his own father.[25]

The detachment of the disguised Edgar from Gloucester is most disconcerting in the scene at the edge of the imaginary Dover Cliff. The kernel of the scene is in Sidney, where the blind father unsuccessfully has besought his loyal son to lead him to the top of a high rock from which he plans to leap to his death. But in the *Arcadia* the father is aware that his travelling companion is his son, and indeed he wishes to commit suicide so that he can cease to be a dangerous burden to him. Unlike Sidney's Paphlagonian king, Gloucester certainly would wish to live if he knew his son were alive. The question to ask is why, despite his obvious decency, does Edgar continue to conceal himself from the father who needs him so deeply? The traditional critical explanation has been to absolve Edgar of the taint of aggression and deviousness, either by reading the scene in exclusively symbolic terms (e.g., as a morality play) or by attributing altruistic motives to him. The latter interpretation posits that Edgar is pursuing a therapeutic strategy that would have been recognizable in Shakespeare's England, whether it be a form of exorcism, or a curing of a wounded spirit by imaginative means, or a delivery from the mortal sin of despair.[26] There is some merit in seeing Edgar as undertaking the office of a therapist, for he is consciously and conscientiously attempting to minister to his father, but it is misleading to stop there. Underneath Edgar's therapeutic program lurk darker, more ambivalent impulses.

Perhaps the best evidence for Edgar's being of two minds is his only statement of intention, a pair of lines that exculpatory interpretations of his behaviour stress heavily. In an aside, Edgar suddenly exclaims, 'Why I do trifle thus with his despair / Is done to cure it' (4.6.33–4). The usual critical assumption is that, being an aside, these lines are a transparent and, as it were, impersonal explanation of motive. But the immediate dramatic context is important: Edgar's explanatory aside follows immediately upon Gloucester's bidding him farewell 'With all my heart,' a phrase expressing a generous integrity of feeling that Edgar realizes he cannot reciprocate. Thus his explanation sounds as if it expresses his uneasy need to convince himself of his good intent. Still more revealing is Edgar's use of 'trifle' to characterize the supposedly curative action he is undertaking, for the word contains a deflected self-accusation, betraying Edgar's worry that he is indeed toying with his father. In this context, Edgar's avowal to himself that he is trifling with his father's despair rather than with his father seems a distinction without a human difference.

The suggestion that, consciously or not, Edgar is toying with his father is intensified by the great farewell speech that Gloucester immediately launches into:

> O you mighty gods!   [*He kneels.*]
> This world I do renounce, and in your sights
> Shake patiently my great affliction off.
> . . . .
>   If Edgar live, O bless him!
> Now, fellow, fare thee well.   [*He falls.*]   4.6.34–6, 40–1

The composed dignity of these lines is a remarkable departure from the impotent rage and desperate superstition Gloucester had expressed before his usurpation. While he is in effect confessing to the gods his failure to carry on as they wish, he speaks as a man who knows himself and quietly accepts his doom. There is great poignancy in the shift from his confessed inability to bear his sorrows to his invocation of a divine blessing for Edgar and good wishes for the companion he thinks is a poor man. But Gloucester's resolute lurch forward is not crowned by the extinction that he seeks and perhaps deserves.

Edgar's silent presence during Gloucester's noble speech and attempted suicide is likely to be disturbing, even though an audience may have grown accustomed to seeing him as an onstage spectator.[27] Indeed, Robert Egan remarks that the Dover Cliff scene is 'nearly as painful to witness, in its profound indignity, as was his [Gloucester's] blinding.'[28] Having in some sense come to terms with the gods, Gloucester is reduced to being a butt of irony. That his beloved Edgar and the 'fellow' standing next to him are one and the same is a comic misprision that seems strangely out of place. Indeed, the situation of a blind father being tricked by his mischievous son occurs in a comic scene in *The Merchant of Venice*, when Launcelot Gobbo decides to 'try confusions' with his father and tells him that his son Launcelot is dead (2.2.33–168).[29] After Gloucester's reawakening, the ironies continue with Edgar's strange beseeching of him to look up and his father's response, 'Alack, I have no eyes' (4.6.60). Throughout the scene the ironies and the trifling are so emphatic that we may recall Gloucester's great cry from earlier in the act: 'As flies to wanton boys are we to th' gods, / They kill us for their sport' (4.1.36–7).[30] In this case, however, we see a son who appears to be rescuing his father for his own sport.

It is, I think, difficult to read or watch Edgar's deception of the physically blind Gloucester in this scene without being reminded of Edmund's deception of the spiritually blind Gloucester in the second act. Even critics who wish to dichotomize the two sons admit that there are similarities between the two situations. Thus, after noting that the Dover Cliff scene is 'an almost exact duplicate' of Edmund's earlier deception, R.B. Heilman argues that the point of the parallel is to clarify the essential difference between the two sons: that, while Edmund deceives his father 'for his own profit,' Edgar does so 'in the interest of that father's spiritual self-mastery.'[31] But there are many kinds of personal profit, and the acquisition of one's father's land and title is only one of them. The punitive teaching of 'spiritual self-mastery' may be another.

If Edgar is delivering therapy, it seems to be aimed more at his own fears of cosmic meaninglessness than at his father's desire to commit suicide. After Gloucester regains consciousness, Edgar attempts to convince him that he has been exorcised of a demon that was left behind on the heights of the cliff:

> As I stood here below, methought his eyes
> Were two full moons; he had a thousand noses,
> Horns welk'd and waved like the enridged sea.
> It was some fiend; therefore, thou happy father,
> Think that the clearest gods, who make them honors
> Of men's impossibilities, have preserved thee.   4.6.69–74

The most obvious interpretation of these lines is the one Edgar provides: Gloucester's supposed fall represents a symbolic death in which his evil spirit is finally exorcised.[32] But the quick shift from the grotesque description of the fiend to 'therefore, thou happy father' suggests that Edgar is performing a buried but more efficacious exorcism on himself. This interpretation is supported by the fact that it is Edgar, not Gloucester, who has imagined himself obsessed with the dark spirits of hatred. Janet Adelman puts it well when she speaks of 'a virtual exorcism for ... the desire to punish.'[33] Certainly, in terms of subsequent behaviour it is Edgar rather than his father who shows the effects of having been exorcised. Gloucester is not as cured of his despair as Edgar wishes: when Oswald declares his intent to kill Gloucester, the old man responds by praising his 'friendly hand' (4.6.230). Edgar, however, remains in disguise, merely speaking in a new, more gentlemanly dialect. He seems to take a covert pleasure in repeatedly calling Gloucester 'father,' perhaps thereby assuaging his need to make a connection with him. But of course it is a connection devoid of shared significance.

Eventually, Edgar does reveal himself to his father, as he recounts in an ornate set speech in the final scene (5.3.205–19), perhaps because 'he wants his father's blessing before going into combat' against Edmund.'[34] In any event, this reconciliation occurs offstage and its consequences are ironic as it precipitates Gloucester's death from a sudden cardiac arrest. Sadly, even after he has received his father's blessing and regained his title from his brother, Edgar still seems possessed by unacknowledged spirits. His unmasking of himself to the dying Edmund contains an attack not only against his brother but also against his father:

> My name is Edgar, and thy father's son.
> The gods are just, and of our pleasant vices
> Make instruments to plague us:
> The dark and vicious place where thee he got
> Cost him his eyes.   5.3.170–4

As Edgar recalls the terrible violence done to his father, he makes an entirely gratuitous moral attack of his own against him. He needs to believe that 'The gods are just,' but he can justify his father's suffering only by dint of labelling it as a proper punishment for adultery, in effect a self-inflicted wound.[35] Edgar's coldly moralizing critique of his father belies the fact that it was actually Gloucester's virtue – his brave loyalty to Lear – rather than his vice that 'cost him his eyes.'

Cordelia's Rescue of Lear: Eclipsing Son and Father

King Lear's daughters differ from Gloucester's sons in a fundamental way: while each of the two sons is divided by ambivalent filial attitudes, the three daughters suffer from no self-divisions. As we have seen, it is a mistake for critics to have labelled Edgar and Edmund as moral exempla, the 'type and antitype of filial piety.'[36] But such a simple and absolute moral dichotomy *does* serve to distinguish the loving Cordelia from her evil sisters, Goneril and Regan. One way to link the children of the two plots is to say that Lear's children outdo in their goodness or evil the efforts of the corresponding children of Gloucester. We feel, I believe, that the bastard Edmund has more justification for his filial anger than do Goneril and Regan, who in turn show more ferocity toward the elder generation than he. By the same token we may also feel that Edgar's filial goodness is much more qualified and much less luminous than Cordelia's. It is as if Gloucester's children are, in both their evil and their good, unrealized versions of Lear's.

If we think of the role of sons being superseded by that of daughters in the play, the key pair to observe is the two good, loyal children, Edgar and Cordelia. They have a great deal in common: both are unjustly banished from court and disowned by their fathers, both risk their lives to protect their helpless fathers, and both, in their different ways, are reconciled with them. These broad parallels have often been commented on by critics, but there is one connection between them that has gone largely unnoticed, even though it also appears prominently in earlier plays about parents and children: both show their filial devotion by rescuing their fathers.

In the Gloucester subplot Shakespeare increases the already considerable emphasis he found in Sidney's *Arcadia* on the legitimate son as the heroic saviour of his father. Like his Sidneian predecessor, Edgar fights to defend his father, but in a different key. In Sidney, the legitimate son, aided by the Arcadian princes, repulses an attack of forty men directed by the evil son. But in Shakespeare the rescue takes a more dramatic form, in that Edgar saves Gloucester from certain death at the hands of a would-be murderer. Soon after the mock suicide at the imagined Dover Cliff, the super-serviceable Oswald comes upon Gloucester and, disregarding the seeming rustic at his side, is eager to kill the blind old man for the reward on his head; armed with only a cudgel, Edgar bravely interposes himself between the two and somehow manages to kill Oswald. This scene bears comparison with those in which the young John Talbot and Prince Hal save their fathers on the battlefield; in all three instances the inexperienced son is revealed to be a person of great courage who fights against considerable odds. Moreover, for all these figures the rescue of the father marks a coming of age and entrance into manhood.

Shakespeare's depiction of Cordelia as a father-rescuer, unlike his treatment of Edgar, involves a fundamental revision of his source materials. The reconciliation of the deposed king with his banished daughter is of course an essential part of the tale, but in Shakespeare's sources (as Bullough notes) the meeting of father and daughter invariably takes place in France, indicating that the king has sought refuge with his loving but essentially passive daughter (7:280). Thus the Cordella of *The True Chronicle History of King Leir* is deeply concerned for her father's well-being but does not actively seek him out. Moved by Cordella's sadness for her deposed father, her husband, the King of Gallia, sends a letter inviting Leir 'to come and visit us' (Bullough 7:369), which the king and his loyal Kent-like companion take up. In what is intended to be seen as a providential meeting, Cordella and her husband the Gallian king are on a pleasure excursion to the seashore, where they come across the pair of exiles. Leir and his companion are so famished that they are at the point of death and even considering cannibalism, but Cordella saves their lives by sharing with them the pastoral banquet that she and her party, all of them disguised as peasants, are sitting down to. While Cordella does perform a rescue of sorts, this is a rescue totally without risk, and almost without intent.

In Shakespeare, however, Cordelia is from the start depicted as a forceful woman who will stand up for the truth and for those who are under attack. Depending on how one reads an ambiguous speech attribution in the Folio text of *King Lear*, it may be that early in the opening scene Cordelia comes to the rescue of Kent by interposing herself between him and Lear, who seems on the verge of attacking his honest, outspoken counsellor.[37] After she has been banished from the kingdom and taken up by the French king, she wastes no time seeking her father out, and, accompanied by her husband, she invades England to save him from her sisters. In 4.4, Cordelia's heartfelt mission to rescue her father is clear in her order to an officer:

> A century send forth;
> Search every acre in the high-grown field
> And bring him to our eye.   4.4.6–8

A few lines later she projects her own active goodness onto the world of nature when she prays to the 'unpublished virtues of the earth' to 'Be aidant and remediate / In the good man's distress' (4.4.16–17). Once again, she beseeches her men to 'Seek, seek for him' (4.4.18). Unlike the Cordella of the source play, whose rescue of her father involves sharing her picnic basket, Cordelia's intervention risks everything. And she will pay the price.

Shakespeare may have been nudged toward depicting Cordelia as an active rescuer by a contemporary legal case involving three daughters (one named 'Cordell') and a mentally disturbed father. In 1603, probably not long before the time that Shakespeare was beginning to write *King Lear*, Cordell Annesley, the youngest of Sir Brian Annesley's three daughters, vigorously sought to protect her senile father from her sisters, who wished to have him declared insane and to have his last will and testament broken.[38] Her campaign proved to be successful. This case seems to have had an important bearing on *King Lear*, in that it stressed the issue of whether or not the old father was insane, which is not a concern in the *King Leir* play or other early versions of the story. And it also provides the figure of a youngest daughter who intervenes to save her helpless father from her grasping sisters.

In depicting Cordelia's rescue of Lear, Shakespeare deviates not only from the received Lear story but also from his own practice of gendering parental rescue in male terms. Before *King Lear*, filial rescue is the exclusive prerogative of sons in Shakespeare, and this attitude is largely typical of Shakespeare's culture, the redoubtable Cordell Annesley notwithstanding. Although the exhortations of catechisms to rescue parents from danger were addressed to children of both sexes, in the Elizabethan imagination rescue was clearly understood as the province of heroic sons. After all, Aeneas was the child who saved the helpless Anchises. In saving her father, then, Cordelia quietly appropriates a male role, and we can see this rescue as a loving, benign version of the brutally masculine conduct that increasingly characterizes Goneril and Regan.[39]

If the filial rescues of Cordelia and Edgar differ from Shakespeare's sources, they also differ in an extremely important way from the rescues in his earlier plays: neither Lear nor Gloucester wants to be rescued. Racked by despair stemming from what he thinks is his responsibility for the death of Edgar, Gloucester wishes to live no longer. When Oswald tells his intended victim that 'The sword is out / That must destroy thee,' Gloucester completes his killer's decasyllabic line: 'Now let thy friendly hand / Put strength enough to't' (4.6.29–30, 30–1). From Gloucester's perspective, this rescue is an unwanted intrusion. Earlier in the same scene, we recall, Edgar had foiled the suicide that his father dearly wished to consummate, and so the rescue compounds the initial injury.[40] With regard to the revival of Gloucester's spirits, Edgar's rescue is no more efficacious than was the supposed miracle of the leap from Dover Cliff. After Oswald's death, Gloucester laments the fact that he still has 'ingenious feeling / Of my huge sorrows' (4.6.280–1). Lear is like Gloucester in that he resists rescue, but – as in all things – the King does so much more imperiously than the Earl. During the storm, Lear had resisted the efforts of Gloucester and Kent to find shelter for him, preferring the intensity of his physical suffering. After Cordelia has landed in England and taken Lear under her protection, we learn that he 'by no means / Will yield to see his daughter' because 'burning shame / Detains him from Cordelia' (4.3.40–1, 46–7 – Quarto only). When several of Cordelia's gentlemen attempt to secure him, Lear cries out 'No rescue' and tries to run away (4.6.190). This resistance by the two old men adds a new level of challenge to Shakespeare's filial saviours; their problem is not only rescuing their fathers from their enemies, but also from themselves.

It is significant that the climax of Cordelia's rescue of Lear near Dover (4.7) occurs immediately after the imaginary Dover Cliff scene that closes with Edgar's saving his father from Oswald (4.6). Clearly,

Shakespeare's juxtaposition of the scenes invites comparison, and there are some general similarities between the two rescues that are immediately apparent.[41] In both scenes, the good child presides over the slow awakening of the father, who returns from a state of delusion and unconsciousness to a life that he suspects may be otherworldly. But these similarities allow the differences between the scenes to stand out in high relief. The sequencing of the two scenes is crucial, for what is missing with father and son in the first is fully realized with father and daughter in the second. Absent from Edgar's ministrations but provided by Cordelia's is nothing less than consolation itself, the healing of the soul.[42] Although the disguised Edgar has heroically rescued his father from his assailant, he cannot rescue him from himself. After having been saved, Gloucester continues to despair; his wish to die at Oswald's hand indicates the failure of Edgar's ambivalent attempt at filial therapy. Conversely, Cordelia rescues Lear less from her murderous siblings than from his own turmoil of shame and remorse, and the delicate inner nature of the rescue removes it from the battlefield heroics of the male world.

Cordelia's rescue is more comforting than Edgar's because it is more truthful and more loving. Earlier in the play, it is appropriate that Edmund draws Gloucester's attention to the forged letter by his mock attempt to hide it, for concealment is a dominant impulse of all three members of the family. Compared to the forthrightness of the Lear family, Gloucester and his sons always seem to be in hiding, and none of them more so than Edgar. A telling verbal echo catches the difference between the deceptiveness of Edgar's rescue and the transparency of Cordelia's.[43] After Gloucester faints and falls, the disguised Edgar says to him 'Do but look up' (4.6.59), whereas Cordelia says to her awakening father 'O, look upon me, sir' (4.7.56). Edgar's 'look up' gestures toward the supposed demon on the top of the imaginary cliff, and it also evokes the world of higher spiritual significance in which he attempts to locate – for Gloucester and for himself – the meaning of life. Quite apart from its strange tone (being directed at a blind man), Edgar's injunction to 'look up' seems an evasion of the reality that must be acknowledged if suffering is to be humanly meaningful.[44] Unlike Edgar, Cordelia does not attempt to impose on her father a philosophy of life, and throughout the scene she holds back and allows him to lead the way. Cordelia's 'O, look upon me, sir' respectfully urges Lear to see beyond his guilt and shame by acknowledging her loving presence.[45] When Lear gave Cordelia to the King of France, he declared:

Thou hast her, France, let her be thine, for we
Have no such daughter, nor shall ever see
That face of hers again.   1.1.262–4

To look upon her is to undo his self-lacerating prophecy.

The tenderness of Cordelia's rescue is most apparent in her acute sensitivity to her father's discomfiture. Instead of insistently reassuring him, Edgar-wise, of his good fortune, she patiently listens and laments, responding instead of directing. As Lear slowly awakens from sleep, several times he worries about being 'abused' and 'mocked,' as if he fears the moment is too good to be true, a cruel ruse. This should remind us that in the previous scene Edgar's cure of his father has been in more ways than one an abuse and mockery. Despite his awareness of his terrible vulnerability, Lear reaches out to his daughter with great poignancy, progressively but cautiously opening himself with each succeeding word: 'For (as I am a man) I think this lady, / To be my child Cordelia' (4.7.68–9). To name his daughter, finally, and to name her to her face, is to re-establish the relationship that he had disowned. Her response says everything that need, and perhaps can, be said: 'And so I am; I am' (4.7.69). In the marvelous simplicity of this mutual recognition, there is a note of the human sublime. The plenitude of Cordelia's love allows, for the first time in Shakespeare, no space for filial ambivalence.

Cordelia's deepest desire is to *restore* Lear not only to his senses and to his role as her father, but also to his proper place as the King of England.[46] When he is asleep, she has him dressed again in his former regalia, and she is careful to address him, upon his awakening, as 'my royal lord' and 'your Majesty,' though she had referred to him as 'father' when he was asleep. Of course, there is a pervasive irony surrounding Cordelia's insistence on Lear's kingship: she cannot know that in the lashings of the storm he rejected the idea of authority with which he formerly identified himself. But it is quite moving how Cordelia draws together the public world of respect and the private world of filial feeling, the two worlds that seem impossible for Shakespeare's fathers and sons to hold together. It is fitting that their most deeply felt emotional exchange takes the form of a traditional ritual of respect. When Cordelia asks Lear to 'hold your hand in benediction o'er me' (4.7.57), she kneels to him in order to receive the 'benison' (1.1.265) that he had denied her earlier. Now, in a much more profound forfeiture of kingly authority than his self-regarding abdication in the opening scene, Lear attempts to kneel to her. Before his downfall and subsequent illumination on the heath, Lear had spoken mockingly to Regan of a father's kneeling to a daughter as the grotesque epitome of disrespect for age and authority (2.4.152–6). Now he passionately initiates that very gesture. The rejection of hierarchy implicit in the kneeling of a father to a child is unprecedented in Shakespeare and unthinkable in his world of fathers and sons.[47]

A clue to the power of this bond between Lear and Cordelia is afforded by a powerful line in a scene which it inspired. In Shakespeare's *Pericles*, written two or three years after *King Lear*, the climactic reconciliation scene between Pericles and his daughter Marina is illuminated by the old man's address to her as 'Thou that beget'st him that did thee beget' (5.1.195). The implications of this magical formulation have been sensitively discussed by C.L. Barber, but one aspect of its historical resonance has gone unremarked.[48] Pericles' line denies the fundamental Elizabethan argument for filial indebtedness to parents, their irreversible anteriority. As Bartholomaeus Battus puts it, 'For albeit we shall be able to requite many things which they [our parents] have bestowed upon us, yet certainly are we never able to requite again unto them our procreation For thou canst by no means beget them again.'[49] Interestingly, when another treatise about parental authority makes this argument about 'the bounteous gift of our dear parents,' it specifies that life is 'such a gift as may admit no manner of recompense, for it can never be possible that the son should beget his Father.'[50] Intentionally or not, the author leaves open the possibility that a *daughter* may be able to give birth to her father. As we saw in the histories and tragedies, a son cannot beget his father, for even if he gives him new life by rescuing him from certain death he is attesting to his father's decline, and perhaps even savouring it. A daughter's motherlike ministrations may, however, deliver her father to the world again.[51]

8 *Macbeth* and the Late Plays: The Disappearance of Ambivalent Sons

In the plays following *King Lear*, depictions of fathers and sons continue to appear with considerable frequency, with four examples in *Macbeth* and three in *The Winter's Tale*. But the sustained frequency masks a diminished importance. In the late plays, plots are no longer driven by the interaction between father and son, and the relationship is never again at the heart of things. To be sure, there are links between father-son relations and larger patterns in the plays, most notably in the rhythm of familial division and reunification that is a defining generic feature of the late plays. Thus, a number of sons are separated from and later restored to fathers. But these reunions of son and father are carried along by the recuperative current of the romance plot rather than providing a vital source of it, Invariably, the most powerful reconciliation scenes involve the active engagement of a daughter, mother, or wife.[1] By contrast, the coming together of sons and fathers is relatively unemotional, and these scenes can more properly be called reunions than reconciliations. That is, the separation of father and son is more a matter of unfortunate happenstance than of emotional conflict; they have not experienced a falling out that would require love and forgiveness to heal.

It is odd that there is so little abrasion between father and son because for the most part these figures are (as in the earlier plays) kings and princes, and thus we might expect a recurrence of familiar conflicts centred on problems of succession. But potential grievances are circumvented by plots that separate fathers and sons into distinct spheres, with little (if any) chance of conflict. In *Cymbeline*, for instance, we see the ultimate distancing of father and son: the father's death precedes the birth of his son, the aptly named Posthumus. Similarly, in

Pericles the death of the royal father predates the action of the play, and so the throne is free to be occupied by young Pericles with his father's blessing from beyond the grave. In *Macbeth* potential conflicts between King Duncan and his successor, Malcolm, are precluded early in the play by the murder of the former. When fathers do remain alive in the late plays, a variety of bizarre plot strategies serves to remove their sons from their ambit, and sometimes fathers and sons are not even aware of each other's existence. Thus, in a strange plot turn the aged and unstable king in *Cymbeline* is protected from the potential rivalry of his spirited sons by dint of their having been kidnapped in their infancy, and the revelations of identity do not occur until the very end of the play. Similarly, in *The Tempest*, a ruler and his only son, Duke Alonso and Ferdinand, are isolated from each other by shipwreck in the opening moments of the play; until the final scene each is convinced that the other has drowned. In instances such as these, the grounds for rivalry between father and son have been removed, and filial autonomy is not a goal to be struggled for.

Given this pervasive separation of father and son and the ensuing diminution of conflict between them, it is not surprising that the figure of the ambivalent son disappears almost entirely. From *Macbeth* onward, the sons in Shakespeare's plays lack the intensity born of inner conflict; these scaled-down figures experience neither the devotion nor the rebellion experienced by their predecessors. (The one son who is conspicuously not scaled-down, Coriolanus, struggles with a mother who plays the demanding paternal role to the hilt.) After the probing, perhaps exhaustive, exploration of opposing impulses in Hal, Hamlet, and Edgar, the late plays replace the double pull of filial deference and defiance with simpler, usually much more complaisant attitudes. Because these sons do not reward detailed examination, it is possible in a single chapter to discuss figures from five different plays.

Among the late plays, *The Winter's Tale* stands apart in its acknowledgment of the dark side of family relationships. It includes two father-son pairs that (with major differences) hark back to earlier representations. In the animated conflict between Prince Florizel and his father Polixenes, we see what had earlier been a familiar situation: the issue of succession is bitterly contested between aging father and virile son. But the difference is that Florizel is in love and, despite his father's threats, is willing to sacrifice his royal inheritance for the apparently humbly born woman he wishes to marry. To imagine such deeply divided figures as Hal and Edgar committing themselves wholly (or even partly) to wooing, or to imagine Hamlet's attachment to Ophelia as unproblematic, is to bring the relative simplicity of Florizel into high relief. The discovery that Perdita is a castaway princess rather than a shepherdess is apparently adequate to undo both the paternal resistance of Polixenes and the filial rebellion of Florizel, leaving the vague impression that all is well between them.

In the late plays, the diminishment of conflict between father and son occurs at the cost of a thinning out of emotional connection and a minimizing of the complexities that in earlier plays had made the relationship troubling and vital. But in *The Winter's Tale* there is one depiction of a father and son in which the erasure of filial ambivalence is not complete. This relationship is quite different from the earlier ones, in that the princely son is not a young man coming of age and ready to compete with his father for mastery. Rather, he is a child of roughly the same age as young Wat in the painting of Walter Ralegh senior and junior. While dynastic politics do not stand between Mamillius and his father Leontes, there is a wrenching conflict of loyalties that divides and ultimately destroys the boy. In Mamillius, we see the origin of attitudes that in the fullness of time could have resulted in filial ambivalence and perhaps even outright conflict between father and son. But death forecloses this potentially complex future.

Macbeth: Genealogical Connection and Emotional Separation

With regard to fathers and sons, *Macbeth* is the key transitional play between *King Lear* and the last plays. In this tragedy, as in the romances that follow it, the father-son bond is thematically important and serves as an image of social and familial unity, but the actual depiction of the relationships reveals the distance between fathers and sons rather than the link connecting them. In *Macbeth* the father-son relationships are free of conflict, but (not coincidentally) they are also largely devoid of mutual feeling.

In *Macbeth* the framing of the relationship suggests that the bond between father and son is crucial to human society because it provides the patrilineal, genealogical connection that sustains the natural growth of family and community through time. In *Macbeth* the symbolic import of fathers and sons is shaped in good part by a contemporary political construction: the unbroken line of sons connecting the legendary Banquo with the Stuart kings of Scotland and especially

214 Fathers and Sons in Shakespeare

James VI, who was crowned James I of England shortly before Shakespeare wrote the play for performance by the King's Men. Before as
well as after he ascended the English throne, James was much given to
reflecting on the political and religious blessings that flowed from the
continuous lineal descent which he derived from the legendary
Banquo.[2] For a monarch deeply invested in a patriarchalist interpretation of the divine right of kings, the ability to trace a direct descent
from the dim, distant past was an invaluable asset, and James made
the most of it.[3]

In characterizing James's relationship to his forebears, Shakespeare
appears to have had in mind a widely disseminated genealogical tree
that traced the King's descent back to Banquo.[4] Such a tree is prophetically alluded to by Banquo himself when he interprets the witches'
prophecy to mean that he will be the 'root and father / Of many kings'
(3.1.5–6). In an obvious way, this genealogical tree ties in with the
play's pervasive imagery of seeds, planting, and growth, suggesting
that patrilineal descent and primogeniture (like patriarchy in general)
are an expression of natural as well as divine order. In a less natural
representation of the Stuart line, the witches devise for Macbeth 'A
show of eight Kings' (s.d., 4.1.111), some of whom carry 'twofold balls,
and treble sceptres' (4.1.121), monarchical symbols associated with the
rule of English kings and especially with the joining of the two kingdoms under King James.[5]

It is certainly true, as many critics have noted, that a powerful
web of symbolism counterpointing birth and growth against steril-
ity and violence pervades the play.[6] These images serve to contrast
the infertility of Macbeth with the fecundity of the men who have
sons, and the usurper's existential isolation has its antithesis in
fathers whose being is reflected in their sons. Thus, Coppélia Kahn
notes that, with the crucial exception of Macbeth, 'The men in the
play are fruitful: Duncan, Banquo, Macduff, and Siward all have
sons, for and through whom they act to perpetuate the natural and
the social order.'[7] This is true enough, so long as we do not assume
that this perpetuation of 'the natural and the social order' includes
mutually sustaining personal relationships between father and son.
It does not follow that, since the unnaturally cruel Macbeth is the
sworn enemy of sons, the father-son relationships of his enemies are
presented in positive terms. Far from having 'amicable relationships,' the play's fathers and sons show little exchange, and still less
expression, of mutual concern.[8] Biological fertility does not prevent

distance and even a certain callousness from arising on the part of father and son.

Barbara Everett has remarked that '*Macbeth* is a tragedy extremely bare in human relationship,' and this affective impoverishment is especially true of its fathers and sons.[9] Rarely do we see a father and his son onstage at the same time, and still more rarely do they actually converse with each other. Thus, we never see Macduff and his little son together, and in the boy's sole appearance the conversation turns on his father's absence; before Young Siward's body is brought to old Siward at the end of the play, this father and son appeared together in only one scene (5.4), and they exchanged no words; Banquo and Fleance appear together briefly in two scenes (2.1, 3.3), but with only a handful of words passing between them; and Duncan and his sons Malcolm and Donalbain appear in three (public) scenes (1.2, 1.4, 1.6), with little if any personal interaction. The sense of distance between father and son is stressed by the motif of running away: Malcolm and Donalbain quickly flee from the scene after the murder of their father, Fleance flees from the assassins who have struck down his father, and Macduff abandons the son who will soon be murdered.

As might be expected, the play's stress on the public aspect of the relationship is most apparent in its depiction of the Scottish royal family. The key interaction between King Duncan and Prince Malcolm is an act of dynastic politics in which there is no personal dimension. In a brief vignette early in the the play, Shakespeare depicts a crucial moment in the history of the inheritance of the Scottish crown. When Duncan designates Malcolm as the Prince of Cumberland and his successor (1.4.35–9), the event marks the shift from the old Scots tradition of tanistry (in which the throne went to a male member of a collateral branch of the king's family) to primogeniture, the inheritance by the eldest son.[10] The custom of tanistry invited competitive violence – in Holinshed's Scottish chronicle Duncan belongs to an appallingly long series of murdered kings – and thus the investiture of Malcolm at the end of the play marks the beginning of the peaceful transference of the Scottish crown from father to son that will lead to the distant but inevitable accession of King James.

In light of Shakespeare's earlier concern with problems of filial succession, it is odd that Malcolm is silent through the scene and does not refer to it later in the play. We are left to puzzle out what his response may be. Surprise? (Macbeth did not expect the proclamation, and conceivably Malcolm did not as well.) Gratitude toward his father? An eagerness to sit upon the throne? Anxiety at the task ahead? A combination of all the above? It is Macbeth, not Malcolm, whose response to Duncan's bequest is immediately revealed in soliloquy, and the newly minted prince's feelings about his father are never made clear. Upon Duncan's murder, Malcolm and Donalbain hastily seize the 'safest way' (2.3.142) and flee from Scotland, not pausing to express sorrow ('our tears are not yet brew'd' [2.3.123]) or to mention revenge. Nor is there is any evidence that their filial tears are ever brewed, for Donalbain does not reappear in the play and Malcolm never mentions his father again. Later in the play Macduff praises Duncan to Malcolm by saying 'Thy royal father / Was a most sainted king' (4.3.108–9), but Malcolm immediately turns the conversation back to himself. (Paradoxically, the person who mentions Duncan most frequently and most feelingly, both before and after his death, is Macbeth.)[11] Though commentators sometimes speak of 'Malcolm's revenging of Duncan's death' at the close, Malcolm says nothing to indicate this is how *he* sees it.[12] Whether this silence represents personal callousness or public commitment on Malcolm's part, it bespeaks a blankness of characterization that would have been unthinkable in an earlier play.

Fleance and Banquo, the begetters of the ostensibly endless line of Stuart kings, are another symbolically freighted father and son who are characterized by an absence of personal interaction. They appear together in only two scenes and exchange a grand total of eight lines, mostly concerning the time and the weather. In the first and longer of these scenes, father and son arrive at Macbeth's castle in the darkness:

> *Ban.* How goes the night, boy?
> *Fle.* The moon is down; I have not heard the clock.
> *Ban.* And she goes down at twelve.
> *Fle.*   I take't, 'tis later, sir.
> *Ban.* Hold, take my sword. There's husbandry in heaven,
>   Their candles are all out. Take thee that too.
>   [*Gives him his belt and dagger.*]
>   A heavy summons lies like lead upon me
>   And yet I would not sleep.   2.1.1–7

When Macbeth immediately appears, Banquo at first fails to recognize him in the darkness and commands Fleance to 'Give me my sword' (1.2.9). It may be, as a critic has argued, that Banquo's handing his sword to Fleance and then receiving it back from him constitutes a 'symbolic ritual' in which 'the father initiates his son to manhood by allowing him to handle his sword.'[13] And certainly Banquo's reliance on Fleance is more assured and more reciprocated than that of another tired father who hands over the family weaponry to a son, the Master Gunner in *1 Henry VI*.

This stress on the symbolic obscures the crucially human fact that, despite the exchange of sword and dagger, the father appears eerily detached from the young son on whom the future depends. (It seems a safe assumption that he has not informed Fleance of the prophecy.) As their addresses to each other ('boy' and 'sir') indicate, the emphasis falls on the formality of the relationship, and the two seem separated from the beginning, as if their talk serves to fill an awkward silence. The swiftness with which Banquo slips into a soliloquy-like meditation on his 'cursed thoughts,' becoming as oblivious to Fleance as the 'rapt' Macbeth was to his fellow commanders after hearing the witches' prophecy, indicates the interior nature of his struggle. Upon the entrance of Macbeth, who does not acknowledge the boy's presence, Fleance recedes further into the background as the two warriors delicately probe each other's intentions and commitments. By the time his dialogue with Macbeth is finished, Banquo seems to have forgotten about Fleance, making no reference to his son when they exit the stage together.[14]

The second and final appearance of Banquo and Fleance (3.3) echoes the earlier scene. Once again, they enter the stage at night with Fleance leading the way, pagelike, with a torch. When they are suddenly set upon by the murderers, the only words spoken by father or son are Banquo's: 'O, treachery! Fly, good Fleance, fly, fly, fly! / Thou mayst revenge. O slave!' (3.3.17–18). This scene, like the previous one, is often read in emblematic terms. Ricardo Quinones, for example, characterizes this 'wonderful metaphoric scene' as 'showing the value Shakespeare placed on the great bond of father and son,' for Banquo and Fleance 'symbolize peaceful succession in which man tries to make his way and bestow the legacy of his person and achievements on his children.'[15] There is, however, a problem with this interpretation. After repeatedly urging 'good Fleance' to 'fly,' Banquo specifies the (self-interested) reason that he wants his son to survive: 'Thou mayst revenge.' Coupled with his previous handing over to Fleance of his sword and dagger, Banquo's injunction to revenge indicates a rather narrow, violent legacy being bestowed upon his son. Perhaps more significantly, Banquo is exhorting his son to look to the past (by pursuing revenge) rather than to fulfil the prophecy about the future. The true 'revenge' of Fleance will come through natural process, through procreation rather than through the paternal sword.

In the play's two other depictions of the relationship, the father and son do not directly interact, and in each there is a strong contrast between the father's complexity and the son's undercharacterized simplicity. The contrast is particularly great between Macduff and his young, unnamed son, for it is never clear why Macduff has abruptly abandoned his family and fled to England. Indeed, the father's flight is the main topic of conversation in young Macduff's exchange with his mother, an exchange that in its intimacy and tonal range could not be more different from those between fathers and sons in the play. Having overheard the dialogue between his aggrieved mother and Lord Rosse concerning his father's ominous absence, little Macduff proceeds to defend him against his mother's charge that 'he wants the natural touch' (4.2.9). The young Macduff's defence of his father is unqualified and unambivalent, as the defence of an older, more knowing son would not likely be. Movingly, the boy attempts to play the protective male role that his father abandoned. When the murderers arrive, he shows a courage that even his father may not have had, as he stands his ground and roundly defies the 'shag-ear'd villain' who proceeds to stab him. We can think of the scene as a pathetic attempt of a too young son to take on the Hamlet roles of rescuing his father's reputation and protecting his mother, actions that emphasize the inadequacy of his absent father.

A convincing refutation of Lady Macduff's criticism about Macduff's wanting the natural touch occurs in the following scene, when he receives the news about his family's slaughter and expresses the deepest paternal grief in all of Shakespeare. Macduff struggles to grasp the enormity of his loss, as he asks 'My children too?' (4.3.211) and 'My wife kill'd too?' (4.3.213) and 'All my pretty ones? / Did you say all? O hell-kite! All?' (4.3.216–17). While Macduff is still stunned by the news, Malcolm (who had expressed no sorrow at the death of his father) curtly advises him to 'Be comforted' (4.3.213). Macduff's response is a critical crux: 'He has no children' (4.3.216).The ambiguous pronoun is functional, for only a man who has never loved children could murder them as Macbeth does, and only such a man could proffer such cold comfort for their deaths as Malcolm does.[16] When, a few lines later, Malcolm exhorts Macduff to 'Dispute it like a man' (4.3.220), Macduff's reply has a very powerful directness:

> I shall do so;
> But I must also feel it as a man:
> I cannot but remember such things were,
> That were most precious to me.   4.3.220–3

These lines are central to the play's exploration of manliness, for in their unguarded way they claim tender feeling as a form of expression as necessary for 'a man' as any other. Sadly, this naked intensity of paternal feeling, elsewhere lacking in the play's father-son relationships, finds expression only in the loss of the son.

Had he wished, Shakespeare could easily have ended the play without introducing another father and son, thus leaving Macduff's lament as the last expression of a father's feeling for a child. Instead, he departed from his main source, Holinshed's account of Scotland, and incorporated a vignette from the same historian's *Chronicle of England* that serves as a negative counter-example to Macduff. The figures of old Siward and Young Siward are reminiscent of the two John Talbots from *1 Henry VI* in that the elder is a celebrated warrior well past his prime while his son is a martial neophyte, one of 'many unrough youths that even now / Protest their first of manhood' (5.2.10–11). Young Siward, however, displays none of young John Talbot's resistance to paternal edict. Though he is only lightly sketched in (father and son do not speak to each other in the play), Young Siward appears to be following in his father's footsteps unquestioningly. He certainly manifests the bravery that is his father's fixation; when this fledgling warrior meets Macbeth on the battlefield, he resolutely denies Macbeth's imputation of fear (twice).[17]

As is his wont with depictions of fathers and sons, Shakespeare complicates and darkens the account he found in his source material. Holinshed notes that in the victory over Macbeth, 'one of Siward's sons chanced to be slain, whereof although the father had good cause to be sorrowful, yet when he heard that he died of a wound which he had received in fighting stoutly in the forepart of his body, and that with his face towards the enemy, he greatly rejoiced thereat, to hear that he died so manfully' (Bullough 7:507). While there may be a hint of disapproval in the discrepancy between old Siward's 'good cause to be sorrowful' and the fact that he 'greatly rejoiced' at the news of his son's manly death, Holinshed's depiction of the warrior father seems mainly positive. But Shakespeare accentuates the negative by counterpointing old Siward's cold response against those of Rosse and Malcolm (and against that of Macduff for his son earlier). Rosse attempts to console old Siward with the thought that 'Your cause of sorrow / Must not be measur'd by his worth, for then / It hath no end' (5.9.10–12), but he need not have worried. Siward is in no danger of excessive, much less endless, grief. After ascertaining that his son's wounds were 'on the front,' Siward declares:

> Why then, God's soldier be he!
>   Had I as many sons as I have hairs,
>   I would not wish them to a fairer death.
>   And so his knell is knoll'd.   5.9.13–16

Siward's eagerness to cast his son's account is unseemly, and his curt last line is perfunctory in its dismissal, as if he has already put paid to the loss; the warrior father sees no cause for reflection in his young son's death and may even feel a certain satisfaction.

Though Siward declares himself finished with his namesake son, Malcolm intervenes to contradict the disturbingly dispassionate father:

> *Mal.*   He's worth more sorrow,
>   And that I'll spend for him.
> *Siw.*   He's worth no more;
>   They say he parted well, and paid his score,
>   And so God be with him! Here comes newer comfort.   5.9.16–19

Like Rosse, Malcolm insists on the sorrow that Young Siward is 'worth,' but Siward's denial of his son's value is vehement, and his metaphor of paying the score, as if a life were a bar bill, is briskly reductive. Siward's final 'And so God be with him' closely echoes his previous dismissal ('And so his knell is knoll'd') and intensifies the sense of a wished-for washing of paternal hands. Some critics have professed themselves moved by what one called 'the sublime conception of Old Siward's stoicism,' but, in the context of the play's critique of a supposedly 'manly' denial of feeling, Siward's coldness seems less philosophical than heartless.[18]

The prominence given to old Siward's cold response to his son's death contributes to the play's examination of manliness and the warrior mentality, and it also returns us to Shakespeare's long-standing interest in the dark side of the paternal moon, the tendency to view sons in exclusively public, institutional terms. Admirable as his commitment may be to remove the bloody tyrant from the throne of Scotland, old Siward is too willing to sacrifice his son to his ideology of martial honour, just as Macduff has sacrificed private for public good by joining Malcolm's army and leaving his family defenceless. Not only does Macduff's remorse at the loss of his children stand in sharp contrast to old Siward's callousness, but even Macbeth, the personification of son-killing, may appear comparatively natural in his feeling that he is cursed by a lack of progeny, having gained merely a 'fruitless crown' and 'barren sceptre' (3.1.60–1).[19]

Pericles, Cymbeline, The Tempest:
Denatured Visions of Father and Son

In the late romances, as in *Macbeth*, there is an ironic discrepancy between the symbolic significance and the actuality of father-son relationships. Once again, the theme of patrilineal succession is important, and the plays may be mindful of King James's claim to be the father of England and respected as such.[20] Certainly, the key romance motif of reunion after long separation applies to fathers and sons as well as to other family members. And yet it seems to be a precondition of these father-son reunions that the relationship be distanced and emotionally thinned out. The late plays, like their forerunner, *Macbeth*, appear to have grown weary of exploring the complex psychological drama of ambivalent sons and their fathers, but not able to move beyond it imaginatively. It is as if the positive vision can be projected only by avoiding what R.D. Laing referred to as 'the texture of the actual lived experience of people in families.'[21] (In only one of the late plays, *The Winter's Tale*, is that texture palpable, and so I set it aside for separate consideration at the end of this chapter.) The stubbornly abiding gaps that separated the male generations in the earlier plays are not so much filled as momentarily dissolved through dream and vision.

Pericles is chronologically the first of the romances, and the entire group's idealized but distanced approach to fathers and sons is adumbrated in an early scene depicting the aftermath of a shipwreck that Pericles has suffered. Pericles is immediately befriended by a tangy group of fishermen, and, in a development not appearing in the play's sources, the fishermen discover a suit of rusty armour in their nets that Pericles recognizes as his father's.[22] This little scene is a reunion of sorts, as providence restores to Pericles the paternal armour that the sea had taken from him. Pericles will proceed to wear this armour in his successful joust at court, and so his inheritance from his father enables him to wed, to gain a father-in-law who reminds him of his own father (2.3.37–8), and ultimately to become a father in his own right. Pericles' (unnamed) father is the (unseen) human face of divine providence.

Especially noteworthy is the novelty of an unproblematic transmission of inheritance from father to son.[23] Pericles characterizes the armour as

> part of my heritage,
> Which my dead father did bequeath to me,
> With this strict charge, even as he left his life,
> 'Keep it, my Pericles, it hath been a shield
> 'Twixt me and death' – and pointed to this brace –
> 'For that it sav'd me, keep it. In like necessity –
> The which the gods protect thee from – may defend thee.'　　2.1.123–9

Unlike the tainted legacies that sons inherit in earlier plays, this is a father's 'strict charge' that mandates his successor's well-being. Rather than demanding revenge of Pericles, it affords him protection and enables him to win the hand of his future wife. In this scene there is no sign of the complexities of filial indebtedness that loomed so large in the histories and tragedies. Interestingly, the issue of debt does arise for Pericles, but it is displaced onto the fishermen. When Pericles asks them for the armour, he says that if his fortunes ever improve, 'I'll pay your bounties; till then, rest your debtor' (2.1.143). Clearly, the debt he owes the fishermen is far more straightforward, and far more easy to discharge, than those that Elizabethan catechisms declared sons owed their fathers. Perhaps it is only by dint of being so removed from the exigencies of the social and political world that Pericles' inheritance from a ghostly father can be depicted as so entirely benign.

The sea and its mysteries also figure in the only father-son relationship in *The Tempest*, and once again father and son are separated by forces beyond their control. Before the audience has seen them together, Alonso the King of Naples and his heir Ferdinand have been isolated from each other by the tempest that opens the play. Once again, there is no conflict about succession, the source of so much abrasion in earlier father-son, king-prince relationships; Alonso thinks he has no living son to succeed him, while Ferdinand believes he already has done so. Nor is there any intimation of previous differences between them in Naples. Thus, their separation and reunion on the island seem to be an entirely tactical matter, being stage-managed by Prospero and having nothing to do with the nature of their previous relationship. As is usually the case in the late plays, father and son do not have a significant shared past, leaving their relation ungrounded.

Compared to the grief of sons, say, in *Hamlet*, Ferdinand's mourning for his father is brief, calmed as it is by Prospero's music and Miranda's beauty. In his first entry he describes himself as having been transformed by music as he was 'Sitting on a bank, / Weeping again the King my father's wrack' (1.2.390–1), where 'King' takes precedence over 'father.' Already he is under the consoling spell of Ariel's music. As in *Pericles*, what we see is not a son's direct expression of mourning but rather a displaced, symbolic representation of what that grief might be. 'Full fadom five,' Ariel's enchanting song to Ferdinand, is about this transformation of filial sorrow into rich wonder:

Full fadom five thy father lies,
    Of his bones are coral made:
Those are pearls that were his eyes:
    Nothing of him that doth fade,
But doth suffer a sea-change
Into something rich and strange.
Sea-nymphs hourly ring his knell:
        Burthen [*within*]. Ding-dong.
Hark now I hear them – ding-dong bell.   1.2.397–405

As in Pericles' seashore remembrance of his father, wonder and mystery replace history. Indeed, this exquisite song is about the father's transformed identity; his mortal body is changed into the timeless delicate beauty of '*something* rich and strange.' This song suggests a fantasy in which the father is removed from the son's world without the pain that love and conflict necessarily entail; he is deeply buried at sea but not defaced or destroyed.

A single magical song resolves a problem that had burdened Hamlet throughout the entirety of an extremely long play. Speaking of the song, a critic notes how 'Music that mourns Alonso's assumed death is also therapy that permits Ferdinand to go on living; he grows through the experience from funeral to marriage without appearing heartless.'[24] But, as is usually the case in the romances, and especially in their father-son relationships, the growth through experience is suggested, not depicted, and takes place at an aesthetic remove from quotidian life. The song works by blurring the distinction between life and art; one cannot be sure if the emotions ascribed to Ferdinand are originating from him or being insinuated into him through Ariel's offices. Ferdinand's immediate response to the song is to declare that 'The ditty does remember my drown'd father' (1.2.406), but his own remembrance of that father fades, being immediately supplanted by the captivating appearance of Miranda. Until he sees him at the end of the play, Ferdinand does not think of his father again.

As is usually the case in the late plays, love flows downward: in ruptured relationships, the intensity of fathers' grief exceeds that of sons. While Ferdinand's mind fixes on Miranda and his hopes for the future, Alonso dwells obsessively on the terrible loss of his son and heir. From his first appearance on stage, in which he resists the facile consolations of his entourage, Alonso's dark grief is his defining, and virtually his only, characteristic. In his first reference to Ferdinand's ostensible death, he laments that 'My son is lost' and then says:

> O thou mine heir
> Of Naples and of Milan, what strange fish
> Hath made his meal on thee?   2.1.110, 112–14

As David Scott Kastan has noted, Alonso 'identifies [his son] not by name but by his dynastic position.'[25] Yet Alonso's grief should not be regarded as exclusively dynastic. Shortly before his reunion with his son, Alonso poignantly characterizes the island to Prospero as the place

> where I have lost
> (How sharp the point of this remembrance is!)
> My dear son Ferdinand.   5.1.137–9

Here he names his son for the first time, and in response to Prospero's expression of sympathy he adds, 'Irreparable is the loss, and patience / Says, it is past her cure' (5.1.140–1). He will not be consoled.

As in the other romances, there is a reunion of father and son at the close, but once again the dramatic force of the reunion is debatable. As an expression of personal feeling, Alonso's insistent articulation of his loss is considerably more powerful than the joy uttered by either father or son when they come together after the masque-like revelation of Ferdinand and Miranda playing chess. Alonso's response is consistent with his open grief for his 'dear son Ferdinand,' and thus he worries in simple, direct language that

> If this prove
> A vision of the island, one dear son
> Shall I twice lose.   5.1.175–7

Of course, it *is* a vision of the island, but it is also real. Ferdinand's response is beautifully evocative, but as usual the son expresses less personal feeling than the father: 'Though the seas threaten, they are merciful; / I have curs'd them without cause' (5.1.178–9). He complements his words with the ritual gesture of kneeling, the sign of his filial deference and obedience; Alonso's reply is the least formal and most accepting of all the paternal responses to filial kneelings in Shakespeare:

> Now all the blessings
> Of a glad father compass thee about!
> Arise, and say how thou cam'st here.   5.1.179–81

Because he has been in deep paternal mourning, which is rare in Shakespeare, his joy is palpable, but one senses that it is not reciprocated by Ferdinand. This relationship is as conflict-free as that of any king and prince in Shakespeare, but the lack of interaction – throughout the play as well as here – prevents it from having much dramatic weight. Compared to the psychological complexity of the fathers and sons in earlier plays, this relationship seems idealized and aestheticized, one that could exist only on a removed island.

In *Cymbeline* there are two sets of separated fathers and sons, and they are even more distanced in time than Pericles is from his armour-giving father and Ferdinand is from Alonso. In the case of Guiderius and Arviragus, the sons of King Cymbeline who were kidnapped from their nursery when the elder brother was only three, their biological progenitor is completely forgotten, replaced by the kindly abductor who claims to be their father. Not content with this quite radical degree of separation, the play depicts another father and son who are separated by the greatest divide possible: they have never met, and indeed the son is named after his condition, Posthumus. The parallel paternal deprivations of Posthumus and of the kidnapped princes are laid out in contiguous passages in the play's first sixty lines, a clear announcement of theme. In the final act of the play, the arc of reunion is completed in two dreamlike scenes: unaware of their relationship to him, King Cymbeline's long-lost sons rescue him from defeat and the long-deceased birth family of Posthumus appears to him in a consoling dream. Even more than in *Pericles* and *The Tempest*, the reunion of father and son is explicitly and essentially visionary, more providential than psychological.

The dilemma of Posthumus is especially compelling. At the beginning of the play we see him as doubly orphaned in that King Cymbeline, the man who had taken him in and sponsored him, has now banished him for disobediently marrying his daughter Imogen. Throughout the play Posthumus's loneliness and lack of guidance are palpable. Though he has won the love of the excellent Imogen, and though he is often praised by others for his honour and virtue, there is something unsettled and dangerously unballasted about him, as we see in the vengeful alacrity with which he endorses the scurrilous false tale of Imogen's adultery.

It is only on the battlefield that Posthumus, the son of a famous warrior and the younger brother of two more, begins to find his familial place and hence himself.[26] He is incorporated into a kind of surrogate military family when he joins with kindly kidnapper Belarius and the two abducted princes to rescue King Cymbeline from the Romans. But his proper family is not restored to him until later. Notwithstanding his successful rescue of the King, the deeply disconsolate Posthumus is arrested by the Britons. As he sleeps in his prison cell, Posthumus's father, mother, and two brothers – all of whom died either before or (in the case of his mother) during his birth – appear to him in a dream ('*as in an apparition*' [s.d., 5.4.29]). The solemn procession (5.4.30ff) is reminiscent of the vision of crowned kings granted to Macbeth, but of course the Scottish king's terrifying vision is of the implacable future while Posthumus's consoling vision restores to him the deceased family he never knew. His words upon waking are very suggestive:

> Sleep, thou hast been a grandsire and begot
> A father to me; and thou hast created
> A mother and two brothers.   5.4.123–5

When he went into battle he prayed to the gods to 'put the strength o' th' Leonati in me' (5.1.31), and now he has gone the gods one better by creating the parents that he desires. As Meredith Skura puts it, 'The play presents a world in which a "posthumus" child finds life only be [*sic*] recreating his dead parents, and where people who had seemed dead come alive in strange ways.'[27] This dream is a sort of reunion, but obviously one that is based in wish-fulfilment rather than in reality, a vision rather than a fact.[28]

The story of the King's kidnapped sons is a happier version of Posthumus's dilemma because Guiderius and Arviragus *think* they know who their father is, and for each of them the presence of a brother further ameliorates the solitariness felt by Posthumus. To be sure, the brothers are unhappy, but their unhappiness stems from their inability to exercise their inherent martial honour in the wilds of Wales, to which their kidnapper, the court-hating Belarius, has removed them. Because Guiderius and Arviragus are true princes in blood and bearing, they find their enforced pastoral retreat to be a great vexation. Between Belarius and his 'boys' (as he fondly calls them) there is a tension reminiscent of earlier father-and-son relationships in Shakespeare, but in a less conflictual form. On the one hand, they are obedient to him, and every day they pay their respects to his deceased wife, who they think is their mother. On the other hand, they chafe at the bit and resist his attempt to limit their experience to the safety of the pastoral life.

Even though Guiderius and Arviragus are simultaneously obedient and resolutely independent, they differ greatly from the ambivalent sons of the earlier plays. Perhaps because they have been raised in a state of nature where there is no concern with succession or usurpation, the young men show no sign of the repressed hostility that marks conflicted sons in the histories and tragedies. They are forthright in their disagreement with their ostensible father, and their insistence on going to war is determined but respectful; they seek the paternal blessing but make it clear that they will leave without it. In an interesting reversal, Belarius is galvanized by their courage, and not only agrees to go with them ('Have with you, boys') but implores them to 'Lead, lead!' (4.4.50, 53). Were Belarius the true father of these boys-turned-men, the scene would be unprecedented in its depiction of a father who defers to his sons and in the process regains his vitality. But instead it stands as an image of what such a moment might look like.

In symbolic terms, and in the context of recurrent Shakespearean themes, the key event is the battle in which the sons (along with Belarius and aided by the arrival of Posthumus) rescue their father, King Cymbeline, from the Romans. This action is very different from the battlefield rescues of fathers by sons in previous Shakespeare plays because of its denatured quality. In effect, this rescue is presented as a vision of a vision, a vision twice removed from the bloody clangour of battlefield reality. First, the rescue is enacted wordlessly onstage, perhaps in some form of dumbshow stylization in which '*the Britains fly*, CYMBELINE *is taken: then enter, to his rescue*, BELARIUS, GUIDERIUS, *and* ARVIRAGUS' (*s.d.* at 5.2.10). Then it is vividly recreated in the long, remarkably evocative description that Posthumus delivers to an unnamed 'Briton Lord' soon after the event (5.3.2–58 with brief interventions from the Lord). Posthumus's description may at first seem to be merely gratuitous duplication since the audience has seen the event, but in fact it deepens the distancing effect first created through the dumbshow. His speech translates the simple action into a haunting dream, evoking a world that the bare stage cannot represent.

The central, oft-reiterated feature of Posthumus's mysterious landscape is a narrow lane in which the battle takes place. In tactical, realistic terms, the narrow lane is important because it allows a handful of Britons to defeat untold numbers of Romans. But the lane represents more than tactical advantage. In its numerous evocations (e.g., 'strait lane,' 'strait pass,' 'Athwart the lane'), it becomes a mysterious, transformative place where life and death meet.[29] The 'narrow lane' proffers itself as a dream symbol, and Freudian commentators have been quick to identify 'battle at a narrow entry' as 'a classic symbolization of oedipal conflict,' while noting that in this instance the son rescues rather than kills his father.[30] Clearly, the Briton Lord is moved by Posthumus's account, and his summary comment makes the event still more elemental and dreamlike: 'This was strange chance. / A narrow lane, an old man, and two boys!' (5.3.51–2).

This rescue of King Cymbeline – the last rescue of a father by his son(s) in Shakespeare's canon – is markedly different from all the earlier instances of the motif. Given the non-verbal quality of the event, there is no way of knowing what is on the minds of the rescuers or the rescued. Certainly, there is no reason to suspect the presence of the ambivalence and hidden aggression that characterize the filial rescues of young John Talbot, Hal, Hamlet, and Edgar, for the good reason that Cymbeline's sons have no idea that the King is also their father. In the world of Shakespearean drama, it is as if a simply heroic, unambivalent rescue of a father by a son can happen only when neither is aware of the other's identity and when, for good measure, the entire scene is depicted in emblematic, dreamlike terms.

The Winter's Tale: Traces of Conflict and Ambivalence

While it shares many conventions with *Pericles*, *Cymbeline*, and *The Tempest*, *The Winter's Tale* suffers from being categorized as simply the fourth romance. Despite its evocation of wonderment and providential design, *The Winter's Tale* never loses its grip on the hardest realities of family life. Like the other romances, it ends in scenes of reconciliation, with two families being reunited both within themselves and with each other, but these largely joyous scenes of familial remembering convey an awareness of the inevitability of disseverment and of the gaps that continue to separate those who have been reunited. In *The Winter's Tale* the phenomenon of parting – in all its myriad forms – is depicted as central to life; the imagery and vocabulary of separation, including many variations on the word 'part,' are deeply woven into the play's fabric.[31] The pervasive fact of separation characterizes not only the play's action but also its remarkably inventive plot structure, which is broken into two discrete, discontinuous sections. (Appropriately, both sections are prefaced by what ultimately proves to be a futile attempt to deny a looming separation: in both a person on a long visit asks permission to return to his home but is prevented for a while from doing so.)[32] These two parts are separated by a great temporal gap of sixteen years at the centre of the play, a symbolic emptiness suggesting that in this play recovery and reunion occur within a great hiatus at the core of things. Nowhere is this gap more apparent than in the play's depiction of fathers and sons, which in its emphasis on conflict is closer to the histories and tragedies than to the other romances.

The Winter's Tale is similar to *Hamlet* and *Part One* of *Henry IV* in its complex juxtaposition of two sets of similar-but-different fathers and sons: Polixenes and Florizel in Bohemia and Leontes and Mamillius in Sicily. The parallels between the romance's two father-son plots are particularly insistent in that the two regal fathers were themselves childhood companions, while their princely sons were born within a month of each other (5.1.117–18). But Shakespeare adds a brilliant complication: we see Leontes with Mamillius when the boy is roughly seven years old, but we do not see Polixenes with Florizel until another sixteen years have passed, bringing the Bohemian prince to the full flush of young manhood. Corresponding with the age differences between Mamillius in the first part and Florizel in the second is a division of emphasis in their troubles with their fathers. For Florizel, the issue of political succession and the threat of a withheld inheritance separates him from his father, while for little Mamillius the gap is created by a more domestic, affective problem: a father's need to create a mirror of himself in his son.

The political register in which Polixenes relates to his (absent) son is already apparent in the opening scene of the play, when Florizel is only six or seven. In response to Leontes' question about paternal affection ('My brother, / Are you so fond of your young prince as we / Do seem to be of ours?' [1.2.163–5]), Polixenes conjures up what appears to be at first a charming domestic scene:

> If at home, sir,
> He's all my exercise, my mirth, my matter;
> Now my sworn friend, and then mine enemy;
> My parasite, my soldier, statesman, all.   1.2.165–8

Polixenes is recollecting domestic pleasure in terms that rather ominously recall his role of monarch. Especially striking is 'My parasite, my soldier, statesman,' all of which are unexpected terms inviting reflection. Polixenes may simply be trying to say that he finds an entire world in what he calls Florizel's 'varying childness' (1.2.170), a playful filial substitute for every aspect of his duties as ruler. But the grown-up, political valence of the terms persists, reminding us that we hear the Bohemian king describing the Bohemian prince. The line 'Now my sworn friend, and then mine enemy' is especially important for it conjures up the Machiavellian politics of court and also points to the conflict that will arise between the king and prince of Bohemia in the second part of the play.

Some sixteen years later, that foreshadowed conflict is voiced in Polixenes' first reference to his now-grown son. Worried about the behaviour of his successor, he asks a counsellor: 'Say to me, when saw'st thou the Prince Florizel, my son?' (4.2.25–6), a question that calls to mind King Henry IV's first reference to *his* wayward prince: 'Can no man tell me of my unthrifty son?' (*R2*:5.3.1). By referring to his 'issue' first as 'Prince Florizel' and only second as 'my son,' Polixenes speaks even more exclusively as a king than does Henry. As Polixenes elaborates his grievance, we learn that Florizel (again like Hal) has been 'of late much retir'd from court' and is also notably delinquent in his 'princely exercises' (*WT*:4.2.31–2).

In addition to recalling King Henry, Polixenes begins to sound the concerns of Gloucester in *King Lear*, being worried about the dangers of filial disobedience and the vulnerabilities of authority exercised by the aged. Sixteen years after saying that Florizel 'cures in me / Thoughts that would thick my blood' (1.2.170–1), he now sees his son as a source of melancholy. When Polixenes and Camillo attend the sheep-shearing feast in disguise, they don the white beards of the old men they are destined to become before long. Shortly before he explodes at Florizel, Polixenes is understandably upset to hear that his son is planning a clandestine wedding, but the elaborate specificity of his questions about age and debility bespeaks a different fear:

> Is not your father grown incapable
> Of reasonable affairs? is he not stupid
> With age and alt'ring rheums? Can he speak? hear?
> Know man from man? dispute his own estate?
> Lies he not bed-rid? and again does nothing
> But what he did being childish?   4.4.397–402

Polixenes may be tacitly reassuring himself that he has not (yet) grown incapable, but the threat of being overthrown by his more virile successor is in the air. To be sure, a few lines later he adopts a calmer, more reasonable stance when he concedes that 'my son / Should choose himself a wife' (4.4.406–7), but when he insists that Florizel should confer with his father and his son flatly refuses, the gap opens again.

In response to Florizel's remark that his father must not learn of his wedding, the infuriated Polixenes explodes from his disguise:

> Mark your divorce, young sir,
>   [*Discovering himself.*]
> Whom son I dare not call. Thou art too base
> To be acknowledg'd. Thou, a sceptre's heir,
> That thus affects a sheep-hook!   4.4.417–20

Among the many reminiscences of Shakespeare's earlier fathers, the references to acknowledgment and disinheritance bring Gloucester and Lear especially to mind. After fulminating against the old shepherd and Perdita, he returns to threatening his son with disinheritance, an issue that does not appear in the corresponding relationship in Shakespeare's primary source, Robert Greene's prose-romance *Pandosto*.[33] As Lear and Gloucester had done, Polixenes senses his lack of control and begins to bluster, declaring that if Florizel so much as sighs for Perdita,

> we'll bar thee from succession,
> Not hold thee of our blood, no, not our kin,
> Farre than Deucalion off.   4.4.429–31

Perhaps Polixenes realizes that his (Lear-like) threat to disinherit his son and to deny all relationship to him is empty, for he quickly exits from the sheep-shearing festival, limply ordering Florizel to 'Follow us to the court' (4.4.432). But, instead of following, Florizel is obdurate: 'From my succession wipe me, father, I / Am heir to my affection' (4.4.480–1).

Prince Florizel is like Prince Ferdinand in *The Tempest* in that reciprocated romantic love affords him a happy alternative to his responsibilities as son and prince. Unlike earlier princes like Hal and Hamlet, these princes of the romances are anchored by the committed love of a good woman. But Ferdinand and Florizel differ from each other because on Prospero's island Ferdinand can choose to marry Miranda without securing the approval of his supposedly drowned father (*Temp*:5.1.190–1), whereas Florizel must disobey Polixenes, who knows about, and passionately disapproves of, his son's relationship with the apparently base-born Perdita. (Like Polonius, he has dispatched spies to report on his son's behaviour.) But the threat of a broken succession is of course easily sidestepped with the revelation that Perdita is indeed a true-born princess who brings a kingdom for a dowry. Indeed, once Perdita's identity is discovered, the play makes no reference at all to a restoration of harmony between the Bohemian King and Prince. Indeed, after Polixenes' explosion of anger at Florizel and Perdita in the sheep-shearing scene, not a single word is exchanged between father and son for the remainder of the play.[34] Nor, in the Gentlemen's lengthy prose account of the numerous reconciliations in Sicily (5.2), is there a reference to any sort of interaction between Polixenes and Florizel. Perhaps we may infer that the discovery of Perdita's royal birth has

removed the grounds of conflict between father and son and also the
need to depict their reconciliation.

Unlike the loud but easily resolved conflict over political succession
that separates Polixenes and Florizel, the relationship of Leontes and
Mamillius is domestic, affective, and tragic. Though he is, like Florizel,
a prince, Mamillius is so young that his connection with his father is
much more personal than civil, not yet hardened into a political
mould. Leontes' comment that when he looked on Mamillius's face,
'I did recoil / Twenty-three years, and saw myself unbreech'd'
(1.2.154–5) indicates his son is not yet dressed in the short pants
('breeches') that marked the beginnings of recognized male identity.
Thus he is no older than seven or eight, the usual time for boys to grad-
uate from unisex clothing.[35] When Leontes, Hermione, and Mamillius
appear onstage for the first time (1.2), we see that rare thing in Shakespeare, a son in the happy company of both parents.[36] The sense of
domestic harmony is enhanced by a still rarer phenomenon: a child
playing in the presence of his royal father. Of course this harmony
proves to be desperately fragile – usually in Shakespeare the triangle
of mother, father, and son proves to be highly unstable[37] – but for a
moment it looks as if the roles of the domestic family-father and the
civil king-father may be brought into accord rather than remaining, as
so often in Shakespeare, dissonant. The visual tableau is supported, for
a moment, by what we hear, as Leontes and Polixenes gladly affirm
their affection for the little sons that restore their health.

In the context of Shakespeare's career-long depiction of fathers and
sons, this scene stands out for the insistence with which Leontes proceeds to identify himself with his son. In the histories and tragedies,
fathers were inclined to see, and to fear, the differences between their
sons and themselves, sensing their progeny would not become adequate successors. Leontes, however, reverses this process as he wishes
to associate himself with the innocence of his son. As Leontes begins to
doubt the integrity of his once innocent boyhood friend, he identifies
himself with his son Mamillius more intensely. It is as if Leontes is
replacing the memory of young Polixenes with the presence of his own
son, so that Mamillius now becomes the 'twinned lamb' that his friend
had been in his boyhood.[38]

In good part, Leontes' identification with his son derives from his
desire to convince himself of his son's legitimacy and his wife's
fidelity. Hence he is insistent on their physical similarity. After asking
Mamillius 'Art thou my boy?' he says of his son's nose, 'it is a copy

out of mine,' and he is happy to claim that women 'say we are /
Almost as like as eggs' (1.2.118, 122, 129–30). For the duration of the
play, Leontes never loses this sense of sons as replicas, and at the end
his emphasis on Florizel as an exact reprint of Polixenes even borders
on the risible:

> Your mother was most true to wedlock, prince;
> For she did print your royal father off,
> Conceiving you.   5.1.123–5

To be sure, other characters in the play mention the similarity of a
family member to a parent, and thus when a Gentleman itemizes the
evidence for Perdita's being the daughter of Hermione he cites the
'majesty of the creature in resemblance of the mother' (5.2.35–6). But
Leontes' repeated insistence on his son's exact replication of himself
reveals his desperate need to see his son as his reflection and should
not be taken as verifiable fact.

As it happens, Leontes is not altogether wrong in insisting on the
similarity between his son and himself, but the resemblance is not
what he thinks. Instead of discerning the lineaments of the man in the
child, as Leontes thinks he is doing, the audience is likely to do just the
opposite: to perceive that the father is now acting in a very childish
fashion.[39] Like son, like father. In his fantasizing about the puzzling
world around him and in his fear of processes he cannot understand
or control, including pregnancy, Leontes is more like a child than he
wants to know. His rage against his best friend and his wife resembles
a temper tantrum to which he has given free rein; against the mature
reason of everyone around him, he will insist on his blinkered view of
things.

Ironically, Leontes creates a terrible gap between himself and
Mamillius when he insists on their shared identity, for his escalating
hysteria about his wife insinuates a complementary confusion and
anxiety into his son. In his first words to his son, Leontes asks, 'Mamillius, / Art thou my boy,' and his son's response is immediate and
unequivocal: 'Ay, my good lord' (1.2.119–20). But after hearing his
father's bizarre free associations concerning animals and horns,
Mamillius is guarded and frightened, responding to 'Art thou my
calf?' with 'Yes, if you will, my lord' (1.2.127). Finally, after hearing his
father's rant about cuckoldry and ponds being fished by neighbours,
Mamillius speaks with palpable fear in his voice, though his father

does not hear it. So, when Leontes suddenly asks 'How now, boy?' Mamillius responds, 'I am like you, they say' (1.2.207–8). That Leontes professes to find 'some comfort' in this troubled response of his son indicates how oblivious he is to the feelings of the lad who is his supposed copy.

Leontes' language reflects his attempt to erase the differences between himself and his boy, for he repeatedly slides from bantering with his son to dark soliloquizing about sexual corruption. Increasingly, he nominally addresses his son but really speaks to himself. Thus, his oft-repeated, punning injunction to 'Go play, boy, play' has the ironic effect of destroying Mamillius's tranquillity and his innocent play. As his fantasy of betrayal takes hold of him, Leontes loses his grip on the reality of his son's presence; A.D. Nuttall astutely notes of Leontes that 'The speeches he addresses to Mamillius are extremely poignant, because Mamillius so nearly succeeds in saving his father from his inwardly erupting delusion.'[40] A telling moment occurs in an early address to Mamillius, when Leontes asks 'What? hast smutch'd thy nose? / They say it is a copy out of mine' (1.2.121–2). It is a small but momentous shift when Leontes moves from concern about his boy's dirtied nose to an insistence on his innocent resemblance to himself.

The sickness of Leontes' interaction with Mamillius is defined by contrast in the following scene (2.1), where we see the boy with his pregnant mother and several serving ladies. Hermione knows that she is not identical to her son, and, by lovingly observing his difference, she can respond to his needs. In the opening words of the scene, Hermione may seem to be even more oblivious to Mamillius's feelings than her husband was, as she charges her waiting ladies to 'Take the boy to you; he so troubles me, / 'Tis past enduring' (2.1.1–2). This sounds like yet another banishment of Mamillius, and the 'past enduring' is reminiscent of Leontes' explosive anger earlier. But what we see is no more than the discomfort of a harassed mother very near her term; twenty lines later she will invite him back into her arms: 'Come, sir, now / I am for you again' (2.1.21–2). In contrast to the male characters' attempts to prevent departures from occurring and gaps from developing, this little vignette is illuminating. Unlike Leontes and Polixenes, Hermione speaks her mind directly to her son without attempting to elevate the relationship into metaphysical significance. And so, after a brief breathing spell, she calls her little 'sir' back again, insisting that he sit next to her, and giving him her entire attention.

This is the truest, quietest scene of separation and reconciliation in the play, until Leontes arrives to shatter it.

Though his father has extolled boyhood innocence and insistently located it in his son, it is mistaken to say that Mamillius 'is present to incarnate that innocence.'[41] The interplay between him and the ladies indicates he is not the lamb that his father wishes him to be, for in the opening line of the scene Hermione complains that he is troubling her 'past enduring' and hands him over to her serving women. Not only does Mamillius seek revenge by trying to play the women off against each other, but also he reveals a shrewd knowledge of the art of women's cosmetics, speaking of an eyebrow that is a 'semicircle, / Or a half-moon made with a pen' (2.1.10–11). This perception, gained by observations of the women at their toilette, is not entirely unlike his father's suspicion of the arts of female betrayal, though grounded in reality and free of his father's hateful hysteria. Moreover, young as he is, Mamillius is aware of the danger of being superseded in the family's politics of affection; the ladies warn him that, since 'a fine new prince' will usurp his mother's attention soon (2.1.17), he had best not spurn companions whom he may need later.

The best evidence of the boy's loss of innocence, and his father's part in it, is the tale he tells his mother. Instead of projecting her ideas on Mamillius, as Leontes had done, Hermione sensitively asks him to 'tell 's a tale' (2.1.23) and praises his storytelling prowess. The winter's tale that he begins to tell of 'sprites and goblins' and of a man who 'Dwelt by a churchyard' (2.1.26, 30) is a fictional transformation of his recent, terrifying experience with his father, perhaps with the suggestion that his father has been possessed by an evil spirit.[42] The telling of the tale seems to conjure up the presence of its protagonist; in a deviation from Shakespeare's principal source, Leontes himself immediately bursts in, disrupting the scene.[43] Leontes' first demand is to separate Mamillius from his mother's embrace ('Give me the boy' [2.1.56]), and this separation quickly becomes more angry as it escalates into a punishment of both Hermione and Mamillius: 'Bear the boy hence, he shall not come about her. / Away with him!' (2.1.59–60). It is not clear if he thinks he is protecting the boy from his mother or punishing him for his intimacy with her, but this forcible separation of Mamillius from Hermione marks the last time the boy will see her or the audience will see him.

When next we hear of Mamillius, he is on his sickbed, and Leontes continues the lethal identification of his son with himself:

> To see his nobleness,
> Conceiving the dishonor of his mother!
> He straight declin'd, droop'd, took it deeply,
> Fasten'd and fix'd the shame on't in himself,
> Threw off his spirit, his appetite, his sleep,
> And downright languish'd. 2.3.12–17

The speech is grotesque because his father intends this description of his son's mental and physical collapse to be praise of his 'nobleness.' Clearly Leontes is projecting his own recent disillusionment about Hermione onto his son. There is an external resemblance between father and son, in that Leontes opens the scene by speaking of his own lack of sleep ('Nor night, nor day, no rest' [2.3.1]), and then goes on to describe how Mamillius no longer sleeps (2.3.16).[44] But the reasons for the shared insomnia are quite different, for Leontes is wrong when he thinks that the boy, like himself, suffers from 'Conceiving the dishonor' (2.3.13) of Hermione. Ironically, despite the father's identification with him, Mamillius is presumably identifying with the suffering of his mother.[45] Indeed, it may well be that this sudden snatching of Mamillius from his mother is a signing of the little boy's death warrant, as his very name suggests his dependency on her nurture.[46]

The force of Leontes' commitment to self-delusion is apparent in his response to the oracle proclaiming Hermione's innocence. In Robert Greene's *Pandosto*, the play's source, the Duke repents as soon as he hears the oracle delivered, and later news is brought that his son is 'suddenly dead.'[47] But Shakespeare's Leontes flatly denies the truth of the oracle and continues to refuse to entertain the possibility that he could be wrong. It is only when the devastating announcement of the death of Mamillius is reported to him, shattering his desperate identification with his son, that he realizes the simple, terrible truth of his errors.[48] In Richard Wheeler's formulation, 'It is the death of Mamillius ... that restores the connection to reality which Leontes has lost in his madness, even as it empties that reality of its life.'[49]

Despite its transformative impact on Leontes, the death of Mamillius has been minimized by critics who are taken with the idea of *The Winter's Tale* as a conventional Romance in which losses are restored. This view argues for a metaphysical restoration of Mamillius to his parents in the form of Florizel, and thus we learn that Mamillius 'dies but is fulfilled in Florizel' and that 'Florizel ... re-presents Mamillius.'[50] To be sure, there are numerous parallels between the two princes who are exactly coeval and also the only sons of best friends who were themselves like brothers. Moreover, if Mamillius *had* remained alive at the end of the play, he and Florizel would have been brothers-in-law. And in a sociological sense it may be accurate to say that 'The male network is solid and copious enough' to supply a replacement for Mamillius.[51] Yet, despite all this, Prince Mamillius can be said to be meaningfully replaced by Prince Florizel only in the narrowest terms of dynastic politics. From the perspective of his grieving parents, there can be no meaningful replacement for him.

After his death, Mamillius is not named by anyone in the play, and this silence might be taken as evidence that he is forgotten and so fully replaced by Florizel that he is not missed. Apparently fearing that audiences have forgotten him, some directors have brought him back as a statue or ghost at the end.[52] But these theatrical interpolations are unnecessary and perhaps counterproductive. Swinburne, who was much taken with Mamillius, remarked that 'at the very end ... it may be that we remember him all the better because the father whose jealously killed him and the mother for love of whom he died would seem to have forgotten the little brave spirit.'[53] Swinburne is right, I think, to stress that the *apparent* forgetting of Mamillius stimulates a compensatory remembering in the reader (and, to a lesser degree, in the enraptured audience). Moreover, on the parents' part silence need not indicate forgetting, as several of Leontes' remarks in act 5 reveal.

The first scene of the fifth act begins with courtiers advising Leontes to marry again, and with Paulina's scotching of the idea by inducing as much guilt as she can in him for the death of 'she you kill'd' (5.1.15). After the unexpected arrival of Prince Florizel and his lovely princess has been announced, Paulina links the imminent appearance of Florizel with the lost Mamillius:

> Had our prince,
> Jewel of children, seen this hour, he had pair'd
> Well with this lord; there was not full a month
> Between their births.   5.1.115–18

Leontes' response to Paulina reveals a pained vulnerability:

> Prithee no more; cease. Thou know'st
> He dies to me again when talk'd of. Sure
> When I shall see this gentleman, thy speeches

> Will bring me to consider that which may
> Unfurnish me of reason. They are come.   5.1.119–23

When Paulina had accidentally-on-purpose referred to Leontes' killing of his wife, he had remonstrated weakly by saying 'Now, good now, / Say so but seldom' (5.1.18–19). Now, his abrupt 'Prithee no more; cease' reveals his alarm at the broaching of the unmentionable. The shift to the beseeching tone of 'Thou know'st / He dies to me again when talk'd of' suggests that Leontes has pleaded with Paulina before not to mention Mamillius, and the rest of the sentence could hardly be more eloquent as an explanation of his silence.[54] This inability – and thus refusal – to speak of Mamillius conveys more sorrow than could any direct expression of grief. The physical absence begets a verbal absence.

It is revealing that neither Paulina nor Leontes mentions Mamillius by name. She speaks of 'our prince / Jewel of children,' and Leontes further distances the boy by referring to 'him.' Also, he alludes to the terrible story of the past in vague, unspecified terms: '*that which* may / Unfurnish me of reason.' Leontes knows whereof he speaks with regard to being deprived of sanity, and he does not refer to the phenomenon lightly. Upon the immediate entrance of Florizel and Perdita, Leontes does not, of course, mention Mamillius, though he can hardly fail to be thinking of him. For the spectator or reader who has not forgotten Leontes' insistence on his son's resemblance to himself at the beginning of the play, there is a poignant echo when he now praises Florizel's mother, 'For she did print your royal father off, / Conceiving you' (5.1.125–6). Paulina's earlier comment on the similarity of Mamillius and Florizel hangs in the air.

In this scene and later, the closest Leontes comes to mentioning Mamillius is when he laments to Florizel and Perdita that 'I lost a couple, that 'twixt heaven and earth / Might thus have stood, begetting wonder' (5.1.132–3). A few lines later, he invokes divine punishment when he contrasts his 'issueless' situation with that of Polixenes, adding:

> What might I have been,
> Might I a son and daughter now have look'd on,
> Such goodly things as you?   5.1.176–8

These lines are moving because of their slight awkwardness, their sense of a much happier life briefly glimpsed. But of course he has not permanently lost the 'couple' of his two children; indeed he is actually looking on the daughter whom he thinks is gone. Despite the frequent talk of men about the importance of princes, it is Leontes' bond with his daughter that provides for his succession and makes his reconciliation with Hermione possible.[55]

Because the succession is restored through Perdita and because no reference is made to Mamillius, it is important to ask how much the boy's death matters at the end of the play.[56] In the final scene, neither Leontes nor Hermione mentions Mamillius. There is of course much in the scene to render both the reunited husband and wife speechless – for him a statue of his wife apparently come to life and for her a daughter miraculously recovered. But one senses a particular reticence about Mamillius. Not only is he not named, but perhaps he cannot be. To name the intolerable, irreparable loss would be to make the reconciliation of his father and mother much more difficult, perhaps even impossible. This ending calls to mind the play's beginning. When the two courtiers discuss Mamillius in the opening scene, the visiting Bohemian says to the Sicilian, 'You have an unspeakable comfort of your young prince Mamillius' (1.1.34–5). In this context 'unspeakable' is a conventional marker of inexpressibility; it is part of the stock-in-trade of courtly hyperbole, signifying nothing. At the end of the play, however, the loss of Mamillius is in the most literal, devastating sense 'unspeakable.'

In this late play, Mamillius can be seen as a forerunner of sons who had appeared earlier in Shakespeare's career. In the boy's dilemma we may glimpse the (unrepresented) childhood of the ambivalent young princes who are the principle subject of this study. Like them, Mamillius is heir and successor to a father who is oblivious to the feelings of the son on whom he wishes to impose himself. The disturbed Leontes views his boy as an extension of himself, a replicant created fully in the paternal image. Thus, for Mamillius, as for Hamlet and his fellow princes, to succeed the royal father poses the threat of accepting a frightening inheritance. Given his youthfulness, the political and moral implications of that inheritance cannot be apparent to Mamillius, and in this regard he differs from earlier ambivalent sons. Nevertheless, the inheritance quickly comes to be terrifying, as its precondition is the boy's entire alienation from the nurture of his mother. Unable to defy his father's commands or to articulate his own needs, he is trapped inside the ghost story that he attempted to share with his mother. Unlike Hal and Hamlet and their fellows, he does not grow up to rescue his father and to inflict his subtle revenge against him. But his premature death does serve to rescue his father from his madness and also grievously to punish him for his failure to recognize his child's autonomy. It is revealing that, even in these late plays in which ambivalent sons have largely disappeared, there is in the diminished form of Mamillius a final revisiting of the issue in a figure who is destroyed before he can grow into the dilemma that awaits him.

9 Biographical Coda: William Shakespeare, Son of John Shakespeare

In the foregoing chapters, I have attempted to observe a self-denying ordinance regarding speculation about Shakespeare the private person. The plays were the thing. It is, however, natural to be curious about possible connections between Shakespeare's life and work, especially with regard to a theme so likely to bear the impress of his own family as fathers and sons. Of course, the undertaking can easily become quixotic, if not downright foolish, and contemporary criticism has tended to shy away from bringing the biographical record to bear on the plays.[1] Beyond the inherent riskiness of interpreting great drama biographically – *all* the voices are Shakespeare's (or perhaps none) – there is a specific problem: while Shakespeare's plays are richly suggestive and expressive, there is very little extra-literary evidence to allow us to reconstruct their creator's inner life. The works are difficult to interpret because there is so much significant detail within them; conversely, the affective life is difficult to interpret because (apart from the plays) there is so little evidence for it. The obvious solution is to wed the simple outlines of the life story and the complexity of the works together, but the most frequent offspring of the marriage is a stillborn logical circularity: biographical speculations shape literary interpretations, which in turn confirm the speculations.

Though it may be impossible to escape this circularity altogether, I have attempted to minimize the problem by confining biographical speculation to this final chapter, where it provides a bookend to correspond with the initial bookend of historical contextualization in chapter 1. Standing in the middle are the chapters of literary analysis that interpret the plays' father and son relationships without recourse to the biographical record. This sequencing ensures that the biographical guesswork is deferred until the end so that it follows *after* – and more importantly follows *from* – what has gone before. Thus, the plausibility of my necessarily hypothetical reconstruction of William Shakespeare's relationship with his father rests on its consonance with historical patterns in the Elizabethan family, with recurring interactions between fathers and sons in the plays, and with the extant biographical records of the Shakespeare family.

Should the reader wonder why this chapter discusses Shakespeare more as a son than as a father, the answer is simple: the factual record concerning his son Hamnet is too slight either to support or to challenge hypotheses derived from the plays. The salient facts about Hamnet are poignantly few: that he was the fraternal twin of Judith and the only son of William and his wife Anne, that he (and the rest of his immediate family) lived in Stratford while William resided in London, and that in August of 1596 he died from unknown causes at the age of eleven and a half. These meagre facts fuel common speculation that the boys who die young in the plays are Hamnet figures (e.g., Arthur in *King John*, young Macduff in *Macbeth*, and Mamillius in *The Winter's Tale*) and that the fathers who lament deceased sons, often with a heavy admixture of guilt, are Shakespeare figures (e.g., Macduff, Northumberland in *2 Henry IV*, Leontes in *The Winter's Tale*, and Alonso in *The Tempest*). A biographer's melodramatic assertion that after his death 'The shade of young Hamnet would stalk his father's lines for many a play to come' may be true, but there is not a firm enough base of biographical fact to confer much substance on these hauntings.[2]

To recapitulate very briefly the gist of earlier chapters, the primary configuration of father and son in the plays involves a dutiful son being pressured to perform an action that he senses is foreign to his values and threatening to his autonomy. For the son, an ambivalent state of mind results; he resists doing his father's bidding but is unwilling or unable to deny his father's right to command him. The son's resistance is accompanied by his extreme reluctance to articulate his dilemma, an internal censorship that extends even to the normally private, self-communing discourse of the soliloquy. Shakespeare's fictional sons do eventually act, and the action usually involves the rescue of the father from his enemies. Without exception, these filial restorations figure more largely in Shakespeare's plays than in the sources they are based on. They are also considerably more complex, being expressions of filial autonomy as well as deference. Characteristically, Shakespeare's sons save their fathers in such a way as to remind them of their weakness, and, in an attempt to settle accounts, the son usually follows his double-edged rescue with an act of concealed revenge against the father whose life he has restored. Rescue is not synonymous with reconciliation.

Though Shakespeare's depiction of it is rooted in cultural tensions of his time, filial ambivalence was not an acknowledged Elizabethan reality. From a modern, post-Freudian perspective, ambivalence toward fathers is a natural and healthy, perhaps even an inevitable, attitude for sons to have; as Freud insisted, it is crucial for children to liberate themselves from the authority of their parents because 'the whole progress of society rests upon the opposition between successive generations.'[3] But it was not always thus. In the religious and political discourse of Elizabethan fathers and sons, there is little, if any, recognition of the possibility that decent and dutiful sons could feel anger toward their fathers, let alone justifiable hostility. Instead, the official emphasis is on the strict separation of 'natural' and 'unnatural' sons, the former serving their fathers with instinctual love and the latter perversely abandoning them. This moral dichotomy characterizes the Elizabethan prototypes of sons (e.g., Aeneas and Icarus), and it is present in many of the key narrative and dramatic sources for Shakespeare's plays, such as Sidney's story of the King of Paphlagonia who has symmetrical, binary sons: a kind, natural, legitimate son and a cruel, unnatural, illegitimate son. But, as we have seen in *King Lear* and other plays, Shakespeare usually complicates the conventional depiction of sons by combining within one character elements of the opposed moral archetypes; he suggests that filial aggression can be as 'natural' as filial sacrifice and likely to coexist in surreptitious forms alongside it.

To the reader who has persevered to this point, my inference is entirely predictable: that Shakespeare was himself probably an ambivalent son. It may be true, in a recent biographer's formulation, that 'William is likely to have felt the strongest loyalty, sympathy, and love for his father,' but that assessment is partial.[4] It is equally likely, for reasons that will soon be apparent, that he also felt the opposite emotions toward his father. Given his persistent exploration of dutiful but angry sons, figures who are not conflicted in their prior appearances in his source materials, it is plausible to think that Shakespeare found in himself the primary source for his insights.[5] Another reason to suspect that Shakespeare may have participated in the filial ambivalence he depicted lies in the uncommon obliqueness with which he represents the phenomenon. In part, the subtlety of Shakespeare's characterization of these sons and the consequent need to interpret them inferentially can be attributed to an artistic fidelity to nature: this is how angry, repressed sons talk and act. But there seems to be another, less mimetic element at work. These representations of ambivalence are so easy to miss, in reading as well as in performance, that one wonders whether the author (or at least part of him) was not content for them to pass unobserved, much as Hal and Hamlet make attacks on their fathers that are hidden almost to the point of invisibility.

The Elder and the Younger Shakespeare

John Shakespeare, the dramatist's father, was a substantial presence in sixteenth-century Stratford, being long-lived, litigious, and engaged in a variety of civic and business affairs. Though he left many traces in the Stratford records, there is no contemporary account of his personality, no comment on him as a husband, father, or business associate. Unfortunately, the document that is closest to being a contemporary comment on his character is of very dubious value. In the middle of the seventeenth century – decades after the death of both John Shakespeare (1601) and William Shakespeare (1617) – the Archdeacon of Rochester, Thomas Plume, entered into his notebook a brief anecdote about the increasingly celebrated dramatist: 'He was a glover's son. Sir John Mennes once saw his old father in his shop – a merry cheeked old man – that said "Will was a good honest fellow, but he darest have cracked a jest with him at any time."'[6] Shakespeare's biographers display a curiously contradictory attitude toward this account. On the one hand, they invariably note that the description of the 'old father in his shop' attributed to Sir John Mennes cannot be relied upon, for Mennes was only two years old when John Shakespeare died. On the other hand, they are loath to disregard such a rare piece of evidence, especially since it accurately identifies the elder Shakespeare as a glover and also suggests an amicable relationship between the jest-sharing father and son. The usual gambit is to attempt to salvage the anecdote by advancing the possibility that it contains some sort of essential truth. But the 'report' is credible only to those who are determined to believe it. Quite apart from the impossibility of Mennes' having seen what the anecdote has him claim, the words supposedly spoken by John Shakespeare do not ring true. Indeed, there is good reason to think, as appendix 2 shows, that Mennes invented the scene he purports to describe.

John Shakespeare's career began as a Tudor success story but ended in financial decline and disappointment. The eldest son of a modestly successful tenant farmer, John Shakespeare was remarkably energetic and ambitious until his forties. After rejecting the precedent of his father by leaving the land, he moved to Stratford, bought two houses, opened a glove-maker's shop, and made a socially and economically advantageous marriage to Mary Arden, the favourite daughter of the well-to-do yeoman from whom his father rented his house and fields.[7] One success followed another. Though local records usually identify his occupation as glove-maker, John Shakespeare had irons in many fires: he engaged in large transactions as a wool merchant, bought and rented houses, lent money at high interest, stored agricultural produce, and may have had a sideline as a butcher as well. His energy and competence were recognized by the Corporation of Stratford, and he moved steadily up the civic hierarchy, beginning as an ale-taster and ascending by degrees to constable, affeeror (a court official who assessed fines), burgess, alderman, and high bailiff (an office corresponding to mayor). After his term as bailiff was completed, he served as chief alderman to the man who succeeded him. Then disaster struck.

William Shakespeare was in his twelfth or thirteenth year when his father's fortunes suddenly began to plummet. Biographers have advanced many causes for the decline, including (in order of likelihood) rash business practices, a general economic downturn in the Midlands, changes in the licensing and practice of wool merchants, an obdurate commitment to Catholicism that led to fines and harassment, and perhaps a drinking problem for good measure.[8] The weakest cause is certainly the hypothetical trouble with alcohol, which is usually accompanied by a fanciful identification of John Shakespeare with Sir John Falstaff. Outside the plays, there is no evidence to support it. Similarly, the argument for associating the elder Shakespeare's decline with his persistence in his supposed Catholic beliefs does not withstand scrutiny, as John Bearman demonstrated in an important study.[9] The most probable cause of John Shakespeare's decline was a combination of economic factors, with the ill-effects of the general downturn and the more vigilant licensing of business practices being greatly exacerbated by his risky habit of relying too heavily on credit to keep his numerous enterprises afloat. Regardless of the causes, the results are clear. John Shakespeare withdrew from the civic life of Stratford that had absorbed so much of his energy, no longer attending meetings or even paying his taxes. More ominously, he began to liquidate the assets that he had so assiduously acquired, selling land for ready money.

What must have been an especially humiliating reversal for the family involved the loss of a house and tract of land near Stratford at Wilmcote. This property (known as Asbyes or Aston Cantlow) was a bitter loss because it constituted the better part of Mary Arden's dowry and because John and Mary lost possession of it to a family member. In his time of troubles, John Shakespeare mortgaged the Wilmcote property to his wife's brother-in-law, Edmund Lambert, for cash with which to pay off some debts, and doubtless he expected to recover it when the redemption fell due.[10] But when the time came to redeem the mortgage, John Shakespeare apparently could not raise the money, and the property remained in the hands of the brother-in-law. Following Lambert's death in 1587, John and Mary Shakespeare attempted to wrest the property or a large cash payment from his heir (their nephew) by bringing a suit in the Court of King's Bench in Westminster, which they eventually dropped. But family dreams die hard, and some nine years later William Shakespeare joined his father and mother in applying to the Court of Chancery for the recovery of the land. After depositions were made, the Shakespeares decided not to pursue the case, presumably because they felt it could not be won. For husband, wife, and eldest son, the loss may have felt like a permanent stigma.[11]

All of Shakespeare's biographers agree that John Shakespeare's sudden decline in status and wealth must have had a profound effect on his sensitive adolescent son. As a child, young William would have been aware of and proud of the deference that in Stratford had been shown to his father and, by association, to himself. As the family of the town's bailiff, the Shakespeares were privileged to worship in the front pew in Holy Trinity Church, and John Shakespeare would have been accompanied by attendants impressively dressed in scarlet when he was on official business. Like most Elizabethan children in provincial towns, William would have been fully exposed to the catechisms about honouring one's father, catechisms in which an explicit connection invariably was drawn between the rule of the domestic father in the family and that of the civic fathers who commanded the obedience and respect of everyone in the land. Aware of his authority in both spheres,

John Shakespeare presumably exercised it with a sense of complacent entitlement, as did other self-made men of the age.[12] When such a self-assured father forfeited his offices, young William would have felt acutely the loss of public prestige and presumably would have seen his father in a new light. Since John Shakespeare remained at home to avoid fines being served on him, William would frequently have found himself in the presence of this once-successful man.

The effect on William is likely to have been a mixture of pity and anger toward his fallen father. It is plausible to think that the imaginative boy sympathized with a father who had become uncharacteristically disconsolate and perhaps felt defeated by a world he could no longer deal with. Thus, Peter Ackroyd and others have linked John Shakespeare's fall with William's sympathy for extreme misfortune in the tragedies, suggesting it would have helped to create in his son's mind 'an idealised patriarchy or an idealised relationship between father and son.'[13] But this interpretation is itself perhaps too idealized; it rests on the assumption that the elder Shakespeare would have been relatively easy to identify with after his fall. In a similarly ahistorical vein, C.L. Barber and Richard P. Wheeler comment briefly on the 'extreme patriarchal authority' exercised by Elizabethan fathers but then rather wishfully add that 'It seems highly unlikely that Shakespeare's father can have maintained such authority within his own house from the time he abdicated public authority, if he had not already lost it some time before.'[14] There is, however, no reason to think that John Shakespeare or any other Elizabethan father in similar circumstances would have easily relinquished the patriarchal prerogatives vested in him by church and state. Moreover, then as now, a common paternal response to failure outside the home was a stronger insistence on authority within it.

Biographers tend to minimize (if they mention it at all) the pressure to support his father that William's status as eldest son would have placed on him. As we saw in chapter 1, in Elizabethan families the eldest son stands in a special relationship to the father as the primary inheritor of property and as the transmitter of patrilineal values. As his father's legal successor and metaphysical continuation, he is inevitably the recipient of paternal advice and anxiety. From the outset of the family troubles, the obligation placed on William would have been great, and it would have increased steadily as he grew older. What could he do to reverse his father's and his family's decline? Insofar as he had internalized the deferential filial attitudes to which every Elizabethan child was exposed, William would have known it was his duty to sacrifice himself for the father who had given him life and to whom his entire obedience was due. As we will see in a moment, there is evidence that he did indeed attempt with some success to rescue his fallen father.

But, unless William were a saintly teenager, it seems fair to postulate that – sooner or later – he would have felt anger at his father for the social embarrassment and the diminishment of life prospects that his decline entailed. In more ways than one, the father's losses also would have been his eldest son's. To the degree that young William took pride in identifying with a father who had received the deference of the community, the loss of that approbation would have carried a personal sting. But issues of social status would have taken second place to the most disturbing of the new realities: financial decline. Not only would the family have had to observe new economies in its day-to-day functioning, but the reduced prospects for the future would also have been troubling. For William, the forfeiture of land and property was clearly a diminution of his own prospective inheritance as the eldest son. The loss of the Arden lands may have been especially hard for William to swallow, as they represented a link (however tenuous) with the ancient nobility of England, and their seizure by his aunt's husband would have reflected badly on his out-manoeuvred father. It would have been natural for William to feel at least some degree of resentment toward his father, even if he largely sympathized with him, and in a bitter mood he may have felt the animus that a critic implies: 'William had seen [his father] rob his mother and himself of her inheritance by his decline.'[15]

William would have had still more cause for resentment if the traditional story is true that his father removed him from school because of financial pressures. According to Nicholas Rowe, Shakespeare's generally well-informed first biographer, John Shakespeare had sent his son to the Stratford grammar school, 'But the narrowness of his circumstances, and the want of his assistance at home, forc'd his father to withdraw him from thence.'[16] If William had harboured dreams of attending university and advancing himself socially, as sons of several of his father's Stratford associates had done, then the removal from school may have felt like a catastrophe. Even if William did not especially enjoy school, as his later satire of schoolmasters may indicate, he could not have been happy that the shape of his life was being dictated by his father's needs. A second biographical speculation, unverified but (like the first) venerable, has it that after his removal from school William was apprenticed to his father to learn the glover's trade.[17] If this happened, young William would certainly have felt a demotion in terms of his life chances and also in terms of his autonomy. To be put to more-or-less menial work for his own father may have felt like a form of bondage in the home, especially since his father was accustomed to deference and doubtless expected it of his son.

Whatever the degree of conflict between paternal authority and filial autonomy, it would likely have come to a head with William's hurried marriage to Anne Hathaway in 1583, an event followed by the birth of their daughter Susanna only six months later. In John Shakespeare's eyes, the problem is less likely to have been intercourse before wedlock, or even pregnancy, than premature marriage. With a single voice, Elizabethan fathers cautioned their sons to be prudent and to defer marriage until they had established themselves as breadwinners, after the requisite seven years of apprenticeship had passed. The typical age for young men to marry was twenty-eight or twenty-nine – William was all of eighteen.[18] By contrast with his improvident son, it is very likely that John Shakespeare had served a full apprenticeship and was in his late twenties when he asked for the hand of Mary Arden. Certainly, he was financially independent, for he had already purchased two freehold properties in Stratford. Not only was William marrying much younger than his father but also much less advantageously; as William's newly impecunious father surely would have noted, Anne Hathaway brought only a modest cash dowry to a household that included William's three younger brothers and a younger sister. Given the severely straitened circumstances of the family, John Shakespeare may well have felt that William was behaving in an irresponsible and even reckless fashion, becoming a prodigal son while still living at home. Since William was underage, his father must have given his consent to the marriage, but it may have been with clenched teeth. It may even be, as Germaine Greer has suggested, that in the face of parental opposition William and Anne attempted to 'force the issue by chancing a pregnancy.'[19]

There is at least one more probable bone of contention between the elder and the younger Shakespeare: William's employment with a theatrical troupe. No one knows for certain when and how Shakespeare first became professionally involved with the theatre, but he must have made the move to London sometime between 1585 (when the twins Judith and Hamnet were born) and 1590 at the very latest. There is no evidence of his father's response to the decision, though we can surmise how he must have reacted. John Shakespeare was apparently not an enemy of the theatre (when he was Stratford's bailiff he allowed travelling companies to stage plays in town), but it is unlikely that he would have been sympathetic to his eldest son's choice of acting in public playhouses as a vocation.[20] Indeed, in those years the theatre was scarcely looked upon as a vocation at all, let alone an honest one. 'Common players,' as professional actors were called, were often criticized by the merchant class, who regarded them as foreign to the social hierarchy and thus related to vagabonds, 'sturdy beggars,' and the like.[21] Also, there were numerous religious objections to be made. When the Puritan minister William Gouge lists the 'unlawful callings' that he faults parents for allowing their children to pursue, the first damnable vocation is predictably 'popish and idolatrous orders,' and the second is 'to be stage-players.'[22]

Though the first of the purpose-built theatres, The Theatre, had been successful following its opening in 1576, it seems highly unlikely that a man of John Shakespeare's age and provincial background could have imagined the financial takings that London's new public theatres would make possible. Those profits, it should be remembered, accrued to the theatres' owners, not to mere actors or playwrights, and no one could have imagined William's improbable and rapid ascent to joint-sharer. What John Shakespeare would have seen is his eldest son rejecting the traditional forms of business in favour of an enterprise that, in addition to being morally questionable in the eyes of many, offered very little promise of stability and steady income. On this issue, the gap in understanding between the generations was probably unbridgeable.

If John Shakespeare did resist his son's leaving Stratford to take up with an acting company, it is tempting to think he may have employed (in good Elizabethan fashion) the parable of the Prodigal Son to warn young William of the dangers he faced. If so, in later life a delicious irony would not have been lost on his son: instead of dissipating his share of his inheritance, as the Prodigal did, Shakespeare left his indigent, irresponsible father behind in order to regain the inheritance that his progenitor had lost. The Prodigal Son returns home from the den of London iniquity not in tatters but in splendour, able to restore the family fortunes.

Rescuing John Shakespeare

In the deferential social world of Elizabethan England, sons did not quickly or automatically outgrow the filial obeisance that had been inculcated in them; it was not uncommon for grown men with children of their own to doff their hats to their fathers and even to kneel for the parental blessing. Some sons felt guilty about becoming more success-ful and more socially elevated than their fathers. One of the most pow-erful expressions of this adult dutifulness appears in the 'additions' that Shakespeare wrote for the collaborative play *Sir Thomas More*. After he has risen from what he calls 'an humble bench of birth' to become Lord Chancellor of England, Shakespeare's More soliloquizes on the possible 'corruption' posed by his having surpassed his father:

> him [to] bind by my place
> To give the smooth and dexter way to me
> That owe it him by nature.[23]

In this reversal of roles, the son compels his father to be deferential, despite the natural debt he owes his progenitor. Suggestively, Dennis Kay observes that this speech 'echoes Shakespeare's life more closely than it does More's.'[24]

As we saw in the introduction and chapter 1, a standard theme of Elizabethan catechisms on honouring one's parents was the exhorta-tion of children to go beyond mere outward shows of obedience by committing themselves to rescue their parents in times of danger. In church and in the schoolroom, impressionable children were subjected to this lesson, and young William Shakespeare could scarcely have avoided hearing about the debt of filial sacrifice. It is likely, given the rapid decline of his father's fortunes, that he also heard at home about the necessity for dutiful children to waive their own desire. There must have been times when William, like many sons in his plays, felt his filial obligation was unfair and unrepayable, 'a debt never promised' in Prince Hal's bitter phrase. If so, his anger did not eradicate his com-mitment to pay his debt to his father by restoring him to his former for-tunes.[25] Like the rescues of fathers by ambivalent sons in the plays, William's restoration of John Shakespeare was double sided. By doing for his father what his father could not do for himself, William made good John's losses and restored much of his former status. As in the plays, the outstanding fact about this filial rescue is its expression of devotion to his father. Less obviously, it confirmed John's dependence on William's superior wealth and mastery, and there is also evidence to indicate the subtle presence of aggression.

Shakespeare's restoration of his father was made possible by – and was an advertisement for – the fact that he had soundly established himself. Though he had written a number of popular plays since his arrival in London probably in the late 1580s, the decisive turning point in his fortunes occurred in 1594 when he became a shareholder in the Lord Chamberlain's Men, a newly founded acting company. The Lord Chamberlain's Men rapidly became the most successful company in London, providing Shakespeare with a share of healthy box-office receipts and with a ready venue for his plays. He flourished. In 1596, probably the year in which he completed the enormously successful *Henry IV, Part One*, Shakespeare had the means and the will to come to his father's aid, and he attempted to do so in several ways.

Part of Shakespeare's intended rescue involved an attempt to regain the property that his father had lost, especially the house and land at Wilmcote that Mary Arden had brought with her when she married John Shakespeare. Ten years after their first attempt in 1586, the family brought forward a suit in Chancery Court, one of the highest courts in the land, to restore the ownership of the property to John Shakespeare. It would seem that the dramatist must have put up the considerable monies necessary to reopen the case; according to the extant document, the litigation was brought forward not by John and Mary alone but by William as well. As noted earlier, the Shakespeare family seems to have withdrawn its appeal, for after depositions (no longer extant) had been made the case was never adjudicated.

At the same time that he was pursuing the maternal Arden property lost by his father, Shakespeare addressed – this time more successfully – another symbolic wound his father had suffered.[26] Sometime in the mid-to-late 1570s, when he was at the height of his public and financial success, John Shakespeare had begun proceedings with the Office of Heralds to secure a coat of arms and 'gentle' status for himself and his family. The original application has not survived, but we may assume that it was based on John's status as a bailiff and on the antiquity of his wife's Arden origins. Nothing came of the application; it seems likely that John was forced to abandon it when his fortunes plummeted. As a leading citizen and sometime bailiff of Stratford, John had a plausible claim to bear a coat of arms, but the process needed to be helped along by payments to the College of Heralds, who were prepared to confirm the gentlemanly status only of people who could pay for the privilege. In 1596, the same year as the unsuccessful reopening of the appeal for the lost estate, the application for a coat of arms for the Stratford Shakespeares was renewed in the name of John Shakespeare. It is the unanimous opinion of Shakespeare's biographers that this ultimately successful application was made by the son in the name of his father. (The granting of arms was always made in the name of the eldest living male of the line.) Some twenty years after his original application, and through the good offices of his son, John Shakespeare officially became a gentleman. But a bitter irony would not have been lost on William Shakespeare: the grant was made only after Hamnet's death had 'doomed the male line of the Shakespeares to extinction.'[27]

More clearly than the reopening of the law case, this renewal of the request for a coat of arms bespeaks the son's ambivalence toward his father. Clearly, the request is a gift to the aging father, a restoration of the honour that William as a child had seen slip away. But there is a twist, perhaps several twists. Behind the filial generosity there may also be lurking an 'aggressive repetition' in which a son betters his father by completing the work at which his progenitor had failed.[28] Coats of arms are (unlike knighthoods) passed down from generation to generation, but in this case the coat of arms has been passed up from the younger generation to the older, in an odd form of inverted, quasi-benign usurpation.[29]

The possibility of unspoken or semi-concealed aggression may extend to details in the coat of arms and the motto that accompanies it (see fig. 3, below). Since John Shakespeare's original request does not survive, it is impossible to be certain if the application made in 1596 differs from it, reflecting the son's intervention. But one detail is especially interesting. In the 1596 bequest it is specified that the tilted spear is to have a silver tip ('the point steeled proper'); the effect of this detail may be to create the visual suggestion that the spear is really a writing pen with a silver nib. As Katherine Duncan-Jones notes, quill pens were the standard writing instrument of the day, but 'gold or silver pens [were] awarded as prizes to outstanding skilled penmen,' and the penlike lance could remind onlookers of such an award. Duncan-Jones does not point out, however, that the metamorphosis of the spear into a pen would shift the meaning of the coat from being a glorification of chivalrous forebears to a tacit celebration of the conquering pen of William Shakespeare, which had made the procurement of the coat of arms possible. The pen is mightier than the spear.

Figure 3 Sketch of the Shakespeare Coat of Arms by Ralph Brooke, York Herald (1602). Courtesy of the Folger Shakespeare Library.

A second intriguing detail, one very likely invented by William Shakespeare, is the Old French motto for the coat: 'Non sanz droict' (not without right).[30] The motto is ambiguous, as 'droict' can refer to the chivalric justice that the spear upholds, or to the victory of the (suggested) pen, or to the worthiness of the Shakespeare family to receive the coat of arms. If it refers to the grant of arms, a note of defensive insecurity creeps in, highlighted by the fact that the assertion is couched as a double negative rather than a strong positive.[31] These complications are exacerbated by a grammatical ambiguity that confused the recording clerk in the Office of Heralds. The first two times the clerk penned the phrase, he wrote it – first in capitals and then in lower-case letters – as 'Non, sanz droict.' Such a reading would imply that the claim is without merit or substance. Realizing that this negative meaning was inappropriate and presumably unintended, on his third attempt the clerk dropped the comma and arrived at 'Non sanz droict,' the assertion of righteous deserving.

I want to suggest that the clerk's process of interpretation – an original negative reading followed by a correction to make the meaning positive – may have pleased Shakespeare, for it could have been the response the ambiguous motto was calculated to elicit.[32] In Elizabethan literature there are a number of trick passages in which the meaning is comically inverted by mispunctuation; indeed, Shakespeare uses the trick himself in a play written at roughly the same time as the reapplication for the coat of arms.[33] In *A Midsummer Night's Dream*, a rattled Peter Quince delivers the Prologue to his Pyramus and Thisbe drama in a way that rides roughshod over the intended punctuation, turning a respectful address into an inadvertent attack on his noble audience (5.1.108–17). If Shakespeare intended 'Non sans droict' to be first misread and then corrected to the expected, decorous meaning, this motto would read like some of the ambiguous comments made about Lord John Talbot in *1 Henry VI*, where the reader may first take the statement as negative but will reinterpret it to turn it into the praise that editors have assumed the context demands.[34] Similarly, chivalry becomes a stalking horse in *The Reign of Edward III*, a play published anonymously but often attributed to Shakespeare in recent criticism, when the embittered Black Prince employs an ambiguous Latin motto to criticize the father who refused to rescue him.[35] Thus Shakespeare may have relished the fact that the motto for the coat of arms does double duty, cleverly hinting at the falseness of the undertaking while also, being reinterpreted as the occasion demands, justifying the claim of John Shakespeare and his heirs to gentle status.

William and John Shakespeare in the Plays

This is not the place to return to my analyses of Shakespeare's plays and move through them a second time, systematically feeding speculations about William and John into the text. But if my hypothesis that Shakespeare was himself an ambivalent son is convincing, it should be possible to look at his representations of fathers and sons with a fresh eye. At the very least, this characterization of the relationship may illuminate details and strike resonances not apparent in a biography-free reading of the plays. Shakespeare's history plays are an excellent register for seeing this biographical dimension, partly because they are so deeply concerned with fathers and sons and the issue of succession. In these popular history plays, many of which were written when he was establishing himself on the London stage, Shakespeare is making the financial rescue of his father possible by writing drama in which rescuing fathers is a central motif.

As one might expect, the biographical resonances are especially rich in *1 Henry VI*, which Shakespeare wrote after having recently left Stratford. In different ways, both sets of fathers and sons in the play – the Master Gunner and his Boy and, more centrally, Lord John Talbot and young John Talbot – may cast light on Shakespeare's relationship with his father. Indeed, they give us two different but complementary depictions of the relationship. In the shaken, exhausted Master Gunner, who is desperate to do something to 'procure me grace' (*1H6*:2.2.7) but must depend on his disobedient son to carry out his plan and preserve his position, we may have a glimpse of John Shakespeare's similarly vulnerable situation. In only a handful of lines, none of which has a source in the historical chronicles, Shakespeare depicts a habit of paternal authority and arrogance rapidly collapsing. And in the sly, disobedient son, who uses the language of reverence to express his rebellion against his father, we may have a glimpse of the future playwright under the wing of his still authoritative but compromised father. Of special interest is Shakespeare's sharp observation of fatherly behaviour when the Master Gunner asserts his superiority over his boy ('Sirrah') in a futile attempt to maintain his own threatened dignity. Like so many of Shakespeare's fathers to come, the Master Gunner finds himself in danger of sudden eclipse and becomes dependent on the youthful energy of a son whom he does not trust, and for good reason. The boy fulfils his father's strategy, but only by disobeying him and shooting the English Earl himself, and this raises an ambiguity that hangs over the scene: is the boy rescuing his father or usurping him, or some combination of both?

The Master Gunner and his Boy differ from most of Shakespeare's depictions of fathers and sons in that they are commoners, and French commoners at that. Shakespeare's usual depictions are closer to what Freud says of boys' fantasies about rescuing their fathers: 'This phantasy is commonly enough displaced on to the emperor, king or some other great man; after being thus distorted it becomes admissible to consciousness, and may even be made use of by creative writers.'[36] With Lord John Talbot, the legendary scourge of the French, and his son young John Talbot, we move into Freud's realm of great men, in which the father of the fantasizing creative writer becomes translated into someone larger than life but still very human. Lord John is especially evocative of Shakespeare's father John, as he is a once great warrior who is now betrayed by his friends and surrounded by his enemies. On the battlefield Lord John stands alone with his suddenly transformed son, who was called to France to be instructed in war but who now proceeds to rescue his paternal teacher. After saving his father, young John leaves him in order to fight his own battle, and the two figures die in each others' arms. But, rich in fantasy material as the scene is, Shakespeare the dramatist explores a complex psychological interaction in which the son's autonomy is tested.

As noted in chapter 2, there is a curious doubleness in the depiction of the two Talbots, in that Shakespeare revises his historical sources in opposing directions by magnifying both the unity of father and son and the distance between them. The best way to make sense of this two-sidedness is to interpret the dramatist's primary intention as an attempt to glorify the unity of father and son, so that they become inter-generational twins, sharing a single name and spirit in two bodies. But this fantasy begets an opposing view, and Shakespeare repeatedly insinuates the likelihood that in reality the father is imposing, or at least trying to impose, his values and his script onto his son. If the elder and younger John Talbot stand together in opposition to the French and also to their quarrelling compatriots – a Daedalus and Icarus imprisoned in a hostile world – they also stand apart from each other in subtle ways. Playing around the edges of the heroic, sentimental representation is the awareness that it is Lord John Talbot and the martial honour he embodies that have trapped and will destroy young John Talbot, much as Daedalus's invention of wings inadvertently dooms Icarus. In 1 Henry VI the fantasy of ennoblement is very strong, but the awareness of irony is always present as well.

It is not surprising that, after Shakespeare's success in London was firmly established, the motif of filial rescue frequently appeared in the plays. The dovetailing of Shakespeare's theatrical depiction of filial

rescue and his attempt to restore his father's status is strikingly apparent in *Henry IV, Part One*, where Prince Hal's rescue of his father at
Shrewsbury Field stands in a metaphorical relation to Shakespeare's
restoration of his father by winning the coat of arms that earlier John
had failed to secure.[37] Most scholars assign this play to 1596, the year
in which Shakespeare initiated the unsuccessful attempt to regain the
Arden lands as well as the successful reapplication for a coat of arms.
It may well be that securing the coat of arms had been on Shakespeare's mind for some time. In his previous history play, *Richard II*,
Bullingbrook vows to 'furbish new the name of John a' Gaunt' (his
father) in a speech containing heraldic details that prefigure the coat of
arms later awarded to John Shakespeare (1.3.69–77).[38]

The connection between the filial rescues of Shakespeare and Prince
Hal is extremely suggestive if one understands both actions as ambivalent gestures, aggressive actions taken against the fathers as well as
heroic deeds undertaken on their behalf. Both rescues prove something to the father, and in the process reprove him. King Henry is
angry at Prince Hal for leaving the court and behaving in a dissipated,
prodigal way that reflects badly on the usurper's claim to the throne;
thus, Hal's rescue of the King is clearly a victory over the Douglas and
also over the father who had earlier branded him as 'degenerate'
(3.2.128). One wonders if Shakespeare felt a similar sense of triumph
over the father *he* rescued. As I speculated earlier in this chapter, John
Shakespeare was probably displeased when, in his paternal hour of
need, his eldest son dropped his many responsibilities in Stratford in
pursuit of a theatrical career that would have seemed at best a will o'
the wisp. If so, there is an implicit reproach to John Shakespeare in the
fact that his rescue was brought about through the good offices of a
once disobedient son who had become a common player (as Hal play-
fully had done in the tavern) and, through his success, proven his creative instincts to have been right.

The implicit parallel between the filial rescues of Prince Hal and
Shakespeare is even more complex, for in each case the rescuing son
has reason to suspect the falseness of the paternal claim he supports.
As I stressed in chapter 4, Prince Hal is clearly aware that his father has
usurped the throne and thus does not possess the legitimacy he claims.
But in *Part Two* of *Henry IV* Shakespeare shows Prince Hal attempting
to force the truth out of his mind through a clenched determination
that amounts to a willed forgetting of past stains. By the same token,
the ambiguity of 'Non sanz droict/Non, sanz droict' would seem to

indicate that Shakespeare at least suspected that his father's claim to gentle status was a fiction. (There is no evidence, by the way, that William Shakespeare himself ever used the actual coat of arms, which he was entitled to emblazon on various possessions, including his house.) In both cases, there is an element of protesting too much in the son's insistence on the straightforward patrilineal legality of what is at best a fragile claim.[39]

One more parallel between rescue in art and in life may help to explain the knowing, compromised insistence of both Prince Hal and Shakespeare on legality and justice: in both cases they are pursuing their own 'right' as well as that of their fathers. Both sons stand directly to gain from the claim made on behalf of their fathers, and it would be cynical but not completely wrong to say that both are really making the claim for paternal possession on behalf of themselves. Because both sons are the legal successors of their fathers and will become the inheritors of their status, the restoration of the father is also a *de facto* self-elevation of the son.[40] Moreover, in both cases the son would not have a claim at all were it not for the prior possession of the father. Quite clearly, Prince Hal has no claim to the throne apart from the primogeniture enabled by his father's (dubious) possession of it. Similarly, as a mere 'player,' Shakespeare could never claim gentle status on his own deserts but only as his father's son.[41] Righteously, Prince Hal ascends his father's throne in the name of God and justice; likewise, at the beginning of his last will and testament Shakespeare will claim the status for himself as 'gent.'[42]

Related to the element of self-aggrandizement in the rescues is a more disturbing reality: both Prince Hal and William Shakespeare come to resemble the flawed fathers they succeed, and both seem to be uncomfortably aware of the fact. As noted in the discussion of *Part Two* of *Henry IV*, toward the end of the play both King Henry and Prince Hal begin to realize that they are not as different as they had thought. Insofar as they have a reconciliation, it is based on their recognition that their political difficulties and options for dealing with them are similar. Indeed, the eventual parallels between the King and Prince, despite the son's conflict with his father, prove to be numerous. Particularly notable is their treatment of their former colleagues. In his deathbed confidence to his son, the King curtly dismisses the erstwhile friends and co-conspirators who helped him to the crown by saying, 'I cut them off' (2H4:4.5.209). This acknowledgment is significant because five scenes later Hal, as the new King Henry, will cut off Fal-

staff, his old companion and a key contributor to his political education. In a telling symmetry, the two *Henry IV* plays begin with King
Henry IV banishing Worcester, his former co-conspirator, from the
court, and they end with King Henry V banishing Falstaff from the
court.

As we saw in chapter 1, there were striking cultural differences
between the male generations in Elizabethan England, and in the case
of Shakespeare *père et fils* these would have been even more pronounced by the fact that 'the gap between young and old in provincial
towns in the 1580s was particularly great.'[43] For John and William
Shakespeare this gap would have manifested itself in culture and education, as John may have had little or no formal education and 'seems
to have had at most only a partial literacy,' being probably unable to
write and perhaps to read as well.[44] As William presumably showed
an uncommon aptitude for reading and writing, thanks to the
grammar school education he received, John Shakespeare's capacity
for understanding and sympathizing with his son may have been constrained. It seems safe to assume that young Shakespeare, like many
highly gifted sons, would have long been aware of being sharply different from his father, a perception that may have contributed to the
distance between father and son that prevails in the plays. Certainly,
any temperamental differences separating father and son would have
been exacerbated by the Elizabethan expectation that sons imitate and
essentially replicate their fathers.

When Shakespeare was writing *Part Two* of *Henry IV* and *Hamlet* in
his mid-thirties, the plays bespeak an increasing awareness of his similarities to his father, not all of them flattering. In addition to being
father and son, John and William were both eldest sons, and across the
generational divide they began to resemble each other, with William
becoming the ambitious, successful businessman that his father had
once been.[45] The similarities between father and son are most apparent in William Shakespeare's complex financial dealings, most of
which involved the Stratford world where his father had made and
lost his fortune. In his commitment to investing in land and agricultural products in the vicinity of Stratford and in his participation in
financial practices that bordered on the unscrupulous and illegal, such
as money lending and grain-hoarding, William Shakespeare quite literally profited by his father's example.[46] It is hard to believe that
Shakespeare's incomparably alert mind would have been unaware
that he was following in his father's footsteps, and we can only guess

at his feelings. In any event, he would not have been the first son to feel that, for better and worse, he was becoming his father.

We may surmise that the dramatist's discovery of filial likeness was not a happy one, especially if there are parallels between Hamlet's imitation of his father and William Shakespeare's imitation of John Shakespeare. In the course of the play, Hamlet's behaviour becomes increasingly modelled on his father's, or, more properly, the Ghost's. Hamlet, we recall, insists at the beginning of the play on the distance between his own base self and his godlike father. Thus, when Hamlet likens the difference between the elder Hamlet and Claudius to that between Hyperion and a satyr, he sees himself as standing in a similar lowly relationship to his exalted, radiant father. In the scenes to follow, however, this paternal image descends, becoming lodged in the armour-clad Ghost who claims to be the spirit of Hamlet's father. As we saw in chapter 6, Hamlet increasingly models his words and deeds on those of the Ghost, disappearing underground and employing surreptitious means to exploit others as his instruments. This process of imitation is most disturbing at the end of the play, where Hamlet borrows the rhetoric of the Ghost, almost word for word, to prevent Horatio from acting as a free agent and thus disturbing the Prince's plans. It is immediately after this imposition on Horatio, and in his dying breath, that Hamlet strikes at his father by naming Fortinbras king and thus gratuitously surrendering the entire inheritance that his father had risked his life to create. An awareness of how he has manipulated Horatio, and of how similar that manipulation is to what the Ghost had done to himself, may be part of the reason Hamlet destroys his patrimony. In this simultaneous awareness of the inevitability and the dangers of filial imitation, there is evidence for the continuing ambivalence that Shakespeare felt toward his father, who was probably extremely ill during his son's composition of the play, dying in early September of 1601.

Several biographical details would seem to support the parallel between Hamlet's unhappy imitation of his father and Shakespeare's of his own father, John. The most suggestive detail concerns William Shakespeare's literal playing of the part of the Ghost. When Shakespeare's diligent first biographer, Nicholas Rowe, set out to discover what roles his subject had played, he learned (from an unspecified source) that 'the top of his Performance was the Ghost in his own Hamlet.'[47] If Rowe's uncorroborated remark is accurate, it raises the tantalizing possibility (mentioned by Stephen Dedalus in Joyce's

Ulysses) that the Ghost may represent not only the authority of John Shakespeare but also some troubling aspect of William Shakespeare's conception of himself as a father. From this perspective, Hamlet may serve not only as a figure for Shakespeare in his youth but also for the middle-aged playwright's son Hamnet, a linkage supported by the Elizabethan confusion of the two names.[48] Thus, if Shakespeare identifies with Hamlet's conflicted struggle for filial autonomy, he may also be conscious of having imitated in some degree the Ghost's imperious treatment of his son and his own father's treatment of himself. But there is no end to mapping the dramatist – as both son and father – onto this most complex, elusive play.

King Lear marks a decisive change in Shakespeare's imaginative engagement with the intertwined figures of father and son because his emphasis shifts from the plight of sons to that of fathers.[49] It may be that this representation of both Gloucester and Lear as helpless and senile indicates Shakespeare's new forbearance of his own father, now well and truly buried. In any event, this shift is all the more interesting in that the familiar dyad of authoritarian father and repressed, ambivalent son is carried over from *Hamlet* into the figures of Gloucester and Edgar (and, to a lesser extent, Edmund) but with new emotional valences. Unlike Lord John Talbot, Henry IV, and the Ghost of King Hamlet, who are in every sense commanding figures and thus not easy for their sons (or perhaps theatre audiences) to commiserate with, Gloucester is a figure of great pathos, especially after his spectacularly cruel blinding. If the eye gouging (for which his bastard son Edmund is ultimately responsible) is appalling, so, too, in its own way is the scene on the imagined Dover Cliff where the loyal son Edgar works a more obscure revenge of his own against a father who could not be more helpless and vulnerable. (Lear's claim to be 'a man more sinned against than sinning' is truer still for Gloucester.) Edgar is not without a degree of sympathy for his father, but that sympathy seems willed and largely withheld. Of course, he has good reason for being alienated from Gloucester – none of his predecessors has had his father pronounce a death sentence on him. Still, in the context of such huge paternal suffering, the dilemma of the ambivalent son may begin to look a little like self-indulgence.

That Shakespeare was himself without a living son and on his way to becoming an old man would have sharpened his perception of Gloucester's suffering. Given that Hamnet had been dead for the better part of a decade and that Shakespeare's two daughters still lived, it is not surprising that the dramatist's imagination began to dwell more powerfully on fathers and daughters than fathers and sons. In the figure of Cordelia, who may be in part inspired by Shakespeare's favourite daughter, Susanna, we see a transformation of the son's role; Cordelia risks her life to rescue her father, as sons had done in earlier plays, but unlike them she performs the act with a commitment of love that dissolves the ambivalence created by the pressure of duty and indebtedness.

In the plays after *King Lear*, ambivalent sons disappear, reflecting a mitigation of earlier conflicts between paternal control and filial autonomy. In a biographically focused discussion such as this, it is tempting to posit a new, more positive understanding of the father-son relationship on Shakespeare's part, the fruit of advancing years and wisdom. One should be leery, however, of such an assumption. It would be safer to say that the lessening of friction between fathers and sons in the late plays is simply a function of the diminished frequency of exchange between them. When they are together, sons are usually too young for fathers to perceive them as a threat, and not many words pass between them. But for the most part the father-son relationship is marked by separation and absence, most notably in the many instances in which either the father or the son is dead. The strongest expressions of affection come from fathers, such as Macduff, Leontes, and Alonso, whose sons have died or (in the case of Alonso) apparently died. As many biographers have speculated, these powerful expressions of paternal grief and guilt for the death of young sons probably register aftershocks of the loss of Shakespeare's only son, Hamnet, who had died almost ten years before his father wrote *Macbeth*.

But what do these late plays imply about William Shakespeare's attitude toward his father? It would seem that, after *King Lear*, the dramatist moved beyond the ambivalence toward John Shakespeare that had energized many of his earlier plays. One can speculate that, not surprisingly, his grief for the loss of Hamnet, and for the end of the male line of family inheritance, proved to have more emotional staying-power than his conflicted feelings toward his father. But there is little reason to think that William and John Shakespeare ever reconciled their differences. As we have seen, from the beginning to the end of Shakespeare's career, there are few signs of reconciliation between his fictional fathers and sons. It may be that the largely unspoken complicities of King Henry and Prince Hal at the former's deathbed are as close as a father and son come to reconciliation, but the scene is rather impersonal – and strikingly so when compared to the reunions of daughters with their fathers in *King Lear* and later plays.[50] Even in the late plays in which the theme of family reunion drives the plot, there is little evidence of deep joy or mutuality when father and son come together again. If there were ever a rapprochement between the two Shakespeares that transcended their personal differences, to say nothing of the patriarchal Elizabethan values that exacerbated those differences, it left little mark in William Shakespeare's plays. Nor did it leave a mark in the public world of Stratford. There is no evidence that John Shakespeare's eldest child, wealthy as he was, ever honoured his gentleman father with a monument or even a memorial plaque in Holy Trinity Church.

A Rustic Grace Note at the Close

Even when one takes into account the reunions of the late plays, the representation of fathers and sons in Shakespearean drama remains largely a story of unresolved feelings, of withheld intimacies and incomplete reconciliations. It would seem that Shakespeare was not interested in representing, or perhaps not able to imagine, a father and son whose relationship is based on strong, mutual feelings of respect and affection. However, in Shakespeare's penultimate (sole-authored) play, *The Winter's Tale*, there is one notable exception to this sequence of estranged, suspicious fathers and sons, one pair that represents a positive alternative to the series of family generations in conflict. Unlike the play's two sets of royal fathers and sons (King Leontes and Mamillius; King Polixenes and Florizel) discussed in the previous chapter, the aged Shepherd and his son the rustic Clown are comic figures rarely discussed by critics. But the fact that there are no proto-types for these characters in Shakespeare's sources for the play suggests that he created this surprisingly genial portrait of a father and son for a reason.[51] For once in Shakespeare, and perhaps once only, a father and a son become a source of unshadowed good feeling.

It is appropriate to end this study with this pair, atypical as they are, for their relationship is predicated on a freedom from the social and economic bonds that usually prove so constraining to fathers and sons in the plays. With the notable exceptions of the Master Gunner and his Boy in *1 Henry VI* and Lancelot Gobbo and his father in *The Merchant of Venice*, there are in Shakespeare few depictions of fathers and sons who do not belong to great families, and so the invention of the Shepherd and the Clown allows him to depict a relationship free from the concerns that spoil the exchanges between the plays' noble fathers and sons. It cannot be a coincidence that there is less conflict between the lowly Shepherd and the Clown than between any other father and son in Shakespeare.

In the play the good-natured quality of the relationship may come as a surprise, for the Shepherd and Clown are introduced in terms that recall father-son tensions in earlier plays. In his first appearance the aged, grumbling Shepherd voices an old man's litany of griev-ances: 'I would there were no age between ten and three-and-twenty, or that youth would sleep out the rest; for there is nothing in the between but getting wenches with child, wronging the ancientry, stealing, fighting' (3.3.59–63). Unlike the play's two rulers, who are invested (dangerously) in trying to make childhood innocence last as long as possible, the Shepherd wishes that boys would leap over the adolescent years that bring so much trouble to 'the ancientry.' (Shake-speare chooses twenty-three as the year in which the Shepherd would readmit sons to society because in sixteenth-century England this was 'the final year allotted to immaturity in a variety of Elizabethan regu-latory statutes, including the Statute of Artificers.')[52] For his part, the Clown appears to be equally critical of his father; when he opens the bags of gold left with Perdita, he says to him: 'You're a made old man; if the sins of your youth are forgiven you, you're well to live' (3.3.120–1).

What these introductory glimpses of the Shepherd and Clown show is less a division between father and son than a healthy awareness of each other's shortcomings. In vivid contrast to the gaps between king and prince in Sicily and Bohemia, gaps which severely inhibit com-munication, we see a rare inter-generational willingness to speak and to co-operate. Despite the Shepherd's grumbling about the fractious irresponsibility of young men, the Clown is clearly engaged with his father in the hunt (in the foulest weather) for their missing sheep. After the discovery of the 'fairy gold' (4.1.123) accompanying the babe, the two look upon the find as a shared windfall, and so the Shepherd says 'We are lucky, boy' (3.3.125, italics supplied).

The sixteen years that separate the pair's first and second appear-ances (in 3.3 and 4.4) seem not to have changed father and son. With the aid of at least some of the gold, the Shepherd and the Clown have prospered greatly, with the son becoming something like his father's partner. In a rare deviation from the norm in Shakespeare, there is no indication of their wealth having created any tension between them, perhaps because it belongs to both. Thus, it seems not to matter – either to father or to son – that the feckless Clown is robbed, and robbed again, by Autolycus; their returns from shearing fifteen hundred sheep promise a plenteous festival and make arguments about lost money and botched filial responsibilities quite superfluous. Nor are the two distanced from each other by the curse of time. Though the Shepherd is 'a man of fourscore three' (4.4.453) and thus belongs to the cohort of Lear and Gloucester, he seems to have no fear of impotence and usurpation. Nor need he. Without insisting on their resemblance, or perhaps even noticing it, the father and his now middle-aged son are as one. In their final appearance at the end of 5.2, father and son enjoy a common satisfaction at having been elevated to the rank of gentleman. The Shepherd even changes his mode of address to his son, shifting from 'boy' (which he uses nine times in 3.3 alone) to the more respectful 'son' in his final lines of the play.[53]

The degree of concord between this father and son is especially noteworthy in that the relationship is a bittersweet fantasy of what Shakespeare's relationship with his father might have been. Beginning with the old Shepherd's opening tirade about young men and their tendency to make trouble, which notably includes William Shakespeare's misdemeanour of 'getting wenches with child' (3.3.61–2), this is a relationship that touches on what likely had been sore points between William Shakespeare and his wool-dealing father. But here they are transformed into matters of mutual acceptance. The happy story of the Shepherd and the Clown is premised on one crucial reversal of John and William's story. In place of the economic calamity that reduced the elder Shakespeare and his family to humiliation, the storm brings the Shepherd a windfall in the form of a foundling babe and a cache of gold, making him a man 'that from very nothing, and beyond the imagination of his neighbors, is grown into an unspeakable estate' (4.2.38–40).

In the play's penultimate scene, the magical success of this lucky shepherd and his feckless son culminates in their amusing advancement to gentle status. Since the Shepherd and Clown have been revealed to be, in a manner of speaking, the father and brother of the Princess Perdita, they are quick to claim to be gentlemen, and the new finery on their backs serves to convince them of their elevation. In their *arriviste* pride, they are eager to assume such time-honoured prerogatives of gentility as thinking themselves justified in swearing that patently false statements are true. To use their phrase, it is truly a 'pre-posterous estate' (5.2.148) to which they have advanced. But more is involved in the scene than social satire, especially when we recall the connection between them and the two Shakespeares.

Like the Shepherd and Clown, the Shakespeares *père et fils* were raised to the gentry by a sudden revelation of their true social station. For both the historical subjects and their fictional counterparts, the new status of being 'gentleman born' (a favourite phrase of the Shepherd and Clown) is belied by the modest station to which they had actually been born, the alchemy of money and good connections having worked a transformation. But here the parallels end, perhaps to the disadvantage of the two Shakespeares. To judge by the continuing friction between fathers and sons in plays such as the two parts of *Henry IV, Hamlet,* and *King Lear,* it would appear that Shakespeare's contribution to his father's gentle status by securing the coat of arms did not clear the air between the two of them, and indeed may have helped to darken it. By contrast, the Shepherd and Clown derive a shared satisfaction from their social advancement. Thus the old Shepherd takes simple pleasure in imagining the good fortune of his line; without envy he tells his son, 'I am past moe ['more'] children, but thy sons and daughters will be all gentlemen born' (5.2.126–7). In place of the heroic but troubling filial rescues that Shakespeare imagined earlier in his career, this mutual elevation of a father and son stems from their simply being in the right place at the right time. For the Clown, there is no burden of filial indebtedness and no call to heed a dread paternal commandment. Moreover, since the Shepherd and the Clown have never been alienated from each other – even though most of the family relationships in this play are full of gaps – there is no need for either to pursue the reconciliation that proved so elusive for earlier fathers and sons in Shakespeare. In this easy, amicable mutuality, we witness the nearest the plays come to closing the distance between father and son.

The only glimmer of competition between rustic father and son appears following the Clown's claim to have been 'gentleman born' since 'any time these four hours' (5.2.136–7). After the Shepherd interjects 'And so have I, boy,' his son responds with a mild correction: 'So you have. But I was a gentleman born before my father; for the King's son took me by the hand, and call'd me brother; and then the two kings call'd my father brother' (5.2.139–41). In what is surely the gentlest usurpation in Shakespeare, the Clown has become the senior partner in the new estate to which they have been advanced. Almost imperceptibly, he has claimed a status that no previous son in Shake-speare's plays had been able to achieve. As 'a gentleman born before my father,' he can be said to have begotten his progenitor, much as William Shakespeare had been responsible for advancing John Shake-speare to gentle status. But the parallel ends abruptly, for the Clown is oblivious to the filial ambivalence that troubled his creator, both com-plicating and deepening his art.

Appendix 1
Shakespearean Fathers and Sons in *Edward III*

A steadily growing chorus of voices asserts that *The Reign of Edward III*, a play published in 1595 without attribution to an author, should be accepted into Shakespeare's canon. The grounds for assigning *Edward III* – in whole or in part – to Shakespeare are too numerous to recount; they range from a variety of shared linguistic features to common threads of dramatic technique, imagery, characterization, and theme.[1] One revealing connection, however, between Shakespeare's accepted canon and *Edward III* has apparently gone unnoticed: the similar interplay in each between sternly authoritative fathers and ambivalent, coming-of-age sons. Of particular importance is the subtle depiction of the young Black Prince as a son with a deeply divided attitude toward his father, Edward III. When the depiction of fathers and sons in *Edward III* is studied in the light of the plays discussed in the foregoing chapters, it is difficult to avoid the conclusion that the author is largely, if not entirely, Shakespeare.

The representation of fathers and sons in *Edward III* is especially close to that in the first part of Shakespeare's *Henry VI*, a contemporary play.[2] As does *1 Henry VI*, *Edward III* depicts a discordant father-son relationship in both the French and English camps, and with a similar strategy. In both plays, the tension between the French father and son is far more explicit than that between their English counterparts. We recall from chapter 2 that the blatant struggle in *1 Henry VI* between the French Master Gunner and his restive son is reflected in the much more subtle conflict between the conspicuously heroic English father and son, Lord John Talbot and his son John Talbot. Similarly, in *Edward III* the differences between King John of France and his eldest son, Charles Duke of Normandy, are quite explicitly depicted, while those between Edward III and Edward the Black Prince are concealed beneath the rituals of chivalric bonding. The heroic Prince Edward can best be understood in the context of Shakespeare's ambivalent sons, being outwardly dutiful but inwardly defiant toward the regal father whose name he bears. As it has done with regard to the sons in Shakespeare's accepted canon, criticism has stressed Prince Edward's explicit, public respect for his father to the exclusion of his subtle protest against him.[3]

In the relatively simple relationship between the French father and son, Prince Charles clearly resists the attempt by King John to squelch his dignity and autonomy. Moved by the urgent remonstrances of a respected ally, the Prince agrees to issue a passport to the English Duke of Salisbury for safe passage through the French lines. But King John seizes Salisbury and, overruling his son, sentences him to immediate death by hanging. Charles's initial response is deferential; he pleads that 'I hope your highness will not so disgrace me, / And dash the virtue of my seal at arms,' and he concludes with a decorous request: 'I do beseech you let him pass in quiet' (4.5.73–4, 79).[4] In spite of the respectful nature of his son's request, the King's response seems designed to humiliate. Not only does King John insist on the 'infamy' of filial disobedience, but he also delivers a devastating claim: 'Thou and thy word lie both in my command. / What canst thou promise that I cannot break?' (4.5.80–1). The implication is that his son has no right to make promises because he has no agency beyond his father's approval. To make matters worse, the King clinches the point in casuistical terms, arguing that Charles need not worry about breaking his word to Salisbury for the simple reason that he has no word of his own to break.

Rather like young John Talbot in *1 Henry VI*, who denies his father's command to flee from battle by arguing for the exigencies of his own honour, Charles stands his ground, as deference gives way to anger:

> What, am I not a soldier in my word?
> Then, arms, adieu, and let them fight that list.
> Shall I not give my girdle from my waist,
> But with a guardian I shall be controlled
> To say I may not give my things away?   4.5.92–6

Prince Charles buttresses his point by citing the English royal family – in a similar situation, he says, King Edward not only would have respected *his* prince's word but also would have feasted the enemy soldiers to whom safe conduct had been promised. King John's response is a sudden, one-line collapse: 'Dwellst thou on precedents? Then be it so' (4.5.103). It is as if his son has called his bluff and won. Interestingly, the once peremptory French King immediately follows his surrender of paternal command with protracted gloating about the battlefield dilemma in which 'the wretched Prince of Wales' now finds himself. Perhaps King John sees the dilemma of the English prince as a threat not only to the English throne, but also as a rebuke to the French Crown-prince who has just invoked his English counterpart in his successful defence of his autonomy.

As opposed to the fractious French king and prince, the two Edwards may seem to have an exemplary relationship, and the onstage rituals in which the King grants armour to the Prince before the battle of Cressy (3.3) and knighthood to him afterward (3.4) suggest as much. As in *1 Henry VI*, however, emotional complexities lie underneath the chivalric surface. A hint of these complications occurs early in the play, when King Edward's headlong, adulterous pursuit of Lady Salisbury is halted by his envisioning the lineaments of his spurned wife in his son's face. As he remarks in an aside,

> Still do I see in him delineate
> His mother's visage: those his eyes are hers,
> Who looking wistly on me make me blush. 2.2.86–8

After his son exits, Edward murmurs, 'Thy mother is but black, and thou, like her, / Dost put it in my mind how foul she is' (2.2.107–8). To be sure, King Edward soon comes to regret his tyrannical pursuit of Lady Salisbury, and he does not mention again his association of his son with his once-despised wife. But the King's early perception that his son is blocking his desires may be relevant to his subsequent distance from him, and it is significant that at the very end of the play there is for the first time an onstage triangulation of father, mother, and son, revealing the Prince's greater closeness to his mother than his father.[5]

As it does in many of Shakespeare's securely canonical plays, the issue of rescue from imminent death brings the relationship of father and son into sharp focus. Usually in Shakespeare it is the father who finds himself in desperate need of rescue, but in *Edward III* it is the son. At the battle of Cressy, Prince Edward is surrounded by the French army, and the King repeatedly refuses to rescue him. The author of *Edward III* alters history to make the King look worse, much as Shakespeare customarily renders fathers in less attractive terms than his sources. In the play's primary historical source, Froissart's *Chronicle*, some of the beleaguered Englishmen send a messenger requesting the King to intervene. After first ascertaining that the Prince is not dead or wounded, the King declines to rescue him, declaring he will not act 'so long as my son is alive.' And he indicates a certain solicitude for his son by commanding the messenger to say to the captains that they should 'suffer him [Edward] this day to win his spurs; for if God be pleased, I will this journey be his and the honour thereof.'[6]

In *Edward III*, however, this brief vignette is expanded into a sequence of fifty lines that invites the audience's criticism of the King's decision. In place of Froissart's single unnamed messenger, the play depicts King Edward being exhorted *seriatim* by three different suppliants, all of whom are respected warriors. In these exchanges, the contrast between the captains' urgent concern for Edward's safety and the King's calm detachment (on an overlooking hill) is striking. When the first knight declares "tis impossible that he should scape, / Except your highness presently descend,' the King dismisses his concern: 'Tut, let him fight; we gave him arms today, / And he is labouring for a knighthood, man' (3.4.28–31). When the second knight begs him to act because the Prince is 'close encompassed with a world of odds,' the King's response is oddly divided:

Then will he win a world of honour too,
If he by valour can redeem him thence.
If not, what remedy? We have more sons
Than one, to comfort our declining age.   3.4.34–7

The first pair of lines conveys the King's chivalric rationale as given in Froissart, but the shockingly callous shrug in the second pair reveals considerably more concern for his own well-being than for his son's.

King Edward's refusal to aid his son stands out still more strongly when he summarily rejects the third captain's exhortation. In response, the knight exclaims, 'O cruel father! Farewell Edward, then' (3.4.67), whereupon the first knight is moved to articulate a sentiment that would better have come from the King's mouth: 'Oh, would my life might ransom him from death!' (3.4.69). Given this emphatic insistence on the solicitude expressed by so many knights, it is unconvincing for

E.M.W. Tillyard to defend King Edward by saying he withholds his aid 'on a policy of education,' because 'the prince must learn to find himself.'[7] Such a policy would not have precluded an expression of concern for Edward on the King's part, nor is it clear why the three great captains would be oblivious of the need for the Prince 'to learn to find himself' on the battlefield. To be sure, the King's strategy proves to be successful in military terms, for his son is thrown back on his own resources and defeats his numerically superior enemies in a fashion that forecasts his ensuing pre-eminence as a warrior. But, despite the victorious outcome, the Prince neither forgets nor forgives his father's cold detachment.

Upon his return from battle, Prince Edward's displeasure at his father's refusal to rescue him is apparent beneath his outwardly decorous behaviour. On the surface, young Edward is the very model of filial deference, to judge from his threefold reference to his 'duty,' from his proper addresses to the King ('My gracious lord' and 'noble father'), and from the stage direction that indicates he '*Kneels and kisses his father's hand*' (at 3.4.76). But some odd lines at the end of the scene point toward a quite different attitude. Apparently young Edward is carrying a painted panel, for the King suddenly asks 'What picture's this?' Edward's response is very revealing:

> A pelican, my lord,
> Wounding her bosom with her crooked beak,
> That so her nest of young ones might be fed
> With drops of blood that issue from her heart.
> The motto, *Sic et vos*: 'And so should you.' *Exeunt.*   3.4.122–6

As its division into a 'picture' and a 'motto' indicates, Prince Edward's depiction derives from contemporary emblem literature, where the pelican piercing its breast in order to feed its young with blood is a common symbol of parental sacrifice and divine love.

The sudden intrusion of these pelican lines is rather puzzling, and a recent editor of *Edward III* surmises that, since 'The scene is obviously concluded' before they are spoken, they are 'a misplaced insertion possibly from a slip of paper added to the manuscript.'[8] There is, however, no need to hypothesize textual confusion. Prince Edward's exposition of the conventional picture makes good sense if it is read as conveying an oblique but bitter reprimand of his father.[9] Given the King's obstinate refusal to rescue him, the Prince can hardly be proferring the self-sacrificing pelican as a symbol of his father's devotion. It makes far better sense to see the bleeding pelican as representing the love that his father has failed to personify. The true pelican sentiment, we recall, was articulated by one of the solicitous captains whom the King ignored: 'Oh, would my life might ransom him [the Prince] from death!' (3.4.69).

The ironic application of the pelican emblem to the King is supported by the Prince's translation of the accompanying motto: '*Sic et vos.*' This motto is a traditional tag that stresses the need for all Christians ('*vos*' is plural) to imitate the sacrificial conduct of the pelican.[10] The Prince's translation of the phrase as 'And so should you' is cleverly deceptive, for it is at once an accurate translation of a traditional Christian exhortation relevant to all believers (if 'you' is heard as plural) and also a sharp reprimand to the King (if 'you' is heard as singular). In performance, the slightest increase of stress on 'you' (which is the final word of the scene) or the quickest glance at the King would be sufficient to suggest the Prince's irony. As in Prince Hal's freeing of the Douglas late in *1 Henry IV*, the filial attack is hidden within chivalric ritual.

In act 5, after Prince Edward has conquered the French a second time (at Poitiers), the play closes with another problematic encounter of the King and Prince. Once again, the Black Prince has been left alone to fight a far more numerous French army, once again he has been triumphant, and once again he indicates his filial displeasure in a covert fashion. After Prince Edward has been greeted by his mother and father (she with considerably more feeling than he), the Prince bestows upon his father the 'gift' of the French crown as well as his two valuable captives, King John and Prince Philip, declaring they were 'Got with as mickle peril of our lives / As e'er was thing of price before this day' (5.1.194–5). It is significant for what follows that the King acknowledges neither the gift nor the peril that made it possible. Without saying a word to his son, he addresses the French king, mocking him and vowing to bring him to England and hold him for ransom.

Immediately following the King's failure to acknowledge his son's suffering, Prince Edward delivers a long speech that is divided into two parts, revealing his ambivalence toward his father. The first half of the speech could hardly be more deferential:

Now, father, this petition Edward makes
To thee, whose grace hath been his strongest shield:
That as thy pleasure chose me for the man
To be the instrument to show thy power,
So thou wilt grant that many princes more,
Bred and brought up within that little isle,
May still be famous for like victories: 5.1.216–22

In these lines Prince Edward addresses the King as if he were a deity who chose him to be the 'instrument' to channel his potency into the world. The petition itself – that many more English princes be bred up to win similarly famous victories – would make more sense being addressed to God than to a mere human being.[11] As if he has heard the obsequious falseness of his address to his father, who has scarcely shown his son 'grace' in any sense of the word, Prince Edward suddenly reverses himself and insists on his own hard-fought accomplishments.

What had been an apparent petition to the King quickly becomes an angry insistence on the pain that Prince Edward was forced to undergo because his father's 'pleasure' was to use him as his 'instrument':

And for my part, the bloody scars I bear,
The weary nights that I have watched in field,
The dangerous conflicts I have often had,
The fearful menaces were proferred me,
The heat and cold, and what else might displease,
I wish were now redoubled twentyfold,
So that hereafter ages, when they read
The painful traffic of my tender youth,
Might thereby be inflamed with such resolve.   5.1.223–31

These lines are an assertive, accusatory catalogue of sufferings ('bloody scars,' 'weary nights,' 'dangerous conflicts,' 'fearful menaces,' 'heat and cold') summarized in 'The painful traffic of my tender youth,' a reminder of the Prince's unreadiness to bear the King's burden and of his father's failure to rescue him. As Prince Edward declares in his final line, it is England's princes who will make her enemies 'tremble and retire' (5.1.235), and these princes will be inspired by his own heroic agony. In the fashion of Hamlet in act 5, the Black Prince insists that *his* story be told. Immediately following these lines, King Edward speaks the play's final words, in which he pointedly ignores his son's speech.

If this interpretation of authoritative fathers and ambivalent sons in *Edward III* is convincing, then the thematic parallels with Shakespeare's canon should figure in discussions of the play's authorship. The depiction of fathers and sons not only provides new evidence of Shakespeare's presence in *Edward III* but also indicates the pervasiveness of that presence. Traditionally, the scenes attributed to Shakespeare with the greatest claim to certainty have been in acts 2 and 4, but the tensions between fathers and sons appear throughout the play, from beginning to very end.[12] If the father and son scenes (both English and French) are accepted as having been written by Shakespeare, as I think they should be, then the balance tilts still more decisively toward him as the only begetter of *Edward III*.

Appendix 2
Thomas Plume's Anecdote: The Merry-Cheeked, Jest-Cracking John Shakespeare, Sir John Mennes, and Sir John Falstaff

Sometime in or around 1657, Thomas Plume, the Vicar of Greenwich, wrote in one of his barely legible notebooks an entry concerning William Shakespeare and his father John:

> He [Shakespeare] was a glovers son – Sir John Mennes saw once his old *Father* in his shop – a merry cheekd old man – that said – Will was a good Honest Fellow – but he darest have crackt a jeast with him at any Time.[1]

When F.J. Furnivall published the extract in 1904, he characterized it as 'the only known notice of the look of Shakespere's father, and his opinion of his gifted son, and is a great gain.'[2] Even though Plume recorded it more than fifty years after John Shakespeare's death, the playwright's biographers have been unwilling to forego this 'great gain.' Their tendency is to say, with Park Honan, that the 'report of a merry-cheeked old man who jests with his son is credible.'[3] To be sure, some biographers, such as Stephen Greenblatt and Katherine Duncan-Jones, have expressed caution, but they still remain inclined to see at least traces of truth in the report.[4] There is, however, good reason to question the validity of this charming, perhaps too charming, account of the two Shakespeares. The problems centre on the figure of Sir John Mennes, to whom Plume attributes the report, and they raise the possibility that Mennes's putative description may well be, instead, his invention.

The veracity of one, and only one, detail in the account is impervious to challenge: that William Shakespeare 'was a glovers son.' With the exception of Elizabethan legal documents, which were not drawn upon by scholars until the eighteenth century, this is the first recorded identification of John Shakespeare as a glovemaker.[5] This accurate naming of the elder Shakespeare's trade makes it impossible to reject the entire entry, and it raises the possibility that the remainder is equally trustworthy. But of course the correctness of the opening 'glovers son' remark does not necessarily validate the report that follows it. It may be significant that Plume does not attribute his terse 'glovers son' comment to a source, while he specifies that Sir John Mennes is the origin of the supposed eyewitness account of John Shakespeare that follows. This difference may indicate that for his entry Plume drew on two sources, one being the unidentified provider of the vocational fact and the other being the interesting, unreliable figure of Sir John Mennes.

The most obvious reason to doubt the report that Plume attributes to Mennes surfaced only three days after Furnivall published the entry. In a communication to *The Westminster Gazette*, a correspondent raised the inconvenient truth that Sir John Mennes was only two years old when John Shakespeare died in 1601.[6] In an attempt to salvage Mennes's credibility, the clergyman and antiquarian Andrew Clark (who had provided the extracts from Plume that Furnivall published) made an interesting observation about the entry's immediate context in Plume's notebook. Clark noted a thematic clustering of entries before and after the anecdote that 'suggests a supper-party at Greenwich, partly nautical, partly literary, Vice-Admiral Mennes and the Vicar (Dr Plume) being of it.'[7] But, moving beyond this plausible conjecture, Clark proceeded to state as fact that 'Dr Plume, in afterwards jotting down the conversation, made the mistake of attributing to Sir John's own experience what was merely reported by him.'[8] According to Clark, Mennes did not misrepresent; rather, Plume mis-remembered. While it is possible that Plume made the mistake attributed to him, Clark failed to address a more likely alternative: that Mennes *did* claim to have seen John Shakespeare and thus is the inventor of the account he told.

At such a gathering as Clark postulates, Sir John Mennes would have been the life of the party. Like Dr Plume, he was a royalist, but unlike the bookish clergyman, Mennes led an eventful life, including service at sea against foreign fleets and on land against the parliamentary forces, the provision of medical aid to royalists on the Continent as an 'amateur venerealogist,' and ascension to comptroller of the navy after the Restoration.[9] Mennes had literary interests as well, being an aggressively anti-Puritan man of letters who specialized in verses

mocking pious attitudes; at roughly the same time as the Plume anecdote, Mennes co-authored with his dissolute friend, James Smith, two
volumes of burlesque verse, *Musarum Deliciae* (1655) and *Wit Restor'd*
(1658).[10] Of particular relevance to the conjectural party at Greenwich
is Mennes's reputation for mirth-making at social occasions, his skill at
parlour games, and his extempory wit. In the Naval Office, Mennes
was a senior colleague of Samuel Pepys, who frequently grumbled in
his *Diary* about the older man's 'dotage and folly' but also praised his
'most excellent pleasant company.'[11] Not only was Mennes fond of
reciting from favourite poets like Chaucer, but according to Pepys he
was 'the best Mimique that ever I saw, and certainly would have made
an excellent Actor.'[12] Thus, upon hearing from Plume (or someone else
at the Greenwich party) that John Shakespeare had been a glover, the
quick-witted Mennes would have been quite capable of topping the
observation by conjuring up the scene he reports, a scene in which the
elder Shakespeare resembles a cavalier wit jesting with his straight-
laced son.

That Mennes invented the scene he claims to have recollected is supported by the language he ascribes to the elder Shakespeare. Quite
simply, these words do not ring true or, rather, do not ring Elizabethan.
The most problematic words are 'he darest h*ave* crackt a jeast w*ith* him
at any Time.' The phrase 'cracked a jest' was rarely used, if used at all,
in the elder Shakespeare's lifetime; for instance, none of the twenty-
two uses of 'crack' as a verb in Shakespeare's plays involves telling a
joke.[13] Of course, one could argue that a remark recounted some fifty
years after its utterance – having passed through at least one interme-
diary – is not likely to be quoted verbatim. But in the word 'darest'
there is a second, more damning, anachronism. In this case, the
problem is not one of usage; 'darest' was common in John Shakespeare's time and continued to be used throughout the seventeenth
century. Rather, the anachronism derives from the difference between
Elizabethan and Restoration values. Fathers of John Shakespeare's
generation demanded deference from their children, and it is unthinkable that such a patriarchal figure would have boasted of daring to
joke with his son, no matter how serious the son was. But by the mid-
seventeenth century paternal authority had notably diminished. At
that time it would have seemed especially plausible to imagine John
Shakespeare daring to joke with his son because William was in the
process of being elevated to the status of great writer and eminent per-

sonage, a status he had not gained in his father's lifetime. Indeed, this anecdote is itself a sign of that growing fame.

The most compelling indication that Sir John Mennes invented his account of John Shakespeare is his vignette of 'a merry cheekd old man' cracking jests with an upright, 'good Honest' young man. Unmistakably, this scene calls to mind the interplay between Prince Hal and Falstaff in the *Henry IV* plays, especially *Part One*, and some biographers have taken the parallel between the play and the anecdote as evidence for the authenticity of the latter.[14] Indeed, a recent biographer cited Mennes's anecdote as evidence to support his contention that 'the character of John Falstaff was based directly on Shakespeare's father.'[15] This argument ignores two central facts in the historical reception of Shakespeare's work: that among cavalier wits, like Mennes, *Henry IV* was Shakespeare's most popular play and Falstaff his most celebrated character.[16] Thus, instead of taking the anecdote as evidence for Shakespeare's derivation of Falstaff from his father (and for art's imitation of life), it is safer to see it as Sir John Mennes's attempt to impose Sir John Falstaff upon John Shakespeare (biography aping art). The chances are that Mennes created for William Shakespeare the genial, wit-cracking father that he wished him to have had, a father begotten in the image of two dissipated, witty Sir Johns.

Notes

Preface

1 This painting (by an unidentified artist) is in London's National Portrait Gallery. It is described in Strong, *Tudor & Jacobean Portraits*, 1:257–8.

2 There is a parallel in Hans Holbein's double portrait of Thomas Godsalve and his son John (1528), where the dominant figure of the father is identified (he writes his name and age on a piece of paper) but his mature son is not. See Bätschmann and Griener, *Hans Holbein*, 172–3.

3 Goldberg, 'Fatherly Authority,' 12.

4 For Ralegh and his son, see Beer, *My Just Desire*, Rowse, *Raleigh and the Throckmortons*, 324–6, and Tromly, 'Sir Walter Ralegh.'

5 Aubrey, *Brief Lives*, 418–19.

6 Mindful of the index to a book on *Hamlet* that lists twenty-six entries under 'Father Figures' – beginning with 'Achilles' ('Adam' comes second) and including 'Madness' and 'Poland' – I have attempted to reserve the terms 'father' and 'son' for the biological figures or for obvious substitutions (e.g., Falstaff) for them.

Introduction: Interpreting Shakespeare's Sons

1 Quiller-Couch, 'Paternity in Shakespeare,' 103, 106.

2 For instance, the tendency to identify the meaning of Shakespeare's depictions with orthodox Elizabethan values weakens the learned studies by Bruce W. Young.

3 Buck, 'Shakespeare's Epic,' 162.

4 Holland, 'Sons and Substitutions,' 73.

5 See, for instance, Barber and Wheeler, *The Whole Journey*, and also Sundel-son, *Shakespeare's Restorations*.

6 Kahn's wide-ranging *Man's Estate* is most relevant to my study in its examination of male identity and filial succession in the history plays (chapter 3). To mention some exemplary studies by women of *Hamlet* alone, Anne Barton's Introduction to the New Penguin edition and the two chapters on the play in Barbara Everett's *Young Hamlet* are outstand-ing for their lucidity. Also notable is Mary Elizabeth Campbell's fine dis-sertation on the father-son relationship in the early plays (a number of which I do not discuss), which concludes with a discussion of *Hamlet* stressing the protagonist's 'need – conscious or unconscious – to distin-guish himself from his father' (*Proving His Beauty*, 268). Kay Stock-holder's insight into the conflict between Hamlet and the Ghost, espe-cially at the end of the play, was perhaps unprecedented in the voluminous critical literature (*Dream Works*, 44, and 'Sex and Authority,' 20).

7 Berger, *Imaginary Audition*, 29–30. In an important study entitled *Shake-speare as Literary Dramatist* (2003), Lukas Erne extends Berger's argument by contending that Shakespeare knowingly wrote texts that were too long for performance because he was committed to realizing the literary as well as the theatrical dimension of his craft.

8 Berger's observations on fathers and sons appear throughout the collec-tion of his essays entitled *Making Trifles of Terrors*, especially in the two essays on *King Lear* (25–49, 50–9) and in the two essays on *Richard II* (148–67, 168–88).

9 Danson's brief but incisive study 'Shakespeare and the Misrecognition of Fathers and Sons' examines recognition scenes in which fathers and sons fail to connect.

10 Dreher, 11. Such binary divisions of Shakespeare's daughters have become *de rigueur*. Lenker's *Fathers and Daughters in Shakespeare and Shaw* contains chapters entitled 'Daughter as Passive Verb' and 'Daughter as Active Verb,' while Hamilton's *Shakespeare's Daughters* has chapters enti-tled 'Daughters Who Rebel' and 'Daughters Who Acquiesce.'

11 Battus, *The Christian Mans Closet*, 63.

12 See Scott, *Domination and the Arts of Resistance*.

13 For the concept in Freud, see Schulz, 'Ambivalence.' For a brief account stressing post-Freudian studies, see McGregor's entry 'Ambivalence' in the forthcoming fourth edition of the *Corsini Encyclopedia of Psychology*. I am indebted to Professor McGregor for showing me this material before publication.

14 For Freud's belief that ambivalence was central to the prehistorical relationship of sons to fathers, see *Moses and Monotheism* (*S. E.* 23:131–6).

15 Freud, *S. E.* 21:183. In 'The Devil as a Father-Substitute,' Freud observes
that this ambivalence toward fathers also 'governs the relation of
mankind to its deity' (*S. E.* 19:85).

16 Freud, *Totem and Taboo* (*S. E.* 13:49).

17 Freud, 'Speech at the Goethe House' (*S. E.* 21:212). For Freud's awareness
of his ambivalence toward his own father, Jacob Freud, see Mahl, 'Father-
Son Themes,' 59.

18 The very full index to Norman Holland's wide-ranging *Shakespeare and
Psychoanalysis* does not contain an entry for 'ambivalence.'

19 For the displacement of filial hostility away from fathers and onto substitutes, see *Totem and Taboo* (*S. E.* 13:129); for Freud on jokes and aggression, see *Jokes and Their Relation to the Unconscious* (*S. E.* 8: passim*).*

20 In a brief, suggestive discussion, Schoenbaum remarks that the Freudian
notion of 'filial ambivalence' can be used to account for Freud's late-life
conviction that Shakespeare did not write the plays attributed to him
(*Shakespeare's Lives*, 612).

21 Armstrong, *Shakespeare in Psychoanalysis*, 25. Similarly, but tortuously,
Greenblatt speaks of 'the curious effect of a discourse that functions *as if*
the psychological categories it invokes were not only simultaneous with
but even prior to and themselves causes of the very phenomena of which
in actual fact they were the results' (*Learning to Curse*, 142).

22 Bloom, *Western Canon*, 375.

23 For an engaging and sometimes amusing account of Freud, Shakespeare,
and the Oedipus Complex, see Nuttall, 'Freud and Shakespeare.'

24 Honan, *Shakespeare: A Life*, 27.

25 This passage occurs in Freud's essay 'A Special Type of Choice of Object
Made by Men' (*S. E.* 11:172–3). As often happened, Freud's original
insight was soon codified into dogma. Thus, Karl Abraham's essay 'The
Rescue and Murder of the Father in Neurotic Phantasy-Formations'
insists that, according to 'our established knowledge,' in the unconscious
the rescue of the father stands for killing him (69).

26 As appendix 1 shows, one of many links between *Edward III* (which is
often attributed to Shakespeare) and the plays discussed in the body of
this study is an act of filial aggression disguised as chivalric ritual.

27 Nowell, *Catechisme*, 13v.

28 Cleaver, *Godlie Forme*, 343.

29 Seneca, *De beneficiis*, III.xxxvi. Cf. Schleiner, 'Aeneas' Flight,' 100–1.

30 Whitney, *Choice of Emblems*, 163.

1 Paternal Authority and Filial Autonomy in Shakespeare's England

1 Stone, *The Family*, 7.
2 Stone, *The Family*, 117.
3 The subtitle is from Steven Ozment's *Ancestors*.
4 Houlbrooke and Pollock have written a number of studies *contra* Stone that stress evidence of familial warmth from journals and letters.
5 Shuger, *Habits of Thought*, 218–19. While arguing that Renaissance patriarchy was quite explicitly *not* 'a justification of male despotism,' she does note the presence of painful confusions of filial love with political obedience (246–9).
6 Houlbrooke, *The English Family*, 185.
7 Williamson, *Myth of the Conqueror*, 166–8. For the relations of James and his two sons, see Strong (*Henry Prince of Wales* 14–15) and Graham, 'Performing Heir.'
8 Handover, *The Second Cecil*, 13. The 'archetypal father' phrase is from Helgerson, *Elizabethan Prodigals*, 29. For an account of Burghley's relationships with his two sons, see Pearson, *Elizabethans at Home*, 227–9.
9 In a rich discussion of the differences between the family in Shakespeare's plays and the historical family of his time, Maynard Mack remarks that 'If we imagine an English county populated only by the types represented in the plays, the purposeful artificiality of Shakespeare's family world becomes strikingly apparent' (42). But he also notes that 'the deference system as we find it in Shakespeare's family of art derives directly from its counterparts in history' (*Everybody's Shakespeare*, 52).
10 Aumerle in *Richard II* and young John Talbot in *1 Henry VI* are examples of Shakespeare's changing his sources so that sons with male siblings become sole sons. Similarly, *contra* Plutarch, Coriolanus becomes an only child in Shakespeare's play.
11 A well-known instance of maternal intervention from the fifteenth century is the repeated pleading of the formidable Margaret Paston with her husband on behalf of their trouble-prone eldest son (Bennett, *The Pastons*, 72–5 and Rosenthal, *Patriarchy*, 64). Two of Shakespeare's rare depictions of the triad involve the mother's vigorous, even angry, intervention on behalf of her son: the Duchess of York with the Duke on behalf of Aumerle (*RII*: 5.2, 5.3) and Queen Margaret with Henry VI on behalf of Edward (*3H6*: 1.1). Though in Sonnet 8 the poet imagines 'sire, and child, and happy mother, / Who all in one, one pleasing note do sing,' we see no such harmonious scenes in the plays.

12 Martin, *Father Figures*, 46. Despite his father's exemplary paternal sensi-
    tivity, Martin blames him for hindering his development because 'he
    gave me no choice at all to quarrel with him' (26).

13 Schochet notes that 'There were no significant variations of opinions
    about the meaning of the duty to obey parents among the sects during
    the entire Stuart period' ('Patriarchalism,' 424).

14 Locke, *Some Thoughts*, 133.

15 Tyndale, *Doctrinal Treatises*, 168. See Strauss for the analogy in Luther's
    Germany between 'the *Hausvater* ruling his little flock and God the father
    as sovereign over all his living creatures' (*Luther's House of Learning*,
    121–2). Hankins cites formulations of the father-as-God idea in Aquinas
    and La Primaudaye (*Backgrounds of Shakespeare's Thought*, 223).

16 An indication of the influence of Tyndale's formulations can be seen in
    how closely they are followed in Robert Cleaver's oft-reprinted *A Godlie
    Forme of Householde Government* (1598). The Tyndale passage quoted
    above, for instance, is the ultimate source of Cleaver's discussion of filial
    debts quoted in the introduction.

17 Tyndale, *Doctrinal Treatises*, 199.

18 Tyndale, *Doctrinal Treatises*, 199.

19 Pearson's comment that the lines 'describe the conventional father's idea
    of a child's obedience to parental authority' is misleading (*Elizabethans at
    Home*, 246), as is Honan's citation of 'To you your father should be as a
    god' as evidence of the 'filial ardour' felt by Shakespeare (*Shakespeare: A
    Life*, 27).

20 For *patria potestas*, see Crook, 'Patria Potestas.' Rather wistfully, Pierre
    Ayrault recalls how paternal punishments in Roman times guaranteed
    that 'all the sons' negotiation had such dependance on their fathers' will,
    as ... rivers have that must be fed from their fountains or head' (*Discourse*,
    19). In Arthur Broke's translation of the Romeo and Juliet story, Capulet
    reminds his daughter of 'what revenge of old the angry sires did find /
    Against their children that rebelled, and showed them selves unkind'
    (Bullough 1:337). Cf. Orlin, *Elizabethan Households*, 623.

21 Houlbrooke, *The English Family*, 145.

22 Tyndale, *Doctrinal Treatises*, 199.

23 Donne, 'First Anniversary' (ll. 213–15), in Patrides, *Complete English
    Poems*, 335.

24 *Geneva Bible*, 33.

25 Schochet, 'Patriarchalism,' 429. This article contains useful material not
    included in Schochet's standard monograph, *Patriarchalism in Political
    Thought*.

26 For the treatment of the Fifth Commandment in English catechistical literature, see Ian Green, *The Christian's ABC*, 451–60 and Griffiths, *Youth and Authority*, 88–9.

27 For Elizabethan England as a 'gerontocracy,' see Thomas's classic study, 'Age and Authority in Early Modern England.'

28 Sommerville, *Royalists and Patriots*, 29.

29 *Certain Sermons or Homilies*, 210. Later the Homily notes that 'the rebels do not only dishonour their prince, the parent of their country, but also do dishonour and shame their natural parents' (225).

30 Helgerson, *Elizabethan Prodigals*, 40.

31 Battus, *The Christian Mans Closet*, 68v. John Calvin thought the death penalty appropriate for disobedience to parents (Stone, *Family* [175]), and there was biblical authority for putting to death children who curse their parents, to say nothing of those who smite them (Exodus 22:15, 17).

32 This point is made by Farrell in his suggestive article 'Self-Effacement and Autonomy in Shakespeare,' 97.

33. For Marlowe's imagery relating to fathers and sons, see Ardolino, 'The "Wrath."'

34 *Selimus*, ed. Vitkus, 70.

35 For examples of parricide committed by bastard sons, see Findlay, *Illegitimate Power*, 94–5.

36 Womersley, '3 *Henry VI*,' 469.

37 For a discussion, see Potter, 'Cockering Mothers.'

38 Sackville and Norton, *Gorboduc*, 1.2.382–4.

39 For some Elizabethan condemnations of parental overindulgence, see Pearson, *Elizabethans at Home*, 123–5.

40 Nowell, *Catechisme*, fol. 14.

41 For the effects of the political analogy on the family (with primary reference to marriage), see Orlin, *Private Matters*, 85–130, and Amussen's discussions in 'Gender, Family, and the Social Order,' 201–35 and in *An Ordered Society*, 417.

42 Montaigne, *Montaigne's Essays*, 2:79.

43. Quoted in Duncan-Jones, *Sir Philip Sidney*, 44. A similar avoidance of open affection is reported by the anonymous biographer of Lord Burghley, probably a member of his household, who notes his kindness toward children, 'and yet with so wise moderation and temper as he was inwardly more kind than outwardly fond of them' (*Anonymous Life*, 119).

44 The two fullest studies of the subject, Bruce Young's 'Parental Blessings' and Slater's *Shakespeare the Director*, 76–9, are not adequately attuned to the tensions in these scenes.

45 In an apparent response to the anxiety provoked by the overlapping of domestic and political roles, William Gouge defended filial kneeling by declaring that 'A child may kneel to his parent and to the king. Yet it followeth not that he maketh his parent a king' (*Of Domesticall Duties*, 439). A similar ambiguity arose in the Jacobean church with regard to kneeling in worship, an act that could represent an obeisance either to God or to the monarch, depending on how it was interpreted. See Ferrell, 'Kneeling,' 73.

46 Stewart and Wolfe, *Letterwriting*, 41.

47 Ayraut, *Discourse*, 31.

48 *Selimus*, ed. Vitkus, 70.

49 Quoted in Cartwright, *Baldassare Castiglione*, 2:393.

50 For the centrality of the *De officiis* to humanist thinking, see O'Gorman's introduction to Nicholas Grimald's sixteenth-century translation (13–14).

51 Cicero, *De officiis*. Loeb ed., 79.

52 *Lamentable Tragedy of Locrine*, 51.

53 Quoted in Graham, 'Performing Heir,' 384.

54 Montaigne (2:8), *The Essays*, 151.

55 The painting is reproduced in Bätschmann and Griener, *Hans Holbein*, 173.

56 Howell, *Sir Philip Sidney*, 49.

57 Smith-Bannister, *Names*, 65. One reason for this increase in children named after parents is the decline of entrusting the naming of children to godparents, who often bestowed their own names.

58 For the letters by Burghley and Ralegh to their sons, see Wright, *Advice to a Son*.

59 Rabelais, *Gargantua and Pantagruel*, 193–4.

60 For the importance to Sidney of familial imitation, and its connection with literary imitation, see E. Berry, *Making of Sir Philip Sidney*, 9–25.

61 Wallace, *Life of Sir Philip Sidney*, 68–9. Apparently concerned about her husband's severity, Lady Mary Sidney added an ameliorative postscript to 'my little Philip' and signed herself as 'Your loving mother' (Wallace, 70).

62 Gouge, *Of Domesticall Duties*, 480.

63 The details and quotations in the remainder of this paragraph are from Kocher's important article ('Francis Bacon and His Father,' esp. 151–2, 148).

64 O'Day, *Family*, 29.

65 Nashe, *Christ's Tears over Jerusalem*, in *Complete Works*, 2:83.

66 A limitation of Anthony Esler's thoughtful study of the 'generation gap' in late Elizabethan England, *The Aspiring Mind of the Elizabethan Younger*

Generation, is that it does not discuss the presence of ambivalent, divided attitudes among the restive younger generation. Esler's analysis should be supplemented by Helgerson's fine discussion in *The Elizabethan Prodigals*.

67 Cardano, *Cardanus Comforte*, fol. 45–45v.

68 Erasmus, *A Declaration*, 328.

69 Montaigne, *Montaigne's Essays*, 2:70–1. On similar grounds, a snoopy but kindly father in Jonson's *Every Man in his Humor* decides not to interfere in his son's mischievous plans: 'Force works on servile natures, not the free. / He that's compelled to goodness may be good, / But 'tis but for that fit; where others, drawn / By softness and example, get a habit' (1.2.124–7).

70 Though some pedagogues saw themselves as superior to natural fathers in that they perceived themselves to be fathers of the student's mind or his spirit, developing what was immortal in him, they were not likely to criticize the fathers who controlled their employment. See Bushnell, *Culture of Teaching*, 33–9.

71 Quoted by Brady in her fine discussion of Jonson's 'recoil from authoritarian models of influence' ('Progenitors,' 21).

72 Guazzo, *Civile Conversation*, 48.

73 My discussion of these humanist ideas is indebted to Douglas's excellent article 'Talent and Vocation in Humanist and Protestant Thought.' His findings have been supplemented by Ago's emphasis on Catholic Italy in 'Paternal Authority and Freedom of Choice.'

74 Erasmus, quoted in Douglas, 'Talent,' 285.

75 Houlbrooke, *The English Family*, 170.

76 Douglas, 'Talent,' 295 and Potter, 'Cockering Mothers,' 275–6.

77 Perkins, *Work*, 460.

78 Gouge, *Of Domesticall Duties*, 534–6.

79 See Ben-Amos (*Adolescence*, 16–19) and Griffiths (*Youth and Authority*, chapters 3–7).

80 Archer notes that 'The very insistence with which the authorities pedalled [*sic*] the theory of obligation through catechisms, sermons and proclamations suggests its fragility' ('Apotheosis or Nemesis,' 75).

81 Whitney, *Choice of Emblemes*, 28. An example of an ambitious son rejecting his father occurs in the anonymous *Edmund Ironside*, when the base-born Duke Edricus is embarrassed to be recognized by his solicitous peasant father and denies knowing him: 'My father, grouthead? Sir knave, I say you lie' (2.2.491). Eric Sams, who argues for Shakespeare's authorship of the play, notes some telling parallels with the scene in *1 Henry VI* (5.4) in

which Joan of Arc similarly denies and mocks her father (*Shakespeare's Edmund Ironside*, 237–8).

82 Griffiths, *Youth and Authority*, 5.
83 Schoenbaum, *Compact Documentary Life*, 234.
84 Quoted in Orme, *Medieval Children*, 84.
85 O'Day, *Family*, 88. She also notes that when young Bagot sought to marry a woman deemed by his father to be insufficiently wealthy, he was finally brought to heel by the threat of disinheritance.
86 Griffiths, *Youth and Authority*, 327.
87 Brigden, 'Youth,' 44. Also, see the discussions in Ben-Amos of the mobility of rural youth (*Adolescence*, 69–83) and the travel of urban apprentices (84–108), stressing how the young developed new competences to meet the challenges they faced.
88 Rappaport, 'Reconsidering Apprenticeship,' 253. The Statute of Artificers (1563) was designed in part to tie down youth and to delay their entrance into the labour market by mandating an apprenticeship lasting for at least seven years, not to be finished before the age of twenty-four.
89 Gouge, *Of Domesticall Duties*, 446.
90 The standard telling of the story is in the eighth book of Ovid's *Metamorphoses*, ll. 183–235.
91 Gardiner, *The Portraitur*, 3, 20.
92 Nashe, *Strange Newes*, in *Complete Works*, 1:319.
93 Wright, *Advice to a Son*, 3.
94 Alan Young, *English Prodigal Son Plays*, 274.
95 Watt, *Cheap Print*, 202–5.
96 The Ovidian phrase is from Miller's translation (8:224); Golding's phrase is at 8:301.
97 Turner, *Myth of Icarus*, 84. Also see Rudd, 'Daedalus and Icarus,' 38–41 and Ginzburg, *Myths, Emblems, Clues*, 65–73.
98 Thus, Sidney asks rhetorically, 'Who readeth Aeneas carrying old Anchises on his back, that wisheth not it were his fortune to perform so excellent an act?' (*Miscellaneous Prose*, 92).
99 For 'the resentment of young men towards foolishly wielded patriarchal authority' in Sidney's work, see Duncan-Jones, *Sir Philip Sidney*, 42–3, 186. And see McCoy's summary comment on Sidney's *New Arcadia*: 'Distrust of authority at all levels – parental, political, even providential – pervades this work' (*Rebellion in Arcadia*, 163).
100 *Miscellaneous Prose*, 77. Icarus is also present in Sidney's characterization of the poet as being 'lifted up with the vigour of his own invention' and 'freely ranging only within the zodiac of his own wit' (78).

101 Sidney's association of poetry with Icarian transcendence gives way to an emphasis on poetry as art (imitation and rules), and late in the treatise he declares that 'as the fertilest ground must be manured, so must the highest-flying wit have a Daedalus to guide him' (111–12). For a more elaborate, political interpretation of Aeneas and Icarus in the *Defence* (with interesting glances at truancy and the Prodigal Son), see Maslin, 'Introduction,' esp. 27–9, 44, 58–9.

102 'The understanding must not ... be supplied with wings, but rather hung with weights, to keep it from leaping and flying' (*New Organon*, civ, ed. Anderson, 98).

103 The elder Bacon's motto was inscribed over the entrance to his great house at Gorhambury and also appears on hs portrait in the National Portrait Gallery. See McCutcheon, *Sir Nicholas Bacon's Great House Sententiae*, 3, 15.

104 Bacon, *The Wisdom of the Ancients*, quoted in Turner, *Myth of Icarus*, 43.

2 Henry VI, Part One

1 E. Berry, *Patterns of Decay*, 10.

2 Pierce, *Shakespeare's History Plays*, 35–6. Cf. Kirschbaum's comment that 'Talbot and his son represent order, in the same way in which the son-killing-father and the father-killing-son in *3 Henry VI* represent disorder' ('Authorship of *1 Henry VI*,' 821). Similar but more nuanced is Rabkin's argument that the 'basic motif' of the play is 'the overthrow of the old family structure of a paradisal England' (*Shakespeare and the Problem of Meaning*, 85).

3 Rosenthal, *Patriarchy*, 64.

4 Ferne, *Blazon of Gentrie*, 25.

5 Kahn, *Man's Estate*, 50.

6 Ferne, *Blazon of Gentrie*, 25.

7 Robert Turner, *Shakespeare's Apprenticeship*, 25, and echoed by Rabkin, *Shakespeare and the Problem of Meaning*, 88. The recent proponents of multiple authorship of the play assign the Talbot scenes to Shakespeare. See Gary Taylor, *Shakespeare and Others*, 162 and Burns, *King Henry VI, Part 1*, 83.

8 For Lord Talbot's heroism, see Bulman, *Heroic Idiom*, 30–3; for his chivalry, see Edelman, *Brawl Ridiculous*, 64–7.

9 As Kastan points out (*Shapes of Time*, 21–2), the historical Lord Talbot had another son (also, confusingly, named John) who remained in England

and eventually succeeded to his father's title. Hall's chronicle indicates that Talbot was accompanied in France by 'his bastard son Henry Talbot' (Bullough 3:73). In Shakespeare, the whoreson is not acknowledged.

10 In fact, the historical Talbots fared much better than Shakespeare indicates, being one of only a dozen peerage families to maintain a direct patrilineal succession throughout the fifteenth century (Rosenthal, *Patriarchy*, 44–5). For the motif of succession in the play, see Walsh, '"Unkind Division,"' and R. Jones, *These Valiant Dead*.

11 Burns, *King Henry VI, Part 1*, 17.

12 Speaking of the trilogy as a single play, Riggs notes that 'The Talbots' fame, as it was earned at Bordeaux, embodies the high ethical ideals of the play; and their death effectively removes those ideals from the world of the play' (*Shakespeare's Heroical Histories*, 113).

13 Sidney, *Defence of the Earl of Leicester*, in *Miscellaneous Prose*, 134.

14 Young John's 'do you fly' is reminiscent of Lysander's impudent rebuke to Demetrius (and to Egeus): 'You have her father's love, Demetrius, / Let me have Hermia's; do you marry him' (*MND*:1.1.93–4).

15 In a blunter threat to withhold the blessing, James I warned his son Henry in the dedicatory epistle to *Basilicon Doron* that 'I charge you, as ever ye think to deserve my Fatherly blessing, to follow and put in practise, as far as lieth in you, the precepts hereafter following,' *Political Works*, 4.

16 In light of the fact that young John's rescue of his father comes so soon after the comment that 'I gave thee life,' it is interesting to recall Freud's postulate that the father's claim to have given the son life is the origin of filial rescue fantasies (*S. E.* 11:172–3).

17 See Pearlman, 'Shakespeare at Work.'

18 A further weakness in Pearlman's argument that 4.5 was intended to substitute for 4.6 is that without the latter scene there would be no indication of Lord Talbot's having rescued his son.

19 Whitney, *Choice of Emblemes*, 163.

20 For examples of otherwise excellent accounts that ignore young John's flight and its implications, see Leggatt, 'Death of John Talbot,' Jones, *These Valiant Dead*, and Hibbard, *Making of Shakespeare's Dramatic Poetry*.

21 Young John's silence is emphasized by his failure to respond to Lord Talbot's exhortation: 'Speak to thy father ere thou yield thy breath' (4.7.24).

22 Without reference to tension between the two Talbots, Leggatt makes suggestive comments on young John Talbot's coming of age ('Death of John Talbot,' 16–18).

23 Kahn, *Man's Estate*, 53.

24 For instance, a warrior in *Richard II* swears that if he is lying he will 'never brandish more revengeful steel / Over the glittering helmet of my foe' (4.1.50–1). Similarly, in the anonymous *Edmund Ironside* a character declares that 'in vain have I lift up my wasting arm / and brandishéd my falchion o'er thy foes' (5.1.1663–4, ed. Sams, 106).

25 Commenting on a phrase in *Macbeth* ('like good men / Bestride our downfall birthdom' [4.3.3–4]), Berger makes a similar point about the ambiguous mix of protection and aggression in the gesture of standing over a fallen person (*Making Trifles*, 120).

26 Barthelme, *Dead Father*, 139.

27 I am aware of only one edition that glosses the phrase so as to preserve its ambiguity; in the recent Oxford Shakespeare edition, Michael Taylor brilliantly renders it as 'solicitous of my fall.'

28 Though Hall's account does not mention Icarus and Daedalus, it gave Shakespeare a useful nudge when it referred to the 'subtle labyrinth in the which he [Lord Talbot] and his people were enclosed and illaqueate [ensnared]' (Bullough 3:73). Fabricius stresses the importance of Deadalus and Icarus in all three of the *Henry VI* plays, but his argument that the myth shows how father and son share a common fate is not convincing (*Shakespeare's Hidden World*, 32–7).

29 Rudd, 'Daedalus and Icarus,' 45–6.

30 Michael Hattaway's New Cambridge edition glosses 'pride' (citing the *OED*) as 'valor' both times that Lord Talbot uses it.

31 Thus Kahn suggests that Talbot 'interpret[s] his [son's] action as "pride" and his death as punishment for it' (*Man's Estate*, 53), while M. Taylor argues that 'Talbot seems to be using him here as an example of filial devotion rather than as an example of ambition to be shunned' (*Henry VI, Part One*, 213).

32 Ovid's phrase is *caelique cupidine tractus* (*Metamorphoses* 8:224).

33 According to Spevack's *Concordance*, 'side' appears eighteen times in *1 Henry VI*; the nine occurrences in *King John* represent the second highest frequency. Interestingly, the usages cluster in the two places that the new disintegrationists most firmly attribute to Shakespeare: the Temple Garden scene (2.4), where the Yorkists and Lancastrians take sides, and the Talbot sequence, where John Talbot first takes and then leaves his father's side.

34 The phrase 'that fatal apprenticeship' is from A.D. Melville's translation of Ovid, *Metamorphoses* (177).

35 Ovid's line is *hortaturque sequi damnosasque erudit artes* (8:215). Without

referring to Daedalus, Trevor Peacock (the Lord Talbot of the BBC TV production) characterizes Talbot in terms that are relevant to the Greek father, saying that Talbot is 'hoist by his own petard' in that he 'has taught him [young John] too well and the very thing he loves he loses' (Fenwick, 'The Production,' 31).

36 Ovid, *Metamorphoses*, Loeb ed., 1:419.

37 Riggs, *Shakespeare's Heroical Histories*, 110.

38 Young John's leaving his father is not noted, for example, in George Hibbard's account: 'Actuated by the same chivalric ideals, the two Talbots ... grow ever closer together in the hour of danger and death, until in the battle that follows the father rescues the son, and then the son rescues the father, before both are killed' (*Making of Shakespeare's Dramatic Poetry*, 57). Still more misleading is Berman's statement that young Talbot 'asserts his birthright by sacrifice, choosing to die with his father' ('Fathers and Sons,' 490).

39 Emily Dickinson says that when she read Talbot's words in her garret 'the rafters wept' (Finnerty, *Emily Dickinson's Shakespeare*, 39), and Thomas Nashe speaks of how thousands of spectators wept when Lord Talbot died (though, oddly, Nashe makes no reference to young John) (*Works*, 1:212).

40 The quotation is from Skura (*Shakespeare the Actor*, 229) who, in a discussion of male and female encirclement, cites the deaths-within-arms of Salisbury (1.4.70–111) and of Mortimer (2.5.37–114) to illuminate the supposedly benevolent nature of Lord Talbot's embrace of his son.

41 It is interesting that another father who realizes that he has become his son's tomb is the unnamed warrior in *3 Henry VI* who discovers that he has (unwittingly) killed his son (2.5.114–15).

42 Cicero, *De officiis*, Loeb ed., 99.

43 Ovid, *Metamorphoses*, Loeb ed., 1:335.

44 Neill, *Issues of Death*, 311. Less convincingly, G.K. Hunter interprets these tombs as positive symbols of family solidarity (*Dramatic Identities*, 330–4).

45 For Titus's interpretation of the meaning of Lavinia's 'martyred signs,' see 3.2.35–45. The decorum of the golden statue should be considered in the light of Romeo's comment to the Apothecary that poison is cordial and that gold is 'worse poison' (5.1.80–4).

46 More recently, Hattaway follows the tradition by glossing 'his harms' as 'the injuries he has done us' (*Henry the Sixth, Part One*, 160). Burns avoids the issue of what 'harms' refers to but provides suggestive comments on 'bloody nurser,' including the *pietá* connection (*King Henry VI, Part One*, 250).

47   It is unfortunate that David Lee Miller's interesting study of paternity and the sacrifice of sons, *Dreams of the Burning Child*, does not make reference to this scene.

48   Shepherd, *Marlowe*, 156–69.

49   Of course, the differences between Joan and Lord Talbot are not absolute. Both are, for instance, ultimately forsaken by their countrymen. For the relevance to the Talbots of the male characters' tendency to understand history in idealized, textual terms and the female tendency to stress the (less glorious) manifestations of physical fact, see Rackin, *Stages of History*, 152–7.

50   Marlowe, 159 and Whitney, *Choice of Emblemes*, 163.

51   Rabkin, for example, emphasizes the contrast between Lord Talbot and Joan, arguing that they 'play out their conflicting ideals in symmetrical acts of familial commitment' (*Shakespeare and the Problem of Meaning*, 86).

52   A notable exception is Michael Taylor's brief linkage of the two sets of fathers and sons (*Henry VI, Part One*, 69).

53   Gary Taylor's comment that 'in crudeness of dramatic and verse technique I.i–I.viii have no rivals in the First Folio' ignores the deftness of the Master Gunner vignette, which he does not discuss ('Shakespeare and Others,' 163). Though Burns does not discuss the authorship of the scene, his comment that Shakespeare's contributions to the play show 'a concern for genealogy, patrimony, and identity' would support ascribing the scene to Shakespeare (*King Henry VI, Part One*, 83).

54   An example of the (mistaken) view that the Master Gunner is being supportive is John Wilders's remark that 'His father assures the boy that he is about to have better luck because he has pointed a cannon directly at the tower' (*The Lost Garden*, 35).

55   See, for instance, Marilyn French's comment that 'The gunner has a true son, who obeys him eagerly and uses initiative, and is successful in killing Salisbury' (*Shakespeare's Division of Experience*, 51).

56   There is a similar expression of mock solicitude for a usurped father in the anonymous tragedy *Selimus*. The title character speaks of deposing his father as if he were doing him a favour: ''Twere good for him if he were presséd out: / 'Twould bring him rest and rid him of his gout' (ed. Vitkus, 72).

57   In his article on fathers and sons, Holland briefly discusses the Master Gunner and his Boy, but without mentioning the central fact of the Boy's disobedience ('Sons and Substitutions,' 67).

3 *Richard II*

1 Stone, *Crisis of the Aristocracy*, 769.
2 For the theme in Shakespeare of progeny as an extension of the father through time, see Quinones, *Renaissance Discovery of Time*, 300–20. This sometimes uncritical discussion should be corrected by Mary Elizabeth Campbell's emphasis on Shakespeare's growing awareness of the need for *dis-identification* on the part of sons in her PhD dissertation, 'Proving His Beauty by Succession Thine: Father-Son Relationships in Shakespeare's Early Drama.'
3 For discussions of the relations between fathers and sons in *Richard II*, see Sundelson's emphasis on their 'mutual distrust' (*Shakespeare's Restorations*, 30), the psychoanalytic discussions (stressing unconscious parricidal motives) in M.P. Taylor ('A Father Pleads'), Wangh ('A Psychoanalytic Commentary'), and Fabricius (*Shakespeare's Hidden World*, 152–3), the rich analysis of 'familial politics' by Seelig ('Loyal Fathers'), and (most usefully) Berger's incisive comments (*Making Trifles of Terrors*, 148–210).
4 Shakespeare may have found a hint for his vivid contrast in Holinshed's account of how Richard's officers arrested innocent people and refused to free them unless they were willing to fight against their accusers, 'although the accusers for the most part were lusty, young and valiant, where the parties accused were perchance old, impotent, maimed and sickly' (*Chronicles*, 2:850).
5 For the nostalgia of these old characters and the contrast between past and present, see Phialas, 'The Medieval in *Richard II*,' 308–10.
6 Molly Smith's argument in 'Mutant Scenes' that the Duchess of Gloucester at the beginning and the Duchess of York at the end of the play represent an admirable, coherent alternative to the values of the old men needs to be balanced by Kehler's comments on the self-interest of the Duchess of York ('*Richard II*, 5.3,' 132).
7 Esler's *The Aspiring Mind of the Elizabethan Younger Generation* attributes simple, unmixed attitudes to both generations; it would have benefited especially from some consideration of ambivalent attitudes among the young.
8 For 'conspicuous expenditure' and its dangers, see Stone, *Crisis of the Aristocracy*, 547–86.
9 James Winny's discussion of the prodigal son motif in the play contains much suggestive detail but is too insistent on a 'pattern of events in which a noble father is disgraced by a morally degenerate son who flings

away the fortune earned by his great ancestors' (*Player King*, 85). This pattern is in part the construction of fathers.

10 In a useful study entitled 'An Elizabethan Perspective on *Richard II*,' Rossky gathers a good deal of Elizabethan material about Richard and childhood, arguing that (until late in the action) he remains in what today would be called a 'prolonged adolescence.' My discussion places more emphasis on generational conflict, and especially on the sources of Richard's adversarial attitude toward his immediate forebears.

11 Wangh, 'A Psychoanalytic Commentary,' 224.

12 Ferne, *Blazon of Gentrie*, 25.

13 Though he did not make direct use of it, Shakespeare may have noted in Holinshed the Duke of Gloucester's sharp reprimand to Richard: 'Sir, your grace ought to put your body in pain to win a strong hold or town by feats of war, yet you take upon you to sell or deliver any town or strong hold gotten with great adventure by the manhood and policy of your noble progenitors' (Bullough 2:834–5).

14 Golding's 'Epistle' to his translation of Ovid's *Metamorphoses*, 2. He adds that 'This fable also doth advise all parents and all such / As bring up youth, to take good heed of cockering them too much.'

15 The Oedipal interpretation is to be found in Wangh, 'A Psychoanalytic Commentary.'

16 Garry alertly notes that, 'Because he has rejected the importance of his own heritage, Richard can easily ignore York's indignant defense of Bolingbroke's inalienable hereditary rights' ('Unworthy Sons,' 15).

17 I am indebted to Harry Berger Jr's shrewd analysis of the Bullingbrook-Gaunt relationship, and especially his elucidation of Bullingbrook's rhetoric (*Making Trifles of Terrors*, 148–67).

18 Seelig, 'Loyal Fathers,' 356.

19 Pierce, *Shakespeare's History Plays*, 159.

20 *OED*, 'furnish' 2. Mistakenly, I believe, the *OED* places Bullingbrook's usage under its first meaning ('to remove rust from [a weapon or armour]').

21 Berger, *Making Trifles of Terrors*, 163.

22 When Gaunt complains that his fellow council members did not prevent him from punishing his son, his pronouns reveal that his concern is primarily with himself: 'But you gave leave to my unwilling tongue / Against my will to do myself this wrong' (1.3.245–6).

23 Denials of consolation are surprisingly common in Shakespeare, and usually (as here) they involve a questioning of the consoler's authority. See Tromly, 'Grief.'

24 See the first two definitions of 'journeyman' in the *OED*. The passage points toward Prince Hal's interaction with the apprentice Francis in *1 Henry IV* (2.4).

25 Machiavelli, *The Prince*, 67. The connection is also noted by Hugh Grady, *Shakespeare, Machiavelli, and Montaigne*, 73.

26 J. Kerrigan notes that Bullingbrook does not mention Gaunt in either part of *Henry IV* ('Death of Old Double,' 38).

27 The closest equivalent is the grouping in *3 Henry VI* (1.1.210 ff.) of Henry VI, his wife Margaret, and their son Edward. In this scene Margaret assails Henry for having secured the throne for himself by agreeing with the Yorkists to deny the succession to Edward. In both plays, the outspoken mother cites her pains of childbirth and devotion to her son in the course of disparaging her husband's lack of natural feeling.

28 Holinshed, *Chronicles*, 2:283.

29 *Court of Good Counsell*, sig. G3.

30 See the references to Margaret Paston (ch. 1, n. 11) and to Lady Mary Sidney (ch. 1, fn. 56).

31 Though it may seem as though the Duchess has not heard York's warning or is using her son's former title merely out of habit, this is not so; in the following scene, when she begs the King to forgive her son, she is careful to refer to Aumerle by his new title of Rutland (5.3.96), the only time she uses it.

32 In 2.1, the Folio stage direction indicates that Aumerle is present (though silent) when the dying Gaunt chastises Richard and also when, a few moments later, York criticizes Richard for his breach of the laws of succession. In 3.3, Aumerle is on the ramparts of Flint Castle with Richard when York is below with Bullingbrook's army. And in the deposition scene (4.1), Aumerle is onstage for the entire scene, with York entering and exiting twice (107–58, 162–319) as he goes about Bullingbrook's business.

33 MacIsaac, 'Three Cousins in *Richard II*,' 137.

34 Holinshed, *Chronicles*, 2:849.

35 There is of course a causal relationship between the two scenes, for York's failure – notwithstanding his 'loyal bosom' – to demand obedience from Bullingbrook has helped to create the usurpation of Richard that Aumerle wishes to undo.

36 Rabkin, *Shakespeare and the Problem of Meaning*, 88.

37 M.P. Taylor, 'A Father Pleads,' 54. Taylor goes on to say, less convincingly, that York feels profoundly guilty for having been disloyal to Richard and that his 'bitterly guilty conscience demands a sacrifice,' which is his son (55).

38 In *Elizabethans at Home*, Pearson notes that 'If a good father had a bad son, then the father's own honesty would be questioned, for people would say no son would go astray "unless he were by a father led thereto"' (101).

39 Berger, *Making Trifles of Terrors*, 173. In the same passage, Berger also usefully speaks of York's desire to exorcise his resemblance to Aumerle.

40 Quoted (with reference to Henry IV and Hal) in Goddard, *Meaning of Shakespeare*, 1:168.

41 Black, 'Interlude of the Beggar,' 112, quotes from the service ('Grant that the Old Adam in this child may be so buried, that the new man may be raised up in him'). For a mother speaking of a much more joyous baptism of grown-up children, see *The Comedy of Errors*, 5.1.404–7.

42 Sutherland and Watts, *Henry V, War Criminal?* 90–1.

43 *Court of Good Counsell*, sig. H2v.

44 Forker's gloss notes that 'Literally, this would imply a lapse of three months since the coronaion, at which Hal had to be present since he participated in the ceremony' (*King Richard II*, 443).

4 Henry IV, Part One

1 The first comment is from Alexander, 'Note on Falstaff,' 599; the second is from Lichtenberg and Lichtenberg, 'Prince Hal's Conflict,' 875.

2 Garber, *Coming of Age*, 197.

3 For turning back the clock, see the beginning of the next chapter.

4 Babula, 'Whatever Happened to Prince Hal?,' 47.

5 Interestingly, J.D. Wilson comments briefly on how the usurpation and murder of Richard affect Henry through 'the consciousness both of guilt and of insecurity of tenure' but does not consider how they would affect Hal (*Fortunes of Falstaff*, 60–1). Wilson does not raise the possibility that Hal may not approve of what his father has done.

6 For the relationship between Hal and Hamlet, see 153–4.

7 For the connections of Hal with the Prodigal Son, and for some of the differences between them, see Alan Young, *English Prodigal*, 194–211.

8 In the parable, the Prodigal protests that he is 'no more worthy to be called thy son' (Luke 15:21), and in *Famous Victories* Hal declares that he is 'an unworthy son for so good a father' (Corbin and Sedge, *Oldcastle Controversy*, 167 [scene 6, line 15]).

9 The standard discussions of financial imagery in the play do not place enough emphasis on the issue of Hal and indebtedness. See, for instance, Rubinstein ('Metaphor of Liability') and Kastan (*King Henry IV*, 68–9).

10 For Hal's future-tensed language, see Wharton, *Henry the Fourth*, 25–6.

11 Godshalk's useful article 'Henry V's Politics of Non-Responsibility' could have paid more attention to the sources of Hal/Henry's need to evade the moral weight of responsibility, and especially to the issue of his father's usurpation.

12 For a list of critics supporting the choric interpretation of the speech, see A. Young, *English Prodigal Son Plays*, 201 (fn. 26).

13 Johnson, *Works* 7:458. Cf. Manlove's comment that this speech shows someone 'who is radically confused about his motives, someone who is a mixture of policy and folly, of detachment from Falstaff and involvement with him, who tries to make one side of the equation explain away the other' (*The Gap in Shakespeare*, 18). Manlove's lively and frequently incisive book deserves more attention than it appears to have received.

14 Zitner, Review, 341.

15 There is historical evidence (cited by Kris, *Psychoanalytic Explorations in Art*, 280–1) that young Hal was a favourite of Richard's and accompanied him on the Irish Expedition, where he was knighted by him, but Shake-speare seems to make no allusion to this material.

16 I owe this observation to an unpublished term essay by Valerie Podpol-lock.

17 Kris, *Psychoanalytic Explorations in Art*, 281.

18 Kris, *Psychoanalytic Explorations in Art*, 282.

19 Kris, *Psychoanalytic Explorations in Art*, 279.

20 Fehrenbach minimizes Hal's complexities when he argues that the Prince (like Hotspur and Falstaff) is an 'open book,' whereas the King is 'secre-tive and distant' ('Characterization of the King,' 43). One need not deny Hal's reticence in order to stress the King's.

21 Tilley, *Dictionary of Proverbs*, 557.

22 Seltzer astutely characterizes the 'pay the debt I never promised' line as 'full of repressed resentment' ('Prince Hal and Tragic Style,' 24). The cor-responding line in *Hamlet* is the Prince's less repressed (and perhaps less resentful) cry, 'O cursed spite, / That ever I was born to set it right!' (1.5.188–9).

23 Kahn, *Man's Estate*, 73. See also Goddard, *Meaning of Shakespeare*, 1:172. In addition to the verbal parallels, Hal's strategy in the soliloquy recalls the experience of his father, who disguised his true intentions and after seizing the throne proceeded to falsify the hopes of *his* collaborators.

24 Marsh ('Hal and Hamlet,' 24–9) comments on how the aggressive practi-cal jokes of Hal and Hamlet stem from their aggrieved sense of com-

pelled duty, but he does not consider the possibility that their fathers are a hidden target of the jests.

25 Freud, *S. E.* 8:105. In a long footnote, Freud makes an interesting comment on Falstaff (231).

26 The Francis business is cut even from the BBC television version, a series that generally represents the entire text of plays. On the occasions when it isn't cut, the scene often makes no sense, as in the recent Toronto production in which Francis was played by an old clown. Even the best editions of the play (e.g., in the Oxford and New Cambridge series) fail to give directors much help. There are, however, at least three useful discussions of the jest (Zitner ['Mirror'], Shuchter ['Prince Hal and Francis'], and Sundelson [*Shakespeare's Restorations*, 47–50]), though I think it expresses more anger toward his father than these critics do.

27 Zitner, 'Mirror,' 67.

28 While it is true, as Dessen says, that 'the stage action presents the image of Francis as a puppet jerked by two competing strings,' it is not quite true that 'the spectator sees that Prince Hal is firmly in control' (*Shakespeare and the Late Moral Plays*, 69). Hal is of course controlling Francis, but the larger point is that he cannot control his own life.

29 For Hal's sympathy for Francis, see Zitner, 'Mirror,' 67–9; for Hal's mockery of Francis, see Sundelson, *Shakespeare's Restorations of the Father* (48–50).

30 The most striking instance of Hal's eloquence being 'the parcel of a reckoning' occurs when he predicts the death of Hotspur to his father; indeed, within eight lines Hal uses both 'reckoning' and 'parcel' (3.2.152–9).

31 Schochet notes that children and household servants were 'usually not distinguished' with regard to the substance of obedience, as the latter were regarded as bound by filial (more than contractual) ties ('Patriarchialism,' 417). John Kerrigan comments suggestively on the 'psychological interest which Hal's alienation from his father/master would have held for early audiences' ('Death of Old Double,' 43).

32 New Historicist assumptions about the containment of revolt lead, I believe, Greenblatt (*Shakespearean Negotiations*, 44–5) and Kastan mistakenly to interpret Hal's lines as being 'designed to reconcile Francis to the life he has in the tavern' (*King Henry IV*, 211).

33 Jameson (*Hidden Shakespeare*, 76–8) makes a similar point about the Vintner and comments, 'To the old script of the Prodigal Son, Shakespeare has added lines that bespeak a prodigal whose deepest impulse is

to stay away from home, *not* to be reconciled to his father if reconciliation means submission.'

34 For Boswell's adoption of Johnson as a father, see the former's *London Journal*, 301. Stressing the education that Hal receives from Falstaff, Allen Bloom invokes another surrogate father and son relationship, that between Socrates and Alcibiades (*Love and Friendship*, 407).

35 French, 'French's Acting Version,' 45. Cf. Pierce's comment on the 'reconciliation': 'This father and son standing together are a symbol of unity in the realm just as in *1 Henry VI* Talbot and his son fighting together stand for the unity that will die with them' (*Shakespeare's History Plays*, 186).

36 Hibbard, '*Henry IV* and *Hamlet*,' 9.

37 For Shakespeare's father-son reunions in which emotion is withheld, see Danson, 'Shakespeare and the Misrecognition of Fathers and Sons.'

38 Luke 15:21. Much closer to Hal's rhetoric are the many cringing letters of excuse that Elizabethan sons sent their angry fathers. Stewart and Wolfe comment that 'Apologetic letters from son to father are so common in the period that they almost form a sub-genre' (*Letterwriting*, 41).

39 In a paragraph on Shrewsbury Field, Holinshed begins by observing that 'The prince that day helped his father like a lusty young gentleman' and proceeds to note several sentences later (without specifying an agent) that the king 'was raised' after 'the earl Douglas struck him down' (Bullough 4:191). In his poem, Daniel draws the inference that it was the Prince who saved the King. Directly invoking Hal, Daniel declares: 'Hadst thou not there lent present speedy aid / To thy endangered father nearly tired, / Whom fierce encountering *Douglas* overlaid, / That day had there his troublous life expired' (Bullough 4:214).

40 Dessen, *Shakespeare and the Late Moral Plays*, 84.

41 With appropriate *OED* citations, West usefully glosses the financial imagery but does not draw inferences about the relationship between father and son ('Glossary,' 324).

42 Interestingly, this scene connects with the rescue scene in *1 Henry VI*, as the King's 'Stay and breathe a while' and ensuing language of indebtedness echo Lord Talbot's 'Pause, and take thy breath; / I gave thee life, and rescu'd thee from death' (4.6.4–5).

43 Cf. Philip Williams's observation that 'Hal's reply is curious, suggesting as it does that thoughts of his father's death had indeed not been absent from his mind' ('Birth and Death of Falstaff Reconsidered,' 361). Similarly, John Kerrigan notes that 'By declaring "I might have let alone / The insulting hand of Douglas over you ..." [Hal] intimates an alternative entertained' ('Death of Old Double,' 42).

44 Buck, 'Shakespeare's Epic,' 145.

45 Alexander, 'Note on Falstaff,' 599. But surely 'the arch-enemy of the king' proves to be not Hotspur but the Douglas, whom Hal will later free.

46 'Shakespeare indicates that the patricidal impulses which Hotspur directs at the Father-King figure of Bolingbroke, impulses with which Hal himself is apparently struggling, are displaced aggressions whose just discharge would be toward Hotspur's own father, the Earl of Northumberland' (Faber, 'Oedipal Patterns,' 431).

47 Weil and Weil, *First Part of King Henry IV*, 12.

48 The most suggestive critical comment I have seen is the brief observation by Fabricius that the play ends 'on a rather ambivalent note with Prince Hal's release of the Douglas, the man who attempted to kill his father, on the ground that "His valours shown upon our crests today Have taught us how to cherish such high deeds"' (*Shakespeare's Hidden World*, 212).

49 These influential phrases are from J.D. Wilson, *Fortunes of Falstaff*, 68–9, and are regularly echoed (e.g., 'the release without ransom is one further testimonial to the prince's magnanimity and political maturity' [Bevington, *Henry IV, Part One*, 15]). Pechter elaborates the point, reading Hal's freeing of the Douglas as a contrast to his father's refusal to free Mortimer (1.3) and to Hotspur's talk of redeeming honour but refusing to share it (1.3). Hence 'Hal both redeems the prisoner and generously transfers the honor to another, thereby confirming his promise in the soliloquy to achieve a true nobility of authority under which England may now unite' ('Falsifying Men's Hopes,' 229–30).

50 See Connor, 'Role of Douglas.' Apart from its unlikely ascription of unchivalrous conduct to Hotspur, a problem with this hypothetical stage business is that Hotspur is not likely to allow a co-rival to share in the glory of a climactic struggle with Prince Hal.

51 In an unpublished term essay, Taela Smith noted the relevance of the Douglas's 'insulting hand' to his being freed by Hal.

52 As Danièle Cybulskie remarked in an unpublished term essay, the freeing of the Douglas may also involve a swipe at Hal's surrogate father, since the Scot had menaced and terrified Falstaff on the battlefield as well as the King.

53 In the probably Shakespearean *Edward III*, a French captain turns over the captured Count of Salisbury to the French King, saying 'Dispose of him as please your majesty' (4.5.60). Clearly, the King hopes to hang Salisbury, but Prince Charles (like Prince Hal) intervenes to save him.

54 Zailig Pollock pointed out to me the appropriateness of 'deep defiance' to Hal's devious hostility.

55 Bevington, 48.
56 Pierce, *Shakespeare's History Plays*, 187.
57 See Pechter, 'Falsifying Men's Hopes,' for an intelligent discussion of closure that addresses issues other than the ones I have raised.
58 It is interesting that Samuel Daniel refers to Shrewsbury as 'a loosing [i.e., losing] victory' for the King's forces: 'And dear it cost, and o much blood is shed / To purchase thee this loosing victory / O travail'd king' (Bullough 4:215). Shakespeare's play suggests that, in another sense, the loss is Hal's.

5 *Henry IV, Part Two*

1 There is a good account of such transformations and their moral significance in Traversi's chapter on *2 Henry IV* in *Approach to Shakespeare*, 237–62.
2 For a discussion linking the themes of the play to the problems Shakespeare faced in writing it, see Calderwood, *Metadrama in Shakespeare's Henriad*, 120–33.
3 Pierce, 'Generations,' 51.
4 Berryman says of this line that 'anything like this is inconceivable in the earlier histories' (*Berryman's Shakespeare*, 338). Oddly, the line is not cited in Faber's essay on unconscious Oedipal rivalry between Hotspur and Northumberland, which on the basis of little textual evidence argues that Hotspur's 'persistent aggressive urges derive from his anger at his parent for never having been a parent, for wanting him out of the way' ('Oedipal Patterns,' 437).
5 For a sparkling discussion of doubles and doubling in the two *Henry IV* plays, see John Kerrigan's essay '*Henry IV* and the Death of Old Double.'
6 In an interesting article entitled 'Reforming Prince Hal' Crewe reads the reformation in *Part Two* as an implicit questioning of what he thinks is Hal's too pat, too spectacular reformation in *Part One*.
7 Jenkins, 'Structural Problem,' 231. Cf. Cain's comment that 'the dramatic assumption of *The Second Part* is that the audience will or must forget that the Prince's reformation has already taken place in *The First Part*, for it is obviously here presented with another version of the same thing' ('Further Light,' 33).
8 Cain, 'Further Light,' 38.
9 For the two parts comprising a diptych, see Hunter, *Dramatic Identities*, 303–18.
10 Sherman Hawkins, 'Structural Problem,' 300. In his *Shakespeare's Serial*

History Plays, Grene stresses the importance of looking backward, especially in *2 Henry IV*.

11 Shaaber, 'Unity of *Henry IV*,' 219. On the following page, Shaaber asks: 'Is there really the slightest hint in *1 Henry IV* that the king and prince are not completely and triumphantly reconciled?' For a similar view, see Cain's argument that at the end of *Part One* the reformation of the Prince leads to 'the rehabilitation of the bonds of affection between father and son and the confirmation of their mutual trust and love' ('Further Light,' 37).

12 Though the old editorial tradition of assigning the location of the scene to 'Prince Henry's house' still continues (e.g., in the Riverside and the Norton editions), there is no evidence to support it. In *1 Henry IV*, all of Hal's scenes with Poins take place in Eastcheap, and the talk of 'small beer' suggests that they are in the same setting again (as they will be in their only other shared scene in the play, 2.4).

13 Auerbach, *Mimesis*, 274–8.

14 As Hal and his father use it, 'vile' carries its now obsolete sense of 'socially base' more than its modern sense of 'morally despicable.'

15 J.D. Wilson, *Fortunes of Falstaff*, 76. William Empson mounts a lively and I think convincing rebuttal of Wilson's interpretation of this dialogue ('Falstaff and Mr Dover Wilson,' 140–2).

16 Pierce, 'Generations,' 54. On the next page Pierce adds, unconvincingly I believe, that Hal 'is fleeing from his grief into dissipation, and the result is that a companion like Poins necessarily misunderstands him' (55). On a similar note, Melchiori says that Hal's reference to bleeding inwardly shows his 'committed acceptance of the role of son' (*Second Part of King Henry IV*, 26).

17 Part of the nastiness of this comment, and of the scene in general, stems from the young men's envy of Falstaff's having a sexual partner. Hal comes up with the idea to play the trick only after he has been intrigued to hear about Doll Tearsheet and asked, 'Sup any women with him?' (2.2.151).

18 Since the action is continuous with the King on stage throughout, there is no need for a scene division between Henry's discussion of Hal with his counsellors and the episode with Hal and the crown. See, for instance, Weis, *Henry IV, Part Two*, 238.

19 Corbin and Sedge, *Oldcastle Controversy*, 171 (scene 8, line 30).

20 Goddard, *Meaning of Shakespeare*, 1:195.

21 Pierce, *Shakespeare's History Plays*, 55.

22 Dawson, *Watching Shakespeare*, 108–9.

23 In *Famous Victories* there is a strong note of mutuality. After he gives the crown back to the King and the King returns it to him, the Prince declares, 'Well may I take it at your Majesty's hands; but it shall never touch my head so long as my father lives' (Corbin and Sedge, *Oldcastle Controversy*, 172 [scene 8, lines 53–4]).

24 J.D. Wilson, *Fortunes of Falstaff*, 79.

25 Watson, *Shakespeare and the Hazards of Ambition*, 60.

26 Weis, *Henry IV, Part Two*, 48.

27 Norman Sanders, 'The True Prince and the False Thief,' 33.

28 Philip Williams makes the related point that in *Part One* Hal steals bar bills from the pocket of Falstaff, his sleeping surrogate father, just as he now takes the crown from his sleeping biological father ('Birth and Death of Falstaff Reconsidered,' 362).

29 For 'outward show' vs inward filial reverence, see p. 6.

30 For the discrepancies between the earlier scene and Hal's recounting of it, see Goddard, *Meaning of Shakespeare*, 1:194–6. Oddly for a psychoanalyst, Kris fails to note the discrepancies and seems to accept Hal's account at face-value (*Psychoanalytic Explorations in Art*, 279).

31 Philip Williams, 'Birth and Death of Falstaff Reconsidered,' 361. Similarly, Blanpied speaks of Hal's 'displacing his own motive' in that he 'projects his most dangerous impulses onto the crown, and thereby controls and, in a measure, evades them' (*Time and the Artist*, 193).

32 Unlike Hal's 'if ... let me,' Falstaff's favourite construction is 'if ... then,' where the effect is to reject the moral hypothesis briefly entertained. See, for instance, 'If sack and sugar be a fault, God help the wicked!' (*1H4*:2.4.470–1).

33 Goddard's comment is shrewd and succinct: 'What he [Hal] expressly declares he did not say or feel fits what he did say and obviously did feel with a damning neatness' (*Meaning of Shakespeare*, 1:196).

34 Cf. John Kerrigan's astute remark that Henry 'does not claim to believe him [Hal]' ('Death of Old Double,' 33).

35 John Kerrigan suggests that a 'subterranean set of resemblances' between King and Prince creates in effect a double Henry figure ('Death of Old Double,' 39).

36 Bradley, 'The Rejection of Falstaff,' 76. Bradley completes his sentence by speaking of 'a final emergence of the wild Prince as a just, wise, stern, and glorious King.'

37 Ornstein, *A Kingdom for a Stage*, 166.

38 J.D. Wilson, *Fortunes of Falstaff*, 75.

39 Corbin and Sedge, *Oldcastle Controversy*, 160 (scene 4, line 69).

40 Corbin and Sedge, *Oldcastle Controversy*, 160 (scene 4, lines 78–80).
41 Corbin and Sedge, *Oldcastle Controversy*, 178 (scene 9, lines 149–50).
42 Cf. Erickson: 'The Lord Chief Justice symbolizes the survival of the dead king and serves as the means by which Hal's private submission to his father can be translated into an institutional norm' (*Patriarchal Structures*, 45).
43 Melchiori, *Second Part of King Henry IV*, 175 and Weis, 257.
44 Erickson, *Patriarchal Structures*, 45.
45 Berryman, *Berryman's Shakespeare*, 338.
46 In an interesting reading of the rejection, Paris stresses the continuing attractiveness of Falstaff to Hal: 'He rejects Falstaff so harshly because he is profoundly threatened by the part of himself that is still attracted to Falstaff and all that he represents' (*Character as a Subversive Force*, 88).
47 J.D. Wilson notes that this interpretation of the lines was first advanced by Warburton in the eighteenth century (*Fortunes of Falstaff*, 122).
48 For the motif of brothers in *Henry V*, see Sundelson, *Shakespeare's Restorations*, 58–66.
49 In his lengthy, over-protesting exculpation of himself to Williams, Henry's hypothetical example of 'a son that is by his father sent about merchandise' (4.1.147–8) evokes his own relationship with his father and the family business of running the kingdom.

6 *Hamlet*

1 Following a brief reference in a letter to his friend Wilhelm Fliess (*Letters*, 272–3), Freud articulated the Oedipal interpretation of *Hamlet* in *The Interpretation of Dreams* (*S. E.* 4: 264–6).
2 Greenblatt speculates that Shakespeare may have denied a request that may have been made by his father – who may have been a devout Catholic – that he pay for masses for the soul of Hamnet (*Will in the World*, 311–18).
3 For uncommonly full comments on *Hamlet* in the context of Shakespeare's previous development (with some emphasis on fathers and sons), see Barton, 'Introduction,' 18–25. Oddly, Greenblatt refers to several stepping stones leading to the 'conceptual breakthrough' of *Hamlet*, but does not mention the most obviously relevant play, *1 Henry IV* (*Will in the World*, 324). Similarly, Shapiro, in *A Year in the Life of Shakespeare, 1599*, minimizes the deep resemblances between *Hamlet* and *1 Henry IV*, perhaps because these plays stand on opposite sides of 1599, which he posits as a watershed in Shakespeare's development.

4 Harriett Hawkins notes that 'the Ghost of Hamlet's father is analogous to the pressures exerted on the present by the past' (*Poetic Freedom*, 87).

5 'Hamlet's Older Brother' is the title of States's stimulating chapter (*Concept of Character*, 157–72) on the 'dramaturgic similarities behind the characterizations' of Hal and Hamlet. He does not address the filial ambivalence of the two, my main concern.

6 Drewry, *Hamlet's Fathers*, 2.

7 Gouge, *Of Domesticall Duties*, 432.

8 For an admirably compendious discussion of the tradition behind the speech, see Jenkins's Arden edition (440–3).

9 Hibbard (*Hamlet*, 350) notes the echo and describes Laertes as 'the true son of his father.'

10 Freud, *Letters*, 202.

11 For Laertes and honour, see R. Levin, 'Dramatic Function of Foils,' and especially 25–7 of Dodsworth's interesting chapter entitled 'Honour and the Polonius Household,' in his *Hamlet Closely Observed*. In this fixation on family honour, Laertes stands in relation to Hamlet as Hotspur does to Prince Hal.

12 Barton, 'Introduction,' 40.

13 In addition to the numerous responses to Jones summarized by Holland in *Psychoanalysis and Shakespeare* (164–85), see the discussions in Erlich (*Hamlet's Absent Father*, 19–50) and King (*Hamlet's Search for Meaning*, 100–34), and especially the trenchant analysis in Jacobson ('Hamlet's Other Selves').

14 Jacobson makes the case for Jones's contradiction in 'Hamlet's Other Selves,' 266.

15 E. Jones, 'Hamlet and Oedipus,' 59.

16 As Campbell puts it, 'Part of the audience's mystification must be attributed to Hamlet's own "repression" of his need to dissociate himself from his father' (*Proving His Beauty*, 276).

17 Blits, *Deadly Thought*, 110.

18 Chettle, *Tragedy of Hoffman*, sig. B1.

19 Goddard's comment cannot be improved on: 'As so often in Shakespeare, the metaphors undo the logic and tell the truth over its head' (*Meaning of Shakespeare*, 1:349). See also Snyder, *Wayward Journey*, 118, and Dodsworth's comment on the syntactical postponement created by the phrases about wings and thoughts (*Hamlet Closely Observed*, 61).

20 Edwards comments appositely that Hamlet's 'reaction to the Ghost is like a religious conversion' (*Hamlet, Prince of Denmark*, 45), and this is surely the effect that the Ghost sought. In Erlich's psychoanalytic terms, 'This

seems a fantasy of the father introjected as a voice of conscience, a super-ego, the commanding voice as distinguished from the "baser" mob of instincts' (*Hamlet's Absent Father*, 56–7).

21 Edwards, *Hamlet, Prince of Denmark*, 45.

22 Respectively, R. Berry, 'Hamlet's Doubles,' 211, and Austin, 'Hamlet's Hungry Ghost,' 80. Garber suggests a more sophisticated notion of pos-session by drawing on Freud's idea of a daemonic compulsion to repeat (*Shakespeare's Ghost Writers*, 162).

23 Barish ('Remembering and Forgetting,' 218) links Hamlet's impressively detailed recollection of the Pyrrhus speech to his recent claim to have erased his memory.

24 The first phrase is from Westlund ('Ambivalence,' 248), and the second is from Kastan ('His semblable,' 200). Kastan's article acutely traces the troubling connections between revenge and imitation in the play.

25 Miola, 'Aeneas and Hamlet,' 285.

26 See Hibbard's gloss in the Oxford World's Classics edition.

27 Similarly, Eissler speaks of how Hamlet's repugnance toward the prospect of becoming 'a mere tool in his father's hands' helps to account for his delay (*Discourse on Hamlet*, 103).

28 Quoted from Dent's *The Plaine Mans Path-Way to Heaven* in Rozett (*Doc-trine of Election*, 48).

29 Just as in *1 Henry IV* Prince Hal is aware of similarities between himself and Francis the drawer even as he mocks Francis's lack of mental and physical freedom, so Hamlet will repeatedly attack Gertrude and Ophelia for manifesting the frail dependence on paternal authority that he feels.

30 Rose, '*Hamlet* and the Shape of Revenge,' 134.

31 McFarland, *Tragic Meanings*, 45.

32 One's sense that Hamlet visits on Rosencrantz and Guildenstern the revenge most appropriate for Claudius is supported by his specifying in his forged letter that his former schoolmates should be 'put to sudden death, / Not shriving time allow'd' (5.2.46–7), which recalls the Ghost's lament to Hamlet that Claudius's poison prevented him from repenting (1.5.74–9).

33 Bond, 'Certain Sermons or Homilies,' 210–11.

34 McAlindon, *Shakespeare and Decorum*, 52.

35 Reina Green notes how, in contrast to the conduct literature of the age, '*Hamlet* presents relationships in which sons and daughters are endan-gered by listening to and obeying fathers and father-substitutes' ('Poi-soned Ears,' par 1).

36 Belsey, 'The Case of Hamlet's Conscience,' 142. (Claudius's equation of love and revenge is at 4.7.106–10.)

37 In his richly stimulating British Academy lecture '*Hamlet*: Conversations with the Dead,' Nuttall explores Hamlet's being assimilated to the metaphysical world of the Ghost but does not mention what I take to be the crucial element of Hamlet's imitation of the Ghost's workings.

38 Willson, in 'Hamlet's Ghostly Presence,' notes that 'something of the ghost's otherworldliness has rubbed off on Hamlet' (81).

39 For a comprehensive survey of these strategies and their place in the structuring of the play, see Brennan, *Shakespeare's Dramatic Structures*, 129–41.

40 For a teasing out of the implications of the staging that does not refer to depth, see Zitner, 'Zig-Zag.' Eissler makes interesting comments on how 'the cellarage scene shows rivalry between Hamlet and the Ghost' (*Discourse on Hamlet*, 104, fn 84).

41 Russ, in 'Old Mole in *Hamlet*,' reviews the debate, arguing convincingly that there was no tradition of the mole as a symbol for Satan. De Grazia's stimulating chapter titled '"Old Mole": The Modern Telos and the Return to Dust' (Hamlet *without Hamlet*, 23–44) does not note the association of moles with destructive pioners in the play.

42 Nashe, *Works*, 3:285.

43 As Nigel Alexander notes, 'Polonius now makes it impossible for Ophelia to trust her own judgment, and therefore be true to herself in the terrible transactions of the heart' (*Poison, Play, and Duel*, 134).

44 The quoted phrase is from Arthur Dent's likening of Satanic Pride to gunpowder: 'For as we see it come to pass in the siege of strong holds, when no battery or force of shot will prevail, the last remedy and policy is to undermine it, and blow it up with trains of gun-powder' (*The Plaine Mans Path-Way to Heaven*, 40).

45 In *Henry V* (3.2.57–64), Fluellen notes that the besieged French at Harfleur attempt to countermine the mines of the English. For the relevant passage in Holinshed, see Bullough 4:387, fn 7.

46 Of the final scene of the play, McFarland says 'Now all is surface' (*Tragic Meanings*, 56).

47 With regard to Hamlet's story and his sense of self, Lee interestingly refers to the 'narrative concept of personal identity' advanced by Alasdair MacIntyre (*Shakespeare's* Hamlet, 204).

48 When Freud refers to the episode on ship in the *Interpretation of Dreams*, he speaks as if it were self-evident that Hamlet acted 'in a pre-meditated and even crafty fashion ... with all the callousness of a Renaissance prince,' but

he does not note the contradiction between this apparent craftiness and Hamlet's later account of his behaviour in his story (*S. E.* 4:265).

49   Lee notes that the passage in which Hamlet tells Gertrude of his plans 'sits uncomfortably' with his later assertion of providential causality, and wonders if 'the prince is labouring to conceal the coldness of his calculations' (*Shakespeare's* Hamlet, 237). He is right to comment that the deletion of the passage in the Folio renders Hamlet's motives 'less known' than in Q2 (237). Kermode states, wrongly I believe, that Shakespeare made the cut because 'Hamlet cannot at this point have foreseen the circumstances under which he might turn the tables on his guards' (*Shakespeare's Language*, 124).

50   To his credit, Jenkins sees the contradiction and tries (unconvincingly) to resolve it by declaring that 'Hamlet's confidence in the outcome will prepare the audience for it, but affords no justification for supposing that he has any precise plan for bringing it about (which he ultimately does by sudden inspiration, v.ii.6–53)' (*Hamlet*, 331–2).

51   For a simpler Shakespearean antecedent to Hamlet's willed forgetting, see Henry V's apparent repression of the fact that, before he demands (apparently sincerely) the Archbishop of Canterbury's considered opinion on whether he has a claim to the French throne, he has threatened the Archbishop with punitive financial measures (*H5*:1.1.1–21, 69–89). Godshalk discusses the issue with reference to what he calls Henry's 'subtle politics of non-responsibility' but says little about the degree of self-deception evidently involved ('Henry V's Politics,' 12).

52   Spencer, 341. (Spencer contributed the notes for the edition, and Anne Barton wrote the Introduction.) Dodsworth makes a similar point (*Hamlet Closely Observed*, 261).

53   Gregory, *Oxford Companion to the Mind*, 197.

54   King, *Hamlet's Search for Meaning*, 5.

55   When the French ambassador asks King Henry if he can speak freely of a matter that may anger him, Henry reassures him that 'We are no tyrant, but a Christian king, / Upon whose grace our passion is as subject / As is our wretches fett'red in our prisons' (*H5*:1.2.241–3). Earlier, Claudius says to Rosencrantz and Guildenstern that 'we will fetters put about this fear' (3.3.25).

56   This view of the mutines in the bilboes was advanced by Gord de Villiers in an unpublished essay. In another term essay, Kaline Baker suggested that Hamlet 'may not be chained in the bowels of the ship, but he is chained to his guilty conscience in the deep recesses of his mind that he cannot escape.'

57 Brennan, *Shakespeare's Dramatic Structures*, 135.

58 My interpretation runs counter to that of Barbara Hardy, who says that Hamlet's 'narration of the adventure is terse, vigorous, almost extrovert' (*Shakespeare's Storytellers*, 185) and adds that 'Confiding supplants soliloquy and its novelty, as a form of discourse for Hamlet, is a moral renewal' (187). Hardy does not note the parallels between the Ghost and Hamlet as storytellers, nor does she note the contradictions in Hamlet's tale.

59 Rosenberg, *Masks of* Hamlet, 862. In its careful effects, Hamlet's story points to the long-promised, self-serving tale that Prospero tells a far more innocent auditor (Miranda) at the beginning of *The Tempest*.

60 The comment on 'psychological harmony' is from Halverson ('*Hamlet*: Ethos and Transcendence,' 67); that on the 'new man' is from H. Levin (*The Question of* Hamlet, 94); that on 'regeneration' is from S.F. Johnson ('Regeneration of Hamlet,' 206).

61 G. Williams, 'Hamlet and the Dread Commandment,' 66.

62 Bradley notes Hamlet's echo of his earlier phrase but draws no inferences from it (*Shakespearean Tragedy*, 120). For a discussion of how 'Yorick stands in marked contrast to the authoritarian father figures who haunt Elsinore,' see Watterson, 'Hamlet's Lost Father.' For the Ghost and Yorick as 'structural poles in the play,' see Maslen, 'Yorick's Place in *Hamlet*.'

63 'The Silence of the Ghost' is a heading in Edwards's Introduction in *Hamlet, Prince of Denmark*, 58–61.

64 'Giving up the Ghost' is the title of the chapter on *Hamlet* in the books by Garber (*Shakespeare's Ghost Writers*) and Watson (*The Rest Is Silence*).

65 Burnett notes this echo of the Ghost but does not comment on the more important ones that immediately follow ('*Hamlet* and Secrets,' 36–7).

66 Hammersmith attributes what he aptly calls Hamlet's 'urgent, near ferocity' cry to his 'terror of utter annihilation,' but I believe that Hamlet wants not simply to be remembered but to be remembered in the moral terms he taught to Horatio ('*Hamlet* and the Myth of Memory,' 602).

67 Erickson, who stresses the importance of Horatio's friendship to Hamlet's integrity, notes Hamlet's troubling echo of the Ghost but maintains there is 'a difference' between the two situations: unlike the Ghost, who mandates revenge, 'Hamlet bequeaths his story to Horatio, thus preserving an alternate legacy of nonviolent fraternal cherishing' (*Patriarchal Structures*, 71–2). (But there *is* violence in Hamlet's insistence, and his disregard for his friend's happiness is scarcely 'fraternal cherishing.') William Kerrigan argues that Hamlet is attempting to save Horatio's life and suggests that in commanding him to tell his story Hamlet is 'supply-

ing the only reason that could possibly dissuade his friend from following him' (*Hamlet's Perfection*, 148). Cf. Hibbard, *Hamlet* (63).

68 The interpretations are, respectively, from Rosenberg (*Masks of* Hamlet, 904), from Eissler (*Discourse on Hamlet*, 129), and from Foakes (*Hamlet versus Lear*, 80). For (to my mind) unconvincing attempts to ascribe to Fortinbras such virtues as exemplary obedience, high honour, and legitimacy, see, respectively, G. Williams ('Hamlet and the Dread Commandment,' 60–1), Fowler ('The Case against Hamlet,' 8), and Hayton, '"The King my father?,"' 64.

69 McGuire, in 'Which Fortinbras, Which *Hamlet*?' stresses the ambivalence of the Q2 passages (and especially Hamlet's Fortinbras soliloquy) that do not appear in the other early texts. Shapiro sensibly argues that in the Folio text the deletion of this 'grim, almost savage soliloquy' has the effect of giving 'a more upbeat, hopeful note' to the lines in which Hamlet gives Fortinbras his voice (*A Year in the Life of Shakespeare*, 311–12).

70 Kay Stockholder is to my knowledge the first commentator to stress that the election of Fortinbras conceals an act of filial revenge: 'In a doubly ironic twist Hamlet revenges himself on an idealized father (whose ghost would presumably forever squeak and gibber in the streets of a Denmark ruled by a Norwegian king) by conferring the kingdom upon the son of his father's enemy' ('Sex and Authority,' 20). In *Dream Works* (44) Stockholder sees Hamlet's filial ambivalence in the fact that Fortinbras is both the son of the elder Hamlet's mortal enemy and also a manifestation of the elder Hamlet's martial values. More cautiously, Cantor notes that 'Hamlet's final action in the last scene seems in fact to undo everything his father was said to have accomplished in the first' (*Hamlet*, 74). And see Thompson and Taylor, '"Father and Mother Is One Flesh,"' 253.

71 Everett, *Young Hamlet*, 8.

7 *King Lear*

1 Snyder, '*King Lear.*'
2 For details on various legal arrangements that allowed old men to retire in secure circumstances, including agreements for exchanging ownership of property for guaranteed maintenance as a 'sojourner' in another's house, see Greenblatt ('Lear's Anxiety' in *Learning to Curse*, esp. 94–8), Wilson (*Will Power*, esp. 220–9), and William O. Scott ('Contracts of Love').
3 Gouge, *Of Domesticall Duties*, 428.
4 Stone, *Family, Sex and Marriage*, 105–14. For a sensitive application of

Stone's idea of coldness in Elizabethan family relationships to Shakespeare's plays, see Novy, 'Shakespeare and Emotional Distance.'

5 Everett speaks of the distance separating Gloucester from both Edmund and Edgar, even before he loses his eyes (*Young Hamlet*, 69–70).

6 See, for instance, Jay Halio's comment in his New Cambridge edition: 'Renaissance nobles often sent their children to be brought up in other noblemen's homes, sometimes in their own country, sometimes abroad' (96).

7 Cf. Berger's apposite comment that 'It is ... Edgar, not Edmund, who can deprive Gloucester through the plague of custom and the curiosity of nations' (*Making Trifles of Terrors*, 55).

8 For further linguistic commentary on 'bond,' see Salingar, '*King Lear*, Montaigne, and Harsnett,' 96–8.

9 In *King Lear* Albany states the moralizing corollary to Cordella's lament when he declares to Goneril that 'She that herself will sliver and disbranch / From her material sap, perforce must wither' (4.2.34–5). The image probably derives from the pulpit. Cf. Robert Cleaver on the dependence of children on parents: 'Take away the beam from the Sun, and it will not shine; the springs from the river, and it will dry up; the bough from the tree, and it will wither' (*Godlie Forme*, 344).

10 There is a richly documented historical discussion of bonds and family relationships in *King Lear* in Kronenfeld, *Naked Truth*, 95–122. The temptation to historicize the play's treatment of the family is irresistible. For instance, Rosalie Colie says that 'A rather silly way of speaking of this play is to suggest that it dramatizes, as no other piece of literature in the period does, the actual decline of paternal authority that Stone has tried to measure in the English Renaissance,' but she cannot resist laying out evidence for the argument ('King Lear,' 210–11). For the view that the representation of the family in *King Lear* is orthodox, see B. Young, '*King Lear* and the Calamity of Fatherhood.' In 'The Image of the Family in *King Lear*,' McFarland advances a more complex understanding.

11 For the place of Montaigne's essay in the discourse on fathers and sons of his time, see Rossi, '"De l'affection des pères aux enfants."' For suggestive comments linking Montaigne, and especially this particular essay, to *King Lear*, see Salingar, '*King Lear*, Montaigne, and Harsnett,' 107–32.

12 Montaigne, I, xxvii (Of Friendship), *Montaigne's Essays*, 1:197.

13 For love descending from parent to child, see Shuger, *Habits of Thought*, esp. 224–7. For an example of the idea (and its abuse), see the declaration of King Leir in the anonymous *True Chronicle Historie* that 'As doth the

Sun exceed the smallest Star, / So much the father's love exceeds the child's' (Bullough 7:342).

14 I am grateful to Laura Farina for pointing out the relevance of the Montaigne passage for Gloucester.

15 Dod, *Ten Commandements*, 191.

16 For the parallel between Edgar and Aeneas (without reference to Sidney), see Doebler, 'When Troy Fell,' 329–30.

17 John Reibetanz makes this distinction between the brothers with specific reference to 3.5 and 3.6 (*The Lear World*, 45). Jonathan Miller implies an absolute difference between Edgar and Edmund when he suggests they can be understood in light of the relationship between Christ and Lucifer ('*King Lear* in Rehearsal,' 26–7). Maynard Mack invokes the archetype of Cain and Abel to gloss the difference of Edgar and Edmund and also that between other pairs of Shakespearean sons ('Play and History,' in *Everybody's Shakespeare*, 44–5). From a Jungian perspective, Maud Bodkin argues that Edgar and Edmund represent a splitting of a single son into his dutiful and rebellious components (*Archetypal Patterns in Poetry*, 15–16).

18 See Danson's pithy observation that 'the clear division of labour between Edmund's filial aggression and Edgar's filial piety erodes' ('Shakespeare and the Misrecognition of Fathers and Sons,' 244) and Boose's comment that the distinction between them is 'nearly erased by Shakespeare's choice of character names so similar as to invite transposition' ('An Approach through Theme,' 63).

19 Without much reference to the text, Findlay argues for a mixture of good and evil in each of the brothers, which 'shows the presence of each in the other, the production of wickedness by legitimate society and the potential for virtue in the bastard' (*Illegitimate Power*, 71).

20 Harry Berger Jr astutely notes that 'Edmund's role as Vice and bravo sits uneasily atop other feelings that derive from his dependence on the father he contemns' (*Making Trifles of Terrors*, 58).

21 McFarland, 'The Image of the Family in *King Lear*,' 115. Also, McFarland makes the fine observation that, when Edmund presents his wound to the not very interested Gloucester, the son's cry 'Look, sir, I bleed' (2.1.42) contains 'the deprivation of a lifetime' (116). Similarly, Boose links Regan with Edmund to speak of how 'the insatiable rage of the neglected child overwhelms the play and vents itself indiscriminately against the world of the fathers' ('An Approach through Theme,' 61).

22 Sidney's King of Paphlagonia laments that his bastard son 'threw me out of my seat, and put out my eyes ... delighting to make me feel my misery'

(Bullough 7:405). Moreover, after he has usurped his brother and his father, the Sidneian illegitimate son leads a troop of horsemen in an attempt to hunt them down and kill them. Unlike Edmund's, his violence is hands-on.

23 In an important reinterpretation of the Gloucester family, Harry Berger Jr sketches out the developing tradition of 'the negative view of Edgar' (*Making Trifles of Terrors*, 436–7).

24 In a searching discussion of his roles and fantasies, Adelman says 'Edgar seems to allow everything that he has had to suppress to be the good, the legitimate, son to emerge in his portrait of Poor Tom' (*Twentieth-Century Interpretations of* King Lear, 18).

25 Compare Edgar's response to Lear crowned with weeds ('O thou side-piercing sight' [4.6.85]) with his less troubled response at first seeing his father blinded (4.1.9–11). Cf. Hattaway's remark that Edgar 'empathizes with Lear in a way he never does with his father' ('Possessing Edgar,' 209).

26 For arguments invoking various Renaissance therapeutic strategies, see Schleiner ('Justifying the Unjustifiable'), Butler ('Jacobean Psychiatry'), and Aggeler ('"Good Pity" in *King Lear*').

27 Adelman has good comments on Edgar's spectatorship and distancing of himself from the events he sees in the play (*Twentieth-Century Interpretations of* King Lear, 2–3).

28 Egan, *Drama within Drama*, 26.

29 One difference between the scenes is that Launcelot's 'brief experiment in separateness ends in total surrender' (Sundelson, *Shakespeare's Restorations*, 76), as he declares 'I am Launcelot, your boy that was, your son that is, your child that shall be' (*MV*:2.2.84–6). By contrast, Edgar sustains his disguise for an extended period of time, and his acknowledgment of his identity occurs offstage.

30 In a term paper, Kaline Baker drew my attention to the link between Gloucester's 'flies to wanton boys' lines and his being used as Edgar's plaything.

31 Heilman, 52, and see his comments on how Edmund and Edgar both 'work on' Gloucester psychologically (*This Great Stage*, 241–2).

32 See, for instance, Brockbank's comment that 'the figure is a fantastic projection of the old Gloucester, the old self, that Edgar is exorcizing' (*On Shakespeare*, 239).

33 Adelman, *Twentieth-Century Interpretations of* King Lear, 19. She adds that 'At Dover Cliff, he [Edgar] participates imaginatively in his father's death in a way that converts potential punishment into cure; this conver-

sion allows him to bid farewell to the concept of his father as fiend, and hence of himself as fiend, that had led them to that cliff.'

34 Halio, *The Tragedy of King Lear*, 26.

35 As do many Puritan commentators, Edgar suggests that the sins of children derive from the corruption of their parents. See John Dod's remark: 'that ill sap that doth appear in the bud came first from the root' (*Ten Commandements*, 196). And see Greenham's 'Of the Good Education of Children' in his *Works*.

36 'Edgar and Edmund are type and antitype of filial piety, as are Cordelia and her sisters.' (Doebler, 'When Troy Fell,' 330).

37 At 1.1.156 in the Folio text, the speech heading for the line 'Dear sir, forbear' is '*Alb.Cor.*,' where '*Cor.*' can be an abbreviation for either 'Cordelia' or 'Cornwall.' For a convincing argument for Cordelia, which would have been more convincing had it taken into account Cordelia's rescue of Lear in act 4, see Goldring, '*Cor.*'s Rescue of Kent.' In his Arden 3 edition, Foakes rejects Goldring's interpretation on the grounds that 'the action is more appropriate to men' (169n), but of course Cordelia's later rescue of her father at the head of an army could also be said to be 'more appropriate to men.'

38 The standard discussion of the Annesley case in Bullough (7:270–1, 309–11) should be supplemented by Wilson's revisionist account (*Will Power*, 215–29), which contextualizes the issues in terms of Kentish testamentary tradition, rendering both Cordell and her father less attractive than Bullough does. Also, unlike Cordelia's, the altruism of the real-life Cordell was questionable, since the will of her father's that she strove to uphold favoured her over her sisters.

39 While Cordelia intervenes in the male world of war to rescue, Regan participates in it in order to attack. When a serving man attempts to rescue the helpless Earl from the attack of Cornwall and Regan, Regan cuts him down with a sword, allowing Cornwall to go to work on Gloucester's other eye.

40 In a further twist, soon after the blinding of Gloucester Regan had said (to Oswald) that 'Edmund, I think, is gone, / In pity of his misery, to dispatch / His nighted life' (4.5.11–13), which suggests an irony: 'as Gloucester's good son denies him the death he so desperately wants, his evil son tries to provide it' (Leggatt, *King Lear*, 50).

41 Kernan discusses the scenes as 'two parallel internal plays of regeneration, which children arrange for their fathers in order to restore to them some faith in life' (*The Playwright as Magician*, 121), but he does not comment on the differences which I take to be central. Similarly, Honig-

mann (*Myriad-Minded Shakespeare*, 86–8) notes resonances between the two scenes without commenting on their differences.

42 For the contrast between the dubious consolation provided by Edgar and Cordelia's more heartfelt consolation of Lear, see Tromly, 'Grief,' 34–41.

43 Revealingly, in the anonymous *King Leir* play it is Cordella who remains in disguise upon first seeing her father again, while the Edgar-figure is open and forthright.

44 In the closing moments of the play Edgar will repeat the same request to 'look up,' this time directing it to Lear on the assumption that he, like Gloucester, has fainted – but in fact he has died (5.3.313).

45 For the play's powerful theme of acknowledgment, see Cavell's important discussion in 'The Avoidance of Love' (*Must We Mean What We Say?* 267–353).

46 Everett draws the useful parallel that, 'like Kent, she [Cordelia] longs to see him [Lear] as true Authority, as King and Father' (*Young Hamlet*, 77).

47 Honigmann (*Myriad-Minded Shakespeare*, 87) suggests that, after his fall in 4.6, Gloucester assumes a kneeling position and that 'Edgar hovers breathlessly above him, exactly anticipating Lear and Cordelia in the next scene' But even if Gloucester is kneeling, the gesture is scarcely like Lear's deliberate obeisance to Cordelia.

48 Barber, '"Thou that beget'st."'

49 Battus, *The Christian Mans Closet*, 62v.

50 Ayraut, *Discourse*, 28–9.

51 If the danger in a son's relation to his father in Shakespeare is estrangement and conflict, the danger in a daughter's is union and incest.

8 *Macbeth* and the Late Plays

1 Danson's analysis in 'Shakespeare and the Misrecognition of Fathers and Sons' of the gendered differences between 'recognition scenes' holds true for reunions as well. Perhaps we should not be surprised by this, for in the earlier plays the supposed reconciliation of father and son invariably harboured continuing differences; on neither side was the exposure of feeling and surrender of control full enough to allow for a transformation of the relationship, unlike the reunions involving women.

2 In a chapter titled 'The Imperial Theme' in *The Royal Play of* Macbeth, Paul has gathered interesting materials concerning the background and contemporary resonance of James's claims, but his imposition of these materials on the play is often misleading.

3 For James's patriarchal politics and the controversy over succession, see Schochet, *Patriarchalism*, 47–50.

4 The tree illustrating the descendants of Banquo is frequently reproduced in critical works, e.g., Bullough, 7:517 (facing).

5 Braunmuller, *Macbeth*, 243–4.

6 The best tracing of this rich symbolism is Cleanth Brooks's frequently reprinted essay 'The Naked Babe and the Cloak of Manliness' in *The Well Wrought Urn*, 22–49.

7 Kahn, *Man's Estate*, 175. Cf. Bamber: 'Macbeth is dramatically neither a father nor a son; the dialectic in this play is between Macbeth's individualism and the social cohesion of the world of the fathers and sons' (*Comic Women*, 107).

8 Partee contrasts the 'amicable relationships' of the play's fathers and sons to Macbeth's 'selfish concern to project his own authority in a lineal succession' (*Childhood in Shakespeare's Plays*, 98).

9 Everett, *Young Hamlet*, 102.

10 Braunmuller, *Macbeth*, 16.

11 Leggatt makes the fine point that 'our strongest sense of Duncan's virtues comes not directly from anything he says or does, but in a broken, refracted way through Macbeth's horror at what it means to kill the king' ('*Macbeth* and the Last Plays,' 200).

12 Braunmuller, *Macbeth*, 25.

13 Janton, 'Sonship and Fathership in *Macbeth*,' 50. Cf. Hogan's comment that 'The second act opens on Banquo, the double of Duncan in the area of progenitorship, who casually turns over his dagger to his son, the son who will accede to progenitorship through his innocence' ('*Macbeth*: Authority and Progenitorship,' 388).

14 Perhaps Shakespeare (like Banquo) forgot about Fleance, for the stage direction in the Folio text ('*Exit Banquo*') makes no reference to him, though he must accompany his father so that the stage is clear for Macbeth's immediate soliloquy.

15 Quinones, *Renaissance Discovery of Time*, 352.

16 In the fullest discussion of the crux to date, Clayton interprets 'He hath no children' as referring to Macbeth ('Who "Has No Children" in *Macbeth*?').

17 Suggestively, his death recalls that of Macduff's son, as little Macduff's cry that 'Thou li'st, thou shag-ear'd villain' (4.2.83) is closely echoed by Young Siward's charge to Macbeth: 'Thou liest, abhorred tyrant' (5.7.10). Since in both cases the death of the son is conveyed to the respective father by Rosse, the paternal responses are nicely counterpointed.

18 Maxwell, 'Shakespeare and the Siwards,' 141. Even more than with the other fathers in the play, critics have been too eager to draw a sharp contrast between old Siward and the supposedly sterile, unnatural Macbeth. Hence, Coppélia Kahn finds that 'Young Siward's death is pure' and that old Siward 'seems to attain through his child that sense of completion Macbeth can never know' (*Man's Estate*, 190). In a similar but more far-fetched vein, Grace Tiffany speaks of how 'The glorification of nurturant fatherhood, which expresses itself even in a war-torn environment, extends to the English soldier Siward' ('*Macbeth*, Paternity, and the Anglicization of James I,' 160). Rosenberg, I believe, is on the right track in his understated comment that old Siward 'manifests a touch of the excessive in his refusal, as a "man," to grieve' (*Masks of* Macbeth, 650).

19 Freud seems to have been the first commentator to have stressed the importance of Macbeth's childlessness (in 'Some Character-Types Met with in Psychoanalytic Work,' in *S. E.* 14). Fuller discussions are in Simon (*Tragic Drama and the Family*) and Omberg ('Macbeth's Barren Sceptre').

20 For (sometimes overdrawn) connections between the royal family and relationships in the romances, see Bergeron, *Shakespeare's Romances*.

21 Laing, *Politics of the Family*, 1.

22 Bergeron (*Shakespeare's Romances*, 131) notes that there is no precedent in the sources for this fished-up paternal armour.

23 In contrasting the scene with the gravedigger scene in *Hamlet*, Stockholder makes a similar point ('Sex and Authority,' 21–2).

24 Sturgess, *Jacobean Private Theatre*, 89.

25 Kastan, '"The Duke of Milan,"' 95.

26 Skura, 'Interpreting Posthumus' Dream,' 209.

27 Skura, 'Interpreting Posthumus' Dream,' 213.

28 Nevo, *Shakespeare's Other Language*, 90.

29 It is in this lane that the two 'boys' become men, as they rescue their father from the Romans. There are greater (but related) transformations: the Romans who had been eagles are become chickens, and conversely the Britons who 'would die or ere resist are grown / The mortal bugs o' th' field' (5.3.50–1).

30 Nevo, *Shakespeare's Other Language*, 89. Like Skura ('Interpreting Posthumus' Dream,' 209), Nevo argues that the rescue of the king reverses Oedipus's killing of the king at the crossroads.

31 Cavell notes that 'The play punctuates its language with literal "part" words ... such as depart, parting, departure, apart, party to, partner, and, of course, bearing a part' (*Disowning Knowledge*, 200).

32 Leontes' denial of Polixenes' plea to return to Bohemia at the outset is parallelled at the beginning of the play's second half by Polixenes' denial of Camillo's desire to return to his homeland of Sicily from Bohemia (4.2.1–13).

33 Bergeron notes that 'The political conflict between father and son and the issue of succession do not appear in *Pandosto*' (*Shakespeare's Romances*, 167).

34 Not only do we see no evidence of a father-son reconciliation, but also we do not hear of any. In 5.2 the unnamed Gentlemen recount at considerable length the arrival of Polixenes at the Sicilian court, to which Florizel and Perdita have already fled, and they describe the many reconciliations that ensue. They make, however, no mention of any interaction between Florizel and his father, which is emphasized by a reference to how the young man is embraced by his father-in-law (5.1.52–3).

35 Mack, *Everybody's Shakespeare*, 48.

36 Mack calculates that, among seventy young people in the plays, 'Shakespeare allots a single parent to fifty-eight, a full complement to only twelve; and for fifty of the fifty-eight, the allotted parent is male' (*Everybody's Shakespeare*, 43).

37 Two father-mother-son scenes that descend into confusion, with the mother strongly taking her son's part and the husband rejecting it, occur in the fifth act of *Richard II* (York, Duchess, and Aumerle) and in the first act of *Henry VI, Part Three* (King Henry, Queen Margaret, and Prince Henry).

38 For illuminating comments on Leontes' use of Mamillius as first a substitute for Polixenes and then as projected image of his own imagined innocence, see Erickson, *Patriarchal Structures*, 154–5.

39 Cf. Sean Bilmer's observation (in an unpublished term essay) that 'when Leontes compares himself to Mamillius, the audience should consider that the king is like his son in his immaturity and insecurity, not just because of his paternal relationship to him.'

40 Nuttall, *The Winter's Tale*, 15.

41 Pendleton, 'Shakespeare's Children,' 45.

42 Orgel's observation is perceptive but overstated: 'Mamillius' tale is the story of Leontes: the child has already been destroyed by Leontes' sin, Mamillius' innocence by Leontes' knowledge' (*Winter's Tale*, 33).

43 In Greene, the king sent his guards to arrest his wife, and 'they found her playing with her young son' (Bullough 8:163). Nuttall connects Leontes' violent intrusion into this quiet scene with 'the closely parallel scene in *Macbeth* (IV.ii) where Lady Macduff teases her son before they are cut down by the murderers' (*Winter's Tale*, 30).

44 Cavell, *Disowning Knowledge*, 194.
45 Myra Farrell puts the matter nicely: 'Leontes refuses to entertain the notion that Mamillius's illness may be a reaction to being separated from his mother. Instead, Leontes convinces himself that Mamillius's sickness is a sign of his loyalty to his father' (unpublished term essay).
46 Snyder stresses the negative consequences 'of Leontes' sudden removal of his son from the nursery world and its maternal figures' (*Wayward Journey*, 210–20).
47 Bullough 8:71.
48 Erickson, *Patriarchal Structures*, 157.
49 Wheeler, 'Deaths in the Family,' 153.
50 Bergeron, *Shakespeare's Romances*, 164, 166.
51 Erickson, *Patriarchal Structures*, 167.
52 For examples, see Snyder and Curren-Aquino, *Winter's Tale*, 60. Another way that directors attempt to make Mamillius virtually present at the end is by doubling the parts of Mamillius and Perdita, so that her return suggests his as well (Snyder and Curren-Aquino, 266–7). In my opinion this doubling is a misguided attempt to create a conventional romance ending.
53 Swinburne, quoted in Muir, *Winter's Tale*, 38–9.
54 This line should be compared with the similar but less impassioned exclamation of Alonso when he sees what may be a vision of his son playing chess: 'If this prove / A vision of the island, one dear son / Shall I lose twice' (*Temp*:5.1.175–7).
55 As David Lee Miller puts it, 'The redemption of Leontes depends on the shift from Mamillius to Perdita' (*Dreams of the Burning Child*, 124).
56 In canvassing possibilities for the unverbalized meaning of Mamillius's death, Cavell asks some excellent questions, including, 'Shall we say that the absent boy is meant to cast the shadow of finitude or doubt over the general air of reunion at the end of the play, to emblematize that no human reconciliation is uncompromised' (*Disowning Knowledge*, 193).

9 Biographical Coda

1 For an incisive discussion of the place of biography in Shakespeare criticism, see Wheeler, 'Deaths in the Family,' 127–34.
2 Holden, *William Shakespeare: His Life and Work*, 145. An important exception to this avoidance of biographical evidence is Wheeler's article, 'Deaths in the Family,' which argues that 'the existence of a long history of ingenious but unpersuasive inventions [by critics speculating on bio-

324 Notes to pages 244–8

graphical matters] should not stand in the way of giving the life record a place in our understanding of the texts' (131).

3 Freud, 'Family Romances,' *S. E.* 9:237.

4 Honan, *Shakespeare: A Life*, 42.

5 Beyond his depictions of fathers and sons, there is a pervasive double-ness in Shakespeare's handling of his sources that may reveal a broader ambivalence toward authority and inheritance: though the plots of the great majority of his plays have their origin in pre-existing narratives and plays, he always transforms radically the meaning of the story, making it his own.

6 For a transcript of the original entry, which is full of abbreviations, see appendix 2.

7 Schoenbaum, *Compact Documentary Life*, 15.

8 Greenblatt (*Will in the World*, 62–71) cites and briefly comments on all of these causes, but, in my view, with undue emphasis on the possibility of alcoholism.

9 In addition to demonstrating that the elder Shakespeare's supposed Catholic sympathies need not be invoked to explain his financial downfall ('John Shakespeare: A Papist or Just Penniless?'), John Bearman has written two deeply researched articles questioning the documentary evidence often cited to prove the Shakespeare family's deep allegiance to the Old Faith ('Was William Shakespeare "William Shakeshaft" Revisited' and 'John Shakespeare's "Spiritual Testament": A Reappraisal'). If, *contra* Bearman, one accepts the view that John Shakespeare was a devoted Catholic and that at least as a young man William shared his father's conviction, then my study does not address what may have been an important dimension of their relationship. But I see no reason to think a committed observance on John's part would have precluded the ambivalent filial feelings I attribute to William, and indeed it could have intensified them.

10 A detailed account of the transaction and ensuing legal actions can be found in Poole, 'John and Mary Shakespeare.'

11 Knight's uneven *Autobiography in Shakespeare's Plays* contends that the loss of this property is a central issue in Shakespeare's life and art. Poole's discussion (not cited by Knight) is more cautious, briefly relating the loss to *Richard II* and *The Merchant of Venice* (39).

12 See Esler's study of generational divisions in Elizabethan England, *The Aspiring Mind of the Elizabethan Younger Generation*.

13 Ackroyd, *Shakespeare: The Biography*, 64. Also Barber and Wheeler speak of Shakespeare's 'sympathetic preoccupation with his amiable father's

failure,' which helped to create 'an ideal of cherishing fatherhood' ('Shakespeare in the Rising Middle Class,' 23).

14 Barber and Wheeler, 'Shakespeare in the Rising Middle Class,' 26.

15 Knight, *Autobiography in Shakespeare's Plays*, 95.

16 Vickers, *Shakespeare: The Critical Heritage*, 2:190.

17 The notion of William's apprenticeship to his father was advanced in the seventeenth century by Aubrey and Rowe and was supported by Schoenbaum (*Compact Documentary Life*, 74) as 'a reasonable enough supposition.'

18 B. Smith, *Shakespeare and Masculinity*, 78.

19 Greer, *Shakespeare's Wife*, 76.

20 Duncan-Jones notes John Shakespeare's licensing the performance of plays in Stratford, which she takes as evidence supporting Thomas Plume's 'merry-cheeked' anecdote (*Ungentle Shakespeare*, 9).

21 For an account of the social and economic status of actors, see the opening chapters of Bradbrook, *The Rise of the Common Player*.

22 Gouge, *Of Domesticall Duties*, 535.

23 Munday, *Sir Thomas More*, 121 (3.1.10–12).

24 Kay, *Shakespeare: His Life, Work, and Era*, 183. It should be noted, however, that the biography written by William Roper, More's son-in-law, mentions that even after More's elevation to Lord Chancellor he continued to kneel reverently in his father's presence and ask his blessing (Sylvester and Harding, *Two Early Tudor Lives*, 221).

25 Greenblatt has a good discussion of what he calls Shakespeare's 'Dream of Restoration' in chapter two of *Will in the World*, though he does not connect this 'restoration' with the motif of rescuing fathers in the plays.

26 Knight notes that the reopening of the Lambert case overlapped with the renewed attempt to secure a coat of arms (*Autobiography in Shakespeare's Plays*, 40).

27 Schoenbaum, *Compact Documentary Life*, 224. If Hamnet were still alive when the request was made, Shakespeare may have thought that his son and his offspring would have benefited from the coat of arms. Duncan-Jones reckons the coat of arms project was 'probably under way, or at least decided upon in principle, while Hamnet still lived' (*Ungentle Shakespeare*, 91).

28 Danson uses the phrase to characterize father-son relationships in the second history tetralogy ('Shakespeare and the Misrecognition of Fathers and Sons,' 240).

29 Youings makes the contrast between knighthoods and coats of arms (*Sixteenth-Century England*, 115).

30 In a minority view, the *Riverside Shakespeare* comments that the motto 'may have been chosen ... by John Shakespeare himself,' but provides no rationale (1955). As a glance at a Shakespeare concordance indicates, the dramatist was fond of the word 'sanz/sans,' using it four times in the final line of Jaques's 'All the world's a stage' speech (*AYLI*:2.7.166).

31 Greenblatt wonders, 'Is there a touch of defensiveness in that motto, a slight sense that the claim to gentlemanly status might raise eyebrows?' (*Will in the World*, 79). If this is so, there is a similarity to the protesting too much of Hamlet and Hal.

32 Scott-Giles notes that the additions and alterations to the document 'probably represent information given and suggestions made by William Shakespeare sitting in conference with the heralds' (*Shakespeare's Heraldry*, 29).

33 For examples of punctuation games in Elizabethan literature, see H. Brooks, *A Midsummer Night's Dream*, 110.

34 See, for instance, the discussion of 'the most bloody nurser of his harms' on 60.

35 See my discussion in appendix 1, 274–5.

36 Freud, 'A Special Type of Choice of Object Made by Men,' *S. E.* 11:173.

37 In his important discussion of the history plays, Sherman Hawkins notes the connection between the two events: 'Shakespeare was able to act out this rescue fantasy both in life and in art' ('Aggression,' 48). My interpretation differs from Hawkins's in that I think he does not place adequate emphasis on the element of aggression in Hal's and Shakespeare's rescues and on its ultimate source, the Elizabethan injunction for dutiful sons to sacrifice themselves for their fathers.

38 The relevance of Bullingbrook's speech (1.3.59–77) to the Shakespeare coat of arms was spotted by Scott-Giles, *Shakespeare's Heraldry*, 35.

39 Without mentioning Hal's rescue of his father, Kris points out the general parallel between Hal's and Shakespeare's situations, saying that the 'Non sanz droict' motto 'is one that might well have been used to characterize Prince Hal's striving for the crown' (*Psychoanalytic Explorations in Art*, 288).

40 Without reference to the parallel with Hal, Knight says of the coat of arms that 'Shakespeare would gentle his own condition; Will would become the son of a gentleman, by making his father a gentleman' (*Autobiography in Shakespeare's Plays*, 96).

41 B. Smith, *Shakespeare and Masculinity*, 61. When a rival herald cited the

Shakespeare coat of arms as an instance of an improper grant, he contemptuously wrote under his sketch of the arms: 'Shakespeare the Player.' See Figure 3 on 255.

42 *Riverside Shakespeare*, 1956.

43 Honan, *Shakespeare: A Life*, 86.

44 Greenblatt, *Will in the World*, 24.

45 Cf. McCurdy's observation that 'Increasingly, as he grew older, he seems to have identified with his father, or certain aspects of him' (*Personality of Shakespeare*, 161).

46 In his brief survey of the younger Shakespeare's business interests, Honigmann observes that he 'actively engaged in money-lending over a period of years, perhaps as his father's partner' ('World Elsewhere,' 41). Later he avers that 'William Shakespeare must have been a partner or associate of his parents in their many financial enterprises,' but without supplying much evidence (44).

47 Vickers, *Shakespeare: The Critical Heritage*, 2:192.

48 For the names Hamnet and Hamlet being 'virtually interchangeable' in Elizabethan orthography, see Greenblatt, *Will in the World*, 311. For the connection between the two figures, see Stephen Dedalus's formulation that 'had Hamnet Shakespeare lived he would have been prince Hamlet's twin' (*Ulysses*, 155).

49 In Alexander Welsh's formulation, *King Lear* and *Hamlet* are 'tragedies with marked points of view, one with pity for the old and the other for the young' (*Hamlet in His Modern Guises*, 14).

50 Lawrence Danson notes that 'The evidence throughout Shakespeare's career suggests that the complement of the playwright's strong urge to father-daughter reunion is his equally strong avoidance of the father-son reunion – a reunion that he is nonetheless drawn repeatedly to attempting' ('Shakespeare and the Misrecognition of Fathers and Sons,' 245).

51 Bergeron notes that 'Shakespeare gives the Shepherd a son instead of a shrewish wife, as in *Pandosto*,' the play's principal narrative source (*Shakespeare's Romances*, 164).

52 Mack, *Everybody's Shakespeare*, 49.

53 The Clown graduates from 'boy' to 'son' at 5.2.146, 152, and 161.

Appendix 1

1 In a thorough, balanced treatment, Metz traces the tradition of authorial attributions of *Edward III* from the seventeenth century to 1989 (*Sources*, 6–20). From a position of partisan support for Shakespeare's sole author-

ship, Sams surveys what he calls 'the Evolution of the Current Consensus' (*Shakespeare's* Edward III, 152–60).

2 Sams catalogues numerous verbal parallels between *Edward III* and *1 Henry VI* (*Shakespeare's* Edward III, 236). Wentersdorf notes that '*Edward III* has many points of resemblance in diction, imagery, and treatment of subject matter to the play about Talbot [*1 Henry VI*],' dating the former at 'about 1589–90' and the latter at 'not later than the winter of 1591–92, and possibly a year or two earlier' ('Date of *Edward III*,' 231). For *Edward III*, Metz (*Sources*, 5) opts for a date of 'about 1590–1591,' and Melchiori places it 'in 1592 or early 1593' (*King Edward III*, 5).

3 See, for instance, Metz's comment that while 'a reasonably good case' can be made for Prince Edward as the hero of the play, 'it is evident that the Prince himself believes his father to be the hero' (*Sources*, 38).

4 Though *Edward III* was added to the second edition of the *Riverside Shakespeare*, some questionable editorial emendations in that text lead me to use Melchiori's New Cambridge edition instead. For an example, see note 11, below.

5 In the final scene, the Queen is much more troubled than the King by worries about Prince Edward's safety (5.1.157–75), and accordingly her greeting of her son is more joyous than his (5.1.187–91). In these respects, the scene is reminiscent of the Aumerle scenes in *Richard II*.

6 Metz, *Sources*, 80.

7 Tillyard, *Shakespeare's History Plays*, 134.

8 Melchiori, *King Edward III*, 173.

9 Apparently alone among commentators, Sams makes the crucial observation that 'the prince's message' is 'immediate and personal: his parent too should have been ready to shed blood for a child' (*Shakespeare's* Edward III, 128). The author of *Edward III* may have derived the idea of using the sacrificially nurturing pelican as a personal reprimand from the most influential Elizabethan emblem book, Geffrey Whitney's *A Choice of Emblemes* (1586). Whitney uses the image of the pelican reviving her young to exhort Alexander Nowell, Dean of St Paul's, to produce learned writing as well as sermons: 'Your zeal is great, your learning is profound; / Then help our wants with that you do abound' (*Choice of Emblemes*, 87). The call to 'help our wants with that you do abound' connects suggestively with the King's refusal to rescue the Prince.

10 For the traditional meanings of the motto, see Melchiori (*King Edward III*, 207) and Lapides (*The Raigne of King Edward the Third*, 248–9).

11 In his edition of the play in the *Riverside Shakespeare*, J.J.M. Tobin notes the theological colouring of these lines and revises the text by inserting

after the first line the stage direction '*Kneels in prayer*' and by capitalizing all of Edward's subsequent second-person pronouns to indicate they are addressed to God (1769). Needless to say, this emendation destroys the subtle depiction of the Prince's divided attitude toward his father.

12 The scenes most frequently attributed to Shakespeare are the King's attempted seduction of the Countess of Salisbury in 2.1 (where the line 'Lilies that fester smell far worse than weeds' occurs [2.1.452]) and in 2.2, and in a different vein the scene (4.4) in which the Black Prince nobly philosophizes about death.

Appendix 2

1 Thomas Plume's Library (Maldon, Essex), MS Plume 25, f. 161. I am grateful to Erica Wylie, the Librarian, and her staff for providing excellent reproductions of the passage. (All the published transcriptions I have seen contain errors.) I have expanded Plume's many contractions, as indicated by italicized letters. Rev. Andrew Clark published informative but not always reliable mini-essays on Plume and his notebook-jottings throughout volumes 12 to 15 of *The Essex Review* (1903–6).

2 Furnivall published the extract, along with Plume's anecdotes about Ben Jonson, in *The Westminster Gazette*, 31 Oct. 1904, 4.

3 Honan, *Shakespeare: A Life*, 40. Cf. Emily Pogue's reference to 'this lovely, revealing description' (*Shakespeare's Family*, 24).

4 Greenblatt, *Will in the World*, 67, and Duncan-Jones, *Ungentle Shakespeare*, 8–9.

5 According to Schoenbaum, the identification of John Shakespeare as a glover did not appear in print until Edmond Malone's posthumous biography of the dramatist in 1821 (*Shakespeare's Lives*, 243).

6 A.G., in the *Westminster Gazette*, 3 Nov. 1904, 10.

7 Clark, 16.

8 Clark, 'Dr Plume's Pocket-Book,' 16-17. After A.G.'s embarrassing revelation that Mennes was only two, Furnivall had raised the possibility that the anecdote 'was wrongly fathered on Sir John by Archdeacon Plume' ('The Merry-Cheekt Old Glover,' 4). Another attempt to defend the anecdote at its recorder's expense is E.K. Chambers's suggestion that Plume might have confused Sir John Mennes with Sir Matthew Mennes, his elder brother by some six years (2:247). But Plume knew Sir John well and was unlikely to confuse the two; besides, attributing the sophisticated report to an eight-year-old does not appreciably increase its plausibility.

9 C.S. Knighton, 'Sir John Mennes,' in the *Oxford Dictionary of National Biography* (on-line edition, January 2008).

10 For Mennes and his circle, see Raylor, *Cavaliers, Clubs, and Literary Culture*.

11 *The Diary of Samuel Pepys*, 5:80 and 7:2.

12 *The Diary of Samuel Pepys*, 4:184 and 7:2.

13 Marvin Spevack, *Harvard Concordance to Shakespeare*, 249; for 'crack' in the sense of cracking a jest, see the on-line *OED*, 'crack,' v. 5.

14 A Shakespeare play also seems to lie behind another story Mennes told Plume: that when he was a young man his employer asked him to deliver a letter to the Master of Bridewell, and when Mennes opened the letter he found a request for the Master to whip the bearer soundly. In a Hamlet-like ploy, Mennes says he resealed the letter and sent a porter to deliver it, who duly received the whipping. See Clark, 'Dr Plume's Pocket-Book,' 20.

15 P.E. Razzell, *William Shakespeare*, 10. More carefully, Peter Ackroyd notes that the anecdote is 'perhaps too close to the image of Falstaff' but proceeds to surmise that 'the merry-cheeked roisterer of the history plays may bear some passing resemblance to a domestic original' (*Shakespeare: The Biography*, 17).

16 Stanley Wells notes that at the Caroline court Falstaff 'was already so dominant a character' that reference was made to performances of the two parts of *Henry IV* as 'Falstaff' (*Shakespeare for All Time*, 176). He also observes the prominent place of Falstaff on the frontispiece to *The Wits* (1662), a collection of drolls (brief entertainments) performed during the closure of the theatres (183–4).

Works Cited

Abraham, Karl. *Clinical Papers and Essays on Psycho-analysis.* Edited by Hilda C. Abraham. Translated by Hilda C. Abraham and D.R. Ellison. 1955. Rptd. London: Maresfield Reprints, 1979.

Ackroyd, Peter. *Shakespeare: The Biography.* London: Chatto and Windus, 2005.

Adelman, Janet, ed. *Twentieth-Century Interpretations of* King Lear. Englewood Cliffs, NJ: Prentice-Hall, 1978.

Aggeler, Geoffrey. '"Good Pity" in *King Lear*: The Progress of Edgar.' *Neophilologus* 77 (1993): 321–31.

Ago, Renata. 'Young Nobles in the Age of Absolutism: Paternal Authority and Freedom of Choice in Seventeenth-Century Italy.' In *A History of Young People in the West.* Vol 1: *Ancient and Medieval Rites of Passage.* Edited by Giovanni Levi and Jean-Claude Schmitt. Translated by Camille Naish. Cambridge, MA: Harvard University Press, 1997. 283–322.

Alexander, Franz. 'A Note on Falstaff.' *Psychoanalytic Quarterly* 2 (1933): 592–606.

Alexander, Nigel. *Poison, Play, and Duel: A Study in* Hamlet. Lincoln: University of Nebraska Press, 1971.

Amussen, Susan Dwyer. 'Gender, Family and the Social Order, 1560–1725.' In *Order and Disorder in Early Modern England.* Edited by Anthony Fletcher and John Stevenson. Cambridge: Cambridge University Press, 1985. 196–217.

– *An Ordered Society: Gender and Class in Early Modern England.* Oxford: Blackwell, 1988.

The 'Anonymous Life' of William Cecil, Lord Burghley. Edited by Alan G.R. Smith. Lewiston, NY: Edwin Mellen, 1990.

Archer, Ian. 'The 1590s: Apotheosis or Nemesis of the Elizabethan Regime?' In *Fins de Siècle: How Centuries End 1400–2000.* Edited by Asa Briggs and

Daniel Snowman. New Haven, CT: Yale University Press, 1996. 62–97.

Ardolino, Frank. 'The "Wrath of Frowning Jove": Fathers and Sons in Marlowe's Plays.' *Journal of Evolutionary Psychology* 2 (1981): 83–100.

Armstrong, Philip. *Shakespeare in Psychoanalysis*. London: Routledge, 2001.

Aubrey, John. *Aubrey's Brief Lives*. Edited by Oliver Lawson Dick. Harmondsworth: Penguin, 1972.

Auerbach, Erich. *Mimesis: The Representation of Reality in Western Literature*. Translated by Willard Trask. 1946. Rptd. New York: Doubleday Anchor, 1957.

Austin, Norman. 'Hamlet's Hungry Ghost.' *Shenandoah* 37 (1987): 78–105.

Ayraut, Pierre. *A Discourse for Parents Honour, and Authoritie*. Translated by John Budden. 1614. STC 1012.

Babula, William. 'Whatever Happened to Prince Hal? An Essay on *Henry V*.' *Shakespeare Survey* 30 (1977): 47–59.

Bacon, Sir Francis. The New Organon *and Related Writings*. Edited by Fulton H. Anderson. Indianapolis: Bobbs-Merrill, 1960.

– *Works*. Edited by James Spedding et al. 14 vols. London: Longman, 1858–74.

Bamber, Linda. *Comic Women, Tragic Men: A Study of Gender and Genre in Shakespeare*. Stanford, CA: Stanford University Press, 1982.

Barber, C.L. 'The Family in Shakespeare's Development: Tragedy and Sacredness.' In *Representing Shakespeare: New Psychoanalytic Essays*. Edited by Murray M. Schwartz and Coppélia Kahn. Baltimore: Johns Hopkins University Press, 1980.

– '"Thou that beget'st him that did thee beget": Transformation in *Pericles* and *The Winter's Tale*.' *Shakespeare Survey* 22 (1969): 59–67.

Barber, C.L., and Richard P. Wheeler. 'Shakespeare in the Rising Middle Class.' In *Shakespeare's Personality*. Edited by Norman N. Holland. Berkeley: University of California Press, 1989. 17–40.

– *The Whole Journey: Shakespeare's Power of Development*. Berkeley: University of California Press, 1986.

Barish, Jonas. 'Remembering and Forgetting in Shakespeare.' In *Elizabethan Theater: Essays in Honor of S. Schoenbaum*. Edited by R.B. Parker and S.P. Zitner. Newark: University of Delaware Press, 1996. 214–21.

Barthelme, Donald. *The Dead Father*. New York: Penguin, 1986.

Barton, Anne. 'Introduction' to *Hamlet*. Edited by T.J.B. Spencer. New Penguin Shakespeare. Harmondsworth: Penguin, 1980. 7–54.

Bätschmann, Oskar, and Pascal Griener. *Hans Holbein*. Princeton, NJ: Princeton University Press, 1997.

Battus, Bartholomaeus. *The Christian Mans Closet*. Translated by William Lowth. 1581.

Bearman, Robert. 'John Shakespeare: A Papist or Just Penniless?' *Shakespeare Quarterly* 56 (2005): 411–33.

– 'John Shakespeare's "Spiritual Testament": A Reappraisal.' *Shakespeare Survey* 56 (2003): 184–202.

– '"Was William Shakespeare William Shakeshaft" Revisited.' *Shakespeare Quarterly* 53 (2002): 83–94.

Beer, Anna. *My Just Desire: The Life of Bess Ralegh, Wife to Sir Walter*. New York: Ballantine, 2003.

Belsey, Catherine. 'The Case of Hamlet's Conscience.' *Studies in Philology* 76 (1979): 127–48.

Ben-Amos, Ilana Krausman. *Adolescence and Youth in Early Modern England*. New Haven, CT: Yale University Press, 1994.

Bennett, H.S. *The Pastons and Their England*. 2nd ed. Cambridge: Cambridge University Press, 1975.

Berger, Harry, Jr. *Imaginary Audition: Shakespeare on Stage and Page*. Berkeley: University of California Press, 1997.

– *Making Trifles of Terrors: Redistributing Complicities in Shakespeare*. Stanford, CA: Stanford University Press, 1997.

Bergeron, David M. *Shakespeare's Romances and the Royal Family*. Lawrence: University Press of Kansas, 1985.

Berman, Ronald S. 'Fathers and Sons in the Henry VI Plays.' *Shakespeare Quarterly* 13 (1962): 487–97.

Berry, Edward. *The Making of Sir Philip Sidney*. Toronto: University of Toronto Press, 1998.

– *Patterns of Decay: Shakespeare's Early Histories*. Charlottesville: University Press of Virginia, 1975.

Berry, Ralph. 'Hamlet's Doubles.' *Shakespeare Quarterly* 37 (1986): 204–12.

Berryman, John. *Berryman's Shakespeare*. New York: Farrar, Straus & Giroux, 1999.

Bevington, David, ed. *Henry IV, Part One*. Oxford Shakespeare. Oxford: Oxford University Press, 1987.

Black, James. 'The Interlude of the Beggar and the King in *Richard II*.' In *Pageantry in the Shakespearean Theater*. Edited by David M. Bergeron. Athens: University of Georgia Press, 1985, 104–13.

Blake, Ann. 'Children and Suffering in Shakespeare's Plays.' *Yearbook of English Studies* 23 (1993): 293–304.

Blanpied, John W. *Time and the Artist in Shakespeare's Histories*. Newark: University of Delaware Press, 1983.

Blits, Jan H. *Deadly Thought:* Hamlet *and the Human Soul.* Oxford: Lexington, 2001.

Bloom, Allen. *Love and Friendship.* New York: Simon and Schuster, 1993.

Bloom, Harold. Hamlet: *Poem Unlimited*: New York: Riverhead, 2003.

– *Shakespeare: The Invention of the Human.* New York: Riverhead, 1988.

– *The Western Canon: The Books and School of the Ages.* New York: Harcourt Brace, 1994.

Bodkin, Maud. *Archetypal Patterns in Poetry: Psychological Studies of Imagination.* Oxford: Oxford University Press, 1965.

Boose, Linda E. 'An Approach through Theme: Marriage and the Family.' In *Approaches to Teaching Shakespeare's* King Lear. Edited by Robert H. Ray. New York: Modern Language Association of America, 1986. 59–68.

Boswell, James. *Boswell's London Journal 1762–1763.* Edited by Frederick A. Pottle. 1950. Rptd. Edinburgh: Edinburgh University Press, 1991.

Bradbrook, M.C. *The Rise of the Common Player: A Study of Actor and Society in Shakespeare's England.* Cambridge: Cambridge University Press, 1979.

Bradley, A.C. 'The Rejection of Falstaff.' (1909). In Hunter 1970, 56–78.

– *Shakespearean Tragedy.* 1904. London: Macmillan, 1958.

Brady, Jennifer. 'Progenitors and Other Sons in Ben Jonson's *Discoveries*.' In *New Perspectives on Ben Jonson.* Edited by James Hirsh. London: Associated University Presses, 1997, 16–34.

Braunmuller, A.R., ed. *Macbeth.* New Cambridge Shakespeare. Cambridge: Cambridge University Press, 1997.

Brennan, Anthony. *Shakespeare's Dramatic Structures.* London: Routledge & Kegan Paul, 1986.

Brigden, Susan. 'Youth and the English Reformation.' *Past and Present* 95 (1982): 36–67.

Brockbank, Philip. *On Shakespeare.* Oxford: Blackwell, 1989.

Brooke, Nicholas, ed. *Macbeth.* Oxford Shakespeare. Oxford: Oxford University Press, 1999.

Brooks, Cleanth. *The Well Wrought Urn.* New York: Harcourt, Brace & World, 1947.

Brooks, Harold F., ed. *A Midsummer Night's Dream.* Arden Shakespeare. London: Methuen, 1979.

Buck, William Stuart. 'Shakespeare's Epic of Fathers and Sons.' PhD diss., University of California, Riverside. 1990.

Bullough, Geoffrey, ed. *Narrative and Dramatic Sources of Shakespeare.* 8 vols. London: Routledge and Kegan Paul, 1957–75.

Bulman, James C. *The Heroic Idiom of Shakespearean Tragedy.* Newark: University of Delaware Press, 1985.

Burnett, Mark Thornton. '*Hamlet* and Secrets.' In *New Essays on* Hamlet. Edited by Mark Thornton Burnett and John Manning. New York: AMS Press, 1994. 21–46.

Burns, Edward, ed. *King Henry VI, Part 1.* Arden Shakespeare Third Series. London: Thomson Learning, 2000.

Bushnell, Rebecca W. *A Culture of Teaching: Early Modern Humanism in Theory and Practice.* Ithaca, NY: Cornell University Press, 1996.

Busse, Claire M. 'Profitable Children: Children as Commodities in Early Modern England.' In *Domestic Arrangements in Early Modern England.* Edited by Kari Boyd McBride. Pittsburgh: Duquesne University Press, 2002. 209–43.

Butler, Guy. 'Jacobean Psychiatry: Edgar's Curative Stratagems.' *Shakespeare in Southern Africa* 2 (1988): 15–30.

Cain, H. Edward. 'Further Light on the Relation of 1 and 2 *Henry IV.*' *Shakespeare Quarterly* 3 (1952): 66–86.

Calderwood, James. *Metadrama in Shakespeare's Henriad.* Berkeley: University of California Press, 1979.

– *To Be and Not To Be: Negation and Metadrama in* Hamlet. New York: Columbia University Press, 1983.

Campbell, Mary Elizabeth. 'Proving His Beauty by Succession Thine: Father-Son Relationships in Shakespeare's Early Drama.' PhD diss., Queen's University (Ontario), 1988.

Cantor, Paul. *Hamlet.* Landmarks of World Literature. Cambridge: Cambridge University Press, 1989.

Cardano, Girolamo. *Cardanus Comforte.* Translated by Thomas Bedingfield. 1576. Rpt. Amsterdam: Theatrum Orbis Terrarum, 1969.

Cartwright, Julia. *Baldassare Castiglione, The Perfect Courtier.* 2 vols. London: John Murray, 1908.

Cavell, Stanley. *Disowning Knowledge in Six Plays of Shakespeare.* Cambridge: Cambridge University Press, 1987.

– *Must We Mean What We Say?: A Book of Essays.* Updated ed. Cambridge: Cambridge University Press, 2003.

'*Certain Sermons or Homilies' (1547) and 'A Homily against Disobedience and Wilful Rebellion' (1570).* Edited by Ronald B. Bond. Toronto: University of Toronto Press, 1987.

Chambers, E.K. *William Shakespeare: A Study of Facts and Problems.* 2 vols. Oxford: Clarendon, 1930.

Charney, Maurice. *Hamlet's Fictions.* New York: Routledge, 1988.

Chettle, Henry. *The Tragedy of Hoffman.* Malone Society Reprints. Oxford: Oxford University Press, 1950.

Cicero, Marcus Tullius. *De officiis*. Translated by Walter Miller. Loeb Library. London: Heinemann, 1913.

– *Marcus Tullius Ciceroes Thre Bokes of Duties* [*De officiis*]. Translated by Nicholas Grimald. Edited by Gerald O'Gorman. Renaissance English Text Society. London: Associated University Presses, 1990.

Clark, Andrew. 'Dr Plume's Pocket-Book.' *Essex Review* 14 (1905): 9–20.

Clayton, Tom. 'Who "Has No Children" in *Macbeth*?' In *Shakespearean Illuminations: Essays in Honor of Marvin Rosenberg*. Edited by Jay L. Halio and Hugh Richmond. Newark: University of Delaware Press, 1998. 164–79.

Cleaver, Robert. *A Godlie Forme of Householde Government: For the Ordering of Private Families, According to the Direction of God's Word.* 1598.

Cohen, Derek. 'The Rite of Violence in *1 Henry IV*.' *Shakespeare Survey* 38 (1985): 77–84.

Colie, Rosalie L. 'Reason and Need: *King Lear* and the "Crisis" of the Aristocracy.' In *Some Facets of* King Lear: *Essays in Prismatic Criticism*. Edited by Rosalie L Colie and F.T. Flahiff. Toronto: University of Toronto Press, 1974. 185–219.

Connor, Seymour V. 'The Role of Douglas in *Henry IV, Part One*.' *University of Texas Studies in English* 27 (1948): 215–221. .

Corbin, Peter, and Douglas Sedge, eds. *The Oldcastle Controversy: 'Sir John Oldcastle, Part I' and 'The Famous Victories of Henry V.'* Manchester: Manchester University Press, 1991.

The Court of Good Counsell. 1607. STC 5876.

Crewe, Jonathan. 'Reforming Prince Hal: The Sovereign Inheritor in *2 Henry IV*.' *Renaissance Drama*, N.S. 21 (1990): 225–42.

Crook, J. A. 'Patria Potestas.' *Classical Quarterly*, N.S. 17 (1967): 113–29.

Danson, Lawrence. 'Shakespeare and the Misrecognition of Fathers and Sons.' In *Paternity and Fatherhood: Myths and Realities*. Edited by Lieve Spaas. New York: St Martin's Press, 1998. 236–45.

Dawson, Anthony. *Watching Shakespeare: A Playgoer's Guide*. New York: Macmillan, 1988.

de Grazia, Margreta. Hamlet *without Hamlet*. Cambridge: Cambridge University Press, 2007.

Dent, Arthur. *The Plaine Mans Path-Way to Heaven* (1601). Rptd. Amsterdam: Theatrum Orbis Terrarum, 1974.

Dessen, Alan C. *Shakespeare and the Late Moral Plays*. Lincoln: University of Nebraska Press, 1986.

Dod, John. *A Plaine and Familiar Exposition of the Ten Commandements*. 1604. STC 6968.

Dodsworth, Martin. *Hamlet Closely Observed*. London: Athlone, 1985.

Doebler, John. 'When Troy Fell: Shakespeare's Iconography of Sorrow and Survival.' *Comparative Drama* 19 (1985–86): 321–31.

Donne, John. *The Complete English Poems of John Donne*. Edited by C.A. Patrides. London: J.M. Dent, 1985.

Douglas, Richard M. 'Talent and Vocation in Humanist and Protestant Thought.' In *Action and Conviction in Early Modern Europe: Essays in Memory of E.H. Harbison*. Edited by Theodore K. Rabb. Princeton, NJ: Princeton University Press, 1969. 261–98.

Dreher, Diane Elizabeth. *Domination and Defiance: Fathers and Daughters in Shakespeare*. Lexington: University Press of Kentucky, 1986.

Drewry, Justin Dathan Anders. 'Hamlet's Fathers: An Analysis of Paternity and Filial Duty in Shakespeare's *Hamlet*.' MA thesis, North Carolina State University, 2004.

Duncan-Jones, Katherine. *Sir Philip Sidney: Courtier Poet*. New Haven, CT: Yale University Press, 1991.

– *Ungentle Shakespeare: Scenes from His Life*. London: Arden Shakespeare, 2001.

Edelman, Charles. *Brawl Ridiculous: Swordfighting in Shakespeare's Plays*. Manchester: Manchester University Press, 1992.

Edwards, Philip, ed. *Hamlet, Prince of Denmark*. New Cambridge Shakespeare. Cambridge: Cambridge University Press, 1985.

Egan, Robert. *Drama within Drama: Shakespeare's Sense of His Art*. New York: Columbia University Press, 1975.

Eissler, K.R. *Discourse on Hamlet and* Hamlet: *A Psychoanalytic Inquiry*. New York: International Universities Press, 1971.

Empson, William. 'Falstaff and Mr Dover Wilson.' In Hunter, *Henry IV*. 135–54.

Erasmus, Desiderius. *A Declamation on the Subject of Early Liberal Education for Children*. In *Literary and Educational Writings* 4. Edited by J.K. Sowards. *Collected Works of Erasmus*. Vol. 26. Toronto: University of Toronto Press, 1985.

Erickson, Peter. *Patriarchal Structures in Shakespeare's Drama*. Berkeley: University of California Press, 1985.

Erlich, Avi. *Hamlet's Absent Father*. Princeton, NJ: Princeton University Press, 1977.

Erne, Lukas. *Shakespeare as Literary Dramatist*. Cambridge: Cambridge University Press, 2003.

Esler, Anthony. *The Aspiring Mind of the Elizabethan Younger Generation*. Durham, NC: Duke University Press, 1966.

Evans, G. Blakemore, ed. *The Riverside Shakespeare*. 2nd ed. Boston: Houghton Mifflin, 1997.

Everett, Barbara. *Young Hamlet: Essays on Shakespeare's Tragedies*. Oxford: Clarendon, 1989.

Faber, M.D., 'Oedipal Patterns in *Henry IV*.' In *The Design Within: Psychoanalytic Approaches to Shakespeare*. Edited by M.D. Faber. New York: Science House, 1970. 430–8.

Fabricius, Johannes. *Shakespeare's Hidden World: A Study of his Unconscious*. Copenhagen: Munksgaard, 1989.

Farrell, Kirby. 'Self-Effacement and Autonomy in Shakespeare.' *Shakespeare Studies* 16 (1983): 75–99.

Fehrenbach, Robert J. 'The Characterization of the King in *1 Henry IV*.' *Shakespeare Quarterly* 30 (1979): 42–50.

Fenwick, Henry. 'The Production.' In *The BBC TV Shakespeare. Henry VI, Part 1*. London: British Broadcasting Corporation, 1983. 21–31.

Ferne, John. *The Blazon of Gentrie*. 1586.

Ferrell, Lori Anne. 'Kneeling and the Body Politic.' In *Religion, Literature, and Politics in Post-Reformation England, 1540–1688*. Edited by Donna B. Hamilton and Richard Strier. Cambridge: Cambridge University Press, 1996, 70–92.

Findlay, Alison. *Illegitimate Power: Bastards in Renaissance Drama*. Manchester: Manchester University Press, 1994.

Finnerty, Páraic. *Emily Dickinson's Shakespeare*. Andover: University of Massachusetts Press, 2006.

Foakes, R.A. *Hamlet versus Lear: Cultural Politics and Shakespeare's Art*. Cambridge: Cambridge University Press, 1993.

– 'Hamlet's Neglect of Revenge.' In *Hamlet: New Critical Essays*. Edited by Arthur F. Kinney. London: Routledge, 2002, 85–99.

Foakes, R.A., ed. *King Lear*. Arden Shakespeare. 3rd series. London: Thomas Nelson and Sons, 1997.

Forker, Charles R., ed. *King Richard II*. Arden Shakespeare. London: Thomson Learning, 2002.

Fowler, Alastair. 'The Case against Hamlet.' *Times Literary Supplement*, Dec. 22, 1995. 6–8.

French, Marilyn. *Shakespeare's Division of Experience*. New York: Summit, 1981.

French, Samuel. *King Henry IV (Part One)*. French's Acting Edition, No. 547. London: Samuel French, n.d.

Freud, Sigmund. *The Complete Letters of Sigmund Freud to Wilhelm Fliess*. Translated and edited by Jeffrey Moussaieff Masson. Cambridge, MA: Harvard University Press, 1985.

– *Standard Edition of the Complete Psychological Works*. Translated by James Strachey. 24 vols. London: Hogarth Press, 1953–74.

Furnivall, F.J. Contribution to 'Literary Notes and News.' *Westminster Gazette*. 31 October 1904, 4.

– 'The Merry-Cheekt Old Glover.' *Westminster Gazette*. 4 November 1904, 4.

Garber, Marjorie. *Coming of Age in Shakespeare*. London: Methuen, 1981.

– *Shakespeare's Ghost Writers: Literature as Uncanny Causality*. London: Methuen, 1987.

Gardiner, Samuel. *The Portraitur of the Prodigal Sonne*. 1599. STC 11579.

Garry, Grace Mary. 'Unworthy Sons: Richard II, Phaethon, and the Disturbance of Temporal Order.' *Modern Language Studies* 9 (1978–9): 15–19.

The Geneva Bible: A Facsimile of the 1560 Edition. Edited by Lloyd E. Berry. Madison: University of Wisconsin Press, 1969.

Ginzburg, Carlo. *Myths, Emblems, Clues*. Translated by John and Anne C. Tedeschi. London: Hutchinson, 1990.

Goddard, Harold C. *The Meaning of Shakespeare*. 2 vols. 1951. Chicago: University of Chicago Press, 1960.

Godshalk, W.L. 'Henry V's Politics of Non-Responsibility.' *Cahiers Élisabéthains* 17 (1980): 11–20.

Goldberg, Jonathan. 'Fatherly Authority: The Politics of Stuart Family Images.' In *Rewriting the Renaissance*. Edited by Margaret W. Ferguson et al. Chicago: University of Chicago Press, 1986. 3–32.

Goldring, Beth. '*Cor.*'s Rescue of Kent.' In *The Division of the Kingdoms: Shakespeare's Two Versions of* King Lear. Edited by Gary Taylor. Oxford: Clarendon Press, 1983. 143–51.

Gouge, William. *Of Domesticall Duties* (1622). Rptd. Amsterdam: Theatrum Orbis Terrarum, 1976.

Grady, Hugh. *Shakespeare, Machiavelli, and Montaigne: Power and Subjectivity from* Richard II *to* Hamlet. Oxford: Oxford University Press, 2002.

Graham, Jean E. 'The Performing Heir in Jonson's Jacobean Masques.' *Studies in English Literature* 41 (2001): 381–98.

Green, Ian. *The Christian's ABC: Catechisms and Catechizing in England c. 1530–1740*. Oxford: Clarendon, 1996.

Green, Reina. 'Poisoned Ears and Parental Advice in *Hamlet*.' *Early Modern Literary Studies* 11 (2006): 1–31. http://purl.oclc.org/emls/11–3/greeham2.htm.

Greenblatt, Stephen. *Hamlet in Purgatory*. Princeton, NJ: Princeton University Press, 2001.

– *Learning to Curse*. New York: Routledge, 1992.

– *Shakespearean Negotiations: The Circulation of Social Energy in Renaissance England*. Berkeley: University of California Press, 1988.

– *Will in the World: How Shakespeare Became Shakespeare*. New York: W.W. Norton, 2004.

Greenham, Richard. *The Works and Life of Reverend Richard Greenham*. Edited by Kenneth L. Parker and Eric J. Carlson. Aldershot, UK: Ashgate 1998.

Greer, Germaine. *Shakespeare's Wife*. London: Bloomsbury, 2007.

Gregory, Richard L., ed. *The Oxford Companion to the Mind*. Oxford: Oxford University Press, 1987.

Grene, Nicholas. *Shakespeare's Serial History Plays*. Cambridge: Cambridge University Press, 2002.

Griffiths, Paul. *Youth and Authority: Formative Experiences in England 1560–1640*. Oxford: Clarendon, 1996.

Guazzo, Stefano. *The Civile Conversation of M. Steeven Guazzo*. Translated by George Pettie. 2 vols. New York: Alfred A. Knopf, 1925.

Halio, Jay L., ed. *The Tragedy of King Lear*. New Cambridge Shakespeare. Cambridge: Cambridge University Press, 1992.

Halverson, John. '*Hamlet*: Ethos and Transcendence.' *Anglia* 106 (1988): 44–73.

Hamilton, Sharon. *Shakespeare's Daughters*. Jefferson, NC: McFarland, 2003.

Hammersmith, James P. '*Hamlet* and the Myth of Memory.' *English Literary History* 45 (1975): 597–605.

Handover, P.M. *The Second Cecil: The Rise to Power, 1563–1604, of Sir Robert Cecil*. London: Eyre and Spottiswoode, 1959.

Hankins, John Erskine. *Backgrounds of Shakespeare's Thought*. Hassocks, UK: Harvester, 1978.

Hardy, Barbara. *Shakespeare's Storytellers: Dramatic Narration*. London: Peter Owen, 1997.

Hattaway, Michael. 'Possessing Edgar: Aspects of *King Lear* in Performance.' In *Shakespeare Performed: Essays in Honor of R.A. Foakes*. Edited by Grace Ioppolo. Newark: University of Delaware Press, 2000.

Hattaway, Michael, ed. *Henry the Sixth, Part One*. New Cambridge Shakespeare. Cambridge: Cambridge University Press, 1990.

Hawkins, Harriett. *Poetic Freedom and Poetic Truth: Chaucer, Shakespeare, Marlowe, Milton*. Oxford: Clarendon, 1976.

Hawkins, Sherman. 'Aggression and the Project of the Histories.' In Holland, *Shakespeare's Personality*, 41–65.

– '*Henry IV*: The Structural Problem Revisited.' *Shakespeare Quarterly* 33 (1982): 278–301.

Hayton, Alison G. '"The King my father?": Paternity in *Hamlet*.' *Hamlet Studies* 9 (1987): 53–64.

Heilman, Robert Bechtold. *This Great Stage: Image and Structure in King Lear*. Seattle: University of Washington Press, 1963.

Helgerson, Richard. *The Elizabethan Prodigals*. Berkeley: University of California Press, 1976.

Hibbard, G.R., ed. *Hamlet*. Oxford Shakespeare. Oxford: Oxford University Press, 1987.

– '*Henry IV* and *Hamlet*.' *Shakespeare Survey* 30 (1997): 1–12.

– *The Making of Shakespeare's Dramatic Poetry*. Toronto: University of Toronto Press, 1981.

Hogan, Patrick Colm. '*Macbeth*: Authority and Progenitorship.' *American Imago* 40 (1983): 385–95.

Holden, Anthony. *William Shakespeare: His Life and Work*. London: Little, Brown, 1999.

Holinshed, Raphael. *Holinshed's Chronicles of England, Scotland and Ireland*. 6 vols. London, 1807.

Holland, Norman N. *Psychoanalysis and Shakespeare*. 1964. Rptd. New York: Octagon, 1976.

– 'Sons and Substitutions: Shakespeare's Phallic Fantasy.' In Holland, *Shakespeare's Personality*, 66–85.

Holland, Norman N., ed. *Shakespeare's Personality*. Berkeley: University of California Press, 1989.

Honan, Park. *Shakespeare: A Life*. Oxford: Oxford University Press, 1998.

Honigmann, E.A.J. *Myriad-Minded Shakespeare: Essays on the Tragedies, Problem Comedies, and Shakespeare the Man*. 2nd ed. New York: Macmillan, 1998.

– 'Shakespeare's Will and Testamentary Traditions.' In *Shakespeare and Cultural Traditions*. Edited by Tetuo Kishi et al. Newark: University of Delaware Press, 1994, 127–37.

– '"There Is a World Elsewhere": William Shakespeare, Businessman.' In *Images of Shakespeare*. Edited by Werner Habicht et al. Newark: University of Delaware Press, 1988, 40–6.

Houlbrooke, Ralph. *The English Family 1450–1700*. London: Longman, 1984.

Howell, Roger. *Sir Philip Sidney: The Shepherd Knight*. London: Hutchinson, 1968.

Hunter, G.K. *Dramatic Identities and Cultural Tradition*. New York: Barnes and Noble, 1978.

Hunter, G.K., ed. *Henry IV: Parts One and Two: A Casebook*. London: Macmillan, 1970.

Jacobson, Dan. 'Hamlet's Other Selves.' *International Review of Psycho-Analysis*, 16 (1989): 265–72.

James I. *The Political Works of James I*. Edited by Charles Howard McIlwain. 1918. Rptd. New York: Russell and Russell, 1965.

Jameson, Thomas H. *The Hidden Shakespeare: A Study of the Poet's Undercover Activity in the Theatre*. New York: Funk and Wagnalls, 1967.

Janton, Pierre. 'Sonship and Fatherhood in *Macbeth.*' *Cahiers Élisabéthains* 35 (1989): 47–58.

Jenkins, Harold. 'The Structural Problem in Shakespeare's *Henry IV.*' In *Henry IV, Part Two*. Edited by Norman N. Holland. The Signet Classic Shakespeare. New York: New American Library, 1965. 212–33.

Jenkins, Harold, ed. *Hamlet*. Arden Shakespeare. London: Methuen, 1982.

Johnson, S.F. 'The Regeneration of Hamlet.' *Shakespeare Quarterly* 3 (1952): 187–207.

Johnson, Samuel. *The Yale Edition of the Works*. 15 vols. New Haven, CT: Yale University Press, 1958–78.

Jones, Ernest. *Hamlet and Oedipus*. 1949. Rptd. New York: W.W. Norton, 1976.

Jones, James H. '*Leir* and *Lear*: Matthew 5:33–37, The Turning Point, and The Rescue Theme.' *Comparative Drama* 4 (1970): 125–31.

Jones, Robert C. *These Valiant Dead: Renewing the Past in Shakespeare's Histories*. Iowa City: University of Iowa Press, 1991.

Jonson, Ben. *Every Man in His Humor*. Edited by Gabriele Bernhard Jackson. The Yale Ben Jonson. New Haven, CT: Yale University Press, 1969.

Joyce, James. *Ulysses*. Edited by Hans Walter Gabler. New York: Vintage, 1986.

Kahn, Coppélia. *Man's Estate: Masculine Identity in Shakespeare*. Berkeley: University of California Press, 1981.

Kastan, David Scott. '"The Duke of Milan / And His Brave Son": Dynastic Politics in *The Tempest*.' In *Critical Essays on Shakespeare's* The Tempest. Edited by Virginia Mason Vaughan. New York: G.K. Hall, 1998. 91–103.

– '"His semblable is his mirror": *Hamlet* and the Imitation of Revenge.' In *Critical Essays on Shakespeare's* Hamlet. Edited by D.S. Kastan. New York: G.K. Hall, 1995. 198–209.

– *Shakespeare and the Shapes of Time*. Hanover, NH: University Press of New England, 1982.

Kastan, David Scott, ed. *King Henry IV, Part 1*. Arden Shakespeare. Third Series. London: Arden Shakespeare, 2003.

Kay, Dennis. *Shakespeare: His Life, Work, and Era*. New York: William Morrow, 1992.

Kehler, Dorothea. '*Richard II*, 5.3: Traditions and Subtext.' In *Traditions and Innovations: Essays on British Literature of the Middle Ages and the Renaissance*. Edited by David G. Allen and Robert A. White. Newark: University of Delaware Press, 1990. 126–36.

Kermode, Frank. *Shakespeare's Language*. New York: Farrar, Straus, Giroux, 2000.

Kernan, Alvin B. *The Playwright as Magician: Shakespeare's Image of the Poet on the English Public Stage*. New Haven, CT: Yale University Press, 1979.

Kerrigan, John. 'Henry IV and the Death of Old Double.' *Essays in Criticism* 40 (1990): 24–53.

Kerrigan, William. *Hamlet's Perfection*. Baltimore: Johns Hopkins University Press, 1994.

King, Walter N. *Hamlet's Search for Meaning*. Athens: University of Georgia Press, 1982.

Kirsch, Arthur. *The Passions of Shakespeare's Tragic Heroes*. Charlottesville: University Press of Virginia, 1990.

Kirschbaum, Leo. 'The Authorship of 1 Henry VI.' *Publications of the Modern Language Association* 67 (1952): 809–22.

Knight, W. Nicholas. *Autobiography in Shakespeare's Plays: Lands So by His Father Lost*. New York: Peter Lang, 2002.

Knighton, C.S. 'Sir John Mennes.' In *The Oxford Dictionary of National Biography*. Online ed., accessed January 2008.

Kocher, Paul H. 'Francis Bacon and His Father.' *Huntington Library Quarterly* 21 (1957–8): 133–58.

Kris, Ernst. *Psychoanalytic Explorations in Art*. 1952. New York: Schocken, 1964.

Kronenfeld, Judy. King Lear *and the Naked Truth: Rethinking the Language of Religion and Resistance*. Durham, NC: Duke University Press, 1998.

Laing, R.D. *The Politics of the Family*. 1969. Rptd. Concord, ON: Anansi, 1993.

The Lamentable Tragedy of Locrine. Edited by Jane Lytton Gooch. New York: Garland, 1981.

Lapides, Fred, ed. *The Raigne of King Edward the Third*. New York: Garland, 1980.

Lee, John. *Shakespeare's* Hamlet *and the Controversies of Self*. Oxford: Clarendon, 2000.

Leggatt, Alexander. 'The Death of John Talbot.' In *Shakespeare's English Histories: A Quest for Form and Genre*. Edited by John W. Velz. Binghampton, NY: Medieval & Renaissance Texts and Studies, 1996. 11–30.

– King Lear. Harvester New Critical Introductions to Shakespeare. New York: Harvester Wheatsheaf, 1988.

– 'Macbeth and the Last Plays.' In *Mirror up to Shakespeare: Essays in Honour of G.R. Hibbard*. Edited by J.C. Gray. Toronto: University of Toronto Press, 1984. 189–207.

Lenker, Lagretta Tallent. *Fathers and Daughters in Shakespeare and Shaw*. Westport, CT: Greenwood, 2001.

Levin, Harry. *The Question of* Hamlet. London: Oxford University Press, 1959.

Levin, Richard. 'Hamlet, Laertes, and the Dramatic Functions of Foils.' In
   Hamlet: *New Critical Essays*. Edited by Arthur F. Kinney. New York: Rout-
   ledge, 2002. 215–30.
Lichtenberg, Joseph D., and Charlotte Lichtenberg. 'Prince Hal's Conflict,
   Adolescent Idealism, and Buffoonery.' *Journal of the American Psychoanalytic
   Association* 17 (1969): 873–87.
Locke, John. *Some Thoughts Concerning Education*. Edited by John W. Yolton
   and Jean S. Yolton. Oxford: Clarendon, 1989.
Machiavelli, Niccoló. *The Prince*. Translated by Harvey C. Mansfield Jr.
   Chicago: University of Chicago Press, 1985.
MacIsaac, Warren J. 'The Three Cousins in *Richard II.*' *Shakespeare Quarterly* 22
   (1971): 137–46.
Mack, Maynard. *Everybody's Shakespeare: Reflections Chiefly on the Tragedies*.
   Lincoln: University of Nebraska Press, 1993.
– King Lear *in Our Time*. Berkeley: University of California Press, 1965.
Mahl, George F. 'Father-Son Themes in Freud's Self-Analysis.' In *Father and
   Child: Developmental and Clinical Perspectives*. Edited by Stanley H. Cath et
   al. Hillsdale, NJ: Analytic Press, 1994. 33–64.
Manlove, Colin N. *The Gap in Shakespeare: The Motif of Division from* Richard II
   to The Tempest. Totowa, NJ: Barnes and Noble, 1981.
Marlowe, Christopher. *Doctor Faustus and Other Plays*. Edited by David Bev-
   ington and Eric Rasmussen. Oxford: Oxford University Press, 1995.
Marsh, Derick R.C. 'Hal and Hamlet: The Loneliness of Integrity.' In *Jonson
   and Shakespeare*. Edited by Ian Donaldson. Atlantic Highlands, NJ: Human-
   ities Press, 1983. 18–34.
Marston, John. *Antonio's Revenge*. Edited by W. Reavley Gair. Revels Plays.
   Manchester: Manchester University Press, 1978.
Martin, Kingsley. *Father Figures: A First Volume of Autobiography 1897–1931*.
   London: Hutchinson, 1966.
Maslen, Elizabeth. 'Yorick's Place in *Hamlet.*' *Essays and Studies* 36 (1983):
   1–13.
Maslin, R.W. 'Introduction' to Sir Philip Sidney, *An Apology for Poetry*. Edited
   by Geoffrey Shepherd. 3rd ed. Manchester: Manchester University Press,
   2002.
Maxwell, J.C. 'Shakespeare and the Siwards.' *Review of English Studies* 24
   (1948): 139–41.
McAlindon, T. *Shakespeare and Decorum*. London: Macmillan, 1973.
McCoy. Richard C. *Rebellion in Arcadia*. New Brunswick, NJ: Rutgers University Press, 1979.
McCurdy, Harold Grier. *The Personality of Shakespeare: A Venture in Psychological Method*. 1953. Rptd. Port Washington, NY: Kennikat, 1973.

McCutcheon, Elizabeth. *Sir Nicholas Bacon's Great House Sententiae*. English Literary Renaissance Supplements, 3. Amherst: English Literary Renaissance, 1977.

McFarland, Thomas. 'The Image of the Family in *King Lear*.' In *On* King Lear. Edited by Lawrence Danson. Princeton, NJ: Princeton University Press, 1981. 91–118.

– *Tragic Meanings in Shakespeare*. New York: Random House, 1966.

McGregor, Ian. 'Ambivalence.' In *The Corsini Encyclopedia of Psychology*. 4th ed. Edited by I. Weiner and E. Craighead. Forthcoming.

McGuire, Philip C. 'Which Fortinbras, Which *Hamlet*?' In *The* Hamlet *First Published (Q1, 1603): Origins, Form, Intertextualities*. Edited by Thomas Clayton. Newark: University of Delaware Press, 1992. 151–78.

Melchiori, Giorgio, ed. *King Edward III*. New Cambridge Shakespeare. Cambridge: Cambridge University Press, 1998.

– *The Second Part of King Henry IV*. New Cambridge Shakespeare. Cambridge: Cambridge University Press, 1989.

Metz, G. Harold. *Sources of Four Plays Ascribed to Shakespeare*. Columbia: University of Missouri Press, 1989.

Miller, David Lee. *Dreams of the Burning Child: Sacrificial Sons and the Father's Witness*. Ithaca, NY: Cornell University Press, 2003.

Miller, Jonathan. '*King Lear* in Rehearsal: A Talk.' In *The Undiscover'd Country: New Essays on Psychoanalysis and Shakespeare*. Edited by B.J. Sokol. London: Free Association, 1993. 17–38.

Miola, Robert S. 'Aeneas and Hamlet.' *Classical and Modern Literature* 8 (1987): 275–90.

Montaigne, Michel Eyquem de. *Montaigne's Essays*. Translated by John Florio. 3 vols. London: Dent, 1965.

– *The Essays: A Selection*. Translated by M.A. Screech. London: Penguin, 1993.

Muir, Kenneth, ed. *Shakespeare:* The Winter's Tale. Casebook Series. London: Macmillan, 1969.

Munday, Anthony. *Sir Thomas More: A Play*. Edited by Vittorio Gabrieli and Giorgio Melchiori. New York: Manchester University Press, 1990.

Nashe, Thomas. *Works*. Edited by Ronald B. McKerrow. 5 vols. 1910. Rev. F.P. Wilson. Oxford: Blackwell, 1966.

Neill, Michael. *Issues of Death: Mortality and Identity in Renaissance Tragedy*. Oxford: Clarendon, 1997.

Nevo, Ruth. *Shakespeare's Other Language*. New York: Methuen, 1987.

Novy, Marianne. 'Shakespeare and Emotional Distance in the Elizabethan Family.' In *Shakespeare and Gender: A History*. Edited by Deborah E. Barker and Ivo Kamps. New York: Verso, 1995. 63–74.

Nowell, Alexander. *A Catechisme or First Instruction and Learning of Christian*

Religion (1570). Translated by Thomas Norton. Rptd. Delmar, NY: Scholars' Facsimiles & Reprints, 1975.

Nuttall, A.D. 'Freud and Shakespeare: *Hamlet.*' In *Shakespearean Continuities: Essays in Honour of E.A.J. Honigmann.* Edited by John Batchelor et al. New York: St Martin's, 1997. 123–37.

– '*Hamlet*: Conversations with the Dead.' In *British Academy Shakespeare Lectures 1980–89.* Edited by E.A.J. Honigmann. Oxford: Oxford University Press, 1993. 213–29.

– *William Shakespeare: 'The Winter's Tale.'* London: Edward Arnold, 1966.

O'Day, Rosemary. *The Family and Family Relationships, 1500–1900.* London: Macmillan, 1994.

Omberg, Margaret. 'Macbeth's Barren Sceptre.' *Studia Neophilologica* 68 (1996): 39–47.

Orgel, Stephen, ed. *The Winter's Tale.* Oxford Shakespeare. Oxford: Oxford University Press, 1996.

Orlin, Lena Cowen. *Elizabethan Households: An Anthology.* Washington, DC: Folger Shakespeare Library, 1995.

– *Private Matters and Public Culture in post-Reformation England.* Ithaca, NY: Cornell University Press, 1994.

Orme, Nicholas. *Medieval Children.* New Haven, CT: Yale University Press, 2001.

Ornstein, Robert. *A Kingdom for a Stage: The Achievement of Shakespeare's History Plays.* Cambridge, MA: Harvard University Press, 1972.

Ovid. *Metamorphoses.* Translated by Frank Justus Miller. Loeb Classical Library. 2 vols. 3rd ed. Cambridge, MA: Harvard University Press, 1977.

– *Metamorphoses.* Translated by A.D. Melville. Oxford: Oxford University Press, 1987.

– *Shakespeare's Ovid.* Translated by Arthur Golding. Edited by W.H.D. Rouse. New York: Norton, 1966.

Ozment, Steven. *Ancestors: The Loving Family in Old Europe.* Cambridge, MA: Harvard University Press, 2001.

Paris, Bernard J. *Character as a Subversive Force in Shakespeare: The Histories and Roman Plays.* London: Associated University Presses, 1991.

Partee, Morriss Henry. *Childhood in Shakespeare's Plays.* New York: Peter Lang, 2006.

Paul, Henry N. *The Royal Play of* Macbeth. New York: Macmillan, 1950.

Pearlman, E. 'Shakespeare at Work: The Two Talbots.' *Philological Quarterly* 75 (1996): 1–22.

Pearson, Lu Emily. *Elizabethans at Home.* Stanford, CA: Stanford University Press, 1957.

Pechter, Edward. 'Falsifying Men's Hopes: The Ending of *1 Henry IV*.' *Modern Language Quarterly* 41 (1980): 211–30.

Pendleton, Thomas A. 'Shakespeare's Children.' *Mid-Hudson Language Studies* 3 (1980): 40–55.

Pepys, Samuel. *The Diary of Samuel Pepys*. Edited by Robert Latham and William Matthews. 11 vols. Berkeley: University of California Press, 1970–83.

Perkins, William. *The Work of William Perkins*. Edited by Ian Breward. Abingdon: Sutton Courtenay Press, 1970.

Phialas, Peter. 'The Medieval in *Richard II*.' *Shakespeare Quarterly* 12 (1961): 305–10.

Pierce, Robert B. 'The Generations in *2 Henry IV*.' In *Twentieth Century Interpretations of* Henry IV Part Two. Edited by David P. Young. Englewood Cliffs, NJ: Prentice-Hall, 1968. 49–57.

– *Shakespeare's History Plays: The Family and the State*. Columbus: Ohio State University Press, 1971.

Pogue, Kate Emery. *Shakespeare's Family*. Westport, CT: Praeger, 2008.

Pollock, Linda. *Forgotten Children: Parent-Child Relations from 1500 to 1900*. Cambridge: Cambridge University Press, 1983.

– 'Parent-Child Relations,' in *The History of the European Family*. Edited by David I. Kertzer and Marzio Barbagli. Vol. 1: *Family Life in Early Modern Times 1500–1789*. New Haven, CT: Yale University Press, 2001. 191–220.

– 'Rethinking Patriarchy and the Family in Seventeenth-Century England,' *Journal of Family History* 23 (1998): 3–27.

Poole, Eric. 'John and Mary Shakespeare and the Aston Cantlow Mortgage.' *Cahiers Élisabéthains* 17 (1980): 21–41.

Potter, Ursula. 'Cockering Mothers and Humanist Pedagogy in Two Tudor School Plays.' In *Domestic Arrangements in Early Modern England*. Edited by Kari Boyd McBride. Pittsburgh: Duquesne University Press, 2002. 244–78.

Quiller-Couch, Arthur. 'Paternity in Shakespeare.' Annual Shakespeare Lecture. *Proceedings of the British Academy* 18 (1932): 93–110.

Quinones, Ricardo J. *The Renaissance Discovery of Time*. Cambridge, MA: Harvard University Press, 1972.

Rabelais, François. *The Histories of Gargantua and Pantagruel*. Translated by J.M. Cohen. Harmondsworth: Penguin, 1955.

Rabkin, Norman. *Shakespeare and the Problem of Meaning*. Chicago: University of Chicago Press, 1981.

Rackin, Phyllis. *Stages of History: Shakespeare's English Chronicles*. Ithaca, NY: Cornell University Press, 1990.

Rappaport, Steve. 'Reconsidering Apprenticeship in Sixteenth-Century

London.' In *Renaissance Society and Culture: Essays in Honor of Eugene F. Rice, Jr*. Edited by John Monfasani and Ronald G. Musto. New York: Italica, 1991. 239–61.

Raylor, Timothy. *Cavaliers, Clubs, and Literary Culture: Sir John Mennes, James Smith, and the Order of the Fancy*. Newark: University of Delaware Press, 1994.

Razzell, P.E. *William Shakespeare: The Anatomy of an Enigma*. Hampstead: Caliban, 1990.

Reibetanz, John. *The Lear World: A Study of* King Lear *in Its Dramatic Context*. London: Heinemann, 1977.

Riggs, David. *Shakespeare's Heroical Histories:* Henry VI *and Its Literary Tradition*. Cambridge, MA: Harvard University Press, 1971.

Rose, Mark. '*Hamlet* and the Shape of Revenge.' *English Literary Renaissance* 1 (1971): 132–43.

Rosenberg, Marvin. *The Masks of* Hamlet. Newark: University of Delaware Press, 1992.

– *The Masks of* King Lear. Berkeley: University of California Press, 1972.

– *The Masks of* Macbeth. Berkeley: University of California Press, 1978.

Rosenthal, Joel T. *Patriarchy and Families of Privilege in Fifteenth-Century England*. Philadelphia: University of Pennsylvania Press, 1991.

Rossi, Giovanni. '"De l'affection des pères aux enfants": Sentimental Bonds and Juridical Bonds in Montaigne, *Essais*, II, 8.' In *Property Law in Renaissance Literature*. Edited by Daniela Carpi. Frankfurt: Peter Lang, 2005. 161–78.

Rossky, William. 'An Elizabethan Perspective on *Richard II*: The Child as King.' *Hebrew University Studies in Literature and the Arts* 15 (1989): 55–77.

Rowse, A.L. *Ralegh and the Throckmortons*. London: Macmillan, 1962.

Rozett, Martha Tuck. *The Doctrine of Election and the Emergence of Elizabethan Tragedy*. Princeton, NJ: Princeton University Press, 1984.

Rubinstein, E. '*1 Henry IV*: The Metaphor of Liability.' *Studies in English Literature* 19 (1970): 287–95.

Rudd, Niall. 'Daedalus and Icarus (ii) From the Renaissance to the Present Day.' In *Ovid Renewed: Ovidian Influences on Literature and Art from the Middle Ages to the Twentieth Century*. Edited by Charles Martindale. Cambridge: Cambridge University Press, 1988. 37–53.

Russ, Jon R. '"Old Mole" in *Hamlet*, I.v.162.' *English Language Notes* 12 (1974–5): 163–8.

Sackville, Thomas, and Thomas Norton, *Gorboduc: or, Ferrex and Porrex*. Regents Drama. Edited by Irby B. Cauthen Jr. Lincoln: University of Nebraska Press, 1970.

Salingar, Leo. '*King Lear*, Montaigne and Harsnett.' In his *Dramatic Form in Shakespeare and the Jacobeans*. Cambridge: Cambridge University Press, 1986, 107–39.

Sams, Eric, ed. *Shakespeare's* Edmund Ironside: *The Lost Play*. Aldershot: Wildwood House, 1986.

– *Shakespeare's* Edward III. New Haven, CT: Yale University Press, 1996.

Sanders, Norman. 'The True Prince and the False Thief: Prince Hal and the Shift of Identity.' *Shakespeare Survey* 30 (1977): 29–34.

Sanders, Wilbur. *The Winter's Tale*. Harvester New Critical Introductions to Shakespeare. Brighton: Harvester, 1987.

Schanzer, Ernest. 'Four Notes on *Macbeth*.' *Modern Language Review* 52 (1957): 223–7.

Schleiner, Winfried. 'Aeneas' Flight from Troy.' *Comparative Literature* 27 (1975): 97–112.

– 'Justifying the Unjustifiable: The Dover Cliff Scene in *King Lear*.' *Shakespeare Quarterly* 36 (1985): 337–43.

Schochet, Gordon J. *Patriarchalism in Political Thought: The Authoritarian Family and Political Speculation and Attitudes Especially in Seventeenth-Century England*. Oxford: Blackwell, 1975.

– 'Patriarchalism, Politics and Mass Attitudes in Stuart England.' *Historical Journal* 12 (1969): 413–41.

Schoenbaum, S. *Shakespeare's Lives*. Oxford: Clarendon, 1970.

– *William Shakespeare: A Compact Documentary Life*. New York: Oxford University Press, 1977.

Schulz, Clarence. 'Ambivalence.' In *The Freud Encyclopedia: Theory, Therapy, and Culture*. Edited by Edward Erwin. New York: Routledge, 2002. 16–17.

Schwartz, Murray M., and Coppélia Kahn, eds. *Representing Shakespeare: New Psychoanalytic Essays*. Baltimore: Johns Hopkins University Press, 1980.

Scofield, Martin. *The Ghosts of* Hamlet: *The Play and Modern Writers*. Cambridge: Cambridge University Press, 1980.

Scott, James C. *Domination and the Arts of Resistance: Hidden Transcripts*. New Haven, CT: Yale University Press, 1990.

Scott, William O. 'Contracts of Love and Affection: Lear, Old Age, and Kingship.' *Shakespeare Survey* 55. Edited by Peter Holland. Cambridge University Press, 2002. 36–42.

Scott-Giles, C. Wilfrid. *Shakespeare's Heraldry*. London: J.M. Dent, 1950.

Seelig, Sharon Cadman. 'Loyal Fathers and Treacherous Sons: Familial Politics in *Richard II*.' *Journal of English and Germanic Philology* 94 (1995): 347–64.

Seltzer, Daniel. 'Prince Hal and Tragic Style.' *Shakespeare Survey* 30 (1977): 13–27.

Seneca, Lucius Annaeus. *Moral Essays*. 3 vols. Translated by John W. Basore. Loeb Library. Cambridge, MA: Harvard University Press, 1935.

Shaaber, M.A. 'The Unity of *Henry IV*.' In *Joseph Quincy Adams Memorial Studies*. Edited by James G. McManaway et al. Washington: Folger Shakespeare Library, 1948. 217–27.

Shapiro, James. *A Year in the Life of William Shakespeare, 1599*. Harper: New York, 2005.

Shepard, Alexandra. *Meanings of Manhood in Early Modern England*. Oxford: Oxford University Press, 2003.

Shepard, Warren V. 'Hoisting the Enginer with His Own Petar.' *Shakespeare Quarterly* 7 (1956): 281–5.

Shepherd, Simon. *Marlowe and the Politics of Elizabethan Theatre*. Brighton: Harvester, 1986.

Shuchter, J.D. 'Prince Hal and Francis: The Imitation of an Action.' *Shakespeare Studies* 3 (1967): 129–37.

Shuger, Debora Kuller. *Habits of Thought in the English Renaissance: Religion, Politics, and the Dominant Culture*. Berkeley: University of California Press, 1990.

Sidney, Sir Philip. *Miscellaneous Prose of Sir Philip Sidney*. Edited by Katherine Duncan-Jones and Jan van Dorsten. Oxford: Oxford University Press, 1973.

Simon, Bennett. *Tragic Drama and the Family: Psychoanalytic Studies from Aeschylus to Beckett*. New Haven, CT: Yale University Press, 1988.

Skura, Meredith. 'Interpreting Posthumus' Dream from Above and Below: Families, Psychoanalysts, and Literary Critics.' In Schwartz and Kahn, *Representing Shakespeare*, 203–16.

– *Shakespeare the Actor and the Purposes of Playing*. Chicago: University of Chicago Press, 1993.

Slater, Anne Pasternak. *Shakespeare the Director*. Brighton: Harvester, 1982.

Smith, Bruce R. *Shakespeare and Masculinity*. Oxford Shakespeare Topics. Oxford: Oxford University Press, 2000.

Smith, Molly. 'Mutant Scenes and "Minor" Conflicts in *Richard II*.' In *A Feminist Guide to Shakespeare*. Edited by Dympna Callaghan. Oxford: Blackwell, 2000. 263–75.

Smith-Bannister, Scott. *Names and Naming Patterns in England 1538–1700*. Oxford: Clarendon, 1997.

Snyder, Susan. '*King Lear* and the Prodigal Son.' *Shakespeare Quarterly* 17 (1966): 361–9.

– *Shakespeare: A Wayward Journey*. Newark: University of Delaware Press, 2002.

Snyder, Susan, and Deborah T. Curren-Aquino., eds. *The Winter's Tale*. New
    Cambridge Shakespeare. Cambridge: Cambridge University Press, 2007.
Sommerville, J.P. *Royalists and Patriots: Politics and Ideology in England
    1603–1640*. 2nd ed. London: Longman, 1999.
Spencer, T.J.B., ed. *Hamlet*. New Penguin Shakespeare. Harmondsworth, UK:
    Penguin, 1980.
Spevack, Marvin. *The Harvard Concordance to Shakespeare*. Cambridge, MA:
    Harvard University Press, 1973.
States, Bert O. *Hamlet and the Concept of Character*. Baltimore: Johns Hopkins
    University Press, 1992.
Stern, Jeffrey. 'The Sins of the Fathers: "Prince Hal's Conflict" Reconsidered.'
    In Faber, *The Design Within*, 487–502.
Stewart, Alan, and Heather Wolfe. *Letterwriting in Renaissance England*. Wash-
    ington, DC: Folger Shakespeare Library, 2004.
Stockholder, Kay. *Dream Works: Lovers and Families in Shakespeare's Plays*.
    Toronto: University of Toronto Press, 1987.
– 'Sex and Authority in *Hamlet*, *King Lear* and *Pericles*.' *Mosaic* 18 (1985):
    17–29.
Stone, Lawrence. *The Crisis of the Aristocracy 1558–1641*. Oxford: Clarendon,
    1965.
– *The Family, Sex and Marriage in England 1500–1800*. London: Weidenfeld
    and Nicolson, 1977.
Strauss, Gerald. *Luther's House of Learning: Indoctrination of the Young in the
    German Reformation*. Baltimore: Johns Hopkins University Press, 1978.
Strong, Roy. *Henry Prince of Wales and England's Lost Renaissance*. New York:
    Thames and Hudson, 1986.
– *Tudor & Jacobean Portraits*. 2 vols. London: HMSO, 1969.
Sturgess, Keith. *Jacobean Private Theatre*. London: Routledge and Kegan Paul,
    1987.
Sundelson, David. *Shakespeare's Restorations of the Father*. New Brunswick, N.J:
    Rutgers University Press, 1983.
Sutherland, John and Cedric Watts. *Henry V, War Criminal? and Other Shake-
    speare Puzzles*. Oxford: Oxford University Press, 2000.
Swinburne, Algernon Charles. Selection from *A Study of Shakespeare*. In *Shake-
    speare: 'The Winter's Tale.'* Edited by Kenneth Muir. Casebook Series.
    London: Macmillan, 1969. 38–9.
Sylvester, Richard S., and Davis P. Harding, eds. *Two Early Tudor Lives:* The
    Life and Death of Cardinal Wolsey *by George Cavendish and* The Life of Sir
    Thomas More *by William Roper*. New Haven, CT: Yale University Press,
    1962.

Taylor, Gary. 'Shakespeare and Others: The Authorship of *Henry VI, Part One.' Medieval and Renaissance Drama in England* 7 (1995): 145–205.

Taylor, M.P. 'A Father Pleads for the Death of His Son.' *International Journal of Psycho-Analysis* 8 (1927): 53–5.

Taylor, Michael., ed. *Henry VI, Part One*. Oxford Shakespeare. Oxford: Oxford University Press, 2003.

Thomas, Keith. 'Age and Authority in Early Modern England.' *Proceedings of the British Academy* 62 (1976): 205–48.

Thompson, Ann, and Neil Taylor. '"Father and Mother is One Flesh": Hamlet and the Problems of Paternity.' In Spaas, *Paternity and Fatherhood*, 246–58.

Tiffany, Grace. '*Macbeth*, Paternity, and the Anglicization of James I.' *Studies in the Humanities* 23 (1996): 148–62.

Tilley, Morris Palmer. *A Dictionary of the Proverbs in England in the Sixteenth and Seventeenth Centuries*. Ann Arbor: University of Michigan Press, 1950.

Tillyard, E.M.W. *Shakespeare's History Plays*. 1944. Rpt. New York: Collier, 1962.

Tippens, Darryl. 'Shakespeare and the Prodigal Son Tradition.' *Explorations in Renaissance Culture* 14 (1988): 57–77.

Traversi, D.A. *An Approach to Shakespeare*. 3rd ed., revised and expanded. 2 vols. New York: Doubleday, 1969.

Tromly, Fred B. 'Grief, Authority and the Resistance to Consolation in Shakespeare.' In *Speaking Grief in English Literary Culture: Shakespeare to Milton*. Edited by Margo Swiss and David A. Kent. Pittsburgh: Duquesne University Press, 2002. 20–41.

– 'Sir Walter Ralegh Instructs His Son, Twice.' *Notes and Queries* 56 (2009): 616–19.

Turner, John H. *The Myth of Icarus in Spanish Renaissance Poetry*. London: Tamesis Books, 1976.

Turner, Robert Y. *Shakespeare's Apprenticeship*. Chicago: University of Chicago Press, 1975.

Tyndale, William. *Doctrinal Treatises*. Edited by Henry Walter. Parker Society. Cambridge: Cambridge University Press, 1848.

Vickers, Brian, ed. *Shakespeare: The Critical Heritage*. 6 vols. London: Routledge & Kegan Paul, 1974–81.

Virgil, *The Aeneid*. Translated by Allen Mandelbaum. Toronto: Bantam, 1961.

Vitkus, Daniel J., ed. *Three Turk Plays from Early Modern England*. New York: Columbia University Press, 2000.

Wagner, Joseph B. 'Hamlet Rewriting *Hamlet*.' *Hamlet Studies* 23 (2001): 75–92.

– 'In the Name of the Dead Father.' *Proceedings of the 12th International Conference on Literature and Psychoanalysis*, June 1995. Edited by Frederico Pereira. Lisbon: ISPA. 79–85.

Wallace, Malcolm William. *The Life of Sir Philip Sidney*. Cambridge: Cambridge University Press, 1915.

Walsh, Brian. '"Unkind Division": The Double Absence of Performing History in *1 Henry VI*.' *Shakespeare Quarterly* 54 (2004): 119–57.

Wangh, Martin. 'A Psychoanalytic Commentary on Shakespeare's *The Tragedie of King Richard the Second*.' *Psychoanalytic Quarterly* 37 (1968): 212–38.

Watson, Robert N. *The Rest Is Silence: Death as Annihilation in the English Renaissance*. Berkeley: University of California Press, 1994.

– *Shakespeare and the Hazards of Ambition*. Cambridge, MA: Harvard University Press, 1984.

Watt, Tessa. *Cheap Print and Popular Piety 1550–1640*. Cambridge: Cambridge University Press, 1991.

Watterson, William Collins. 'Hamlet's Lost Father.' *Hamlet Studies* 16 (1994): 10–23.

Watts, Cedric. *Hamlet*. Harvester New Critical Introductions to Shakespeare. Harvester: London, 1988.

Webster, John. *The Duchess of Malfi*. Edited by John Russell Brown. Revels Plays. London: Methuen, 1964.

Weil, Herbert, and Judith Weil, eds. *The First Part of King Henry IV*. New Cambridge Shakespeare. Cambridge: Cambridge University Press, 1997.

Weis, René, ed. *Henry Four, Part Two*. Oxford Shakespeare. Oxford: Oxford University Press, 1997.

Wells, Stanley. *Shakespeare for All Time*. London: Macmillan, 2002.

Welsh, Alexander. *Hamlet in his Modern Guises*. Princeton, NJ: Princeton University Press, 2001.

Wentersdorf, Karl P. 'The Date of *Edward III*.' *Shakespeare Quarterly* 16 (1965): 227–31.

West, Gillian. 'A Glossary to the Language of Debt at the Climax of *1 Henry IV*.' *Notes and Queries* 36 (1989): 323–4.

Westlund, Joseph. 'Ambivalence in The Player's Speech in *Hamlet*.' *Studies in English Literature* 18 (1978): 245–56.

Wharton, T.F. *Henry the Fourth, Parts 1 and 2: Text and Performance*. London: Macmillan, 1983.

Wheeler, Richard P. 'Deaths in the Family: The Loss of a Son and the Rise of Shakespearean Comedy.' *Shakespeare Quarterly* 51 (2000): 127–53.

Whitney, Geffrey. *A Choice of Emblemes*. Edited by John Manning. Facsimile of the 1586 edition. Menston: Scolar, 1989.

Wilders, John. *The Lost Garden*. London: Macmillan, 1978.

Williams, George Walton. 'Hamlet and the Dread Commandment.' In *Shakespeare's Universe: Essays in Honour of W.R. Elton*. Edited by John M. Mucciolo. Aldershot: Scolar Press, 1996. 60–8.

Williams, Philip. 'The Birth and Death of Falstaff Reconsidered.' *Shakespeare Quarterly* 8 (1957): 359–65.

Williamson, Jerry Wayne. *The Myth of the Conqueror: Prince Henry*. New York: AMS, 1978.

Willson, Robert F., Jr. 'Hamlet's Ghostly Presence.' *Hamlet Studies* 11 (1989): 80–6.

Wilson, John Dover. *The Fortunes of Falstaff*. Cambridge: Cambridge University Press, 1943.

Wilson, Richard. *Will Power: Essays on Shakespearean Authority*. Detroit: Wayne State University Press, 1993.

Winny, James. *The Player King: A Theme of Shakespeare's Histories*. London: Chatto and Windus, 1968.

Womersley, D.J. '3 *Henry VI*: Shakespeare, Tacitus, and Parricide.' *Notes and Queries* 32 (1985): 468–73.

Wright, Leonard. *A Display of Dutie, Dect with Sage Sayings*. London, 1589.

Wright, Louis B. *Advice to a Son: Precepts of Lord Burghley, Sir Walter Raleigh, and Francis Osborne*. Ithaca, NY: Cornell University Press, 1962.

Youings, Joyce. *Sixteenth-Century England*. The Pelican Social History of England. London: Penguin, 1984.

Young, Alan. *The English Prodigal Son Plays: A Theatrical Fashion of the Sixteenth and Seventeenth Centuries*. Salzburg: Institut für Anglistik und Amerikanistik, 1979.

– *Tudor and Jacobean Tournaments*. Dobbs Ferry, NY: Sheridan House, 1987.

Young, Bruce W. *Family Life in the Age of Shakespeare*. Westport, CT: Greenwood, 2009.

– '*King Lear* and the Calamity of Fatherhood.' In *In the Company of Shakespeare: Essays on English Renaissance Literature in Honor of G. Blakemore Evans*. Edited by Thomas Moisan and Douglas Bruster. London: Associated University Presses, 2002. 43–64.

– 'Parental Blessings in Shakespeare's Plays.' *Studies in Philology* 89 (1992): 179–210.

Young, David. '*Hamlet*, Son of *Hamlet*.' In *Perspectives on* Hamlet. Edited by William G. Holzberger and Peter B. Waldeck. London: Associated University Press, 1975. 184–206.

Zitner, S.P. 'Anon, Anon: or, A Mirror for a Magistrate.' *Shakespeare Quarterly* 19 (1968): 63–70.

– Review of S.C. Sen Gupta, *Shakespeare's Historical Plays*. *Modern Philology* 64 (1966–7): 339–41.

– 'Zig-Zag in *Hamlet* I, v.' In *Craft & Tradition: Essays in Honour of William Blisset*. Edited by H.B. de Groot and A. Leggatt. Calgary: University of Calgary Press, 1990. 81–8.

Index

DATE DUE